COMPETITION, CARTELS AND THEIR REGULATION

STUDIES IN INDUSTRIAL ECONOMICS

IV

1962

NORTH-HOLLAND PUBLISHING COMPANY
AMSTERDAM

COMPETITION CARTELS AND THEIR REGULATION

EDITED BY

JOHN PERRY MILLER

Professor of Economics, Yale University

1962

NORTH-HOLLAND PUBLISHING COMPANY
AMSTERDAM

PRINTED IN THE NETHERLANDS

INTRODUCTION TO THE SERIES

As business life becomes more complex, so the field of industrial economics grows increasingly important. Though the problems in the micro-world of the firm and the influence of its behaviour on society as a whole are studied extensively there still exist a lack of that collaboration between students of different nationalities which has proved to be so fruitful in other sciences and even in other parts of economics.

Another obstacle to the development of this field of our science is the relatively few contacts in many countries between economists and business men.

The principal aim of this present series is to stimulate study and research in this part of economics and to further an interchange of ideas and results on an international basis. In general it is expected that contributors will not only give the present state of informed opinion in their respective countries on the subjects treated but also include the results of their own study and research. Although this may sometimes lead to some overlapping the editors feel that this may not be undesirable, in so far as its serves to link together the parts of the subject.

As the reader will see, the level of treatment is that appropriate to an audience of graduate academic standard. Nevertheless, the volumes are not addressed to academic scholars only but also to those engaged in management. A knowledge of basic economic principles is assumed.

If the publishing of this series gives an impulse to the fostering of international collaboration in this important section of economics and focuses attention on the necessity for further development of industrial economics and on the mutual benefit economics as well as practical business life may derive from it, the goal of the editors will be achieved.

THE EDITORS

BIOGRAPHICAL NOTES

JOHN PERRY MILLER, B.A., M.A., Ph.D.: Professor of Economics and Dean of the Graduate School, Yale University, New Haven, Conn., U.S.A.
Author of: *Unfair Competition; Pricing Military Procurement.*
Co-Author of: *The New England Economy; The Economic Outlook for the Naugatuck and Farmington River Valleys in the State of Connecticut.*

JOSEPH J. SPENGLER, B.A., M.A., Ph.D.: James B. Duke Professor of Economics, Director of Graduate Studies in Economics, Duke University, Durham, N.C., U.S.A.
Author of: *France Faces Depopulation; French Predecessors of Malthus.*
Co-editor of: *Population Theory and Practice; Demographic Analysis; Essays in Economic Thought.*

WILLIAM BOSERUP, candidatus politices (M.A. [Ec]), University of Copenhagen. Head of Division, The Monopolies Control Authority, Copenhagen, Denmark.
Consultant Editor of: *Guide to Legislation on Restrictive Business Practices,* published by the E.P.A. of the O.E.E.C., Paris.

UFFE SCHLICHTKRULL, candidatus juris (MLL), University of Copenhagen. Assistant Head of Section, The Monopolies Control Authority, Copenhagen, Denmark.

THOMAS WILSON, M.A., Ph.D., O.B.E.: Adam Smith Professor of Political Economy, University of Glasgow, U. K.
Author of: *Fluctuations in Income and Employment; Modern Capitalism and Economic Progress; Inflation.*
Editor of: *Oxford Studies in the Price Mechanism.* Formerly General Editor of *Oxford Economic Papers.*

FRITZ VOIGT, Dr. rer. pol. habil., Dr. iur.: Professor of Economics, Director of Institut für Industrie- und Gewerbepolitik, Director of Institut für das Spar-, Giro- und Kreditwesen, Director of Verkehrswissenschaftliches Seminar, Hamburg, Germany.
Author of: *Die Wandlungen der Marktordnungsverbände; Der volkswirtschaftliche Sparprozess; Die gestaltende Kraft der Verkehrsmittel in wirtschaftlichen Wachstumsprozessen; Die volkswirtschaftliche Bedeutung des Verkehrssystems; Verhaltensweise und Entwicklungsmöglichkeiten der Kartelle; Die Mitbestimmung der Arbeitnehmer in Unternehmungen der Bundesrepublik Deutschland.*
Co-editor of: *Jahrbuch für Sozialwissenschaft.*

RICHARD H. HOLTON, B.S., M.A., Ph.D.: Associate Professor of Business Administration, Director of the Bureau of Business and Economic Research, University of California, Berkeley, California, U.S.A.
Co-Author of: *Marketing Efficiency of Puerto Rico; A Canadian Economy: Prospect and Retrospect.*

ALFRED E. KAHN, B.A., M.A., Ph.D.: Professor of Economics, Chairman of Department of Economics, Cornell University, Ithaca, New York, U.S.A.
Author of: *Great Britain in the World Economy.*
Co-Author of: *Fair Competition, the Law and Economics of Antitrust Policy; Integration and Competition in the Petroleum Industry.*

RICHARD A. HAMBURGER, Dr. Ing., Councillor of the High Authority of the European Coal and Steel Community.

PIERRE URI, formerly Director General with the European Communities.
Author of: *The Brussels Report on the Common Market and Euratom; The Report on the Economic Situation of the Community Countries.*

CONTENTS

CHAPTER 1

ECONOMIC GOALS AND THE ROLE OF COMPETITION: INTRODUCTION

JOHN PERRY MILLER
Yale University, New Haven, Conn., U.S.A.

The free market is an ubiquitous institution to be found in most societies, ancient and modern, developed and underdeveloped, planned and unplanned. Current interest in the functioning of free markets has been heightened by the increasing awareness of the role of the private industrial sector—including manufacturing, construction and distribution—in the process of economic growth. The development of the institution of the free market was a major feat of social engineering and the development of our understanding of its potential was a major intellectual accomplishment. While there is considerable evidence of a "natural tendency" of man to "truck and barter," it is clear that if man's energies and resources are to be used effectively, institutions which will channel these energies and resources appropriately must be developed.

Economic growth in free societies depends upon social, political and economic institutions which are respectful of and conducive to enterprise, i.e., innovation and risk taking, and acquisitiveness and mobility on the part of substantial groups throughout the society. It presupposes various institutions supporting a free market, including the law regarding property and contract, and substantial freedom for individuals and firms acting independently in their own interest to make decisions with respect to investment, output and prices. But it has long been recognized that the public interest and private interest are not always synonymous. For example, freedom to misrepresent one's product, freedom to destroy a competitor's property, freedom to monopolize and freedom to restrain trade are generally recognized as contrary to the public interest. The evolution of the rules for a policy of enterprise and competition has been a tortuous one; as the following chapters indicate, it has followed different paths in various countries.

Current practice reflects differences in objective economic factors, in philosophy and economic understanding, in cultural traditions, and in the historical development of particular societies.

The concept of a policy of competition is ambiguous. There is a general concensus among economists concerning the meaning of the concepts of "pure competition" and "perfect competition," but there is less concensus concerning their usefulness in the study of modern economics for either analytical or normative purposes. Most markets have some blend of "monopolistic" and "competitive" elements. The monopolistic or oligopolistic elements are in part inherent in the system due to economies of scale, the spatial distribution of production and consumption, the limits to knowledge, the cost of rational decisions, etc. But in part they are due to conscious public policies such as copyrights, trademarks, trade names and patents. And in part they are the incidental result of other policies, e.g., tax laws, practices of advertising and laws of incorporation. In the interest of enterprise we encourage limited elements of "monopoly" in the belief that their over-all long run effect will be to promote "competition." In other cases we tolerate monopoly elements believing that in the absence of clearly preferable and workable alternatives we should defer to the freedom of enterprise even though this leads to some monopoly power. Public policy is not concerned solely to promote competition through the antitrust or restrictive practices legislation. Its concern is broader, to identify and encourage those institutional arrangements which will foster economic growth and other public objectives. Because of the pluralistic nature of these objectives, e.g., growth, security, equality, opportunity and freedom, because of differences in economic and cultural conditions, and because of the different rates at which these objectives may be traded off, policies with respect to competition vary in different societies and at different times.

What is the case for a policy of competition? The claims made for a policy of competition are twofold: first, that it supports broad social and political objectives of opportunity and freedom; and second, that, properly conceived, it is the best insurance for steady economic growth. There are those who argue that other forms of economic administration would be more conducive to growth and that in supporting the policy of free competition we pay a price in terms of economic growth in order that we may have the social and political benefits of individual opportunity and freedom. But certainly, whatever one's views concerning the amount of freedom and opportunity and rate of economic growth which may be obtained under a policy of free competition, the case for such a policy rests upon these two pillars.

A policy of competition in a free society means decentralization—decentralization of initiative, in the determination of goals and in administration of economic affairs. Initiative for innovation and change rests in the hands of individuals, firms and other groups. Choice between alternative uses of resources rests primarily in the hands of consumers, labor, and owners of natural and capital resources. Responsibility for organizing and administering the production and distribution processes is decentralized to individuals, private firms and other groups.

The direct coercive power of the state over individuals and of one individual over another is minimized. Coercion, a necessary ingredient in any economic system, takes the form of the impersonal coercion of the market. The individual, while subject to the coercion of the market, faces alternatives in his roles as a consumer and as a supplier of productive services and resources. In his various roles the individual is, then, faced with several opportunities among which he is free to choose.

The second claim of the policy of competition is that it promotes economic development. This will receive special attention in the chapters below. Properly structured free markets may provide incentives to innovation and a mechanism for the diffusion of innovation; they may promote efficient use of resources by individuals and firms and efficient allocation of resources in response to consumer preferences. These four factors—innovation, diffusion, efficiency and the appropriate allocation of resources—represent the core of the essentially economic argument for the policy of competition.

But it must be emphasized that this system of decentralization is one within a set of institutions contrived by man and supported by law. The rigors of the impersonal coercion of the market are mitigated by public and private programs of social security, education and relief. Modern societies have long since abandoned the naked spontaneous market system as a device for economic administration. Monetary and fiscal policies play a large role in setting the environment within which individuals are free to act by affecting the level of effective demand and thereby influencing the incentives to private investment and initiative. Governments sometimes play the role of innovator in some sectors of the economy, e.g., atomic energy. Likewise governments may encourage the consumption of certain products, e.g., school milk programs, and discourage others, e.g., limiting the sale of liquor to minors. While governments may play an important role, both directly and indirectly, even in industrial countries outside the orbit of the Soviet Republics and Communist China, the private sector is predominant and major reliance is placed upon a policy of enterprise and competition acting through free markets.

As indicated above, the concept of a free competitive market is ambiguous. The problem of public policy is to develop a set of rules which will serve to maintain the climate and incentives necessary for enterprise, to channel economic activities and resources so as to promote economic growth and, at the same time, to preserve the essential opportunities and freedoms for individuals.

This is not an easy task. We know too little about the economic effects of alternative market structures, particularly oligopolistic markets, or markets of the few. We are only beginning to understand the differences of business behavior resulting from differences in the political, social and cultural characteristics of various countries. We know little about the changes in market structure and behavior in the process of the development of a country, industry or region. We know little about the potentialities for changing market structure and market behavior by administrative, legislative and judicial action. There is a great deal to be done in exploring and integrating the experiences of both developed and underdeveloped countries in these respects. The time is ripe for extensive comparative analysis—comparisons through time, comparisons of countries and regions and comparisons of industries operating under different systems of law.

The following chapters explore the current state of our knowledge and the experience of various countries in their efforts to promote economic development, freedom and opportunity. In Chapter 2 Professor Joseph J. Spengler surveys the theory of the role of competition and monopoly in promoting economic development. He considers in detail the state of our knowledge concerning the types of market structure and behavior which will promote or retard innovation, diffusion and the efficient allocation of resources.

The postwar period has seen a reconsideration of policy with respect to restrictive agreements in the United Kingdom and on the Continent. In Chapter 4 Professor Thomas Wilson analyzes the effects of restrictive practices, particularly in Great Britain, and in Chapter 5 Fritz Voigt considers the effects of the German experience in the promotion and regulation of cartels. The investigation of restrictive practices in Great Britain during the postwar period represents a substantial contribution to our body of knowledge concerning business practices and their effects under a system which was relatively tolerant of joint business behavior. The gradual elimination of restrictive practices in recent years has been associated with an expansion of British industry, and it is interesting to speculate upon the relationship between these two phenomena. The German experience is somewhat different. Until recent years Germany has likewise been tolerant of collective arrangements. Yet German industry developed substantially and constituted a serious challenge to Britain and other industrialized countries in the early part of the century. How important is government policy with respect to restrictive practices in promoting or retarding economic growth, compared to other economic and cultural factors? The German experience throws a great deal of light upon the potentialities and limits of cartel arrangements both voluntary and compulsory. In Chapter 3 Dr. William Boserup and Dr. Uffe Schlichtkrull present a detailed outline of current policies with respect to restrictive practices and competitive behavior in other European countries. They summarize the variety of experiments in the postwar period and testify to the increasing concern in all countries with promoting a policy of competition.

In Chapter 6, I outline the development and current status of antitrust policy in the United States, the country which has wrestled with these problems for the longest period. In Chapter 7 Professor Richard H. Holton discusses, with specific reference to the United States, the changing structure of distribution and the role it has played in the promotion of competition. The development of new distributive channels in the United States in rivalry with the traditional channels has provided an interesting interplay between the efforts of manufacturers to develop strong market positions by reaching forward to control the channels of distribution or to influence consumers' acceptance through advertising or other sales effort, on the one hand, and the effort of the mass distributors to reach back into the processes of production and limit the power of the manufacturers, on the other. Change and heterogeneity in the process of distribution have served to promote competitive behavior in the United States. Antitrust policy has played its part in this process by facilitating the development of new techniques of distribution.

In Chapter 8 Professor Alfred E. Kahn discusses the role of patents in the promotion of competition and monopoly and the problem of reconciling the grant of limited monopoly power with the policy of competition. Here again this problem has been vividly posed in the enforcement of antitrust policy in the United States during the last twenty years.

The authors of the last two chapters are concerned with the development of competitive markets which transcend national boundaries in Continental Europe. Dr. Richard A. Hamburger discusses the efforts to develop a more rational and competitive sector of the European economy under the Coal and Steel Community. Dr. Pierre Uri is concerned which the broad problems of integrating in a rational and practical way the six countries of the European Common Market, countries whose industrial, financial and fiscal systems have been protected in various ways from one another and from other countries outside the Community. These two experiments in developing rational market structures which transcend historically defined national boundaries hold forth great promise not only for the countries involved but, by their example, for other regional communities.

CHAPTER 2

ROLE OF COMPETITION AND MONOPOLY IN ECONOMIC DEVELOPMENT[1]

JOSEPH J. SPENGLER

Duke University, Durham, N.C., U. S. A.

"Geometry ascended the throne left vacant by philosophy and commonsense; and ingenuous youths and maidens, beguiled into the belief that here was a true picture of the real world, spent the best moments of their young lives in memorizing (generally wrong) endless fantastic patterns of tangencies and intersections."

D. H. Robertson, *Quarterly Journal of Economics*, February, 1950, p. 8.

"Competition guarantees only that *some* efficient capital program will be followed... The intertemporal invisible hand ...while it results in efficiency over long periods of time,... requires only the most myopic vision on the part of market participants... But for society as a whole there is need for vision at a distance."

Robert Dorfman et al., *Linear Programming and Economic Analysis*, p. 321.

My discussion of the relation of types of economic organization to economic development has to do with economic development in both relatively underdeveloped and relatively developed countries; it is confined, however, to those parts of the world in which free enterprise plays a major role and the activities of the state are not so predominant as in the Soviet Union and its sphere of influence. Accordingly, after I review the development of economic opinion respecting the comparative effects of competition and monopoly, I shall differentiate between developed and underdeveloped countries and identify some of the factors with which economic development is associated. Then I shall inquire into the impact of alternative forms of economic and business organization upon the more important of the determinants of economic development and indicate the implications of the associations discovered for economic development in both relatively advanced and relatively backward countries.

I shall not assign highly specific and unchanging empirical content to the terms competition and monopoly, or make use of the criteria which have been developed to classify industries and markets precisely in respect of their competitiveness. These terms can be given precise, unchanging, and always applicable meaning only if they are made very general, or if the world to which they relate is quite stable. A world characterized by economic development does not answer to this description. Development entails change; it is both a cause of instability and a sequel to it. Much of the discussion that follows is centered about economic development. It has to do with kinetic rather than with static situations, with situations in which change, often of a discontinuous sort, is undergone either by the decision-making economic organization, or by the market in which it operates, or by the remainder of the relevant external environment. In such a world a model or a definition can be kept isologous with relevant reality only if it is appropriately modified as this reality changes.

The situations encountered in the world of reality seldom correspond to polar competitive or monopolistic models; as a rule, they approximate hybrid interpolar models, sometimes approaching closer to the one and sometimes to the other extreme. Decision-makers who can significantly modify prevailing selling or buying prices, together with the amounts exchanged, are describable as "monopolistic"; those who cannot do so are describable as "competitive". In either situation, however, the decision maker remains free to innovate and reduce inputs per unit of output, or to transform inputs into novel and (hence) relatively profitable types of output. An industry may perhaps be thought of as relatively competitive when, though it is dominated by one or several firms, the "dominating effect" that might result is kept in check.[2] For purposes of this essay, however, a problem remains even after competitiveness has been defined: How do economic development and welfare vary with competitiveness as defined?

I. Competition Wins Approval

How policy-makers and social scientists approach problems is determined only in part by the analytical tools they have at hand, together with the objectives they seek. This approach is colored also by the predominating ideological and ideational climates. Current interpretations of the comparative roles of competition and monopoly illustrate the pertinence of this dictum; they reflect the subjective climate surrounding economists and policy makers, a climate always partially shaped by views of yesteryear's theorists respecting the comparative impact of competition and monopoly.

The esteem attached to competition, viewed as an optimizing social process, has fluctuated; so also has the degree of disfavor manifested toward monopoly, though in lesser measure. Medieval authors looked with more or less disapproval upon monopoly as did many pre-Smithian writers who remained somewhat in the scholastic tradition. Nonetheless, during the centuries when men subscribed to the tenets of mercantilism, with its emphasis upon economic development in general and upon Asiatic and New-World commerce in particular, temporary or indefinite monopoly often was found to be good. It was believed, and not without reason, that certain ventures purportedly of advantage to the national community were more likely to be carried out if their undertakers were assured such security as monopoly might provide. By the early eighteenth century if not before, however, a solid business community had been established especially in England, Holland, and France, and some members of this community were finding various of the existing restraints upon competition to be objectionable; even earlier in fact there had been objection to a state's conferring monopolistic privileges upon preferred beneficiaries. Meanwhile powerful expression was being given to the presumed ethical and economic superiority of competitive over non-competitive mechanisms and systems by the Physiocrats and, above all, by Adam Smith, the spirit of whose classical endorsement of a system of natural liberty prevailed widely and far into the nineteenth century, except perhaps in Germany where the historical school of economists was dominant. Smith supposed also that a monopoly could not persist in the face of the forces making for competition so long as the state did not undergird such monopoly.[3]

The concepts of competition and monopoly, together with their conditions, were not completely defined until the present century. Smith and his classical successors lay down certain conditions along with qualifications, but did not establish that competition as defined would necessarily eventuate in optimum results. More precise definitions of competition, monopoly, and their requirements were provided by Cournot and his mathematical-economist successors, though it remained for Marshall (and later, Pareto and Pigou) to inquire carefully into the extent to which competition gives rise to optimum economic organization. It was Knight, however, who, by building upon the work of J. B. Clark and completing the definition of perfect competition, made plain how unlikely it was to prevail. He thus stimulated anew the search for concepts of competition either more in keeping with economic reality, or, because less rigorously delineated, more in keeping with the requirements of those charged with formulating or executing regulative policy. Of the policy-oriented concepts resulting, "workable competition", essentially a lineal descendant (via Knight and Chamberlin) of Marshallian competition, is perhaps the most important.[4]

The gradual emergence after 1850, of combinations of firms (i.e., trusts, cartels, pools, etc.) in transport and industry, especially in the United States and Germany, prompted inquiry into means whereby their behavior might be regulated and into the extent to which the preservation of competition was a good thing. In the United States the principal resulting legislation, the Sherman Act, was the expression, not of "a simple faith in unqualified competition", but of a desire to prevent monopoly.[5] It eventuated nonetheless in antitrust decisions that went much beyond what might have been accomplished on the basis of previously regnant commonlaw principles.[6] In England Alfred Marshall, reflecting the belief that the Anglo-Saxon temper was unfavorable to state management of enterprise and confident in the regulative power of public opinion, was interested in preserving "what is essential in the benefits of true competition", among which he included the superiority of the "inventive force of a multitude of small undertakers" to that of large private firms considered as a group.[7] In Germany, and perhaps in other continental European countries, there was less emphasis upon the salutary influence of competition than in England, with its great dependence on external trade. In general, though in internationally varying degree, the emphasis was not so much upon the need to preserve pure competition as upon the need to prevent monopoly, and it remained so until in the present century the supposedly development-favoring properties of monopoly began to be stressed, especially by Schumpeter and others. Even so, these properties did not command much attention until in the 1940's, after the prior, partial rejection (in the 1930's) of the competitive norm. The theorists of the 1930's remained content to concentrate attention upon resource allocation, rate of use of capacity, and related questions.[8] They thus reflected a concern with the distribution of resources among uses that had been more or less dominant since the 1870's. Out of this concern, however, arose some of the findings which eventuated in the newer welfare economics and the critique of competitive processes therewith associated.

The importance of invention and innovation was slow to be appreciated by nineteenth-century economists. This is somewhat surprising in view of the fact that "invention of the method of invention" has been described as "the greatest invention of the nineteenth century."[9] Presumably, however, these economists, aware of the widespreadness of poverty and still apprehensive lest "diminishing returns" really make itself felt, were unable to appreciate how significant were the improvements already under way or how rapidly output and income might in time be increased. In discussions respecting how economic organization might be improved, therefore, most economists gave relatively little attention to invention, innovation, their correlates, and their facilitation.

II. Competition Found Wanting; Monopoly Defended

Up to the time of World War I economists outside Germany generally found a not well-defined but still highly competitive form of economic organization to be superior, on welfare grounds, to alternative forms; but this view was not universally accepted. Public opinion could hardly be expected to be entirely favorable to a social process (i.e., competition) whose workings were not well understood. Moreover, even some economists occasionally found relatively non-competitive forms of organization (other than "natural" and "legal" monopolies) to be superior to their competitive counterparts.

Indirectly indicative of the degree of hostility of public opinion to competition is Marshall's expression of concern lest the recurrent emergence of "anti-social" forms of competition blind men to the fact that, on the balance, competition augments "social wellbeing".[10] The need for such expression was greater, of course, in a British or particularly in a European society than in the American.[11] A highly developed economic rivalry is not particularly welcome in a long established society that is shot through, as was the European, with social-philosophical, ideological, and other vestiges of feudalism, paternalism, etc. It is in keeping, however, with the Weltanschauung prevailing in a land recently settled as was the American by successive streams of ethnically distinguishable immigrants who were bent upon finding better situations for themselves and their descendants in a society reputedly open socially, economically, and geographically. Free competition still enjoys greater social approval in the United States and post-war Germany than in Britain, France, and various other lands, with the result that in America and Germany actual or potential "victims" of free competition are less likely to be guarded against its impact.[12] Nonetheless, even in the United States competition has been condemned as unfair and destructive, and it is probable that the degree of approval given competitive processes has declined in recent decades.[13] Elsewhere, misuse of resources and wastes attendant upon competition have been noted, together with conflicts between public and private and between economic and noneconomic ends.[14] These critiques have not eventuated in positive defenses of monopoly, but in pleas for intervention by the state.

In recent years, however, qualified defenses have been made of temporary arrangements which are "monopolistic" in that the beneficiaries of these arrangements are guarded for a time against the competition of some buyers or sellers. Defenses of such arrangements have usually arisen, as did earlier defenses of patent rights, infant-industry protectionism, etc., out of concern with the process of economic development, or with its acceleration. Best known of these defenses is that of Schumpeter, though it differs greatly from ordinary defenses of protectionism and of patent monopoly.[15] It incorporates a theory of the rise and fall of particular monopolies into a general explanation of "how the economic system generates the forces which incessantly transform it".[16] This transformation process gives rise to new economic structures and the destruction of old ones, and could eventuate in the decomposition and supersession of capitalism itself. In this process monopoly functions as both a precondition to successful innovation and as a temporary sequel thereto.[17] While monopoly is described also as serving to check deflation, the development-favoring effects of this influence are considered secondary to those of innovation.[18]

Schumpeter's notions of innovation and competition are crucial to his analysis. At the time he was forming these notions industrial management had not yet become rationalized as it is today. The role of the individual and of specific innovations loomed larger than it does in the contemporary world in which a bureaucratized management usually is continuously concerned to innovate. As a rule, it was an individual who made the strategic, innovation-producing decision which permitted a development-supporting surplus to emerge.[19] Let C represent the aggregate money cost of a collection I (or its equivalent) of inputs and V, the relevant final aggregate value of the output (or its equivalent) into which this collection I may be transformed; then Schumpeterian innovation may be said to take place when the improvement or change involved greatly increases the spread between C and V. This spread can be increased either by reducing I whilst holding V at its former level, or by converting I into a more or less novel output commanding a much higher value V in the market than did that into which I was transformed formerly, or by simultaneously reducing

I and increasing its correlate *V*. The basis of such an innovation may be the discovery of a new use for a product, a newly introduced invention, a more economical mode of industrial organization, a more effective method of marketing or of using by-products, and so on. Its introducer, the innovating entrepreneur, is likely, at least in a non-trustified economy, Schumpeter reasons, to be a "New" Man or industrial leader who incorporates his innovation in a new firm founded for that purpose and entailing the construction of new plant or the rebuilding of old. His reward consists in the increase in the spread between *C* and *V*, augmented by such expansion of output as proves feasible under the new conditions; how long he can enjoy this particular reward turns on how long it takes other producers to imitate or modify his innovation and bid up the exchange value *C* of a given input collection *I* or depress the value *V* into which *I* is being transformed.

The innovator's situation is thus that "designated by the term Monopolistic Competition", and it becomes weaker as the competition to which he is exposed increases, more or less according to the temporal models utilized to describe the monopolistically competitive process of price and profit adjustment.[20] Even so, the absorption into an economy of a major Schumpeterian innovation, together with the so-called cluster of complementary innovations that come in its wake, tends to produce a much greater break with the past than does the introduction of an ordinary monopolistically competitive situation. According to the theory, the efforts of many new entrepreneurs to profit from the initial innovation by imitating it, improving it, or engaging in activities complementary thereto push up input prices and depress various output prices except in so far as these are sustained, in money terms, by the credit inflation that at first usually accompanies the absorption of an innovation. The competition associated with this innovative process is not primarily price competition, however, although this form of competition plays an adaptive role in the modification of the prices of inputs and of various outputs, some of which are complementary to or substitutive for outputs more immediately affected by innovation. The competition that counts most is the *replacement of old by new* products, resource supplies, methods, markets, etc. For this competition, the "creative response" of the innovator to the environment in which he finds himself and through which he commands "a decisive cost or quality advantage", strikes not at "the margins of the profits and the outputs of the existing firms but at their foundations and their lives"; it is the source of most of the transformation which economies intermittently undergo.[21]

According to Schumpeter's account of the developmental process, monopolistic situations are necessarily transitory. They are transformed in time under the impact of competition, particularly under that arising out of new products, new methods, etc. For this reason Schumpeter seems to have believed that temporary monopoly, even when not merely a sequel to innovation, might accelerate economic development in a world subject to "rapidly changing conditions" and hence to the possibility that the relative significance of newly introduced or improved commodities, technologies, etc., might be markedly and speedily reduced. For economic development depended immediately upon innovation; and this would be undertaken in any particular case only if the prospective costs occasioned thereby to the innovator were sufficiently outweighed by his prospective returns, even though the marginal social benefit associated with the innovation was bound to exceed its marginal social cost under all circumstances. Accordingly, temporary "monopoly", or protection against competition, even though not always a prerequisite to the introduction of an innovation, made for an increase in the rate of innovation. Such protection might have its origin in the nature of an industry, in governmental practice, in inter-firm relations, etc.; it could be associated with patents, secrecy of process, favorable price situations, heavy initial, entry-retarding capital costs, and so on. This protection could not persist, however, being doomed to removal by the "perennial gale of creative destruction" which innovation is always blowing up.[22] It might also be accompanied by a reduction of financial and administrative costs originating in greater size and security, access to greater profits, etc.

The impact of "monopoly" upon technical progress is discussed below; here it need only be noted that Schumpeter's "defense" of monopoly has been criticized, and that its endorsement has sometimes rested upon the belief that the presence of monopolistic elements makes for stability.[23] Solo has rejected Schumpeter's conception of the innovation process, particularly his emphasis upon the role of new entrepreneurs and firms, and has sought to show that "innovation is a regular part of normal business procedure based upon deliberate inventive effort on the part of the firm", and that consequently inputs are used in this just as in any other business activity.[24] M. Abramovitz concluded, on the basis of T. N. E. C. materials, "that the destruction of monopoly controls would make for a higher rate of new investment, both immediately and in the long run", implying also that the rate of technological progress would be stepped up.[25] G. H. Hildebrand, Jr., observed that even if some protection were temporarily given to a firm, it would not necessarily advance applied technology or invest capital at a heightened rate.[26] Stocking and Watkins also question, as has W. Adams, whether the presence of monopoly elements stimulates innovation and investment, and Machlup decides, though the available evidence is not finally conclusive, "against a policy of creating or condoning monopoly positions as investment incentives."[27] P. Hennipman, after reviewing the impact of market structure, market position, and monopoly upon innovation and its diffusion, concluded that the problem was too complex to permit simple or unconditional inferences. He noted also that "a certain measure of monopoly" was an "inevitable concomitant of progress", but declared that established monopoly, even though it might be credited with great innovative ability, tended on the balance to retard rather than to foster economic development.[28]

Chamberlin reasons that both temporary monopoly and competition are essential to continuing technical progress. A potential innovator would be without motive to innovate if he could not gain at least a temporary advantage therefrom. "How can one doubt that if a new product or variation of a product, or a new and more efficient technique of production, could be instantly imitated by others, the incentive to make it would for most people be lost?" Having acquired such a monopolistic situation, however, its beneficiary is under pressure to distribute the benefits resulting and to undertake new innovations only if he is subject to competition, especially from newcomers bent on introducing further innovations as well as upon imitating the monopolist's own innovation.[29] Chamberlin thus approves of an entrepreneur establishing a temporarily monopolistic situation through the introduction of an innovation which is likely to benefit the community at large, but disapproves of entrepreneurial activity that serves only to generate monopolistic profit.[30]

Innovation and technical progress have been assigned an increasingly important place in the literature relating to "workable competition".[31] Thus Sosnick reports that about half the writers he studied believe that "profits should be at levels which reward investment and efficiency and induce innovation", but describes none as endorsing temporary monopoly arising from conditions other than innovation. Moreover, his own inference that the presence of "creative destruction" is essential to "workable market conditions" probably has wide endorsement.[32] According to Papandreou and Wheeler, whether competition remains adequately workable to constitute a "meaningful alternative to a planned society" depends upon the amount of "innovation" realized, together with the extent to which new products and industries result.[33] G. W. Stocking's findings suggest, however, that in the absence of state intervention of the antitrust sort, there would not be enough innovation and development to meet the Papandreou-Wheeler requirements.[34]

The discussions of workable competition and of the manner in which innovativeness and competitiveness are linked point to a fundamental outcome conspicuous in recent literature and of great significance for analyses such as the present in which "ideal-output" conditions are sometimes made a part of the norm by which the desirability of changes in economic organization are to be judged. (1) Let us suppose that the adjustments under consideration are marginal, or at least quite small, and that little if any attention need be given the future, or the equitability of income distribution. Suppose also that in the economy under analysis, as in every real economy, there exist a number of divergences between marginal values and costs. Then, even though a removal of all divergences would increase economic welfare, a reduction of only one or several, with the others remaining unchanged, could diminish rather than increase economic welfare. Account must therefore be taken of the possible side effects of particular, divergence-reducing actions, since the components of an economy (i.e., firms, industries, sectors) are interdependent. (2) If attention must be given to development and hence to the future, a regime of competition, even though it efficiently supplies what is desired when only small and present-facing adjustments are involved, loses some of its attractiveness. Such a regime may assign too little weight to developmental activities, and its executors may be less capable of coping with dearth of information and uncertainty through risk-pooling than are very large units, or a central authority. (3) When, as in a rapidly developing economy, vast structural changes are involved, difficulties of the sort indicated under (1) and (2) are great, with the result that competitive regimes are often likely to prove wanting and that frequently even desirable divergence-reducing measures prove of minor significance. In short, when an economy is imperfectly competitive, increases in "competitiveness" and reductions in value-cost divergences do not necessarily increase economic welfare; and when an economy is undergoing rapid development, measures intended to bring about such increases and reductions may even check the growth of economic welfare as defined.[35]

III. Developed versus Under-Developed Countries

Non-communist countries are classifiable as developed, quasi-developed, and underdeveloped, accordingly as their per capita incomes are high, intermediate, or low since, as a rule, income differences reflect differences in skill, resource-use, etc.[36] The immediate determinants of economic development do not vary generically from country to country. The specific forms they assume do vary internationally, however, as do socio-political milieux and other conditions which affect economic performance.

Of most concern here are circumstances which condition the extent, the variety, and the impact of competition in economic life. Underdeveloped countries and, in lesser measure, quasi-developed countries share many characteristics which, acting in combination, give rise to lowness of per capita income, but only some of these are presently relevant. Upon an economist's research objective must depend his conception of pertinent characteristics, variations in the dimensions of which distinguish economically developed from economically underdeveloped and, though less sharply, from quasi-developed countries. Seemingly relevant characteristics are listed below.[37] This list is of limited usefulness, however, for countries assembled into any one of our three categories (i.e., developed, quasi-developed, underdeveloped) differ appreciably from one another in particular respects.

There follows a list of conditions, many of which environ enterprisers and enterprise in underdeveloped countries.

1. *General*

   (a) The civil service tends to be quantitatively and qualitatively deficient.
   (b) Monetary and financial institutions are underdeveloped.
   (c) Growth-facilitating public institutions are likely to be deficient.
   (d) Asset preferences may be comparatively unfavorable to economic growth.

2. *Capital*

   (a) The capital-population ratio is very low as is the amount of capital available per worker.
   (b) Because of lowness of income, together with institutional conditions that affect the propensity to save, a majority of the population saves little or nothing.

(c) Working capital tends to be in short supply.
(d) The ratio of both voluntary savings and capital formation to national income is very low as is the average amount of capital formed per capita.
(e) Savings and capital are not always mobile, particularly when they originate in agriculture.

3. *Labor*

(a) Because natality is very high whilst mortality is not so high and tending to decline, the rate of growth of both the population and the labor force is high and tending to increase.
(b) A very large fraction of both the population and the labor force is situated in agriculture and rural communities.
(c) Only a small fraction of the labor force is engaged in industry (i.e., outside agriculture, commerce, and services).
(d) Only a small fraction of the population resides in towns and cities.
(e) The labor force is lacking in skills and literacy and often includes relatively high numbers of children.
(f) The labor force includes a relatively small number of paid employees and relatively many who are unpaid or work on own account.
(g) There is considerable seasonal and chronic unemployment as well as under-employment (especially in agriculture and other residual employment categories).

4. *Land and Natural Resources*

(a) In Asia and parts of Africa and the Caribbean area the ratio of the agricultural population to cultivable land is very high, often so high that it could be reduced without reducing output.
(b) Frequently important fuels and minerals are in short actual or potential supply.

5. *Technology*

(a) Advanced technology is known and utilized only infrequently with the result that agricultural output per agricultural worker and per acre, together with non-agricultural output per non-agricultural worker, is usually very low.
(b) Technicians, engineers, etc., are few in number, and there are few or no facilities for their training.
(c) The spread between best or better and inferior methods of production in use is much greater than in advanced countries, with the result that under-developed economies are likely to be dual in technological and business-organizational structure, comprising both relatively advanced and quite backward sectors.
(d) Transport and public utility services are likely to be in very short supply.
(e) In enterprise carried on in underdeveloped economies the ratio of unskilled to highly skilled personnel is much higher than in quite advanced economies, the role of administrative personnel is much less developed, and overhead costs are relatively less important.[38]

6. *Sources of Enterprise*

(a) The middle class is relatively unimportant numerically.
(b) The ratio of really enterprising entrepreneurs to the population is very low.
(c) The ratio of skilled managers (as distinguished from entrepreneurs) to the population is low.

(d) Facilities or circumstances conducive to the augmentation of the supply of entrepreneurs and skilled managers are lacking.

7. *Social Conditions*

(a) The climate of opinion among the intelligentsia and in government circles is likely to be hostile to private enterprise.
(b) Many small landowners, cultivators, and self-employed are very short of liquid or easily liquidable resources.
(c) The status and the socio-economic position of women is inferior.

8. *Market Situation*

(a) The price system is likely to be underdeveloped and hence less suited than required to give adequate policy indications.
(b) Entrepreneurs tend to be confronted by relatively price-inelastic demands for goods and services.
(c) The elasticity of the aggregate supply of particular goods or services tends to be low, especially in the shorter run.
(d) The internal domestic market for many products is likely to be expanding relatively slowly.
(e) The number and the variety of goods and services entering into most household budgets tends to be small, with the result that, in countries of ancient and respected culture and hence partially immune to foreign demonstration effects, the potential marginal propensity to save can be high.
(f) Capital is likely to be in inelastic supply to most enterprisers.
(g) The services of relatively skilled workers and of professional people are in relatively inelastic supply.
(h) Only the services of unskilled and relatively unskilled labor are in quite elastic supply in general and to particular enterpreneurs.
(i) Markets are shot through with bottlenecks and potential discontinuities.
(j) Many but not all of the underdeveloped countries are too small to permit the realization of considerable economies of scale and manoeuver.

Several inferences may now be drawn. First, underdeveloped economies are less competitive than are developed economies. (1) The elasticity of supply of particular products at firm and industry levels tends to be low, especially in the shorter run, with the result that a relatively small number of firms gives rise only to a relatively small amount of competition.[39] Plants are not so likely to be flexible,[40] or susceptible of being converted to the production of goods other than those being turned out. Moreover, shortages of inputs complementary to unskilled labor are particularly operative in the short run, and may, even in the absence of barriers to entry, be harder to overcome in the long run than in advanced economies.[41] (2) The elasticity of the demands confronting many suppliers in the domestic (as distinguished from the external) market is likely to be low, with the result that prices and profit margins will be high. Nor is that which is rational in the short run likely to be tempered by longer run prospects unless, as is not so likely, affluence is increasing appreciably and the market for the products in question is expanding quite rapidly.[42] (3) Condition (2) is likely to be re-enforced by a disposition to live and let live, arising out of an unwillingness of entrepreneurs to encourage competitiveness, increase their economic risks, and expose themselves to the danger of losing the social position associated with entrepreneurship.

Second, because of the obstacles that supposedly stand in the way of economic development under private auspices, the economic role of the state tends to be large in underdeveloped countries, even when the actual and the potential contribution of private initiative is very important though likely to be underestimated.[43] The state may undertake the role of pace-setter, or it may attempt to accelerate development in sectors deemed strategic or critical. In either event it is likely to attempt to increase the rate of capital formation—an attempt unlikely to succeed at first unless steps are taken to increase the marginal propensity to save.

Third, since unskilled labor is in relatively elastic supply in most underdeveloped countries whereas agents complementary thereto (i.e., capital, management, skilled labor) are in short and not easily augmentable supply, expansion of output long depends primarily upon increasing the supply of these complementary agents.[44] Of the two main sectors composing an underdeveloped economy, the large, labor-rich non-capitalistic sector is dominated either by traditional methods of production, as in countries of complicated culture (e.g., parts of Asia), or by less hallowed but still backward methods, as in regions where subsistence-oriented culture and interchange are mixed (e.g., in parts of Sub-Sahara Africa).[45] The small but growing capitalistic sector, wherein alone agents complementary to unskilled labor are to be found, tends to be export-oriented in a raw-material producing country. Economic development consists primarily in the expansion of the capitalistic sector at the expense of the non-capitalistic,[46] in which unskilled labor is superabundant and average income and the marginal productivity of labor are very low. Hence, although the rate of development depends upon the rapidity with which capital and scarce managerial and industrial skills can be formed, it is conditioned by the extent to which unskilled labor can be attracted to the capitalistic sector by wages that remain low enough (say 35–50 per cent above level in the non-capitalistic sector) to permit capitalistic entrepreneurs to realize large surpluses wherewith to support further development. Accordingly, whatever pushes up this wage (e.g., trade unions, minimum-wage requirements, etc.), or increases the supply price required in the non-capitalistic sector, tends to slow down capital formation and economic development.[47] In the end, of course, this price rises under the impact of expansion and of such waste in the use of labor, together with retardation of technical progress, as flows from the presence of an abundance of cheap labor.[48]

Fourth, corporations, particularly those of foreign provenance which operate in underdeveloped countries, are likely to have to bear various economic and social overhead costs which in advanced countries are borne by the state. In most underdeveloped countries, despite great deficiencies in the socio-economic infrastructure, governmental expenditures suited to overcome these deficiencies form only a small fraction of the national income.[49] Private corporations can bear such burdens only if they are large, enjoy a somewhat monopolistic situation, and shift the resulting costs to foreign or other consumers of their products. Public corporations subject to these burdens are under similar pressure to recover the resulting outlays from consumers or taxpayers. Under some conditions better use would be made of resources if the state supplied all the overhead facilities in question; then economies of specialization might be maximized and expenditures might be carried to points where public and private marginal benefit roughly coincided. These conditions seldom obtain in underdeveloped countries, however. There the missing facilities have to be supplied by private or public enterprise,[50] with enterprise free to recover the net costs resulting.

IV. Immediate Determinants of the Growth of Output per Capita

The growth of output per capita is dependent upon determinants which may be gathered into three classes: (a) those which are directly and continuously operative; (b) those which are directly but discontinuously operative; and (c) those which are indirectly operative, acting upon and through (a) and (b). Of those included under (a) the most important are growth of personal and impersonal capital currently in use per head and augmentation of applied technological knowledge.

Increments in output attributable to determinants included under (b) arise principally through shifts of inputs to more productive uses, as when excess labor is moved out of agriculture and into more productive employments. In a static economy the need for such shifts ends when inputs have become optimally distributed among and within firms. In a non-static economy, however, the need is always present; for population growth and technical and other changes bring about sub-optimal situations as well as terminate them.

The determinants included under (c) are important in the context of the present essay only in so far as they govern the amount of competition realizable. Illustrative are laws and institutions that condition what sellers and/or buyers may do; financial institutions which affect the assembly and the flow of funds; the legal structure within which business enterprise functions; patent laws; arrangements designed to bring marginal social costs and benefits into balance; and so on.

Of the two determinants, capital formation and technological progress, the latter seems to have played much the greater role in the augmentation of output per worker in developed countries in the past 50–75 or more years. The importance of technological progress has been recognized in a general way;[51] it has also been estimated to have increased output per head much more than has the accumulation of capital. In the United States between 1869–78 and 1919–28 "increase in resource efficiency" augmented gross national product about as much as did "increase in resources".[52] Abramovitz's estimates suggest that because of technical progress, net national product per unit of total input (i.e., man-hours plus capital) grew above 1.5 per cent per year.[53] This rate exceeds that observed in Northern and Western Europe in 1870–1914, but probably falls below that currently realizable in Chile and some Latin American countries.[54] According to R. M. Solow, in the United States in 1901–49 gross output per manhour increased about 100 per cent, of which about seven-eighths was attributable to "technical change" and the remaining one-eighth "to increased use of capital".[55] Technical progress has also increased output per unit of input appreciably in many countries, and failure of the output-input ratio to rise has usually been associated primarily with absence of technical progress.[56]

While it is clear that the role of technological progress in economic development is greater than that of capital accumulation, particularly in advanced countries and in those underdeveloped countries in which technological advances may constitute the only means of escape from a Malthusian trap,[57] the role of capital formation nonetheless is both important and strategic. Utilization of improved methods is possible, as a rule, only if enough capital is currently available and, above all, in capital-short, technologically retarded countries in which both equipping workers and adapting advanced technology call for a great deal of capital. Furthermore, the role of capital is underestimated, because some forms of capital formation (e.g., in agriculture) are imperfectly estimated, and because gross and net investment in education and relatively advanced technical and professional training is inadequately recorded. Estimates of the contribution of technological progress usually rest on the assumption that growth which cannot be imputed to increase in man-hours and physical equipment is attributable to technological progress. This progress is thus made to include at least those effects which are consequent upon increasing returns, or upon investment in education and the improvement of man's individual qualities, a form of investment requiring public subsidy, since its marginal private return tends to fall short of its marginal social return.[58]

Comparative misinvestment of capital also limits its contribution to economic growth and may therefore make for underestimation of its potential importance. The capacity of newly invested resources to eventuate in output and growth is conditioned by the uses to which they are put; it may be less at times, for example, if too much is put in plant and too little in equipment. The tendency to misinvest mobile resources may vary with the mode of business organization, if these are differentially biased. From the standpoint of the economy as a whole, however, misallocation probably results largely because the "interest rate" is not known (or possibly is not determinable), or because capital is allocated partly on the basis of non-economic or quasi-economic criteria (e.g., by governments, as proposed in a recent Indian plan). As was noted earlier though, it is impossible to determine non-arbitrarily when investment in development is optimal; optimality is a function of time and may not therefore be realized until a certain amount of time has elapsed. Emphasis upon shortrun criteria may (in part because they tend to be myopic) result in the inference that investment is non-optimal even though it is optimal (insofar as optimality is specifiable in a dynamic world) over the relevant period of time.[59]

Though the aggregate advantage to be had from income increasing redistributions of inputs among uses sometimes is small, such shifts (included under [b]) have played an important role and will continue to do so if factor mobility is facilitated.[60] The need to shift excess labor out of agriculture remains great in many underdeveloped countries with relatively large and growing rural populations; that it will not easily be achieved, however, the limited success of Japan (together with the experience of Europe) suggests. Of continuing importance in a dynamic world is the shift of resources toward technologically progressive industries, the demand for whose products is expanding. Output thus tends to increase relatively rapidly when technical progress is relatively great in industries, the elasticity of demand for whose products is relatively high and into which resources are free to move and thereby also stimulate capital accumulation. Such expansion slows down when "monopolistic" barriers develop and impede the shift of resources and the capital formation therewith associated.[61]

V. Forms of Business Organization

Large-scale entrepreneurial organization plays a much smaller role in underdeveloped than in developed economies both because these economies and their heavy-industry sectors remain small and because there is a shortage of agents of production (e.g., capital, skilled management) requisite for the creation of large organizations.[62] Much of the activity within the private sector is carried on by small firms, or by cottage and handicraft industries, together with self-employed workers. As a backward country develops, of course, the relative importance of larger firms increases, as Japanese experience suggests. In consequence, as Indian and Middle-Eastern experience indicates, the relative importance of the corporate form increases while that of simpler organizational forms (e.g., partnership, proprietorship) declines.[63]

While the presence of a multiplicity of small producers makes for competition in the sectors in which they carry on, the smallness of the industrial sector and the domestic market, together with the operation of economies of scale, often makes for the concentration of a large fraction of production in the hands of a very small number of firms in underdeveloped economies.[64] The resulting conduciveness to imperfectness of competition is accentuated when decision-making is further concentrated by such arrangements as the managing agency system common in India where the industrial sector employs little more than one-twentieth of the self-supporting workers.[65] This tendency may be held in check, of course, by potential imports, or, if an industry is supplying a foreign market, by the competition of foreign producers supplying this same market.

Governments have resorted to a variety of organizational arrangements intended to initiate or to accelerate economic development in sectors in which private initiative has been found wanting or inadequate to meet the risks and costs involved.[66] (1) The financial management of an enterprise may be undertaken by a governmental department, but this arrangement, while it has sometimes proved successful in established industries, is not suited to develop new industries. (2) The state may finance wholly or in part a company that operates under ordinary company law, or (3) it may establish a "public corporation" which finances its operations through borrowing and reinvestment of profits. None of these forms, though attractive in the abstract, is sufficiently likely to work well in practice, or to facilitate the establishment of new industry. It is too likely to become enmeshed in inflexibility-producing rules and regulations.[67] (4) The state may enter into an operating arrangement with a domestic or a foreign company whose remuneration and working conditions are contractually fixed; this arrangement too often proves unsatisfactory.[68] The pricing of output in accordance with the requirements of economic development may readily be accomplished with one or the other of the two forms most commonly used, (2) or (3), but the supply of this output may be attended by high costs if defects peculiar to one or the other form are not avoided.[69] If private enterprise is unable, even when its milieu is congenial, to establish a feasible industry, or unwilling to price properly, form (2) or (3) constitutes a workable alternative, provided that its potential shortcomings are guarded against.

VI. Active vs. Passive Sectors

Economic development is of two sorts, that taking place in the dynamic or active sectors of any economy in consequence of supply- or demand-modifying changes originating therein, and that taking place in essentially passive sectors under pressure to adjust to earlier changes in the active sectors. Differences between these two sorts of change are prominent only when investment decisions are non-infinitesimal in character, as is usual in rapidly expanding economies, be they advanced or retarded. In fact, it was with the post-war rise in growth rates that concern again began to be expressed, not that the price mechanism would imperfectly reflect costs and benefits, but that in the absence of appropriate action, particular industries might grow faster than the demand for their products or the supply of their inputs and thus give rise to development-retarding imbalance. It has come to be recognized, however, that growth usually entails, in sequence, intersectoral variation, imbalance, and adjustment, with the degree of imbalance and adjustment consequent upon a given sectoral expansion dependent upon a country's external trading relations.[70] A growing economy tends to be unbalanced; its expansion is made up of a series of spurts, some growth-generating and adjustment-compelling and others merely adaptive.[71] Some investment (e.g., motor car plants) "initiates a chain of further investment whereby the original investment is sustained, elaborated and supplemented" whereas other investment (e.g., rubber plantations, road-making equipment) is consequential upon prior initiatory investment. Industries differ, however, in their propensity to innovate and in their capacity to compel adjustment to innovation; this propensity appears to be strongest in some branches of manufacture whereas this capacity is greatest in innovating industries which *both* supply certain industries and require products of others.[72] The role of progressive countries is somewhat analogous to that of progressive industries; they may initiate growth processes to which those of other countries respond, given sufficient freedom of trade and communication.[73]

Economic development will take place so long as some of an economy's sectors are actively expanding and thus compelling others to adjust thereto. This means that an economy will continue to develop so long as entrepreneurial organization in some sectors is disposed to innovate and expand, since then entrepreneurs in other sectors will be under pressure to expand their activities accordingly. Portions of surpluses originating in some industries or sectors may supply others which are relatively expanding and hence capital-short; technical improvements originating in some firms or research institutions may be introduced into other firms or sectors and adapted thereto; and so on. If, as Marx implied, every entrepreneurial organization "is bent on making value expand itself",[74] or if, as Baumol concludes, "the institutionalized structure and psychology" of the larger, oligopolized firms "provides a powerful and sustained force making for the expansion of the economy",[75] development is assured since "drone" and "Fabian" as well as "imitative" entrepreneurs will be under pressure to follow in the wake of "innovating" entrepreneurs.[76] If, however, some forms of organization are much more disposed than others to expand or to adapt, then enough of these must be kept in existence, particularly in potentially dynamic sectors, if economic development is to be assured. Under all circumstances, however, progress will be greater in proportion as adjustments are expeditiously made to imbalances arising out of change in dynamic sectors.

VII. Mobility and Capital Formation

Variation in an economy's competitiveness may affect factor mobility, capital formation, and technological progress. Four modes of inquiry are possible: (1) a comparative study of countries; (2) historical studies of specific countries; (3) interindustry or intersectoral comparisons within given countries; or (4) essentially analytical studies. Mode (4), supplemented by empirical findings, will be used.

A dearth of suitable empirical data makes difficult recourse to approaches (1) and (2). International differences in the rate of development have various causes, of which difference in competitiveness is but one among many and is difficult to gauge and translate into comparable terms. It may be true, as suggested earlier, that a part of the superiority of American to British and continental European manufacturing productivity is attributable to the greater competitiveness of the American economy, but it is difficult to draw conclusions from a comparison of European economies in respect of competitiveness and productivity.[77] It is difficult also to determine the degree to which competitiveness has varied within a given economy and to associate these variations with variations in the rate of growth of output not attributable to other causes. Presumably the degree of competitiveness in economies such as the American declined somewhat in the later nineteenth century only to stabilize or even increase slightly in the present century; the net impact of this change on the course of economic development is very difficult, however, to isolate empirically.[78]

It is inferable on analytical and empirical grounds that factor mobility is positively associated with the degree of competition and that the shifts described as essential under (b) in Section IV proceed more rapidly when an economy is competitive than when it is not. It is probably inferable also that those conditions [listed in IV under (c)] which are the product of governmental policy are more likely to be adversely influenced by pressure groups when economic decision-making and the control of industry are highly concentrated than when this is not the case.[79] In sum, many if not most determinants of economic development included in categories (b) and (c) will be more favorable to growth under conditions of competition than under conditions of oligopoly, monopoly, etc.

The net effect of variation in an economy's competitiveness upon its rate of capital formation is less easy to establish, even given that technological progress suffices to keep *ex-ante* savings and investment in balance. Insofar as competition is imperfect and inputs are suboptimally distributed among uses, aggregate output is below the level attainable as, therefore, is capital formation under *ceteris paribus* conditions. But conditions tend to change; in consequence of this imperfection, profits and/or rents are likely to constitute a larger fraction of the national income, and this fraction may pass into the hands of recipients with a relatively high marginal propensity to save.[80] Should the rate of capital formation rise sufficiently as a result, the absolute rate of consumption would eventually move above the level at which it would have been in the absence of this capital formation.[81] Such tendency would be accentuated if the existence of monopoly made possible economically feasible production that would not otherwise have been undertaken.

The argument that imperfectness of competition fosters development by favoring capital formation is acceptable only in so far as the resulting stimuli to saving are not offset by negative stimuli and by other unfavorable concomitants of imperfectness of competition. In particular, account must be taken of the fact that outputs of monopolistic and oligopolistic firms may be inputs to enterprises whose capacity for expansion or for producing at relatively low cost is crucial to development; for capital formation by these enterprises as well as investment and development in general are retarded when the inputs in question are supplied under conditions of more or less contrived scarcity and the excessive prices therewith associated.

Scarcity occasioned by contrived monopoly or oligopoly must be distinguished from scarcity that is inherent in the growth process and hence automatic, but that gives rise only temporarily to considerable disparity between long-run "competitive" and "monopolistic" pricing and output. In general, if a country's politico-economic institutions are such as to enable it to fix upon the "desired" amount of saving and investment and the associated rate of growth, the present burden of this saving and growth will be less in proportion as ideal-output conditions of production and exchange compatible with this growth rate are approximated. Unfortunately this observation does not help much. It is difficult to specify "ideal output" conditions for a dynamic economy, and even more difficult to translate these conditions into policy terms. Even so, recourse to monopoly and oligopoly can be justified on capital-formation grounds, only if they actually foster capital formation and no better means to this end is realizable in practice.[82]

Contrived monopoly and oligopoly are much less likely to stimulate capital formation in an underdeveloped country than is automatic, temporary scarcity of the sort associated with innovation. (In this and the next paragraph it is assumed for analytical purposes, though the postulate is contrary to fact, that the rate of innovation is independent of the degree of competition obtaining.) It is true that whatever makes for savings-augmenting inequality in such an economy will conduce to development, since so large a fraction of private savings must originate in profits and rents, and since capital requirements are always adequate to absorb whatever *ex-ante* savings are forthcoming. But it is also true that an expanding underdeveloped economy is a disequilibrium economy in which disequilibrium itself gives rise temporarily to inequality and hence to abnormally large profits and savings.[83] In the more active sectors of such an economy, supply lags behind demand. Hence, profits are relatively high and capable of financing considerable economic development even when output is priced at levels much below those associated with the coincidence of short-run marginal cost and marginal revenue. Then development flourishes, particularly if the active sectors are those specializing in higher-order goods. Impermanent monopoly or oligopoly of the contrived sort may contribute to economic development, but only in so far as it supplies non-essential consumer goods (rather than inputs to development-generating industries) and therewith diverts excessive purchasing power to potential savers and capital-formers from spenders who might otherwise consume large quantities of these goods and hence of a nation's available inputs.[84] Generally, the profit-generating power associated with temporary disequilibrium suffices to supply much of the surplus needed for expansion. This is particularly so when there has come into being, as in India, a small but growing corporate sector capable of realizing economies of scale and hence of elevating output per worker much above the levels attainable even in better-run, very small undertakings.

Under various conditions the presence of monopoly or strong oligopoly retards investment even though it generates surpluses. It does so if enterprisers generally believe investment opportunities to be lacking.[85] It tends to do so if oligopolists do not fear trade-union inroads upon their profits, or are not bent upon increasing longer-run output in their own or other sectors.[86] Consumption may be checked and savings accentuated if enough purchasing power is diverted to individuals with relatively low propensities to consume from those with relatively high propensities. It is unlikely, however, that monopoly and oligopoly would give rise to enough redistribution of income in advanced countries to affect the average propensity to save greatly.[87]

From what has been said emerges the conclusion that temporary monopoly and oligopoly may be described as favorable to national capital formation only in so far as the conditions obtaining do not permit recourse to superior alternatives. Permanent monopoly is unfavorable as is persistent and strong oligopoly. What counts is aggregate capital formation; how big this should be depends upon the value premises postulated, and will be affected, as a rule, by governmental action; how it should be achieved turns largely on how the present burden of forming a stipulated amount of capital may be minimized. A specific "monopolist" may realize a relatively great profit by fixing price and output at levels associated with the coincidence of marginal revenue and marginal cost. But his limitation of output tends to reduce the profit of both firms supplying him with inputs and firms purchasing his output.

In sum, monopoly and oligopoly tend to reduce output in general, even with innovation given and with the presence of market-controls somewhat favorable to expectations. They do this by preventing an optimum distribution of resources among uses, compatible with the amount of capital formation desired, and thereby increase the real cost of a given amount of saving. In so far as the monopolist is producing a commodity essential to development (e.g., steel) his restriction of its output short of the "competitive" level checks development, particularly if nonavailability of this commodity denies employment to resources complementary thereto. The desideratum consists in forming capital at some given rate, but subject to the constraint that inputs be distributed among uses compatibly with as "ideal" a set of output conditions as can be approximated.

While it is generally true that monopoly and oligopoly, especially when contrived, are not comparatively favorable to capital formation under *ceteris paribus* conditions, it is also true that the presence of larger, incorporated companies conduces to the maintenance of a high rate of dynamic saving. (1) Realization of economies of scale and innovation, together with the savings thereby made possible, presupposes sufficiency of size, as probably does the preservation of states of longer-run expectations favorable to economic development. (2) Within limits the longer-run decision-affecting horizon (as distinguished from shorter-run, production-planning horizons) usually is greater in respect of larger than of smaller firms; this tendency makes for capital formation, a consequence of great importance in underdeveloped countries in which dearth of capital is the main immediate growth-limiting factor.[88] (3) In countries in which (unlike in some Latin-American lands) incorporation is regulated by modern laws, a relatively large fraction of the profits of all but quite small corporations tends to be reinvested. Furthermore, these savings tend to flow into more dynamic activities than does a great deal of non-corporate investment.[89]

The argument just advanced is subject to several qualifications, however. In advanced countries half or more of national savings is likely to be supplied by individuals rather than by incorporated and unincorporated enterprise, with a very small fraction of the individuals supplying most of the personal savings. In underdeveloped countries by contrast, savings are supplied predominately by enterprise, especially by unincorporated undertakers.[90] Furthermore, smaller firms, corporate and otherwise, are of two main sorts: (a) those which, proving successful, continue to reinvest profits until their size has become commensurate with the opportunities seemingly accessible in the lines in which they are engaged, after which only some seek to grow faster than the economy; (b) those which, because their operators are inefficient (as is often true in family firms) or indisposed to invest profits and expand, manifest little or no tendency to grow and often fail. The (b) group contributes nothing to invention and innovation. The situation and performance of the (a) group resemble those of successful small nations; they contribute significantly to capital formation, to the imitation of innovations, and in time even to invention and innovation, though at times only with the help of private or governmental research institutes.[91]

VIII. Size of Firms and Technological Progress

It has been argued that largeness of firm, in so far as associated with economies of size, is potentially favorable to capital formation as well as temporarily conducive to departure from competition. Size of firm may also affect the rate of technological progress. This effect, if realized, would make for increase in size of firm, a consequence presently disregarded.[92]

Economic growth attributable to technological progress is the end result of a sequence of actions: (a) addition to the pool of scientific knowledge; (b) invention, or the development of "an operational method of creating something new" or doing something more efficiently; (c) innovation, or the introduction of a newly invented product or process into commerce; (d) supplying the financial assistance essential to introducing innovation and its results into use; (e) securing sufficiently widespread acceptance of innovation and its results.[93] The degree of correlation obtaining between any two of these steps varies, however, as does the extent to which the sequence of steps is under the control of a single decision-maker seeking either a satisfactory profit or a maximum profit for a designated period.[94] Entrepreneurs in underdeveloped economies are largely concerned to draw on external sources for scientific findings and to adapt foreign technology to local requirements.

Steps (a) and (b) are closely connected only in the long run. Purely scientific knowledge is now being increased principally through highly organized, rational efforts instead of through dispersed, comparatively unorganized, hit and miss activities of the early nineteenth century sort.[95] While much of what is known is technically and economically obsolete, more or less of what is applicable may not be in use. The ratio of actual performance to possible performance may be low, for example, because steps (b), (c), etc., have not been taken. In the longer run, however, the magnitude of the pool of scientific knowledge sets limits to what can be accomplished, though the pool itself tends to be enlarged in consequence of pressure arising from the approach ot these limits.

Although much basic research is prompted by the endeavors of firms to achieve their goals, the additions consequently made to the pool of scientific knowledge will be limited. Such efforts, even when successful, are only partially rewarded inasmuch as they give rise to "substantial external economies". They may also result in failure, particularly if a firm is small and unable to diversify adequately, or if it is incapable of realizing a suitable return within the time horizon of its resource-allocating plan.[96] Only certain types of firms are virtually certain to find support of basic research (other than that intended to cut firm costs) profitable. Firms need to be sufficiently large and diversified; or be in industries in which "innovation and associated obsolescence proceed rapidly" (e.g., in the pharmaceutical industry);[97] or rest upon "a broad technological base" which insures that "whatever direction the path of research may take, the results are likely to be of value to the sponsoring firm";[98] or be controlled by entrepreneurs with invention-exploiting capacity.[99] Consequently much less even of industry's than of the nation's expenditure upon research and development has been devoted to "basic" research in recent years, and this has been largely concentrated in four industries; in fact Brode puts at 85 per cent the fraction of "basic" research supported by the federal government.[100] For these reasons and because many important technological contributions are unanticipated by-products, not easily exploited by the discoverer, it is inferable that industry as such will continue to underwrite only a minor fraction of the annual increment to the nation's pool of scientific knowledge. Augmentation of this pool will probably continue to depend largely upon government support and the activities of non-industrial research agencies;[101] its growth will be retarded if the nation's scarce, resource-oriented facilities are largely devoted to non-basic inquiry.[102]

Activity (b), invention, is the product of firms, individuals, and governmental institutions, with the contribution of firms increasing somewhat over time and that of individuals diminishing somewhat.[103] The introduction of an invention into use is more difficult, however, when activity (c), innovation, is separated from activity (b).

A relatively large fraction of disclosed invention made under the aegis of firms is the product of a relatively small fraction of the nation's corporations. This statement is supported by patent statistics, even though these are imperfect indicators in that the economic importance of patents varies greatly, many being duplicative or inferior or economically unworkable, and in that the ratio of patents to inventions and improvements probably is falling and must be far below unity.[104]

Of the patents issued in the United States in 1939–55, 58.5 per cent were issued to corporations; and 58 per cent of these went to only 394 corporations in a universe of more than 20,000 corporations with one or more patents. Of the 16,199 patents issued to United States corporations in 1955, 7,678 went to 4,177 corporations receiving 10 or less; 3,214 went to 16 corporations receiving over 100; the balance, 5,307 went to 212 corporations receiving 11–90.[105] This concentration partly reflects the concentration of research and patenting in a few industrial sectors (e.g., aircraft, electrical equipment, chemicals).

A relatively large fraction of the expenditure made by firms upon research and development was made by large firms. Thus whereas in 1953 only 8.3 per cent of the manufacturing firms with less than 100 employees conducted research and development, 94.3 per cent of those with 5,000 or more employees did so, and the proportion generally increased with company size. Moreover, while all or virtually all companies with 5,000 or more employees did so in every branch of manufacture, the proportion so doing among companies with 500 or less employees ranges from around only 40–50 per cent in aircraft, electrical equipment, and chemicals to below 10 per cent in petroleum, food production, etc. Small firms sometimes sought to overcome a dearth of research facilities by employing outside organizations to do this. Of the firms with less than 100 employees which conducted or financed research and development, 20.3 per cent relied solely upon outside organizations whereas only 5.1 per cent of those employing 5,000 or more employees did so.[106] Companies with 5,000 or more employees were responsible for 39.3 per cent of all employment and 72.6 per cent of all research and development expenditure in manufacturing industries; the corresponding percentages for firms employing less than 500 employees were 35.1 and 10.3.[107]

Were sufficient data relating to innovation available, they would probably indicate innovation to be more concentrated than invention, since innovation tends to be costly and risky and must be carried on at the firm level. Data relating to patents and inventions do not indicate that largeness of firm is a necessary prerequisite to technological progress or a guarantor of it; but they do suggest that technologically dynamic manufacturing industries are dominated in greater measure by large firms than are technologically static industries.[108] Innovation tends to be more concentrated than invention, because the propensity of firms to innovate their own and other inventions is greater among invention-producing than among invention-non-producing firms, and because the former are relatively more likely to be able to finance innovation and to persuade potential users to adopt newly innovated processes and products.

Larger firms enjoy several other advantages over smaller firms in respect to innovation. They can cope more effectively with cultural resistance to new processes and products, though if this resistance is strong they will require governmental support before undertaking an innovation. They are better able also to finance innovation and overcome obstacles to technological progress arising from scarcity of capital or from bias on the part of capital-suppliers against investment in innovation.[109] Economic concentration is affected accordingly; for the differential access of inventors and innovators to finance makes for a relatively great concentration of economic activities in the hands of a few firms even as credit rationing makes for skewness in the distribution of personal income.[110] Because of the higher cost of funds to small firms as well as the risks involved in invention and innovation, finance for these purposes is not as readily available to small firms, in sufficient quantity and at relatively low rates, as to large and diversified firms.[111] Yet there are many inventions which smaller firms are peculiarly adapted to exploit. The rate of technological progress may be increased through the establishment of institutions suited to provide economically warranted credit for the exploitation of inventions. It may also be increased through the public support (as in agriculture) of invention which may then be gratuitously exploited by entrepreneurs (e.g., as the often highly productive findings of agricultural research are exploited by farmers, frequently with the assistance of the agricultural extension service).[112]

The capacity of an innovated invention to contribute to economic development depends largely on the widespreadness of its use. The rate of diffusion of an innovation depends upon conditions internal as well as external to its potential imitators. While it is technologically easier to imitate than to innovate, the capacity of a firm to use domestic or foreign innovations (say on a royalty basis as in Japan or Australia), or to imitate them, presupposes the presence of minimal technological and personnel conditions.[113] Less firm-size may be required, however, to imitate an innovation than to introduce it initially. Underdeveloped countries experiencing the establishment of new firms are under less disadvantage because of this circumstance. They may also benefit from the circumstance that under some conditions it is economically easier for a newly established firm, or for a newly introduced foreign subsidiary firm, than for an old and established firm to introduce or imitate an innovation. Whether this potential advantage is made to materialize, however, turns on qualities of a new firm's leadership.[114] Among the circumstances external to a firm that affect its capacity or its disposition to imitate are the competitive pressure it is under from either the cost or the product-marketing side, together with its degree of access to patented and non-patented innovations.[115]

The rate of innovation also depends upon circumstances both internal and external to a firm. Among the former may be included such factors as the extent to which a firm's management is progressive, the pressure it is under to utilize idle resources, size of firm, and so on.[116] Of these factors size of firm is the most important in the context of the present discussion. It is not possible, of course, to connect technical progressiveness systematically with size of firm, even within given industries, in part because such progressiveness is a cause as well as a consequence of firm size. When inquiry is focused on the situation of the moment technical progressiveness appears to be associated, at least within limits, with size of firm; statistical manifestations of innovativeness and of relatively heavy research expenditure are prominent only among firms that exceed some critical minimum size, failure to have reached which appears to be associated with technological non-progressiveness. Even though research expenditure may not be highly correlated with size among firms in excess of this minimum, and though many medium-size and comparatively small firms seem to be technically progressive, it is probably much easier to institutionalize invention, discovery, and innovation in large than in small firms. This inference might have to be modified, however, if research and associated non-business functions were performed not only by firms themselves but also by private or public institutions specializing in the supply of invention (as now do various private research organizations). This inference does not, however, imply that the magnitude of these firms of critical minimum size is such as necessarily to give rise to strong oligopolies. The economy may be too large, or it may trade freely with other economies. Moreover, so long as entry into industry is free and research organizations are accessible and disposed to guard a client's secrets, small-firm entrepreneurs with the requisite skills (e.g., ability to choose and implement new or potential opportunities; willingness to assume risks) can compete effectively and in time fully realize economies of scale, organization, etc.[117]

While bigness often facilitates innovation and is essential to certain types, it is not an index of innovativeness any more than smallness is an index of lack of innovativeness. A big firm can survive many expensive failures, offsetting them with successful innovations, whereas a small firm cannot do so. At the same time a firm that has survived the high mortality of youth (i.e., the first 5 to 15 years) and acquired some size may, even though it is not very innovative, continue to grow as the economy grows; for, upon becoming well established, small firms grow about as fast as large firms, at least in times of prosperity and ready availability of funds.[118] As Dewey observes, although "the large firm accounts for 'some' technological progress" and there exist opportunities "which small firms cannot exploit", one need not "bow down in worship before the research laboratories of the large firm".[119] A universe made up largely of small firms could realize a high rate of innovation, given these conditions: (a) willingness to innovate new products as well as cost reduction despite the risks involved; (b) strong public support of basic science; (c) the availability of research organizations to which technical problems can be presented for partial solution.

Of the external determinants of innovation and its diffusion, the presence of a sufficiency of competition is of primary importance, although the behavior of firms is conditioned by the technical progressiveness and the rate of growth of the industry in which they are situated.[120] Competition must be defined, however, to allow for the carrot of profit as well as for the stick of rising costs and falling prices. It need only signify that an entrepreneur is free to enter an industry and produce as much as he wishes, together with the stipulation that no independently acting firm "can appreciably influence prices in the long run".[121] We may then define a firm as competitive even though it is temporarily realizing great profits as a result of successful innovation;[122] and we may regard a newly emerging industry as competitive even though as yet it consists of only one or several firms. This definition recognizes that competition makes for the undertaking and diffusion of invention and relies largely upon the market to determine which innovations deserve support.[123] For, given the costs, risks, and uncertainty involved, firms tend to innovate only if (a) they feel sufficient pressure from the cost or the demand side; and (b) they may count upon an innovation, if successful, to shield them temporarily against this pressure and permit them to realize relatively high profits in that interval. That competition makes for innovation is suggested by the frequency with which competitive pressure has forced the use of superior methods, and by findings such as Stigler's that the greatest decline in labor input per unit of output had occurred in industries in which competitiveness had apparently increased most markedly.[124] Even when competitive pressure is present, however, firms may be indisposed to innovate what subsequently prove to be significant inventions, particularly if these are contributions of independent inventors. As a result such inventors often find it necessary to innovate their own inventions.[125]

IX. Ideal Output Conditions vs. Economic Development

It has been argued that, when an economy develops in circumstances approximating those associated with a high degree of competition, development tends to proceed in rough accordance with the "ideal-output conditions" envisaged in static models. It was indicated earlier, however, that one cannot unqualifiedly apply static norms in an economic world that is imperfectly competitive and growing. (a) Reducing only one divergence between marginal value and cost may decrease instead of increase economic welfare when numerous such divergences exist. (b) When the changes contemplated are future-oriented and large-scale (instead of marginal), the outcome cannot be anticipated with precision, particularly if the time-period to which the decisions relate is not well specified. In so far, therefore, as (what Boulding calls) "the simple rubrics of comparative statics" fail to provide norms in the light of which one may choose among the available forms of organization, there is need for an alternative set adapted to situations in which development, change, and futurity are prominent. At present such a set is not available, and it is not always very helpful to make use of the concept of "ideal-output conditions" so long as its content remains obscure. Even so, concentration on qualifications (a) and (b) may obscure the efficacious effects of an intensification of competition. For, when this takes place, not one but many divergences between value and cost are likely to be reduced, and decision-makers almost certainly will be under great pressure to make output-increasing improvements, the total effect of which may well outweigh the gains to be had from mere efforts to behave in accordance with welfare criteria.

Instead of attempting to put appropriate content into the concept of "ideal-output conditions", we shall make use primarily of development-oriented criteria and of estimates of the probable effects of changes in the size and number of firms and the extent of their competitiveness. Accordingly, suppose a particular rate of growth is desired. It may be realized through recourse to any one of a variety of combinations of capital formation, invention, and innovation (or adaptation of a foreign innovation). Should individual preferences not make available enough inputs to actualize one of these suitable combinations, existing preferences would need to be overriden by the state. To the extent that such overriding proved necessary, the decision to use inputs to realize the stipulated growth rate would be political rather than purely economic.

The cost or burden of realizing such stipulated rate of development would tend to be minimized in so far as the following rules were followed. (1) Of the adequate combinations of capital formation, invention, and innovation available, that one ought to be chosen which minimized the aggregate of inputs required; undoubtedly it would be one heavily weighted with invention and innovation. (2) Since development is retarded by the actual or the emerging shortage of particular factors or inputs (i.e., "bottleneck" or limitational factors), facilitation of the chosen rate of development would immediately entail the correction of the physical or technological causes of these shortages and the removal of such institutional or market arrangements as made the supply of these inputs less than was compatible with economic use of the capacity available to produce them. (3) In so far as *ex-ante* voluntary savings fell short of requirements and the state had to intervene to step up the rate of saving and capital formation, it might proceed in one of various ways. Presumably it would favor a method that, given certain arbitrary assumptions, minimized the burden of supplying the extra savings, subject to the constraint that rules (1) and (2) were complied with and that the aggregate supply of "effort" was not diminished.

Application of principle (1) could involve some conflict with that of (2). Principle (1) presupposes a considerable emphasis upon innovation and hence upon the presence of firms of sufficient size to innovate. Under the circumstances, oligopoly might emerge in industries supplying "bottleneck" inputs and slow down their output and the growth of industries dependent upon these inputs. It is argued by some, however, that oligopoly may be comparatively competitive, and that "competitive oligopoly", because of its supposedly strong innovative tendencies, is the organizational form relatively most favorable to economic development.[126] In so far as this supposed competitiveness is not present, external pressure or other action by the state is indicated.

Pursuit of a stipulated rate of growth, if high, would facilitate capital formation, since even pricing in accordance with marginal cost would stimulate considerable business saving, particularly in industries producing scarce or "bottleneck" products. As noted earlier, in underdeveloped countries most of the private savings would originate with entrepreneurs.[127] In any event, it may be supposed that action in accordance with principles (1) and (2) would not diminish the propensity to save.

Principles (1) and (2) are not likely to be markedly violated in a large economy with large markets unless firms are permitted greatly to exceed optimum size, and this outcome may be averted through effective antitrust or similar action. When a country's domestic markets are large, output becomes concentrated in the hands of a few firms only if these become very large. There is some evidence to the effect that the skewed and eventually stable size-distribution assumed by firms in an industry is the result of a stochastic process.[128] We shall, however, assemble the sources of firms growth into three categories which are essentially economic and technological in character.

Since only the second of these three sources of growth is closely associated with a firm's capacity for technical progress, it is not likely that such capacity would make for a size incompatible with the presence of a considerable measure of competition in the industry affected. (1) A firm may continue to grow primarily because the economy is growing, so long as none of the main restrictions upon a particular firm's growth proves permanently limitational. Under these circumstances, however, some of the firms composing an industry will grow no faster than the economy, and others will grow less rapidly, with the result that each firm's share of the market diminishes and the industry becomes more competitive in the conventional sense.[129] (2) A firm may for a time grow faster than the industry of which it is a part, in consequence of economies of scale (limited largely to individual plants) and (especially when a firm embraces a number of plants) of economies of finance, management, marketing, research, etc. Increases in size incompatible with the maintenance of competitiveness are seldom encountered in single-plant firms, since the optimum-size plant usually is small in relation to the market and has not been increasing significantly.[130] Even when a firm is multi-plant in structure, increase in size need not greatly augment its market-influencing power, so long as this increase rests upon marketing, financial, managerial, and research economies, and upon such diminution in instability, risk, and uncertainty as are associated with increase in size and in variety of output. For economies realizable in the production of any particular product are limited;[131] and in proportion as a firm's newly added assets are devoted to product lines it has not theretofore supplied, it becomes exposed to competition from a greater number of firms. (3) A firm may grow by merging with other firms, or by acquiring the assets of other firms. Growth of this sort sometimes enables the resulting single organization to achieve improvements in the use of the research facilities, scarce managerial personnel, and under-utilized resources contributed by the combining firms. Such growth tends to reduce competition, however, when the combining firms are actually or potentially competitive.[132]

The second and third of these types of firm-growth tend to diminish competition in small or underdeveloped countries, so long as foreign competitors are denied ready access to markets in these countries. For the capacity of a plant whose size is optimal, given existing technologies and comparative factor scarcities, may form so large a fraction of an industry's capacity and a nation's consumption that quasi-monopoly or powerful oligopoly results. Then the supply of "bottleneck" factors may be restricted, with the result that development is retarded.[133] Under these circumstances an underdeveloped country is confronted with two choices: (a) requiring the plants in question to behave as competitively as is feasible, given the manner in which capital is raised and innovation and imitation of innovation are supported; or (b) converting these plants into public or state companies. In either instance foreign processes could be introduced, though they might prove less effective than if developed by a foreign subsidiary firm. Choice (a) would probably be superior to choice (b) unless the public or state corporation were quite free to engage first-rate managerial personnel, and these were free in turn to make all essential managerial and entrepreneurial decisions, subject to the constraint that these decisions bring about expeditiously the development sought.

X. Conclusion

The three major immediate determinants of economic development, listed in order of importance, are: (1) technical progress, (2) capital formation and (3) factor mobility. Competition has been represented as a social process operating in a non-static economy and there making for two not always wholly compatible growth-favoring outcomes: (1) optimal marginal equivalences, and (2) development-fostering changes. Development proceeds nicely *ceteris paribus* when competition is such as to make for both these effects, in part because growth consequent upon outcome (2) offsets harm consequent upon failure to approximate outcome (1).[134] Competition so functions when entry into every industry is unbarred, when each firm is free to produce as much as it pleases, and when, though an individual firm may influence prices appreciably in the short run, it cannot do so in the longer run. Competition so defined is incompatible with the persistence of monopoly and strong oligopoly. It is compatible with temporary monopoly, or with instable oligopoly, if such form of organization conduces to enough technical progress to counterbalance temporary but sometimes marked departures from what are describable as optimal marginal equivalences.

Factor mobility, so essential in an economy undergoing change, presupposes a considerable amount of competition of the sort that reduces departures from optimal marginal equivalences. Technical progress depends upon a number of factors, among them the presence of enough firms of sufficient size. It tends to be greatest *ceteris paribus* when continuing invention and innovation are essential to a firm's continuing to realize profits in the face of the competition it continually faces from similarly behaving rivals. This form of competition, since it both generates and reduces departure from optimal marginal equivalences, is compatible with the presence of departures therefrom; it may be intensified through appropriate action by the state.

Both competitive outcomes make for capital formation, at least within limits. The presence of strong oligopoly and persisting monopoly retards investment, thereby holding down the growth of national income and savings, given the propensity to save. The removal of persisting monopoly and the conversion of a strong into a "competitive" oligopoly will therefore augment the growth of both national income and savings and investment. The decision to form a nation's capital at a certain rate and to grow commensurately is political in so far as the realized rate exceeds that to which individual preferences could give rise.

NOTES

1. I am greatly indebted to my colleague, Professor C. E. Ferguson, author of a forthcoming work dealing with welfare economics and workable competition, for many helpful suggestions.
2. On the issues touched upon above see FRANÇOIS PERROUX, "The Domination Effect and Modern Economic Theory", *Social Research*, vol. 17, June, 1950, p. 206; R. W. PFOUTS and C. E. FERGUSON, "Market Classification Systems in Theory and Practice", *Southern Economic Journal*, vol. 26, October, 1959, pp. 111–18; A. G. PAPANDREOU, "Market Structure and Monopoly Power", *American Economic Review*, vol. 39, September, 1949, pp. 883–98; also FRITZ MACHLUP, "Statics and Dynamics: Kaleidoscopic Words", *Southern Economic Journal*, vol. 26, October, 1959, pp. 91–110.
3. R. DE ROOVER, "Monopoly Theory Prior to Adam Smith: A Revision", *Quarterly Journal of Economics*, vol. 65, November, 1951, pp. 492–524. See also M. S. HEATH, "Freedom, Economics, and Corporate Organization", *Southern Economic Journal*, vol. 24, January, 1958, pp. 251–58; C. J. RATZLAFF, *The Theory of Free Competition*, Philadelphia: University of Pennsylvania Press, 1936, chs. 3–8; VERNON A. MUND, *Monopoly*, Princeton: Princeton University Press, 1933, chs. 2–5; KARL PRIBRAM, *Cartel Problems*, Washington: The Brookings Institution, 1935, pp. 94–95, 101.
4. F. H. KNIGHT, *Risk, Uncertainty and Profit*, Boston: Houghton Mifflin Co., 1921; GEORGE STIGLER, "Perfect Competition, Historically Contemplated", *Journal of Political Economy*, vol. 65, February, 1957, pp. 1–17; PAUL A. SAMUELSON, *Foundations of Economic Analyses*, Cambridge: Harvard University Press, 1947, ch. 8. See also MUND, *op. cit.*, ch. 7; RATZLAFF, *op. cit.;* SHOREY PETERSON, "Antitrust and the Classic Model", *American Economic Review*, vol. 47, March, 1957, pp.

60–78; Calvin B. Hoover, "The Relevance of the Competitive Laissez-Faire Economic Model to Modern Capitalistic National Economies", *Kyklos*, vol. 8, fasc. 1, 1955, pp. 40–55; J. R. Hicks, "Annual Survey of Economic Theory: The Theory of Monopoly", *Econometrica*, vol. 3, January, 1935, pp. 18–20; Robert Dorfman, P. A. Samuelson and R. M. Solow, *Linear Programming and Economic Analysis*, New York: McGraw-Hill Book Co., 1958, chs. 13–14.

5. William L. Letwin, "The Origins of Antitrust Policy", *Journal of Political Economy*, vol. 64, April, 1956, p. 158. See also Peterson, *op. cit.;* Charles J. Bullock, "Trust Literature: A Survey and Criticism", *Quarterly Journal of Economics*, vol. 15, February, 1901, pp. 167–216.
6. Donald Dewey, "The Common-law Background Of Anti-trust Policy", *Virginia Law Review*, vol. 41, October, 1955, pp. 759–86, and *Monopoly in Economics and Law*, Chicago: Rand McNally & Company, 1959, chs. 9–11.
7. Alfred Marshall, "Some Aspects of Competition" (1890), in A. C. Pigou, ed., *Memorials of Alfred Marshall*, New York: Kelley & Millman, Inc., 1956, pp. 256–91, esp. pp. 274–81, 282, 290. See also Alfred Marshall, *Industry and Trade*, London: Macmillan and Co., Ltd., 1919, Bk. III.
8. Tibor Scitovsky, "Economies of Scale and European Integration", *American Economic Review*, vol. 46, March, 1956, pp. 83–88, and "Monopoly And Competition In Europe and America", *Quarterly Journal of Economics*, vol. 69, November, 1955, pp. 610–12; Egon Sohmen, "Competition and Growth: West Germany", *American Economic Review*, vol. 49, December, 1959, pp. 86–103; Gideon Rosenbluth, "Measures of Concentration", in George J. Stigler, ed., *Business Concentration and Policy*, Princeton: Princeton University Press, 1955, pp. 70–77; also Pribram, *op. cit.*,pp. 241–82; Edward H. Chamberlin, ed., *Monopoly and Competition and Their Regulation*, London: Macmillan & Co., Ltd., 1954, pp. 3–187.
9. Alfred North Whitehead, *Science and the Modern World*, New York: The Macmillan Company, 1947, p. 141.
10. Alfred Marshall, *Principles of Economics*, London: Macmillan and Co., Ltd., 1920, pp. 5–10; this observation appeared already in the fifth (1907) edition.
11. E.g., see Friedrich von Wieser's critique of competition in *Social Economics* (1914, 1924), translated by A. Ford Hinrichs, New York: Adelphi Company, 1927, pp. 207–11, 217, and Part IV; Henry R. Seager and Charles A. Gulick, Jr., *Trust and Corporation Problems*, New York: Harper & Brothers, 1929, chs. 4–6, 24–28; S. Moos, "Laissez Faire, Planning, And Ethics", *Economic Journal*, vol. LV, April, 1945, pp. 17–27; Chamberlin, ed., *op. cit.*
12. C. F. Carter and B. R. Williams, *Industry and Technical Progress*, London: Oxford University Press, 1957, p. 164; Paul Stanchfield, "American Productivity and Full Employment", *Monthly Labor Review*, vol. 74, February, 1952, p. 126. See also Chamberlin, ed., *op. cit.;* Marshall, *Industry and Trade*, Bk. I, ch. 8, Bk. III; Rudolf Frei, ed., *Economic Systems of the West*, 2 vols., Basel: Kyklos-Verlag, 1957, 1959; Sohmen, *op. cit.;* J. K. Galbraith, "Monopoly and the Concentration of Economic Power" in H. S. Ellis, ed., *A Survey of Contemporary Economics*, Philadelphia: Blakiston Co., 1948, ch. 3.
13. H. W. Macrosty, *Trusts and the State*, London: G. Richards, 1901; John P. Miller, *Unfair Competition*, Cambridge: Harvard University Press, 1940; Seager and Gulick, *op. cit.;* Arthur R. Burns, *The Decline of Competition*, New York: McGraw-Hill Book Company, Inc., 1936; Bernard W. Dempsey, *Functional Economics*, Englewood Cliffs, N. J.: Prentice-Hall, Inc., 1958, chs. 17–18, 21; Milton Handler, "Unfair Competition", in Edgar M. Hoover, Jr., and Joel Dean, *Readings in the Social Control of Industry*, Philadelphia: The Blakiston Co., 1942, pp. 76–180.
14. See K. Rothschild, "The Wastes of Competition", in Chamberlin, ed., *op. cit.*,

pp. 301–14; F. C. Bator, "The Anatomy of Market Failure", *Quarterly Journal of Economics*, vol. 72, August, 1958, pp. 351–79; J. de V. Graaf, *Theoretical Welfare Economics*, Cambridge: Cambridge University Press, 1957, pp. 169–70; J. R. Hicks, *Essays in World Economics*, Oxford: Clarendon Press, 1959, pp. viii–xiv, 46; L. J. Zimmerman, *The Propensity to Monopolize*, Amsterdam: North-Holland Publishing Co., 1952.

15. E. g., see Fritz Machlup's excellent review of economic opinion respecting patents in *An Economic Review of the Patent System*, Study No. 15, issued by the Subcommittee on Patents, Trademarks, and Copyrights of the Committee on the Judiciary, United States Senate, 85th Congress, 2d session, pursuant to S. Res. 236, Washington, 1958; Everett E. Hagen, "An Economic Justification of Protectionism", *Quarterly Journal of Economics*, vol. 72, November, 1958, pp. 496–514; W. A. Lewis, "Economic Development With Unlimited Supplies of Labour", *Manchester School of Economic and Social Studies*, vol. 22, May, 1954, pp. 181–91; and Jacob Viner's description of Malthus's demographic argument in support of agricultural protection, in *International Trade and Economic Development*, Glencoe: Free Press, 1952, pp. 128–29.
16. See Richard V. Clemence, ed., *Essays of J. A. Schumpeter*, Cambridge: Addison-Wesley Press, Inc., 1951; this is cited hereinafter as Schumpeter, *Essays*. His conception of economic development is most fully treated in his *The Theory of Economic Development*, Cambridge: Harvard University Press, 1934, and in *Business Cycles*, New York: McGraw-Hill Book Company, Inc., 1939. His treatment of monopoly is most fully developed in *Capitalism, Socialism and Democracy*, New York: Harper & Brothers, 2d. ed., 1942, esp. ch. 8. See also Richard V. Clemence and Francis C. Doody, *The Schumpeterian System*, Cambridge: Addison-Wesley Press, 1950; Carolyn S. Solo, "Innovation In the Capitalist Process: A Critique Of The Schumpeterian Theory", *Quarterly Journal of Economics*, vol. 65, August, 1951, pp. 417–28; Manuel Gottlieb, "The Ideological Influence in Schumpeter's Thought", *Zeitschrift für Nationalökonomie*, vol. 19, Heft 1–2, 1959, esp. pp. 15–21, 27–31; W. P. Strassmann, "Creative Destruction and Partial Obsolescence in American Economic Development", *Journal of Economic History*, vol. 19, September, 1959, pp. 335–49.
17. Schumpeter, *Capitalism, Socialism and Democracy*, chs. 7, 12–14; *Essays:* pp. 170 ff., 216 ff. That, despite the Indian Summer through which American capitalism is presently passing, Schumpeter's forebodings "remain broadly valid" and are likely to be realized in the absence of a discerning leadership and an avoidance of intermittent panics, has recently been argued by James R. Schlesinger and Almarin Phillips, "The Ebb Tide Of Capitalism", *Quarterly Journal of Economics*, vol. 73, August, 1959, pp. 448–65. "The structure of forces affecting American social policy will drive it more and more in the direction of control... The problem to be solved is that of carefully insulating controls so that the essentials of capitalism and freedom may be preserved in those areas where control is inappropriate". *Ibid.*, p. 462.
18. Schumpeter, *Capitalism, Socialism and Democracy*, p. 95.
19. See Heinz Hartmann, "Managers And Entrepreneurs: A Useful Distinction", *Administrative Science Quarterly*, vol. 3, March, 1959, pp. 429–51. Hartmann is interested primarily in redefining the respective roles of manager and entrepreneur in terms of their formal authority in the industrial organization; "within the organization" the entrepreneur "alone is the source of all formal authority" whereas "management enjoys only residual and delegated authority." *Ibid.*, pp. 450–51. Schumpeter recognized that individual initiative was giving place to bureaucratized initiative. E.g., see *Essays*, pp. 70–71.
20. On equilibration in monopolistic competition see Harold Demsetz, "The Nature

Of Equilibrium In Monopolistic Competition", *Journal of Political Economy*, vol. 67, February, 1959; also Dewey, *op. cit.*, pp. 96–108.

21. See SCHUMPETER, *Capitalism, Socialism and Democracy*, esp. chs. 7–8, and *Business Cycles*, ch. 3.
22. SCHUMPETER, *Capitalism, Socialism and Democracy*, chs. 7–8, esp. pp. 87–91, 101, 106, and p. 95 on the deflation-checking effect of price inflexibility. See also GEORGE W. STOCKING and MYRON W. WATKINS, *Monopoly and Free Enterprise*, New York: Twentieth Century Fund, 1951, pp. 104–07; EDWARD S. MASON, "Schumpeter on Monopoly and the Large Firm", *Review of Economics and Statistics*, vol. 33, May, 1951, pp. 139–44; and FRITZ MACHLUP's "balance sheet of 'debts and credits' in the account of monopolistic restrictions", *The Political Economy of Monopoly*, Baltimore: Johns Hopkins Press, 1952, pp. 72–74.
23. E.g., see ZIMMERMAN, *op. cit.*, pp. 66–68; and K. E. BOULDING, "In Defence Of Monopoly", *Quarterly Journal of Economics*, vol. 59, August, 1945, p. 527 on innovation, and pp. 527, 531, 534, 537–38, where restrictions upon competition are described as having originated largely in attempts to avoid deflation. That monopoly, in given situations, produces effects for which remedy is sought in inflation, has been well described by MARTIN BRONFENBRENNER, "Monopoly And Inflation In Contemporary Japan", *Osaka Economic Papers*, vol. 3, March, 1955, pp. 41–48. See also J. K. GALBRAITH's description of the inflation-generating role of oligopoly and the comparative immunity of the oligopolistic sector to disinflationary monetary and fiscal policies which prove effective in the competitive sector, in "Market Structure and Stabilization Policy", *Review of Economics and Statistics*, vol. 39, May, 1957, pp. 124–33. WILLIAM BAUMOL makes a convincing argument, however, for the proposition that the oligopolistic sector does not differ so greatly from the competitive sector in respect of inflation and disinflation, in *Business Behavior, Value and Growth*, New York: Macmillan Company, 1959, pp. 78–82. See also MACHLUP's critique of the argument that monopolistic restrictions are stabilizing on balance, in "Monopoly And The Problem Of Economic Stability", in CHAMBERLIN, ed., *op. cit.*, pp. 391–95.
24. *Op. cit.*, pp. 424–28. E. D. DOMAR points out that a new firm is more likely *ceteris paribus* to innovate because it "has no interest in preserving the old product" as well as because its "actions are not inhibited by possible capital losses". See "Investment, Losses and Monopolies", in *Income, Employment, and Public Policy*, New York: W. W. Norton & Company, 1948, p. 37, also p. 41.
25. "Savings and Investment: Profits vs. Prosperity", *American Economic Review*, vol. 32, No. 2, Part 2, Suppl., June, 1942, pp. 84–86.
26. "Monopolization and the Decline of Investment Opportunity", *American Economic Review*, vol. 33, September, 1943, pp. 593–97. H. S. ELLIS's findings are in line with HILDEBRAND's. See C. O. HARDY, K. B. WILLIAMS, and H. S. ELLIS, *Prices, Wages and Employment*, Postwar Economic Studies, No. 4, Washington: Board of Governors of the Federal Reserve System, 1946, pp. 70–74, 85–86; also G. C. ALLEN, "Economic Progress, Retrospect and Prospect", *Economic Journal*, vol. 60, September, 1950, pp. 473–74.
27. See "Monopoly And ... Stability", in CHAMBERLIN, ed., *op. cit.*, pp. 395–97; STOCKING and WATKINS, *op. cit.*, pp. 106–07, 385, and ch. 14; WALTER ADAMS, ed., *The Structure of American Industry*, New York: Macmillan and Company, rev. ed., 1954, pp. 517–18, and "Competition, Monopoly and Countervailing Power", *Quarterly Journal of Economics*, vol. 67, November, 1953, pp. 487–91.
28. See CHAMBERLIN, ed., "Monopoly: Impediment Or Stimulus To Economic Progress?", *op. cit.*, pp. 421–56, esp. pp. 454–56.
29. "Monopolistic Competition Revisited", *Economica*, vol. 18, November, 1951, pp. 357–58.

30. As CHAMBERLIN has long implied and HUNTER points out, "product differentiation" may be treated as a beneficial form of innovation in that it constitutes a "part of what the consumer considers to be his economic welfare". Hence such "imperfection" of competition as arises out of warrantable differentiation needs to be distinguished from "imperfection" arising from cost conditions that prevent equalization of the relevant marginal productivities. See ALEX HUNTER, "Product Differentiation And Welfare Economics", *Quarterly Journal Economics*, vol. 69, November, 1955, pp. 537, 546–47.
31. In J. M. CLARK's original paper he noted only that technical progress might make for greater substitutability, but he now assigns it a much more important role. See "Toward a Concept of Workable Competition", in HOOVER and DEAN, *op. cit.*, pp. 474–75, and "The Uses Of Diversity: Competitive Bearings Of Diversities In Cost And Demand Functions", *American Economic Review*, vol. 48, No. 2, May, 1958, pp. 474–82. Technical progress is barely touched upon by E. A. G. ROBINSON, in *Monopoly*, London: Nisbet & Co., 1941.
32. STEPHEN H. SOSNICK, "A Critique Of Workable Competition", *Quarterly Journal of Economics*, vol. 72, August, 1958, pp. 391, 415.
33. A. G. PAPANDREOU and J. R. WHEELER, *Competition and Its Regulation*, Englewood Cliffs: Prentice-Hall, Inc., 1957, pp. 204–06, 485–89.
34. E.g., see STOCKING, "On the Concept of Workable Competition as an Antitrust Guide", *The Antitrust Bulletin*, vol. 2, September, 1956, pp. 3–39, and "Economic Change and the Sherman Act: Some Reflections on 'Workable Competition'," *Virginia Law Review*, vol. 44, May, 1958, pp. 537–82.
35. See J. E. MEADE, *Trade and Welfare*, London: Oxford University Press, 1955, chs. 2, 4–5, 7–8; R. G. LIPSEY and R. K. LANCASTER, "The General Theory of Second Best", *Review of Economic Studies*, vol. 24, 1956–57, pp. 11–32; R. H. STROTZ, "Myopia and Inconsistency in Dynamic Utility Maximization", *ibid.*, vol. 23, 1955–56, pp. 165–80; L. W. MCKENZIE, "Ideal Output And The Interdependence Of Firms", *Economic Journal*, vol. 61, December, 1951, pp. 785–803; G. B. RICHARDSON, "Equilibrium, Expectations, and Information", *ibid.*, vol. 69, June, 1959, pp. 223–37; R. M. SOLOW, "Competitive Valuation In A Dynamic Input-Output System", *Econometrica*, vol. 27, January, 1959, pp. 30–53; J. DE V. GRAAF, *op. cit.*, chs. 6–8, 10, 12.
36. PAUL STUDENSKI, *The Income Of Nations*, New York: New York University Press, 1958, pp. 229–33; United Nations, *Per-Capita Product of Fifty-Five Countries: 1952–54*, Statistical Papers Series E, No. 4, New York: United Nations, 1957; SIMON KUZNETS's series "Quantitative Aspects Of The Economic Growth Of Nations", *Economic Development and Cultural Change*, vols. 5–7, 1956–59.
37. Concerning the characteristics of underdeveloped countries see HARVEY LEIBENSTEIN, *Economic Backwardness and Economic Growth*, New York: John Wiley & Sons, Inc., 1957, ch. 4; BENJAMIN HIGGINS, *Economic Development*, New York: W. W. Norton & Company, Inc., 1959; CHARLES P. KINDLEBERGER, *Economic Development*, New York: McGraw-Hill Book Co., 1958; W. ARTHUR LEWIS, *The Theory of Economic Growth*, London: G. Allen & Unwin, 1955; H. F. WILLIAMSON and J. A. BUTTRICK, *Economic Development: Principles and Patterns*, Englewood Cliffs: Prentice-Hall, Inc., 1954; United Nations, *Processes And Problems Of Industrialization In Under-Developed Countries*, New York: United Nations, 1955; and *Management Of Industrial Enterprises In Under-Developed Countries*, New York: United Nations, 1958.
38. See SAMUEL E. HILL and FREDERICK HARBISON, *Manpower and Innovation in American Industry*, Princeton: Princeton University Industrial Relations Section, 1959; SEYMOUR MELMAN, *Dynamic Factors in Industrial Productivity*, Oxford: Basil Blackwell, 1956, Part 2 and ch. 17 on rising administrative overhead;

MICHAEL C. DALY, "The Effect of Overhead Costs Upon the Structure of the American Economy", *Southern Economic Journal*, vol. 8, July, 1941, pp. 22–39.

39. On the effects of supply elasticity see JOAN ROBINSON, *Collected Economic Papers*, New York: Augustus M. Kelley, Inc., 1951, pp. 32–33; also A. J. NICHOL, *Partial Monopoly and Price Leadership*, New York: Privately Printed, 1930, p. 22; PAPANDREOU, *op. cit.*, pp. 890–91. But see ZIMMERMAN, *op. cit.*, chs. 3–4, on how excess capacity may promote "monopoly".
40. On flexibility see GEORGE J. STIGLER, "Production And Distribution In The Short Run", *Journal of Political Economy*, vol. 47, June, 1939, pp. 305–27, sec. 2.
41. See WILLARD D. ARANT, "Competition Of The Few Among The Many", *Quarterly Journal of Economics*, vol. 70, August, 1956, pp. 332–38; also JOE S. BAIN, *Barriers to New Competition*, Cambridge: Harvard University Press, 1956, ch. 1.
42. M. ABRAMOVITZ's remark respecting advanced economies seems to be relevant here: "Business men are more likely in an industry's early days to adopt competitive tactics as a regular policy... the relatively rapid changes associated with an industry's early stages are favorable to competitive action, and ... the contrary is true of the later stages of an industry's growth". See "Monopolistic Selling In A Changing Economy", *Quarterly Journal of Economics*, vol. 52, February, 1938, pp. 210–11, also 199–200, 205, 212–13; also YALE BROZEN, "Time Demand, And Market Position", *Journal of Business of the University of Chicago*, vol. 31, April, 1958, pp. 95–106; PRIBRAM, *op. cit.*, pp. 231, 243–44, 248, on the tendency to cartellisation to be less strong, and that to competition to be greater, when markets are expanding; and A. C. PIGOU, *Employment and Equilibrium*, London: Macmillan and Co., 1941, pp. 47–49 on tendency of elasticity to rise as affluence increases.
43. On this last point see P. T. BAUER and B. S. YAMEY, *The Economics of Under-developed Countries*, London: James Nisbet & Co., Ltd., 1957; N. S. BUCHANAN and HOWARD S. ELLIS, *Approaches to Economic Development*, New York: The Twentieth Century Fund, 1955, Part III.
44. E.g., see LEWIS, "Economic Development...", *loc. cit.*, and "Unlimited Labour: Further Notes", *Manchester School of Economic and Social Studies*, vol. 26, January, 1958, pp. 1–32; M. D. MORRIS, "Some Comments on the Supply of Labour to the Bombay Cotton Textile Industry, 1854–1951", *Indian Economic Journal*, I, October, 1953, pp. 138–52; also S. P. SCHATZ, "A Dual-Economy Model of an Underdeveloped Country", *Social Research*, vol. 23, Winter, 1956, pp. 419–32. Raw labor was long in elastic supply in nineteenth-century European economies undergoing development and apparently even in parts of New England though the United States as a whole remained a labor-short country. On the problem of labor commitment see WILBERT E. MOORE and A. S. FELDMAN, *Labor Commitment and Social Change in Developing Areas*, New York: Social Science Research Council, 1960.
45. E.g., see E. K. HAWKINS, "The Growth of a Money Economy in Nigeria and Ghana", *Oxford Economic Papers*, vol. 10, October, 1958, pp. 339–54; United Nations, *Structure And Growth Of Selected African Economies*, New York: United Nations, 1958; P. T. BAUER, *West African Trade*, Cambridge: Cambridge University Press, 1954; International Bank for Reconstruction and Development, *The Economic Development of Nigeria*, Baltimore: Johns Hopkins Press, 1955.
46. E.g., see LEWIS's Papers cited in note 44 above; also G. D. N. WORSWICK, "Mrs. Robinson on Simple Accumulation", *Oxford Economic Papers*, vol. 11, June, 1959, pp. 125–42; G. O. GUTMAN, "Development with Subsistence Agriculture", *ibid.*, vol. 9, October, 1957, pp. 323–29.
47. LEWIS estimates that wages in the capitalistic sector must be 30 or more per cent higher than in the non-capitalistic sector if labor is to be attracted and held. See "Economic Development...", *loc. cit.*, p. 150, also 151–67 on capital formation.

Lewis may overestimate the elasticity of supply of rural labor and its capacity to facilitate capital formation. E.g., see DIPAK MAZUMDAR, "Underemployment in Agriculture and the Industrial Wage Rage", *Economica*, November, 1959, pp. 328–40, on why the supply of rural labor may not be highly elastic and its supply price may be relatively high. Wages often are higher in the capitalistic sector than they need to be, with the result that capital formation is checked if the workers are not taxed suitably. E.g., C. A. MYERS describes Indian labor as "no longer cheap", though plentiful, with earnings of factory workers more than double those of agricultural laborers. See *Labor Problems in the Industrialization of India*, Cambridge: Harvard University Press, 1958, pp. 12–13, 178–79, 247. A somewhat similar relationship was found in Egypt. See WALTER GALENSON, ed., *Labor and Economic Development*, New York: John Wiley & Sons, 1959, pp. 3, 156–57. See also P. T. BAUER, "Regulated Wages in Underdeveloped Countries", in Philip D. Bradley, ed., *The Public Stake In Union Power*, Charlottesville: University of Virginia Press, 1959, pp. 324–49. On the productivity—increasing influence of better diets made possible by higher wages, see LEIBENSTEIN, *op. cit.*, ch. 6, and HARRY T. OSHIMA, "Underemployment in Backward Economies: An Empirical Comment", *Journal of Political Economy*, vol. 66, June, 1958, pp. 259–64.

48. E.g., see United Nations (Economic Commission for Latin America), *Labour Productivity Of The Cotton Textile Industry In Five Latin-American Countries*, New York: United Nations, 1951, pp. 11–13.
49. E.g., see ALISON M. MARTIN and W. A. LEWIS, "Patterns of Public Revenue And Expenditure", *Manchester School of Economic and Social Studies*, vol. 24, September, 1956, pp. 203–44; also H. T. OSHIMA, "Share of Government in Gross National Product", *American Economic Review*, vol. 47, June, 1957, pp. 381–89.
50. E.g., see GALENSON, *op. cit.*, pp. 4–6; A. H. HANSON, *Public Enterprise And Economic Development*, London: Routledge & Kegan Paul Ltd., 1959, pp. 464–74.
51. E.g., see INGVAR SVENNILSON, *Growth And Stagnation In The European Economy*, Geneva: United Nations, 1954, pp. 7–9, 20–22, 206; RICHARD L. MEIER, *Science and Economic Development*, New York: John Wiley & Sons, Inc., 1956; GILBERT BURCK and SANFORD PARKER, "Productivity: The Great Age of 3%", *Fortune*, vol. 52, November, 1955, pp. 102 ff.; and "The Mighty Multiplier", *ibid.*, vol. 50, October, 1954, pp. 108 ff.; ARNOLD C. HARBERGER, "Using The Resources At Hand More Effectively"; *American Economic Review*, vol. 49, No. 2, May, 1959, pp. 142–44.
52. JACOB SCHMOOKLER, "The Changing Efficiency of the American Economy: 1869–1932," *Review of Economics and Statistics*, vol. 34, August, 1952, p. 230; also J. W. KENDRICK's estimate for 1889–1953, reported in Solomon Fabricant, "Investing in Economic Knowledge", Thirty-Eighth Annual Report, New York: National Bureau of Economic Research, May, 1959, p. 60.
53. MOSES ABRAMOVITZ, *Resource and Output Trends in the United States since* 1870, Occasional Paper 52, New York: National Bureau of Economic Research, 1956, p. 8. See also SOLOMON FABRICANT, *Basic Facts on Productivity*, Occasional Paper 63, New York: National Bureau of Economic Research, 1959.
54. JAN TINBERGEN and J. J. POLAK, *The Dynamics of Business Cycles*, Chicago: University of Chicago Press, 1950, pp. 127–28. Higher rates are reported for Norway and Finland in recent decades, in Unsigned, "The Human Factor and Economic Growth", *The Index*, No. 1, 1959, p. 2. On Chile and Latin America, see HARBERGER, *op. cit.*, pp. 143–44.
55. "Technical Change and the Aggregate Production Function", *Review of Economics and Statistics*, vol. 39, August, 1957, p. 320. See also comments by LUIGI L. PASINETTI and ROBERT M. SOLOW, in "On Concepts and Measures of Changes in Productivity", *ibid.*, vol. 41, August, 1959, pp. 270–86.

56. E.g., see United Nations, *Labour Productivity Of The Cotton Textile Industry*, pp. 11–13; JOHN JEWKES, "The Growth of World Industry", *Oxford Economic Papers*, vol. 3, February, 1951, pp. 8–13.
57. RICHARD R. NELSON, "A Theory Of The Low-Level Equilibrium Trap In Underdeveloped Economies", *American Economic Review*, vol. 46, December, 1946, pp. 894–908. See also LEIBENSTEIN, *op. cit.*, chs. 8–10, 14; CLIFFORD GEERTZ, "Capital-Intensive Agriculture in Peasant Society: A Case Study", *Social Research*, vol. 23, Winter, 1956, pp. 445–47.
58. E.g., see THEODORE SCHULTZ, "Investment In Man: An Economist's View", *The Social Service Review*, vol. 33, June, 1959, pp. 109–17.
59. See papers by SOLOW and STROTZ, cited in note 34; also RYUTARO KOMIJA, "A Note On Professor Mahalanobis's Model of Indian Economic Planning", *Review of Economics and Statistics*, vol. 41, February, 1959, pp. 29–35.
60. HARBERGER, (*op. cit.*, p. 140) estimates that if all the monopolistic and similar barriers were eliminated in Chile, national income would rise only about 15 per cent. KUZNETS estimates that about four-tenths of the rise in output per worker in the United States between the 1870's and the 1940's was associated with inter-industry shifts as distinguished from intra-industry changes. See SIMON KUZNETS, etc., *Income And Wealth of the United States*, Cambridge: Bowes & Bowes, 1952, pp. 123–26; also A. MADDISON, "Productivity In An Expanding Economy", *Economic Journal*, vol. 62, September, 1952, pp. 592–93.
61. SCITOVSKY attributes the lag in the growth of European behind American living standards not only to the lesser increase of efficiency in Europe but also to "the lesser shift of demand and resources toward industries of actually or potentially increasing efficiency" and to "the resulting lesser stimulus to, and hence lower level of investment". See "Economies of Scale and European Integration", *loc. cit.*, p. 88. See also J. J. SPENGLER, "Product-Adding vs. Product-Replacing Invention", *Kyklos*, vol. 10, Fasc. 3, 1957, pp. 249–80.
62. On the nature of this form of organization see FREDERICK HARBISON, "Entrepreneurial Organization As A Factor In Economic Development", *Quarterly Journal of Economics*, vol. 70, August, 1956, pp. 364–79. "The functions of the modern entrepreneurial organization, whether it be privately or publicly owned and operated, may be categorized as follows: (1) the undertaking or managing of risk and the handling of economic uncertainty; (2) planning and innovation; (3) co-ordination, administration, and control; and (4) routine supervision". *Ibid.*, p. 365. See also OM PRAKASH, "The Problem Of Entrepreneurship In Socialist Economy", *Indian Journal of Economics*, vol. 39, July, 1958, pp. 59–70.
63. On the prevalence of smaller-scale activities and on some of the shortages and conditions responsible see THEODORE HERMAN, "The Role of Cottage and Small-Scale Industries in Asian Economic Development", *Economic Development and Cultural Change*, vol. 4, July, 1956, pp. 365–70; CHARLES A. MYERS, "Recent Developments in Management Training in India", *Indian Journal of Public Administration*, vol. 4, April-June, 1958, pp. 154–64; HENRY G. AUBREY, "Small Industry in Economic Development", *Social Research*, vol. 18, September, 1951, pp. 269–312; AYANORI OKASAKI's pamphlet, *La grande industrie et la population des ouvriers du Japon*, Tokio: Institut d'étude des problèmes démographiques, 1954, esp. pp. 17, 28–29; FREDERICK HARBISON and IBRAHIM ABDELKADER IBRAHIM, *Human Resources For Egyptian Enterprise*, New York: McGraw-Hill Book Co., 1958, ch. 2; United Nations, *The Development Of Manufacturing Industry in Egypt, Israel And Turkey*, New York: United Nations, 1958, pp. 9, 28–38, 103–09.
64. E.g., see United Nations, *A Study Of The Iron And Steel Industry In Latin America*, New York: United Nations, 1954, pp. 52, 112–22; United Nations, *The Development Of Manufacturing Industry...*, chs. 4, 8.

65. On the managing agency system see ANDREW F. BRIMMER, "The Setting Of Entrepreneurship In India", *Quarterly Journal of Economics*, vol. 69, November, 1955, pp. 553–76. Under the Indian Companies Act, 1956, the managing agency system was subjected to controls designed to "prevent concentration of wealth" and to "ensure a minimum standard of good behavior in company promotion and management". See G. D. and J. K. JATHAR, *Indian Economics*, London: Oxford University Press, 1957, p. 187. See also HELEN LAMB, "The Indian Business Communities and the Evolution of an Industrial Class", *Pacific Affairs*, vol. 28, June, 1955, pp. 101–16.
66. No attention will be given to the roles played by more general governmental agencies (e.g., general development corporations, industrial development and industrial finance agencies, agricultural development agencies, river-development agencies, etc.), or to collectivistic efforts intended to countervail bureaucratization or to institutionalize initiative as in Russia. Concerning these matters see HANSON, *op. cit.*, pp. 207–335; *idem*, ed., *Public Enterprise*, Brussels, International Institute of Administrative Sciences, 1955; REINHARD BENDIX, "Industrialization, Ideologies, and Social Structure", *American Sociological Review*, vol. 24, October, 1959, pp. 619–23.
67. On types (1) and (3) see HANSON, *Public Enterprise*, pp. 336–56, 360–474, also HANSON, ed., *op. cit.;* ASOK CHANDA, *Indian Administration*, London: George Allen and Unwin, Ltd., 1958, pp. 194–204, 262–65; R. KELF-COHEN, *Nationalization In Britain*, New York: St. Martin's Press, 1959, pp. 224–26, 257, 295–97.
68. HANSON, *Public Enterprise*, pp. 356–59.
69. Even when the accounting results of a state enterpreneur are satisfactory, this outcome may be due to the fact that his inputs have been priced below the level ruling in input markets. See LOUIS MARK, JR., "The Favored Status of the State Entrepreneur in Economic Development Programs", *Economic Development and Cultural Change*, vol. 7, July, 1959, pp. 422, 427–30.
70. E.g., see RAGNAR NURKSE, *Problems of Capital Formation In Underdeveloped Countries*, New York: Oxford University Press, 1953, pp. 11–15, and "Balanced Growth on Static Assumptions", *Economic Journal*, vol. 66, September, 1956, pp. 365–67; J. M. FLEMING, "External Economies and the Doctrine of Balanced Growth", *ibid.*, June, 1955, pp. 241–56; JOHN SHEAN, "International Specialization and the Concept of Balanced Growth", *Quarterly Journal of Economics*, vol. 73, May, 1958, pp. 183–97; PAUL STREETEN, "Unbalanced Growth", *Oxford Economic Papers*, vol. 11, June, 1959, pp. 167–90. The fundamental issue is well treated by HOLLIS B. CHENERY, in "The Interdependence Of Investment Decisions", in M. ABRAMOVITZ, ed., *The Allocation of Economic Resources*, Stanford University Press, 1959, pp. 82–120.
71. E.g., see STREETEN, *op. cit.*, pp. 172–90; HIGGINS, *op. cit.*, chs. 5, 16; ALBERT O. HIRSCHMAN, *The Strategy of Economic Development*, New Haven: Yale University Press, 1958, chs. 3–5; P. WILES, "Growth versus Choice", *Economic Journal*, vol. 66, June, 1956, pp. 244–55.
72. A. J. YOUNGSON, *Possibilities of Economic Progress*, Cambridge: Cambridge University Press, 1959, pp. 84–87; HIRSCHMAN *op. cit.*, ch. 6; W. P. STRASSMANN, "Interrelated Industries And The Rate of Technological Change", *Review of Economic Studies*, vol. 27, October, 1959, pp. 16–22.
73. Witness the impact of the South Manchurian Railway, or the diffusion of growth processes through nineteenth-century Europe. See EDWIN P. REUBENS, "Opportunities, Governments, and Economic Development in Manchuria 1860–1940", in H. G. J. AITKEN, *The State and Economic Growth*, New York: Social Science Research Council, 1959, pp. 158–74; G. L. MEIER and R. D. BALDWIN, *Economic Development*, New York: John Wiley & Sons, Inc., 1957, Part 2.

74. Karl Marx, *Capital*, Chicago: Charles H. Kerr & Company, 1906, Vol. 1, p. 649.
75. *Op. cit.*, chs. 10–11, esp. p. 100.
76. R. Richard Wohl, ed., *Change and the Entrepreneur*, Cambridge: Harvard University Press, 1949, pp. 23–24. The four-fold classification of entrepreneurs is Clarence H. Danhof's.
77. See Marvin Frankel, *British And American Manufacturing Productivity*, (Bulletin Series: No. 81), Urbana: University of Illinois Bureau of Economic and Business Research, 1957, pp. 69, 75–76, 114–16, also ch. 7. See also works cited in note 8 above, and compare P. Sargant Florence, *The Logic of British and American Industry*, London: Routledge and Kegan Paul, Ltd., 1953, pp. 121–35; also F. H. Harbison and E. W. Burgess, "Modern Management In Western Europe", *American Journal of Sociology*, vol. 60, July, 1954, pp. 20, 21–22.
78. E.g., see George J. Stigler, *Five Lectures On Economic Problems*, London: Macmillan Company, 1950, pp. 46–65, and "The Statistics Of Monopoly And Merger", *Journal of Political Economy*, vol. 64, February, 1956, pp. 33–40; M. A. Adelman, "The Mea urement of Industrial Concentration", *Review of Economics and Statistics*, vol. 33, November, 1951, pp. 295–96, and comments in *ibid.*, vol. 34, May, 1952, pp. 156–76; the review of major empirical studies in Dewey, *op cit.*, chs. 5–7.
79. E.g., see J. J. Spengler, "Power Blocs and the Formation and Content of Economic Decisions", *American Economic Review*, vol. 40, No. 2, May, 1950, pp. 413–30; Corwin D. Edwards, *Maintaining Competition*, New York: M Graw-Hill and Co., 1949, pp. 102–06.
80. On the inequality-producing effect of monopoly see Sidney Weintraub, *An Approach to the Theory of Income Distribution*, Philadelphia: Chilton Company, 1958, ch. 4. In the text above I neglect the effects of differences in marginal tax rates upon propensities to save, since these differences are not associated with degree of monopoly as such.
81. E.g., see K. E. Boulding, "The Fruits of Progress and the Dynamics of Distribution", *American Economic Review*, vol. 43, No. 2, May, 1953, pp. 481–83.
82. On some of the issues involved see I. M. D. Little, *A Critique of Welfare Economics*, Oxford: Clarendon Press, 1957, chs. 7–8; F. D. Holzman, "Consumer Sovereignty And The Rate Of Economic Development", *Economia Internazionale*, vol. 11, May, 1958, pp. 193–207; Otto Eckstein, "Investment Criteria For Economic Development And The Theory Of Intertemporal W.lfare Economics", *Quarterly Journal of Economics*, vol. 71, February, 1957, pp. 56–85; Francis M. Bator, "On Capital Productivity, Input Allocation and Growth", *ibid.*, pp. 86–106; references in note 35 and accompanying text.
83. J. K. Galbraith employs the concept "disequilibrium" in a different sense in "The Disequilibrium System", *American Economic Review*, vol. 37, June, 1947, pp. 287–302.
84. Two facts are noteworthy. First, in underdeveloped countries receivers of wages and salaries are little disposed to supply savings for the financing of development; it is the beneficiaries of inequality who are in a position to supply a large amount of savings. E.g., see W. A. Lewis, *The Theory of Economic Growth*, pp. 100–01, 225–44; International Bank for Reconstruction and Development, *The Basis of a Development Program for Colombia*, Baltimore: Johns Hopkins Press, 1950, pp. 51–54. Second, many beneficiaries of inequality fail to provide much financial support for economic development. Milton Friedman suggests that income associated with impermanent monopoly is much less likely to be spent on consumables and unproductive assets than is income associated with permanent monopoly. See *A Theory of the Consumption Function*, Princeton: Princeton University Press, 1957, pp. 233–39. Criticisms of Friedman's thesis, even should they prove valid, are

not necessarily relevant to its applicability to underdeveloped countries. See the critiques of H. S. HOUTHAKKER, "The Permanent Income Hypothesis", *American Economic Review*, vol. 48, June, 1958, pp. 396–404; and of RONALD BODKIN, "Windfall Income and Consumption", *ibid.*, vol. 49, September, 1959, pp. 602–14.

85. On the surpluses associated with imperfect competition see M. KALECKI, *Theory of Economic Dynamics*, London: George Allen and Unwin, 1954, pp. 18, 30–31; B. S. KEIRSTEAD, *An Essay in the Theory of Prifits and Distribution*, Oxford: Basil Blackwell, 1953, ch. 2; JOAN ROBINSON, *Economics of Imperfect Competition*, London: Macmillan and Co., 1933, pp. 323–25. On oligopoly vs. monopoly and investment see JAMES DUESENBERRY, *Business Cycles and Economic Growth*, New York: McGraw-Hill, 1958, ch. 6.

86. E.g., see BAUMOL, *op. cit.*, chs. 10–11; KENNETH K. KURIHARA, "Distribution, Employment and Secular Growth", in *idem*, ed., *Post-Keynesian Economics*, New Brunswick: Rutgers University Press, 1954, pp. 253–54, 272–73; also HILDEBRAND, *op. cit.*, pp. 593–94; ABRAMOVITZ, "Savings and Investment", *loc. cit.*, pp. 81–88. The presence of monopsony may accentuate or alleviate investment-depressing effects associated with monopoly. E.g., see M. BRONFENBRENNER, "Monopsony And The Consumer Interest", *Indian Economic Review*, vol. II, February, 1954, pp. 1–20.

87. See M. BRONFENBRENNER, TARO YAMANE, and C. H. LEE, "A Study in Redistribution and Consumption", *Review of Economics and Statistics*, vol. 37, May, 1955, pp. 149–59; M. BRONFENBRENNER, "A Contribution to the Aggregative Theory of Wages", *Journal of Political Economy*, vol. 64, December, 1956, pp. 459–69. On factors affecting saving see IRVING FRIEND and I. B. KRAVIS, "Entrepreneurial Income, Saving and Investment", *American Economic Review*, vol. 47, June, 1957, pp. 269–301; S. KUZNETS, "Economic Growth and Income Equality", *ibid.*, vol. 45, March, 1955, pp. 1–28; HAROLD LYDALL and J. B. LANSING, "Distribution of Personal Income and Wealth", *ibid.*, vol. 49, March, 1959, pp. 43–67.

88. E.g., see FRANZ GEHRELS, "Factor Substitution and Growth Stability", *American Economic Review*, vol. 47, September, 1957, pp. 629–33.

89. American corporations typically reinvest 40–60 per cent of their disposable earnings; the former figure coincides more closely with the long term result. See JOHN LINTNER, "Distribution of Incomes Of Corporations Among Dividends, Retained Earnings, And Taxes", *American Economic Review*, No. 2, May, 1956, pp. 97–113. In India in the 1940's corporations reinvested about 58 per cent of the corporate industrial sector's profits. See Employers' Association, *Role of Private Enterprise in India—In Retrospect & Prospect*, Calcutta: Employers' Association, c. 1951, pp. 9–10, 22. British corporate performance was similar. *Ibid.*, p. 22; P. SARGANT FLORENCE, "New Measures of the Growth of Firms", *Economic Journal*, vol. 67, June, 1957, p. 247. In Britain very large corporations reinvest a somewhat larger fraction of net earnings than do smaller corporations. *Ibid.*, p. 247; also S. J. PRAIS, "The Financial Experience of Giant Companies", *ibid.*, pp. 252, 263. In the United States, according to data supplied to me by the National Industrial Conference Board and based on U.S. Treasury tax returns compilations for 1954–56, retained profits as per cent of net post-tax profits were negative for corporations with less than $100,000 of assets, and generally higher for corporations with assets of 0.1 to 5 million dollars than for those with greater assets. On corporate and non-corporate additions to assets see U.S. Department of Commerce, *U.S. Income And Output*, Washington: U.S. Department of Commerce, 1958, pp. 11–12, 16, 194–95; also LYDALL and LANSING, *op. cit.*, pp. 62–67. Earnings-reinvestment policy and the extent to which exposure to competition prompts firms to borrow or sell securities are treated by J. R. MEYER and EDWIN KUH, in *The Investment Decision*, Cambridge: Harvard University Press, 1957, ch. 9.

90. Before 1930 and after 1945 corporations supplied about 20 per cent of national saving in the United States; government, about 10 per cent; and individuals (including farmers and unincorporated businesses, which together accounted for less than one-sixth of the personal total), about 70 per cent. See R. W. GOLDSMITH, *A Study of Saving in the United States*, vol. I, Princeton: Princeton University Press, 1955, pp. 8–9, ch. 4. According to I. FRIEND and S. SCHOR, in 1950 59% of personal and family savings were supplied by 4 per cent of the families or individuals. See "Who Saves?", *Review of Economics and Statistics*, vol. 41, No. 2, Part 2, May, 1959, p. 239. See note 127 below.
91. See A. D. H. KAPLAN, *Small Business: Its Place and Problems*, New York: McGraw-Hill Book Co., 1948, chs. 5–7; R. O. EVERETT, ed., "Small Business", *Law and Contemporary Problems*, vol. 24, Winter, 1959, esp. pp. 27–88, 132–46, 192–240; S. H. WELLISZ, "The Coexistence Of Large And Small Firms: A Study Of The Italian Mechanical Industries", *Quarterly Journal of Economics*, vol. 71, February, 1957, pp. 116–31; FLORENCE, *The Logic of British and American Industry*, pp. 22–36, 55–82; R. B. HEFLEBOWER, "Economics of Size", *Journal of Business of the University of Chicago*, vol. 24, October, 1951, pp. 265–68; S. KUZNETS, "Economic Growth of Small Nations", in A. BONNE, ed., *The Challenge of Development;* Jerusalem: Hebrew University, 1958; P. N. DHAR shows that the size of the surplus available for reinvestment is greatly increased by mechanisation in small industries, but that the extent to which it is ploughed back into the business is much affected by the background and aspirations of the proprietor. See "Some Aspects Of Technical Progress In Small Scale Industries", *Indian Economic Review*, vol. 3, February, 1956, pp. 74–75. See also BAUER, *West African Trade*, pp. 28–39, 313–14, 334–38, on trading and saving.
92. On the tendency of invention to result in monopoly see JACOB SCHMOOKLER, "Invention, Innovation, And Competition", *Southern Economics Journal*, vol. 20, April, 1954, pp. 384–85.
93. This sequence is based upon the sequence of propensities upon which, according to W. RUPERT MACLAURIN, the conversion of pure science into economic growth depends. See his "The Sequence From Invention to Innovation And Its Relation To Economic Growth", *Quarterly Journal of Economics*, vol. 67, February, 1953, pp. 97–111.
94. Concerning the diverse goals of firms and conditions affecting them see HERBERT A. SIMON, "Theories Of Decision-Making In Economics And Behavioral Sciences", *American Economic Review*, vol. 49, June, 1959, pp. 262–65, and J. G. MARCH and H. A. SIMON, *Organization*, New York: John Wiley and Sons, 1958, *passim*.
95. See RICHARD R. NELSON, "The Economics Of Invention: A Survey Of The Situation", *Journal of Business of the University of Chicago*, vol. 32, April, 1959, pp. 105–07; CARTER and WILLIAMS, *op. cit.*, ch. 3; also National Resources Planning Board, *Research- A National Resource*, II, Washington: U. S. Government Printing Office, 1941, *passim*. At the international level scientific contributions and activities are highly correlated. See B. J. ZWOLINSKI and F. D. ROSSINI, "Analysis of References in Critical Tables", *Science*, vol. 130, December 25, 1959, pp. 1743–46.
96. See RICHARD R. NELSON, "The Economics of Invention...", *loc. cit.*, pp. 103–04, pp. 112–15, and "The Simple Economics of Basic Scientific Research", *Journal of Political Economy*, vol. 67, June, 1959, pp. 297–306, esp. pp. 302–04.
97. J. C. FISHER, "Basic Research in Industry", *Science*, vol. 129, p. 1657. Hastening obsolescence may be one objective of innovation. E.g., see WILLIAM H. BROWN, "Innovation In The Machine Tool Industry", *Quarterly Journal of Economics*, vol. 71, August, 1957, pp. 412, 423–24.
98. NELSON, "The Simple Economics...", *loc. cit.*, pp. 302–03. Only 1 in 20 of the

research projects of America's largest chemical corporations "has proved successful". See National Science Foundation, *Review of Data on Research & Development*, No. 13, March, 1959, p. 4.

99. W. R. MACLAURIN, "The Process of Technological Innovation", *American Economic Review*, vol. 40, March, 1950, pp. 90–112, and "Technological Progress In Some American Industries", *ibid.*, vol. 44, No. 2, May, 1954, pp. 178–89; YALE BROZEN, "Invention, Innovation, and Imitation," *ibid.*, vol. 41, No. 2, May, 1959, pp. 243–44. M. ABRAMOVITZ, "Economics of Growth", in B. F. Haley, ed., *A Survey of Contemporary Economics*, Chicago: Richard Irwin, Inc., 1952, pp. 158 ff.

100. It has been estimated that only about 3 per cent of industry's and no more than 10 per cent of the nation's expenditure upon research in the United States in the 1950's was devoted to basic research; apparently less than 0.5 per cent of gross national product was thus used. See CHESTER I. BARNARD, "A National Science Policy", *Scientific American*, vol. 197, November, 1957, pp. 46–49; NELSON, "The Simple Economics...", *loc. cit.*, p. 297; National Science Foundation, *Science and Engineering in American Industry*, Washington, 1956, pp. 18–21, and *Review of Data on Research & Development*, No. 14, August, 1959, p. 4; also W. R. BRODE, "Development of a Science Policy", *Science*, vol. 131, January 1, 1960, p. 11. Whether research is basic or not is not always clear. Furthermore, a firm may be engaging in basic research, but not disclosing this fact.

101. Provisions for enlarging this pool differ from country to country. See DAVID M. GATES, "Basic Research in Europe", *Science*, vol. 128, August 1, 1958, pp. 227–35.

102. E.g., see FRITZ MACHLUP, "Can There Be Too Much Research", *Science*, vol. 128, November 28, 1958, pp. 1320–25; also S. MELMAN, *The Impact of the Patent System on Research*, Study No. 11 of the Subcommittee on Patents, Trademarks, and Copyrights of the Committee on the Judiciary, U. S. Senate, pursuant to S. Res. 236, Washington: U. S. Government Printing Office, 1958, chs. 7–9.

103. JACOB SCHMOOKLER, "Inventors Past and Present", *Review of Economics and Statistics*, vol. 39, August, 1957, pp. 329–30. SCHMOOKLER's findings run counter to E. L. VAN DEUSEN's, in "The Inventor in Eclipse", *Fortune*, vol. 50, December, 1954, pp. 132 ff., and they suggest that the flow of inventions from the general public will remain important. The findings of J. JEWKES *et al* are of similar import, in *The Sources of Invention*, London: Macmillan and Co., 1958. See also THOMAS WILSON, "Science and Industry", *Lloyds Bank Review*, No. 46, October, 1957, pp. 35–37. Inasmuch as private firms usually insist on college degrees for technical personnel, non-college graduates, relatively many of whom are inventive, find it necessary to invent as individuals. See SCHMOOKLER, "Inventors"... *loc. cit.*, p. 330.

104. MELMAN, *The Impact...*, pp. 32–37. Machlup writes: "The bulk of technological advances, especially the millions of small improvements in production techniques which probably account for a large part of the increases in labor productivity, have nothing to do with patent protection". See MACHLUP, *An Economic Review...*, p. 63.

105. P. J. FEDERICO, *Distribution of Patents Issued to Corporations* (1939–55), Study No. 3 of the Subcommittee on Patents, Trademarks, and Copyrights of the Committee on the Judiciary, the U. S. Senate, pursuant to S. Res. 167, Washington: U. S. Government Printing Office, 1957, pp. 3–5, 16–18.

106. National Science Foundation, *Science and Engineering...*, pp. 6–11, 58–62, also pp. 33–35, 81–82 on inter-industry differences in expenditure.

107. *Ibid.*, p. 65. Average cost per scientist and engineer varies somewhat with type of industry and with firm size in given industries. *Ibid.*, p. 80. Clear-cut relationships

between research and development expenditures and firm assets or sales are not apparent, in part perhaps because sales-oriented expenditures may be adapted to the size of the prospective market. See *ibid.*, pp. 33–36, 81–82; also H. S. TURNER, "How Much Should a Company Spend on Research", *Harvard Business Review*, vol. 32, May-June, 1954, pp. 101–112.

108. Maclaurin has described as most dynamic of the manufacturing industries those engaged in oil refining and in the manufacture of heavy chemicals, photographic supplies, aircraft, radio, television, and electric lighting equipment (to which list pharmaceuticals may be added), all of which appear to be dominated by large firms. Least progressive are food processing, cotton textiles, coal mining, and mass housing, in the last three of which industries small or medium firms predominate. See MACLAURIN, "Technological Progress...", *loc. cit.*, pp. 180–81, and "Patents Technological Progress—A Study of Television", *Journal of Political Economy*, vol. 58, April, 1950, pp. 142–57.

109. Maclaurin, "The Sequence...", *loc. cit.*, pp. 108–10, and "The Process of Technological Innovation", *loc. cit.*, pp. 110–11. On British experience respecting the shortage of capital for the support of invention and innovation, see CARTER and WILLIAMS, *op. cit.*, ch. 13.

110. On the skewness-producing effect of the fact that persons with relatively large incomes have relatively greater access to income-producing credit, see STANLEY LEBERGOTT, "The Shape Of The Income Distribution", *American Economic Review*, vol. 49, June, 1959, pp. 343–45. Lack of finance is but one of the obstacles found by individual inventors, according to CARTER and WILLIAMS, *op. cit.*, pp. 72–75.

111. On the risks, etc., see NELSON, "The Economics Of Invention", *loc. cit.*, pp. 110–15. DEWEY describes the ability of the large firm to borrow capital on relatively favorable terms to be a "true" economy of scale. See *op. cit.*, p. 41; also BROZEN, "Invention, Innovation, and Imitation", *loc. cit.*, pp. 240–41, on the disadvantage of small firms seeking capital through sale of securities. On cost of funds see also DUESENBERRY, *op. cit.*, ch. 5; MEYER and KUH, *op. cit.*

112. E.g., on the exploitation of agricultural research see ZVI GRILICHES, "Research Costs and Social Returns: Hybrid Corn and Related Innovations", *Journal of Political Economy*, vol. 66, October, 1958, pp. 419–31; T. W. SCHULTZ, *The Economic Organization of Agriculture*, New York: McGraw-Hill Book Co., 1953, pp. 114–22. The need of small firms for capital to exploit invention seems to be much less stressed in writings on small business than are other needs for capital. On the public support and finance of invention see also MACLAURIN, "The Sequence...", *loc. cit.*, p. 109; H. H. VILLARD, "Competition, Oligopoly, And Research", *Journal of Political Economy*, vol. 66, December, 1958, pp. 494–97.

113. On associations between innovation and personnel requirements see HILL and HARBISON, *op. cit.*, pp. 53–56, 67–69. And on the development-retarding effect of a shortage of trained personnel, see CARTER and WILLIAMS, *op. cit.*, ch. 9.

114. On some of the factors involved see FRITZ MACHLUP, "The Optimum Lag of Imitation Behind Innovation", reprinted from *Festskrift til Frederik Zeuthen*, Copenhagen: Nationalokonomisk Forening, 1958, pp. 239–56; BROZEN, "Invention, Innovation, And Imitation", *loc. cit.*, esp. pp. 240–45; MARVIN FRANKEL, "Obsolescence and Technological Change", *American Economic Review*, vol. 45, June, 1955, pp. 296–329; and CARTER and WILLIAMS, *op. cit.*, ch. 16, on conditions that make a firm progressive, and p. 160 on advantage of early start.

115. Even though it be granted that a patent system increases both (a) the rate of invention and (b) the disclosure of the technological advances incorporated in particular patents, it remains true that a reduction of the legal lifetime of patents may result in an increase in (b) without diminishing (a). The cost to society of

delayed imitation of innovations would be reduced, MACHLUP believes, if the length of the period of patent protection were reduced below 16–18 years; and this gain would not be at all offset by a diminution in the rate of invention and innovation. See "The Optimum Lag...", *loc. cit.*, p. 256; also *An Economic Review Of The Patent System*, pp. 66–73, 76–80. See also National Resources Committee, *Technological Trends And National Policy*, Washington: United States Government Printing Office, 1937, *passim*. It is not wholly clear that, as some believe, firms are more responsive to prospectively profitable innovation or imitation when product-change rather than cost-reduction is involved; nor, if there be such difference in response, has its association (if any) with variation in firm size been examined. E.g., see G. F. BLOOM, "Wage Pressure and Technological Discovery", *American Economic Review*, vol. 41, September, 1951, pp. 603–17; YALE BROZEN, "Determinants Of The Direction Of Technological Change", *ibid.*, vol. 43, No. 2, May, 1953, pp. 288–302.

116. On the part played by quality of management see CARTER and WILLIAMS, *op. cit.*, pp. 52, 66, ch. 16, and "The Characteristics of Technically Progressive Firms", *Journal of Industrial Economics*, vol. 7, March, 1959, pp. 87–104. EDITH PENROSE reports many inventions and technical advances to be traceable "to the desire of a firm to take advantage of already possessed services not used in current production". See "Limits To The Growth And Size Of Firms", *American Economic Review*, vol. 45, No. 2, May, 1955, p. 537. On possible effects of some elements endogenous to a firm or its organizational structure see JAMES G. MARCH and H. A. SIMON, *Organizations*, New York: John Wiley and Sons, 1958, ch. 7; R. M. CYERT and J. G. MARCH, "Organizational Structure And Pricing Behavior In An Oligopolistic Market", *American Economic Review*, vol. 45, March, 1955, pp. 129–39.

117. On these economies see E. A. G. ROBINSON, *Structure of Competitive Industry*, Chicago: University of Chicago Press. 1958. On the relations between size and technical progressiveness see NELSON, "The Economics of Invention...", *loc. cit.*, pp. 108–09, and "The Simple Economics...", *loc. cit.*, pp. 302–03; VILLARD, *op. cit.*; CARTER and WILLIAMS, *Industry and Technical Progress*, pp. 122–127, 186. On the distinction between technical research and peculiarly entrepreneurial functions, see G. J. STIGLER, "Industrial Organization and Economic Progress", in Leonard D. White, ed., *The State of the Social Sciences*, Chicago: University of Chicago Press, 1956, pp. 269–82, esp. pp. 275, 279–82; G. W. NUTTER, "Monopoly, Bigness, And Progress", *Journal of Political Economy*, vol. 64, December, 1956, pp. 522, 525–26.

118. For data on the length of life of companies see WILLIAM L. CRUM, *The Age Structure Of The Corporate System*, Berkeley: University of California Press, 1953, p. 176; G. H. EVANS, JR., *Business Incorporations In The United States* 1800–1943, New York: National Bureau of Economic Research, 1948, pp. 7–9; GUNNAR LINDGREN, "How Long does a Company Live?" *Oxford Economic Papers*, vol. 5, October, 1953, pp. 235–47. On why large firms persist see SEYMOUR FRIEDLAND, "Turnover And Growth Of The Largest Industrial Firms, 1906–1950", *Review of Economics and Statistics*, vol. 39, February, 1957, pp. 79–83. See also next section. On firm size and growth see MEYER and KUH, *op. cit.*, ch. 10; S. HYMER and B. P. PASHIGIAN, "Firm Size and Rate of Growth" (Abstract), *Econometrica*, vol. 27, 1959, p. 315.

119. *Op. cit.*, p. 41.

120. CARTER and WILLIAMS, *Industry And Technical Progress*, pp. 117, 157–59, 190–92. The favorableness of a high rate of industrial growth to the profits of firms and their inclination to technical progress may be partly offset by the high variability sometimes characteristic of this rate and the consequent increase in uncertainty.

The variousness of the factors which may affect technical progress is suggested by R. S. Sayers's "The Springs of Technical Progress in Great Britain, 1919–39". *Economic Journal*, vol. 60, June, 1950, pp. 275–91.

121. This definition is employed by Stigler to meet the conditions of a changing economy. See "Industrial Organization...", *loc. cit.*, pp. 272–73. Cf. also J. P. Miller, "Competition And Countervailing Power: Their Roles In The American Economy", *American Economic Review*, vol. 44, No. 2, May, 1954, pp. 22–23.

122. Carter and Williams, *Industry and Technical Progress*, p. 169; also pp. 168–69 on the failure of competition to foster technical progress in depressed industries. "The profit-oriented motive to innovate is likely to be largest in an economy that approaches neither a world of monopolies nor a world of diminutive units in densely populated industries". See Machlup, "The Optimum Lag...", *loc. cit.*, p. 240.

123. It is not true, of course, that an innovation's profitability is necessarily an index of its "social usefulness". See Machlup, *An Economic Review Of The Patent System*, pp. 30, 54, ff. Furthermore, when expansion is financed largely out of profits, it may be inadequately subjected to market tests, Carl Kaysen observed, in "The Social Significance of the Modern Corporation", *American Economic Review*, vol. 47, No. 2, May, 1957, pp. 315–16.

124. See Stigler, "Industrial Organization...", *loc. cit.*, pp. 276–79. See, however, A. Phillips's finding that between 1899 and 1939 labor input per unit of output fell most markedly in industries dominated by large-scale units already in 1904, in "Concentration, Scale and Technological Change in Selected Manufacturing Industries 1899–1939", *Journal of Industrial Economics*, vol. 4, March, 1956, pp. 192–93. On the effect of competition generally see Carter and Williams, *Industry and Technological Progress*, pp. 165–68; Nutter, *op. cit.*, pp. 525–26; Brozen, "Invention, Innovation, and Imitation", *loc. cit.*, pp. 243, 256; and Jacob Schmookler, "Invention, Innovation, and Competition", *loc. cit.*, pp. 384–85 where it is argued that severance of the link between invention and innovation may be essential to keeping the economy sufficiently competitive to sustain a high rate of innovation.

125. Maclaurin, "The Process...," *loc. cit.*, pp. 108–110; Nelson, "The Economics of Invention...", *loc. cit.*, pp. 108–110; Yale Brozen, "Research, Technology, And Productivity", in L. Reed Thripp, ed., *Industrial Productivity*, Madison, Wis.: Industrial Relations Research Association, 1951, pp. 27 ff.,; Carter and Williams, *Industry And Technical Progress*, pp. 72–75, esp. p. 74 where it is said "that the amount of private invention of industrial significance is small".

126. Villard believes "competitive oligopoly" to be the structural form most conducive to the increase of productivity since it presupposes firms (1) "large enough or few enough to afford and benefit from research and (2) ... under competitive pressure to innovate—utilize the results of research". *Op. cit.*, p. 491. Baumol's view is similar. *Op. cit.*, chs. 10–11, 15. M. A. Adelman considers the "drive toward size" to be a major force making for competition. See "Business and Public Policy", *Journal of Business of the University of Chicago*, vol. 24, October, 1951, p. 274.

127. In the United States enterprise is the source of close to one-third of all savings; in India corporate savings (about 5 per cent of all savings), together with household direct investment, constitute somewhat more than half of all savings. See Goldsmith, *op. cit.* p. 9; V. V. Bhatt, "Savings and Capital Formation", *Economic Development and Cultural Change*, vol. 7, No. 3, Part 1, April, 1959, pp. 336–37, 340. Estimates of corporate savings and unincorporated enterprise income for many countries is given by S. Kuznets in "Quantitative Aspects Of The Economic Growth Of Nations, IV," *ibid.*, Part 2, pp. 78–80.

128. E.g., see H. A. Simon and Charles P. Bonini, "The Size Distribution of Business

Firms", *American Economic Review*, vol. 48, September, 1958, pp. 607–17; IRMA G. ADELMAN, "A Stochastic Analysis Of The Size Distribution Of Firms", *Journal of the American Statistical Association*, vol. 53, December, 1958, pp. 893–904; also FLORENCE, *op. cit.*, pp. 22–37.

129. This process has been described by PENROSE, *op. cit.*, pp. 530–43, and "Towards A Theory Of Industrial Concentration", *Economic Record*, vol. 32, May, 1956, pp. 66–77.

130. JOHN JEWKES "The Size of Factory", *Economic Journal*, vol, 62, 1952, 251; JOHN M. BLAIR, "Technology And Size", *American Economic Review*, vol. 38, No. 2, May, 1948, pp. 121–52. Of 20 industries studied by Bain, "a minimum optimal plant" accounts for less than 2.5 per cent of American national capacity in 11 industries and for more than 7.5 per cent in 5. See BAIN, *op. cit.*, pp. 56–67, 72–73, also pp. 80, 110–13, 184–87, 211–14. See also F. T. MOORE, "Economies Of Scale: Some Statistical Evidence", *Quarterly Journal of Economics*, vol. 73, May, 1959, pp. 232–45; DAVID SCHWARTZMAN, "The Methodology of the Theory of Return to Scale", *Oxford Economic Papers*, vol. 10, February, 1958, pp. 98–105; FLORENCE, *op. cit.*, pp. 55–73.

131. E.g., see CALEB A. SMITH, "Survey Of The Empirical Evidence On Economies Of Scale", in Stigler, ed., *Business Concentration and Price Policy*, pp. 213–30 and MILTON FRIEDMAN's comments, *ibid.*, pp. 230–38; BAIN, *op. cit.*, pp. 84–93, 110–13, 137–41, 187–89, 192–201, 211–14; FLORENCE, *op. cit.*, pp. 74–83.

132. PENROSE, "Towards A Theory...", *loc. cit.*, pp. 74–76; FLORENCE, *op. cit.*, pp. 130–35, 273–324; D. R. ROBERTS, "A General Theory of Executive Compensation Based on Statistically Tested Propositions", *Quarterly Journal of Economics*, vol. 70, May, 1956, pp. 270–94, esp. p. 294; H. H. HINES, "Effectiveness of 'Entry' By Already Established Firms", *ibid.*, vol. 71, February, 1957, pp. 143, 145; R. F. LANZILLOTTI, "Pricing Objectives in Large Companies", *American Economic Review*, vol. 48, December, 1958, pp. 941–53; G. J. STIGLER, "Monopoly And Oligopoly By Merger", *ibid.*, vol. 40, No. 2, May, 1950, pp. 22–34, and "The Statistics Of Monopoly And Merger", *Journal of Political Economy*, vol. 64, February, 1956, pp. 33–40; J. W. MARKHAM, "Survey Of The Evidence And Findings On Mergers", in Stigler, ed., *Business Concentration and Price Policy*, pp. 141–212; J. M. BLAIR, *et al.*, "The Lintner-Butters Analysis of the Effect of Mergers on Industrial Concentration, 1940–1947", *Review of Economics and Statistics*, vol. 33, May, 1951, pp. 63–75; Federal Trade Commission, *Report On Corporate Mergers And Acquisitions*, Washington: U. S. Government Printing Office, 1955, and *Industrial Concentration And Product Diversification In The 1,000 Largest Manufacturing Companies: 1950*, Washington: U. S. Government Printing Office, 1957.

133. As was noted earlier, in 11 of 20 American industries optimal plant capacity accounted for 0.1 to 2.5 per cent of national capacity; in 4 it accounted for 1.375 to 6 per cent, and in 5 for 5 to 30 per cent of national capacity. See BAIN, *op. cit.*, p. 72. While optimal plant capacity would probably be lower in most underdeveloped countries, it would not fall nearly as short of optimal capacity in America as the underdeveloped country's national capacity would fall short of the American.

134. P. WILES asserts that "a determination never to violate... welfare equations... slows up the rate of growth", and that "rapid growth diminishes the harm done by violation not only of consumer sovereignty but also of rational allocation in general". "We must choose, to some extent, between choice and growth". See "Growth Versus Choice", *Economic Journal*, vol. 66, June, 1956, pp. 248, 251, 255.

CHAPTER 3

ALTERNATIVE APPROACHES TO THE CONTROL OF COMPETITION*

An Outline of European Cartel Legislation and its Administration

WILLIAM BOSERUP AND UFFE SCHLICHTKRULL

The Monopolies Control Authority, Copenhagen, Denmark

I

At the XXVIth Conference of the Inter-Parliamentary Union held in London in 1930, a resolution was passed unanimously[1] which stated, among other things,

> "...that cartels, trusts and other analogous combines are natural phenomena of economic life towards which it is impossible to adopt an entirely negative attitude. Seeing, however, that those combines may have a harmful effect both as regards public interests and those of the State, it is necessary that they should be controlled. This Control should not take the form of an interference in economic life likely to affect its normal development. It should simply seek to establish a supervision over possible abuses and to prevent those abuses.
>
> An efficacious means of fighting such abuses and a basic condition for eventual control is to be found in publicity, which implies the obligation for cartels and similar combines to announce their existence and to register in the books of the State. To this should be added a stipulation making compulsory written agreements for such combines.
>
> Conventions which have not been made in writing, or which have not been communicated and submitted to the competent authority within the given time, should not be entitled to claim legal protection.
>
> Registered cartels, trusts and similar organisations should be made publicly known within a given time by the office of registry, whereas the agreements themselves should only be published, either partly or as a whole, in the event of well-ascertained abuses, according to the gravity of the case.
>
> In order to examine and to decide whether registered agreements do not contain provisions dangerous to public interests or to the State, and in order to examine and decide whether abuses have been committed, there should be created in each

* This chapter reflects the situation in the summer of 1960.

State a Committee on Trusts and Cartels, independent of the Government and as strictly limited in number as possible, on which the consumer and the worker should be represented.

The Committee on Cartels should be entrusted ex officio with all inquiries of a general nature, whereas particular cases should only be made the object of an inquiry at the request of the highest competent official authority. The conclusions of the Committee should be made public.

On the basis of the conclusions reached by the Committee, the competent central authority should be entitled to institute proceedings for the punishment of abuses and in certain cases to obtain that treaties should be declared void before the competent courts.

The XXVIth Conference of the Inter-Parliamentary Union recommends that its national Groups shall endeavour to obtain adoption of these principles by their Governments."

In many respects this is a remarkable document.

The first point of interest is the date of the document. In 1930, at which time anti-trust legislation had been in existence for many years in the United States, for instance, Europe was, as it appears, still in the preliminary stages. At that time only two countries, namely Norway and Germany, had special acts, the German Cartel Ordinance (Kartell-Verordnung) of 1923, and the Norwegian Anti-trust Act of 1926. The reason why the cartel legislation in Europe had such a late start, however, was not that the tendencies towards concentration within trade and industry resulting in cartels, trusts or other forms of combines limiting the free competition and the freedom of trade had come into existence so much later than in the United States. Nor was it because the perspectives of these tendencies had not been realised before. On the contrary, already during the years before the First World War, jurists and economists, especially in Germany but also in other European countries, had paid intense attention to the growing cartellization and its various effects, and, even as early as 1897, in Austria, a bill had been proposed with a view to regulating cartel activities, but it was not passed. Also the Norwegian and Swedish Governments took the cartel problems under observation and appointed committees to make investigations in preparation for possible future cartel legislation. However, this work was stopped because of the First World War, and after the Armistice other economic and political problems came to the fore.

Further, the London resolution is interesting because it states certain basic principles and sketches a system of control and regulation which has, to a great extent, influenced the Cartel legislation in most of the West European countries, although, of course, certain differences will be found in the legislation of the various countries.

The Principle of Control and Intervention

We have seen that the London resolution in principle accepts cartels, trusts and similar combinations as being natural economic phenomena and advocates that only effects which are adverse to the public interest should provoke interference on the part of the State. The fact that the combinations in question limit the competition—which by the nature of things they will generally do—is not in itself a criterion of their harmfulness. In this respect the resolution differs fundamentally from the American viewpoint as expressed in The Sherman Act. As is well known, this Act not only contains a definite prohibition against "any monopolization of trade and commerce" but also declares "every contract, combination in form of trust or otherwise, or conspiracy, in restraint of trade and commerce... to be illegal". And although during the passage of time the practical application of the rules of Common Law has taken the brunt of this rather rigorous provision of the Sherman Act by interpreting the words "restraint of trade and commerce" to mean "*unreasonable* restraint of trade and commerce", there is still a fundamental difference between the American system and a system recommended by the London resolution and adopted by most of the European countries: while the American system is based upon "the principle of prohibition and illegality", the European legislation in principle accepts cartels, trusts and other combinations, even if they involve restraints of trade and commerce, and will interfere only in cases where it appears that their consequences are to the detriment of the public interest. This may be called "the principle of control and intervention".

The Principle of Publicity

Complementary to the principle of control and intervention we find another fundamental view-point in the London resolution: the light of publicity must be thrown on the cartels, trusts and similar combinations having a restraining effect on competition. The purpose of this is twofold, namely to establish a basis for the control of private restrictive business practices permitting immediate intervention when necessary, and to attempt to prevent abuse of restrictive arrangements, for, as a rule, it will not be to the interest of trade and industry to have such arrangements made known to the public. As pointed out in the London resolution, the implementation of the principle of publicity will require provisions prescribing duty of notification for cartels, trusts and other combinations and arrangements of a restrictive nature, as well as the establishing of a register and a controlling body. As a supplementary measure the notified and registered matters may be published in one form or another and the contents of the register made available to the public. Besides, the principle of publicity will also call for provisions prescribing publishing of the abuses revealed by investigations made by the controlling authorities.

Cartel Control Organization

The London resolution also contains fundamental statements and recommendations concerning the organization of the cartel control and the judicial reaction against established abuses of restrictive arrangements. Thus it is suggested in the resolution that inquiries into the question whether registered agreements or arrangements contain provisions detrimental to the public interest be referred to a special cartel commission. The commission, the resolution continues, shall be *independent of the government*, and both *consumers'* and *workers' interests* shall be represented in it, although it should be as *strictly limited in number* as possible. The insistence on independence is quite natural as the commission will have a certain similarity to a law court in its operation, although it is not supposed to exert any formal jurisdiction. The demand that consumers' and workers' interests should be represented in the commission implies the assumption that it should be comprehensively composed; thus the main trades and industries as well as economic and judicial expert knowledge should also be represented.

The system advocated by the London resolution consists of three main components: 1) the aforementioned cartel commission, which shall investigate, establish the facts, and make recommendations to 2) the competent central authority which *may* subsequently decide to commence legal proceedings before 3) the ordinary Law Courts with a view to having harmful restrictions of competition declared void and also, if warranted by the circumstances of the case, to having the person or persons responsible punished.

As mentioned before, the fundamental principles expressed in the London resolution have come to influence the subsequent European cartel legislation to a rather great extent. This will be shown in the following passages giving a short survey of the cartel legislation in the various European countries. We have selected the countries where the legislation in this field is of particular interest.

1. NORWAY

Norway is one of the pioneer countries in Europe in the field of cartel legislation, and in an Act passed in 1920—several years before the London resolution—we find for the first time the principle of publicity put into practice. The Act was a provisionary emergency act, the direct purpose of which was to carry on the exceptional wartime measures of price control and price regulation, etc., because of the still abnormal supply conditions in evidence during the early post-war period. But, at the same time, the Act became a forerunner for the permanent cartel legislation, already under preparation for some time, as it laid down that monopolies and dominating enterprises, as well as restrictive agreements and combinations, should be notified to and filed with a public register, the management of which should be in charge of the price control authorities. The register should be open to the public.

The subsequent permanent Act, the so-called "Trust-Act" of 1926, preserved this system of notification and registration, but with the modification that the register should be at the disposal of the controlling authorities only. Under certain circumstances, however,—especially where the public interest was concerned—the authorities could inform non-authorized persons of the contents of the register.

The present Norwegian cartel act, Act on Control of Prices, Dividends and Restrictive Arrangements of 1953, short title "The Price Act"[2], is, as indicated by its name, more than a cartel control act, since it confers rather extensive powers to the Government to make regulations outside fields characterized by restrictions of competition. For our purpose, however, we shall deal only with the part of the Act concerning restrictive practices, and here no great changes have been made in relation to the old "Trust Act" in respect of the provisions concerning duty of notification, public registration, obligation to furnish information, and publication. In the following we shall give a short account of the provisions laid down by the Price Act in these respects.

(a) *Notification*

The Act prescribes *immediate* duty of notification (i.e. a duty to report on one's own initiative) for "large-scale enterprises" and for restrictive agreements and combinations and, also for restrictive regulations made by the large-scale enterprises subject to the duty of notification.

The Act defines a *large-scale or dominating enterprise* firstly as an enterprise manufacturing or selling 25 per cent or more of the country's total production or trade volume of the commodities or of the services in question, and secondly as an enterprise which is a sub-branch of or under controlling influence of a foreign firm or combination* which must be presumed to have a substantial influence on the prices in one or several countries for one or several commodities or services.

Moreover, the authorities are empowered to *impose* the duty of notification on an enterprise which, although not having a market share of 25 per cent or more, is found to be holding a dominating position—or in the words of the Act: "when they carry on a business which is of importance to one or more trades within the country".

The question whether the *restrictive arrangements* are based on binding or guiding agreements or provisions is of no consequence in respect of the obligation to report.

Failure to comply with the duty of notification is an offence under the Act, and a provision lays down the rule that restrictive arrangements are illegal when not reported, i.e. that they are not only non-binding on the parties, but it is absolutely prohibited to practice them and even to attempt to do so.

(b) *Obligation to Furnish Information*

It is the obligation of all citizens to furnish any such information to the authorities as may be demanded; the authorities have also a right to examine ledgers, business documents, and accounts, and to look over the premises of business. Failure to comply with the obligation to furnish information to the authorities is made an offence under the Act.

(c) *Registration*

All notifications made under the Act are filed in the register, but in addition, the controlling authorities may, *ex officio*, register any information they may possess for the elucidation of the matter registered. Furthermore, the authorities are empowered *ex officio* to make temporary registrations of restrictive practices subject to noti-

* This rule applies also to combinations including both Norwegian and foreign members.

fication but which have not been duly reported by the party or parties concerned.

The registration does not imply approval of the registered matter.

Information regarding technical devices and processes shall be withheld from the register if it is found that they have a justifiable claim to secrecy.

As of October 31, 1958, the register contained a grand total of 803 registrations, distributed as follows: 533 associations and combines, 191 agreements and arrangements, and 79 dominating enterprises.

(d) *Publication*

The rules concerning publication in the Price Act go further than the London resolution as the cartel register, which contains not only information about the making of cartel agreements and about the existence of trusts, etc. but also about the contents of agreements and decisions, is now available to everyone. Moreover, an officially issued bulletin ("Pristidende") gives surveys of the registered matters. The bulletin, furthermore, publishes the decisions made by the competent authorities in pursuance of the Act in cases where the question is one of intervention against restrictive business practices.

(e) *Cartel Authorities*

The Norwegian system is more complex than the pattern set up in the London resolution. The reason for this is, to a certain degree, that the scope of the Norwegian Price Act comprehends more than the control of and the intervention against restrictive business practices, and therefore, a comparison with the London program is not immediately possible.

As the central organ within the Norwegian system may be considered *the Price Directorate* ("Prisdirektoratet"). The duties charged on the Directorate are the keeping of the cartel register, the settling of questions regarding the duty of notification and, furthermore, a controlling and investigating activity in general. *The Price Council* ("Prisrådet") is the Norwegian organ corresponding nearest to the "Cartel Commission" of the London resolution, but it has been given more powers than implied in the resolution.

The Price Council consists of 5 members appointed by the Government (the King). The Act does not prescribe any definite qualifications of the members. In the preparatory works for the Act, however, it is stated that the members should be independent of outside business interests and possess a thorough and comprehensive knowledge of trade and industry together with economic, judicial, and—if possible—technical insight[3]. The duty of the Price Council is mainly to make decisions regarding abolishments, wholly or partly, of restrictive practices with harmful effects. Furthermore, the Council acts as a court of appeal for decisions made by the Price Directorate on questions concerning duty of notification. The Government (the King), finally, is entitled to amend or abolish provisions laid down by an association regulating competition, if they are deemed to have harmful effects; before such action is taken, an opinion from the Price Council must be required. Cases concerning violations of prohibitive provisions are referred by the Price Directorate to the ordinary Law Courts.

2. DENMARK

In Denmark the challenge of the London resolution to the governments of countries represented at the conference led, to begin with, only to a meagre result, namely an Act of 1931 aimed only at *price agreements* made by trusts, cartels and similar combinations. Under the Act, a committee was set up which on the basis of complaints—but not *ex officio*—could investigate price agreements and their effects. If the committee found that the agreements resulted in unfair prices, it could institute legal proceedings against the parties to the agreements before the ordinary law courts, which had the sole power of deciding whether the agreements or the means by which they were enforced were illegal. No cartel register was established.

Not until the subsequent Act, the Price Agreement Act of 1937, was the principle of publicity made effective through the establishment of a cartel register and by means of provisions covering the duty of notification and the obligation to supply information. The Act went considerably further than its predecessor also in other respects.

In the present Danish act, The Monopolies and Restrictive Practices Control Act of 1955—short title "The Monopolies Control Act"[4]—the principle of publicity is expressed in a system similar to the Norwegian one, but not quite as far-reaching.

(a) *Notification*

The Act prescribes *immediate* duty to report any such agreements made between enterprises and any such decisions made within organizations or combinations which exert or may be able to exert a substantial influence on price, production, distribution, or transport conditions throughout the country or in local market areas.

Enterprises and combinations holding a dominating position are subject to a special notification when the controlling authorities in each individual case so demand. This notification should also comprehend the general price fixing and the restrictive policies of enterprises or combinations.

All subsequent amendments to the matters registered shall be notified to the register without prior demand.

Default in complying with the duty of notification is an offence under the Act. The agreements subject to duty of notification have no legal standing whatsoever, if they are not reported before the expiration of the time limit (8 days).

(b) *Obligation to Furnish Information*

The Danish rules on this point correspond to those in Norway.

(c) *Registration*

Only matters of which the authorities have been notified can be filed in the register. However, the register contains only an excerpt of the notification while the document of notification together with any supplementary documents are kept in a special file, which is also open to the public. *Ex officio* registrations can be made by the competent authorities only of their decisions concerning abolishments of registered agreements or decisions.

Under very special circumstances, *secret* registration can be made.

As of December 31, 1959, the register contained a grand total of 2292 registrations of agreements, combinations and associations, and dominating enterprises. Of these, however, only 1317 are still in force.

(d) *Publication*

A notice of the registration is inserted in the Danish Official Gazette, and in addition the registrations are published in a special Registration Journal. Furthermore, the register is open to the public, so in this respect the Danish Act, just as the Norwegian one, goes further than the London resolution.

General surveys of the economic structure of various fields of trade and industry made by the controlling authorities, and also the decisions made by the competent authorities concerning questions of intervention, are published in an officially issued periodical ("Meddelelser fra Monopoltilsynet").

Finally, an annual report is published on the activities of the controlling authorities.

(e) *Cartel Authorities*

The central cartel authority in Denmark is the *Monopolies Control Authority* ("Monopoltilsynet"), which consists of a Council and a Directorate. The Directorate makes inquiries on its own initiative or on the basis of complaints and has the management of the cartel register, while the Council in principle makes all the decisions in pursuance of the Act, both in respect of interventions against harmful restrictive practices and in questions concerning duty of notification and registration. The enterprises or organizations affected by the decisions of the Council have a right to lodge an appeal of the decisions with a special court of appeal, *The Monopolies Appeal Tribunal* ("Monopolankenaevnet"), after which the appeal lies first with the High Court and thereafter with the Supreme Court.

The Council consists of 15 members. The chairman is appointed by the Government (the King), the other members by the Minister of Commerce. A majority of the members must possess a comprehensive knowledge of conditions within trade and industry and consumer problems and shall, in addition, be familiar with judicial, national, economic, and technical issues. Furthermore, a majority of the members shall be independent of enterprises within trade and industry and of trade organizations directly affected by the Act. The minority, on the other hand, represents the various trade interests.

The Monopolies Appeal Tribunal consists of 3 members appointed by the Minister of Commerce. One of the members is appointed after consulting the central organizations of trade and industry. The chairman shall possess qualifications similar to those of a Justice of the Supreme Court (at present he is, in fact, a Justice of the Supreme Court), and one of the members shall possess knowledge of economics.

3. SWEDEN

In Sweden, special cartel legislation is comparatively recent. The first cartel act in the proper sense of the word did not appear until 1946, namely the Act on Supervision of Restrictive Business Practices within Trade and Industry.* This Act, which prescribed, inter alia,

* It is true that before the appearance of this Act Sweden had an Act of 1925 concerning investigations of monopolistic enterprises and combinations. However, this Act only empowered the Government to have such investigations made on given occasion,

public registration of retrictive agreements, has now been replaced by the following two Acts: Restrictive Practices Control Act of 25th September 1953* and an Act of 1st June 1956 concerning the obligation to furnish information in respect of prices and restrictions of competition[5].

The interesting feature of the Swedish anti-trust legislation is that the preventive element of the principle of publicity plays a greater role here than in other countries as under the law the authorities have no other means of counteracting harmful restrictions of competition than just this measure of publication.

The Swedish system may be summarized briefly as follows:

(a) *Information*

No immediate duty of notification is prescribed, but every citizen, firm or corporate body is obliged, *on request,* to give the authorities all such information that may serve to throw light on prices and the circumstances of competition within trade and industry. However, the obligation to furnish information does not apply to business secrets of a technical nature.

It is an offence under the Act to fail to comply with a request for information or to furnish false information.

As the anti-trust law in Sweden does not confer any legal rights on the authorities in regard to enforcing abolishment of, or amendments to, agreements or arrangements implying harmful restrictions of competition, the consequence is that failure to comply with the obligation to furnish information cannot result in invalidity of any agreement or the like.

(b) *Registration*

Particulars on agreements, collective decisions or measures restraining competition which have reached the authorities through the information furnished or in other ways are entered in the register. Contrary to the practice in Norway and Denmark, no registration can be made in Sweden of enterprises or combinations for the sole reason of their occupying dominating positions on the market.

The register is open to the public, but hardly as a reflection of the

by an especially appointed commission for each case, but the Act did not confer executive powers either on the Government or on the commission for the counteracting of any harmful effects revealed by the investigations. The Act was applied only in a limited number of cases.

* Amended by an Act of 1st June 1956.

special principle of cartel publicity. Rather it is a result of the time-honoured general principle of publicity in the administration existing in Sweden. In cases where special circumstances are in evidence, secret registration, however, may be permitted.

As of March, 1959, the register had on file 1759 agreements, of which 892 were still in force.

(c) *Publication*

The registrations are published in an officially issued periodical ("Pris- och Kartellfrågor"). The same periodical also contains accounts of the general surveys made by the authorities together with statements of genuine cases of complaints brought before the authorities. As will appear from the above, no real enforcible decisions are made, but the point of view taken by the authorities is almost always followed by the parties.

Also the legal procedure itself followed in these cases of complaint is in principle public and takes very much the same form as a hearing before the Courts.

(d) *Cartel Authorities*

In Sweden three institutions constitute the cartel authorities, namely the National Price and Cartel Office ("Pris- och Kartellnämnden"), the Commissioner for Freedom of Commerce ("Ombudsmannen för näringsfrihetsfrågor"), and the Freedom of Commerce Board ("Näringsfrihetsrådet"). *The Price and Cartel Office* manages the cartel register and, in addition, functions as an investigating office for the Commissioner and the Freedom of Commerce Board.

The Commissioner, who shall be—or shall have been—a Justice, receives complaints concerning harmful effects of restrictive business practices and has the complaints investigated. If he finds that detrimental effects are in evidence, he submits the case to the Freedom of Commerce Board. If he does not find sufficient grounds for submitting a complaint to the Board, the person or persons affected by the restrictive practices or an association of consumers or wage earners can, however, put the matter before the Board of their own accord.

The Freedom of Commerce Board consists of 9 members appointed by the Government. The chairman and the vice-chairman shall be—or shall have been—judges; a third member shall possess special knowledge of business problems and conditions. These three members form the "neutral" group of the Council. Of the remaining 6 members, three shall represent the interests of trade and industry, and the other three the general interests of consumers and wage earners.

As mentioned before, the Freedom of Commerce Board has no means of enforcing an abolishment of restrictive practices resulting in harmful effects. Its only course is to make recommendations to the parties concerned and to publish its decisions. So far this procedure seems to have been sufficient to produce the desired changes.

If, however, the Board cannot put an end to the harmful effects of a restrictive practice, it shall, if the case is of importance, report the matter to the Government.

4. THE NETHERLANDS

In the Netherlands the structure of the cartel legislation is somewhat different from that of the Scandinavian countries. The explanation of this difference is probably to be found primarily in historical facts. In 1935, the year of the first Dutch cartel act, the country bore still the heavy mark of the economic depression of the interwar period, a depression which had had a severe impact on Dutch economic life. The Act, The Entrepreneurs' Agreements Act, therefore, aimed at both a too strong and a too weak competition. The Act warranted the legal right to the Government on one hand to set up compulsory cartels in order to check a ruining competition, and, on the other hand, to declare agreements in restraint of competition which were considered harmful to the general interest to be without binding effect.

The Cartel Decree of 1941 follows the same lines and incorporates a *non-public* cartel register as a new feature in aid of the administration, and in the present Act, The Economic Competition Act 1956, we find the same dualism as in the previous Acts[6]. For the purpose of this essay, of course, it is the part of the Act directed against privately established restrictions of competition which is of main interest.

Although the cartel register has not become public under the Act of 1956, other features of publicity are in evidence, as will be seen below.

(a) *Duty of Notification*

The Economic Competition Act prescribes that all regulations of competition shall be reported to the cartel register. The duty of notification includes all regulations of competition, irrespective of scope and importance, but exemptions may be made for certain categories in general or—in exceptional cases—for short-term arrangements.

But, contrary to the case in Norway and Denmark, individual enterprises or combinations shall not be registered only because they hold a dominating position on the market. (They are comprehended, however, by other provisions of the Act. Thus the cartel authorities can issue instructions concerning prices, delivery, and selling conditions).

Failure to comply with the duty of notification is an offence under the Act and will make certain categories of restrictive practices void.

(b) *Obligation to Furnish Information*

On request from the cartel authorities any person is obliged to furnish such information considered necessary to make the authorities able to judge whether a regulation on competition or the practising of it is contrary to the general interest, or whether a dominant position exists which has consequences contrary to the general interest. Furthermore, if facts are demonstrated that arouse suspicion of such matters detrimental to the general interest as mentioned above, the cartel authorities may require, from those considered to be concerned, inspection of such books and documents as they deem necessary.

(c) *Registration*

The notifications are filed in the cartel register which is not open to the public.

(d) *Publication*

As a measure against a regulation of competition deemed to be to the detriment of the public interest, the authorities are empowered to make it subject to publication. Under the same condition, the authorities can also inform the public of enterprises or combinations occupying a dominant market position irrespective of the fact that such a position—as we have seen—does not in itself afford grounds for registration.

With the exception of a single rule of minor importance (Section 27, subsection 2) which shall not be discussed here, the Dutch cartel legislation does not warrant any other forms of publicity than the ones mentioned.

(e) *Cartel Authorities*

The central cartel authority is the *Minister of Economic Affairs* who is responsible for the management of the cartel register, and who institutes investigations. However, in all matters concerning measures to be adopted in pursuance of the Act—including questions of declaring restrictive practices to have no binding effect, or the issuing of instructions to market dominating enterprises—the opinion of the Consultative Committee must be obtained first.*

The Consultative Committee shall consist of at least 12 ordinary members** appointed by the Crown. The Act does not stipulate any conditions as to special qualifications of the members, but in practice, of course, it is presumed that expert knowledge is to be represented in the Committee. On the other hand, a demand for a certain amount of political independence, at any rate, is found in the provision of the Act which excludes Ministers, Under Secretaries of State, ministerial officials, and Members of Parliament.

Extraordinary members may be appointed to deal with special subjects.

It is the sole duty of the Committee to make recommendations to the Minister (the Government). The decisions are made by the Minister, possibly in co-operation with the Minister responsible for the special field affected by the case in question. Certain decisions, however, are made by the Council of State.

Appeal against the decisions made by the Minister may in a number of specially defined cases (Section 33) be lodged with a special section of the Court for the Industrial Organization (The Chamber for Competition Affairs).

5. IRELAND

The Irish Restrictive Trade Practices Act 1953[7] is the first Act of its kind within the Irish Republic. Inasmuch as the Act itself does not lay down any direct rules of prohibition, it is based on the principles of control and intervention, but the Act has widened its scope in comparison to that of the London resolution by introducing a system conferring on the state authorities a considerable influence on competition within the economic life of the country. This is done partly by means of *orders* which through prohibitions against certain arrangements ensure the freedom of competition within certain trades, and partly

* This provision, however, does not apply in respect of provisional non-binding declarations or instructions, as the Minister has been empowered to take such steps in cases where quick intervention is necessary and where consequently there is not time for awaiting the Committee's opinion on the case.

** At present the Committee has 18 members.

through the issuance of *Fair Trading Rules* to a certain trade. These Fair Trading Rules are official recommendations in respect of Trade Practices, and although they have no legal force, it must be assumed that they possess such a suggestive power that in actual fact they have the effect of a sort of compulsory cartel, even though they do not serve one-sidedly as a protection of the trade against ruining mutual competition but are set up in consideration of the public interest, which, in the first place, must be presumed to mean the interest of the consumers. Sometimes, however, the true interest of the public lies in the cushioning of the effect of too hard a competition.

In the Irish system there is no official publicity, as we usually understand it, around the cartel activities. The legislation has no provisions as to notification, registration, and publication of private regulations of competition. It is the traditional principles of legal procedure, rather, that underlie the provisions concerning publication found in the Irish Act. Thus a provision of the Act saying that, before the competent authority (The Fair Trade Commission) issues Fair Trading Rules, the Commission shall make public its intention to do so in order to give anyone interested an opportunity to state his objections, is founded in the general principle of contradiction. Likewise, the provisions prescribing that the enquiries of the Commission shall be held in public, together with the legal means to procure information and other rules of legal procedure, are rooted in time-honoured principles underlying the administration of justice in general.

The Irish cartel authorities are the Fair Trade Commission and the Ministery for Industry and Commerce. The *Fair Trade Commission* consists of not less than 3 and not more than 5 permanent members appointed by the Minister. The Act does not require any special qualifications of the members, but they must not be Members of Parliament. The Minister may appoint extraordinary members. The Commission may on its own initiative, or on request of a trade organization, lay down and publish Fair Trading Rules; furthermore, it controls in general restrictive practices, and institutes on its own accord, or on request of the Minister, enquiries into the conditions which obtain in regard to the supply and distribution of any kind of goods.

The Commission submits a report on the matter to the Minister and may recommend the issuing of an order abolishing or limiting the restrictive business practices which in the opinion of the Commission are detrimental to the public interest.

Then the *Minister* decides whether there are grounds for issuing an order. An order has no legal standing, however, until it has been confirmed by Parliament.

Violation of an order is an offence under the Act.

6. FRANCE

Not until after the Second World War was special legislation concerning restrictive business practices introduced in France. The essential legal rules are laid down in a few articles of The Price Ordinance 1945 (Articles 37, 59 bis–59 quater, and 62), while the rules concerning the enforcement are to be found partly in another Ordinance of 1945, and partly in Decree of 27 January 1954 (No. 54–97), as amended by Decree of 17 August 1959.[8]

Like the American anti-trust legislation, the French system is based on the principle of prohibition and invalidity. The principle of publicity common to the cartel legislation in other countries—compulsory notification, registration and publication—are not found in France. But the ordinary public administration of justice and the usual judicial means of obtaining information, i.e. the duty of giving evidence, *editio instrumentorum,* the right of search, etc., apply, of course, also to legal prosecution for violations of the prohibitive provisions of The Price Ordinance.

Recently, however, a special provision concerning publication has been added to the French cartel legislation by Article 20 of Decree of 17 August 1959. This provision is interconnected with the existing opportunity of having cases regarding illegal restrictions of competition settled out of court when the parties to the agreement, combine, etc. in question accept a suggestion made by the competent authority (the Minister of Economic Affairs) as to the abolishment or modification of the restriction of competition in question (see below). As a new feature of the Act, the above mentioned Article prescribes that the annual report submitted by The Technical Commission on Combines containing the recommendations of the commission and the decisions of the Minister shall be published in the "Journal Officiel". This rule, however, is hardly to be considered as a manifestation of the principle of publication laid down in the London resolution, but is merely a natural adjunct to the general rules on public administration of justice.

The arrangement of the administrative functions under the French cartel legislation is somewhat complex. It is necessary to distinguish between the clearly defined prohibitions laid down in Article 37 of the Price Ordinance, and the somewhat vaguer provisions about "ententes", etc. in Article 59 bis, cf. Article 59 ter.

It is anyone's right to file a complaint directly with the *Cours Tribunaux* for violation of Article 37. The ordinary procedure, however, is to apply to *le Service des Enquêtes Economiques*, a department under "la Direction Générale des Prix et des Enquêtes Economiques". If the director of the department mentioned finds sufficient grounds for furtherance of the case, and if the director general (in certain cases also the Minister) agrees, he may suggest an extra-judicial conclusion of the case in which event the defendant pays a certain amount of money to the Treasury. If the defendant will not accept this solution, or if the director does not consider the case suitable for such a solution, it is referred to the prosecuting authorities as a criminal case to be brought before the "Cours Tribunaux".

In principle, also, cases concerning "ententes" (Article 59 bis) may be brought directly before the "Cours Tribunaux", Article 59 bis being a provision of prohibition, the violation of which is an offence under the Act. By the establishing of The Technical Commission on Combines ("la Commission Technique des Ententes") by Decree of 27 January 1954, an institution was set up, however, which was especially suited to investigate and evaluate the judicial, economic, and social problems related to "ententes". In practice, all such cases are now put before this commission.

The Technical Commission on Combines consists of 14 members appointed by decree: the chairman, who must be a Justice either of Conseil d'Etat, la Cour de Cassation, or la Cour des Comptes; 5 members also to be appointed among Judges of specially mentioned Law Courts; 6 members of special professional competence (two of these representing the trade unions); and 2 members possessing expert economic knowledge. The procedure of the Commission has a certain similarity to the legal procedure at the Law Courts. When a case has been studied by the Commission, a report is submitted to the *Minister for Economic Affairs* on the question whether the subject matter of the case is to be considered to be unlawful under the cartel legislation, or not. If the report concludes in the affirmative, suggestions are made as to the further steps to be taken. The Commission is not obliged to suggest criminal prosecution, but is free to propose any suitable regulation of the matter. The Minister is under no obligation to act upon the recommendations of the Commission, but if he finds grounds for intervention, he may invite the parties to the "entente" to have the matter legalized along certain specified lines in order to avoid criminal prosecution. If the parties will not accept such a proposal, the Minister refers the case to the prosecuting authorities for criminal prosecution before before the Law Courts.

7. AUSTRIA

In 1938—after the Annexation—the German Cartel Act was introduced in Austria; it soon led to the establishment of economic plans by the State and to the formation of compulsory cartels. After the war, the organization necessary for enforcing the Act was lacking. So the first systematic regulation in the field of cartels was introduced in Austria by the enactment of the Cartel Act of 1951.

This Act institutes a system somewhat different from the legislation in the afore-mentioned countries. Cartel agreements are not generally banned, but in order to be valid, an agreement, its modifications and supplements must be entered into the *Cartel Register*. Registration is subject to the consent of the *Cartel Tribunal*. Before making a decision, the Cartel Tribunal shall obtain an opinion from a *Joint Commission* consisting of members of the Federal Chamber of Trade and Commerce and the Austrian Workers' Chambers Diet.

Appeals against decisions of the Cartel Tribunal shall be lodged with the *Superior Cartel Tribunal* at the Supreme Court.

The Act lays down several criteria for refusing registration of a cartel agreement. First and foremost, registration may be refused in case the agreement is not justifiable from the point of view of general national economy.

The duty of notification and registration comprises any form of cartel agreements, also "gentlemen's agreements".

The Register contains a brief summary of the agreements, and is open to the public. The documents filed in the Register may be inspected only by representatives of interests specified by the Act.

The Cartel Tribunal and the Superior Cartel Tribunal consist of a chairman and a number of vice-chairmen and assessors. The members are appointed by the Federal President upon nomination by the Federal Government.

The Federal Chamber of Trade and Commerce and the Austrian Workers' Chambers Diet are entitled to request revision of a cartel agreement by the Cartel Tribunal in order to ascertain whether the prerequisites for its registration are still existing.

The operation of a cartel prior to its registration is considered an offence under the Act.

8. UNITED KINGDOM AND GERMANY

As the cartel legislation in the United Kingdom as well as in Germany is specially dealt with elsewhere in this work, a comment of the cartel law of these countries is omitted here.

II

In the previous section we have dealt mainly with the basic principles of the European cartel legislation and the instruments of *control* of trusts, cartels and other concerted actions in restraint of competition. We shall now proceed to discuss the actual *legal regulation* of these phenomena.

Restraint of Competition

While the European cartel acts may contain dissimilarities in respect of ways and means, we find considerable conformity as to their concepts of the subject-matter of the legislation. The wording may be different, but in the main the factual contents are the same. This is quite natural as, by and large, the conditions of trade and industry are the same in Western Europe. The business practices, therefore, will also take practically the same forms.

As a starting point we may sketch the following pattern for what constitutes the subject-matter of European cartel legislation:

(a) In respect of *control* (especially the provisions concerning notification and registration), the legislation comprehends *all* privately established restrictions of competition, irrespective of their origin and the form in which they appear;

(b) in respect of *intervention* and *prohibition,* the legislation includes *all* private restrictions of competition, irrespective of type and form, which are or may become *detrimental* to general or public interests in the widest meaning of these words.

This formula might be expressed graphically by two concentric circles.

In putting our above model definition to a test on the cartel legislations of the individual European countries, we find that, theoretically, it applies completely for instance to the Norwegian Price Act and the Dutch Economic Competition Act, and approximately so to the Swedish cartel legislation. In respect of the latter, however, this one does not entirely cover the area of the "outer" circle (a), as the Swedish notification and registration rules are applied only to agreements restricting competition, and restrictive decisions and regulations made by trade organizations, but *not* to such restraint of competition as is caused by a monopolistic or other market dominating position. As regards France and Ireland, the cartel legislations of these countries have established no cartel registers, so the French and Irish acts cannot extend beyond the border of the "inner" circle (b), but with this reservation the above pattern is applicable also to the cartel legislation of these countries.

The most outstanding deviations from the formula—but also the less tangible ones—are found in the Danish Monopolies Control Act, as the rules of the said Act on both control and intervention are applicable only to restrictions of competition of a certain proportion and importance. In the words of the Act (Section 2), it "applies to private enterprises, co-operative associations, etc. within trades in which competition, throughout the country or in local market areas, is restricted *in such a manner that the enterprises exert or may be able to exert an essential influence* on price, production, distribution, or transport conditions."* In short, the Danish Act covers but parts of both the "outer circle" (a) and the "inner circle" (b).

But let us revert to the general issue and analyse it a little closer.

We have shown that in general the control and publicity provisions of the European cartel legislation aim at any restriction of competition, that is, in the widest sense, "any such condition implying, or having as a result that competition is not completely free and unlimited"[9]. Considering the nature of the concept it is hardly possible, however, to define it exhaustively, and if a definition was attempted it would, at any rate, necessarily be so vague that it would afford but poor

* It is difficult to state in general when the restriction of competition within a trade has reached such a dominance as implied by the Danish Act. A number of circumstances must be taken into consideration, as, for instance, the nature of the commodity, its relative importance in the consumption, the form and nature of the restriction in question, whether the commodity is protected by customs duty or import restrictions, or whether any possibility of foreign competition exists, etc.

If the restriction of competition stems from the fact that the trade in question is dominated by a few big enterprises, it is, as mentioned on page 67, possible under the Danish Act to have these firms registered as dominating enterprises. In this respect, however, the criteria of dominance are more comprehensive. The question is not decided exclusively on considerations of the share held by the individual enterprise of the total turnover of the commodity concerned. How the remaining share of the turnover is divided between the other enterprises of the trade is also taken into account, especially whether it is distributed on many or few firms. Other points of interest in this connection are, for instance, the nature of the commodity, its importance in the consumption, possible competition from abroad, etc. In Danish registration practice, enterprises representing a market share of even less than 10 per cent of the total trade volume have thus been registered as dominating enterprises in special cases.

guidance[10]. Besides, a perfectly "watertight" definition is not absolutely necessary for the practical purpose of the cartel legislation. In principle neither the form nor the literal contents of the restrictive measure are of decisive importance. The vital point is not whether an agreement between members of a trade or trades about concerted action is binding on the parties or merely of a guiding nature, but *whether* the agreement is effective and *how* it works. Incidentally, it is found to be psychologically true that agreements and to no less degree decisions of a guiding nature in themselves will always have a certain suggestive power, quite apart from the following they can count on, naturally, when they express an obvious common trade interest of some importance.

The general provision of prohibition of the French Price Ordinance, Article 59 bis, states that it comprises "every concerted action, convention, combine (*entente*), express *or tacit*..."; a similar formulation is found in the Irish Restrictive Trade Practices Act, Second Schedule ("any measures, agreements, or acts put into effect... by a person alone or in combination or agreement, *express or implied,* with others..."). The words italicized by us do not constitute any expansion in relation to the concept of restraint of competition as it is generally understood, but are to be considered merely a descriptive detail. Is is obvious that if the cartel legislation is to have any real effect, it must cover also such restrictive practices as "gentlemen's agreements" and "tacit understandings on concerted actions". The fact that, in practice, these less tangible phenomena may present special problems does not alter the case. We are here in the borderland of the field of restraint of competition which has been called "the grey field", an expression characterizing this sphere by its opaqueness. It would be a mistake to underrate its significance; there can be no doubt that the firmer a hold the cartel authorities get on the overt restrictions of competition, the more "the grey field" will expand. In this connection we will dwell for a moment on the Dutch Economic Competition Act. In Section 1, the legislator defines the legal term of the Act *regulation of competition* as follows:"... *any* agreement or decision, subject to civil law, to regulate economic competition between owners of enterprises"; and Section 5 continues to say that "it may be enacted by Order in Council that any regulations on competition to be specified by that order shall cease to have legal force unless they are *embodied in writing* and notified..." The Act, then, also comprehends verbal agreements (and tacit understandings on concerted action, too, we think), but risking the application of the above rule of Section 5 the verbal agreements, on the other hand, have been put into a class by themselves.

As an example from "the grey field" let us imagine an instance where the cartel authorities have abolished a tangible agreement between a group of retailers and a group of wholesale dealers on exclusive dealing, the authorities having found the agreement to be an undue or detrimental discrimination in respect of the retailers outside the agreement; but, in spite of this decision, however, the wholesale dealers or a majority of them still refuse individually to accept orders from the formerly excluded retailers or to put them on an equal footing with the retailers formerly in possession of exclusive buying rights. This conduct need not be due to a secret agreement between the former parties to the abolished arrangement or between the wholesalers themselves, but may stem from a wish on the part of the wholesale dealers to please the old group of customers with whom the goods have been well established, thus ensuring continuity of sale to these retailers to the same extent as earlier. By a greater dispersion of sales—including for instance sale to shops lacking a special atmosphere of first quality—the wholesalers may fear that in the opinion of the consumers the goods may be deprived of their former exclusive character, thus losing some of their attraction also for the traders, which may result in a decline in total sales.

"HARMFUL EFFECT"

To justify an intervention on the part of the authorities, a restriction of competition must have effects contrary to the general or public interests. For the sake of brevity these effects will be denoted in the following by the term used in the Swedish Restrictive Business Practices Act and the Danish Monopolies Control Act: "harmful effects".

Some acts state in particular in which respects restraint of competition may have harmful effects in relation to the interests of the general public. Points mentioned are (a) effect on the price formation, (b) limitation of the free entry into trade and the equal opportunity of carrying on trade, and (c) obstruction of productive and progressive forces in economic life.

(a) *Price Formation*

It is obvious, of course, that the process of price formation and the circumstances under which it functions are of the greatest interest to the public. The influence of restrictive practices on the prices will, therefore, always receive the Government's special attention. In Norway, where the underlying principles of the anti-trust legislation ordinarily are those of control and intervention, this point has been considered of such importance even that the legislator has not been content with provisions empowering the authorities to intervene when unreasonable prices are found as a consequence of restrictive practices, but has inserted a direct prohibition against unfair prices in the Price Act regardless of whether these unfair prices can be proved to originate from a factor of restrictive practices or not (Section 18). Moreover, in addition to the provisions concerning control of private restrictions of competition in general and interventions against those which are unfair or harmful to the public interest, the Norwegian Act has also provisions warranting general governmental regulation of prices.

Direct price agreements are one of the classical types of restraint of competition. They have been known far back in history. We only need mentioning the often quoted paragraph from "Wealth of Nations", saying that "people of the same trade seldom meet together, even for merriment and diversion, but the conversation ends in conspiracy against the public, or in some contrivance *to raise the prices*."[11] —But for that matter all restrictions of competition, irrespective of form and contents, will have some influence on the prices.

The question of when price agreements and other forms of restraint of competition affecting the prices are contrary to the general public interest is left by the legislation for the administration or, in the end, the courts to decide. We find no guidance in the term "unreasonable prices" used in the Danish Monopolies Control Act and the Norwegian Price Act, or in the provision of the Swedish Act which states that "a restraint of competition shall be deemed to have a harmful effect if, contrary to the public interest, it unduly affects the formation of prices...". It is not made clear, even, whether the legislator is thinking only of *unreasonably high prices*. A price war where a single large-scale enterprise, or a group of large-scale enterprises, backed by substantial reserves of capital, attempt to wipe financially weaker competitors out of the market by means of loss-inflicting prices (which do not have to cover even primary costs), is but the beginning of an elimination of a sound price competition and will under any circumstances compel the authorities to intervene later on, should the operation succeed. The question is, then, whether from a liberal point of view it would not be more reasonable to intervene against a price war disturbing an existing market structure characterized by sound and effective competition already at its outset. The legislators of the various countries do not give the same answers to this question. In *Sweden* and *Denmark* it is an open question, and one cannot be sure that the answer will be the same in the two countries. But from the preparatory works for the *Norwegian* Price Act it is evident that the present as well as the previous legislation* is applicable also to *unreasonably low prices*. The same, of course, must be the case in respect of the legislations warranting the cartel authorities the right to establish compulsory cartels and the like (*Holland* and *Ireland*). Conversely, the *French* Price Ordinance has only unreasonably high prices in view, see Section 59 bis, which prohibits any restraint of competition "which has the object or may have the effect of interfering with full competition by hindering the reduction of production costs or selling prices or by encouraging the artificial increase of prices".

It is true, of course, that first and foremost it is the unreasonably high prices caused or sustained by restrictions of competition which must catch the attention of the public and provoke a reaction; and, as mentioned before, the legislations of the various countries leave it to the administrative bodies or the courts to substantiate the contents of the term "unreasonable prices".

In the sometimes very comprehensive preparatory works for the various acts, the many problems that appear, and the circumstances to be taken into consideration in judging whether a price is unreasonable or not, are discussed in detail. These expositions follow almost the same lines and may be summarized as follows:

There are two sides to the case: the costs and the net profit. When competition is neutralized or weakened within a trade, there is the danger that prices may increase too much either because the entrepreneur in question deliberately takes advantage of the situation to make large profits, or because less attention is paid to the expenditures. *In the former case* the question is: What is a fair profit, including a reasonable interest of the invested capital? In this connection it is necessary also to assess the actual economic risk involved in the production and distribution concerned.

In the latter case one is confronted with the problem of efficiency, which problem is again split up in a number of sub-questions. In the Danish Monopolies Control Act these problems are dealt with in Sec-

* By an amendment of 1932 to the Norwegian Trust Act (1926) an express *prohibition* against unreasonably low prices was laid down in addition to the prohibition already in force against unreasonably high prices.

tion 12, subsection 4. This provision states that when cartels or dominating enterprises have been ordered to reduce their prices, the authorities shall fix the maximum prices in such a way that enterprises operating on a technically and commercially sound and adequate basis shall be able to cover their necessary costs, inclusive of depreciation allowances, and expenses paid in connection with the purchase or replacement purchase of the commodity, its production, transport and distribution. In addition, the prices shall be fixed at such a level as to secure the enterprises a reasonable net profit in consideration of the risk involved in manufacturing or distributing the commodity in question. In this provision, the relevant points of view to be taken into account, when considering and judging the reasonableness of a price, are stated very clearly.

As already mentioned, the question whether a restriction of competition has any influence on the price formation, which may result in unreasonable prices or profits, is in principle independent of the type of restriction concerned. The restrictions may take the form of horizontal or vertical price agreements or decisions, binding or guiding; they may also appear as quota-agreements, agreements as to the sharing of the market, specialization agreements, horizontal or vertical agreements on control of new establishments, or agreements on exclusiveness, etc.; but even without any express or tacit agreements being evident as causes for the restriction of competition we may find prices of more or less monopolistic origin. Such a monopolistic price formation not being a result of a conspiracy is found rather frequently in Europe where several of the national markets are relatively small, and where monopolies and quasi-monopolies may easily arise with sound technical and economic justification. This phenomenon is probably the fundamental reason why the European legislation does not condemn monopolization *per se*, as is the case in the United States. On the other hand, European legislation considers it vital that monopolistic (or dominating) enterprises, and primarily their price policies, are controlled, and provisions to this effect are incorporated in most European cartel acts.* We have already seen examples of this in respect to notification and registration. As a further example it may be mentioned that under the Danish Act not only price increases made collectively (i.e. by cartels or similar combines or trade organizations) but also price increases made by a dominating enterprise must be approved by the authorities before they take effect.

* As an exception the French cartel legislation may be mentioned.

In some countries certain types of price agreements or decisions are considered in advance to be contrary to the public interest and are consequently forbidden or declared to be non-binding on the parties. This is the case in respect of (i) imposed resale prices and (ii) tender cartels.

(i) *Imposed Resale Prices*

Imposed resale prices, especially in connection with branded goods, have found widespread use in Europe[12] during the years where for a long time—in most countries until recent years—it has been possible, generally speaking, to maintain and enforce them through the courts, supported as they were by established judicial principles. There are even examples that they have been expressly protected by law.* But with the growing realization of the economic, social, and political perspectives of the various forms of restraints of competition, as reflected in the modern cartel legislation, the attitude of the judiciary towards resale price maintenance has also changed in most countries.

Imposed resale prices may take the form of fixed prices, minimum prices, or maximum prices. In practice, however, it is rare to find privately imposed maximum resale prices, and seeing that it is chiefly the fixing of a *lower price limit,* of course, which may influence the price formation in a way adverse to the public interest, the legislators have focused their attention solely on minimum resale prices (or margins) and fixed resale prices (or margins). When the law employs the expressions "minimum resale prices (or margins)" or "minimum prices (or margins)", these terms, naturally, also include fixed resale prices (or margins).

A distinction is made between binding and suggested minimum resale prices. An imposed minimum resale price is binding when it is stated expressly or when it is clearly implied that underselling of the price will result in retaliatory measures on the part of the suppliers (refusal of supply, for instance).

In several countries the anti-trust legislation contains special provisions in accordance with which certain types of minimum resale prices *a priori* are considered to be contrary to the public interest. This is the case in France, Sweden, Denmark, United Kingdom, and Norway. Notwithstanding certain differences as to form of legislation, Germany and Ireland also may be mentioned in this connection.

* From 1912 to 1926, the Danish act on unfair competition contained a provision which made underselling of imposed prices an offence punishable under the law.

The scope of these provisions, however, vary from country to country.

1. FRANCE

Under the Price Ordinance, Article 37, paragraph 4, as formulated by Decree of 9 August 1953, *binding minimum prices and margins—the vertically fixed (resale prices) as well as those based on horizontal agreements—are prohibited,* which means that any action for the purpose of enforcing or maintaining the desired prices or the "punishing" of underselling is a punishable offence under the law. Exemptions may be granted, however. "Such exemptions, which shall in any event be subject to a time limit, may be granted on the grounds, inter alia, of the novelty of the goods or services concerned, of exclusive rights under a patent, a license or a registered design, or of the requirement of a specification involving a warranty of quality or condition, or of an initial publicity campaign". (Article 37–4, subsec. 2).

2. SWEDEN

Under the Restraint of Competition Act, Section 2, it is *prohibited to fix binding minimum resale prices* unless special permission for such a vertical binding of the prices has been granted. It is also forbidden to fix *resale prices* intended only to be recommendations, if it is not *expressly stated that they may be undersold.* Violations of these prohibitions are punishable under the law. Under Section 4 of the Act, exemptions may be granted only "if the restraint of competition can be expected to result in lower costs, substantially benefiting the consumers, or otherwise to contribute to the public interest, or if there are other special reasons for granting such exemption".

Until now only in a few cases permission has been given to fix binding minimum prices. The most significant exemption concerns books and music.

3. DENMARK

Section 10 of the Monopolies Control Act has a provision in accordance to which it is not permissable to enforce agreements or decisions fixing *minimum prices or margins binding on the subsequent resellers* unless the agreement or decision in question has been approved by the authorities.

So contrary to what is the case in Swedish law, it is not prohibited (or punishable under the law) to establish a vertical binding of prices and margins. But an agreement about observing a fixed minimum price or margin on resale is not enforceable in the law courts. Retaliatory measures against underselling are not punishable under the law, but may possibly entail other legal consequences, liability for damages and injunctions ordering delivery, for instance.

The law lays down that binding minimum resale prices must be approved only "if warranted by circumstances of special importance". From the preparatory works for the Act it appears that by this the legislator has been thinking of, inter alia, extraordinary distribution circumstances and cases where a system of fixed prices affords special advantages to the consumers (for instance that the article in question may be exchanged in any shop within the trade). Moreover, it has been especially underlined that the use of a branded article by certain resalers as a loss-leader may also warrant the granting of permission to maintain minimum resale prices for the article concerned. It is very difficult to decide, however, when *in concreto* one is confronted with a genuine case of loss-leader practice. No guidance is found in the preparatory works for the Act. It must be presumed, at any rate, that a considerable undersale of the suggested resale price must be in evidence. Also, as far as we can see, there must be a further presumption that it can be shown that the loss-leader practice has—or in all probability will have—a general adverse effect on the sale of the goods concerned, such as, for instance, that other dealers lose interest in the article and concentrate their sales promotion work on competing articles.

Although often adduced, the loss-leader argument has never as yet won a Danish petitioner an approval of resale price maintenance.* Besides, only very few exemptions have been granted from the prohibition against enforcement of resale prices. The most important of these exemptions concern books, music, periodicals, perfume and cosmetics, wine and spirits, and tyres and tubes for automobiles and bicycles. The reason for the exemptions in respect of perfume and cosmetics, and of wine and spirits is to be found in a special system of collection of excise duties for these commodities, making fixed

* In a few cases the Danish cartel authorities have, however, approved ordinary sales clauses to the effect that if the article in question is used as loss-leader, the supplier reserves his right to cease to deliver, subject to the approval of the cartel authorities in each individual case. So far no cases have occurred where the authorities have found the underselling to be of such considerable size as to justify a granting of permission to stop supplies in accordance with these clauses.

retail prices expedient. As far as tyres and tubes for automobiles and bicycles are concerned, the motivation for the exemption was the fear that the resellers should raise their margins if the prices were to be of a guiding nature only.

4. UNITED KINGDOM

The Restrictive Trading Practices Act 1956, Section 24, declares it unlawful to make or carry out any agreement or arrangement for collective enforcement of conditions as to resale prices. But any supplier—as far as the goods delivered by him is concerned—is free to enforce conditions as to resale prices (*individual enforcement*), and this is the case not only in respect of his direct buyers but also "against any person not party to the sale who acquires the goods with notice of the [resale price] condition" (Subsection 1 of Section 25)—provided that the buyer in question has bought the goods "for the purpose of resale in the course of business" (Subsection 2 (a) of Section 25).

5. NORWAY

By a decree of 18 October 1957 in pursuance of the Price Act, the legal position as to the fixing and maintenance of resale prices and margins is as follows:

Collective fixing of *binding* as well as *suggested* resale prices and margins is prohibited and punishable under the law.*

Individual fixing of *binding* resale prices or margins is also prohibited and punishable under the law.

In both instances exemptions may be granted by the authorities when special circumstances speak for it, and if such exemptions are compatible with the public interest. This possibility of exemption, however, is administered with the greatest caution; until now, permission to fix binding minimum prices has been given only in respect of very few commodities, the most important being books and wireless sets and accessories.

It is permitted *individually* to fix *suggested* resale prices and margins without obtaining any approval, but it is a condition that the seller makes it clear that the resellers are free to quote lower prices or margins; if this prescription is not complied with, the control authorities can forbid such price and margin recommendations. All individual suggested prices and margins, of course, are governed by the ordinary

* A Bill proposing the prohibition of *horizontal* price agreements is being discussed in Norway at present.

control and regulation provisions of the Price Act. Any attempt to influence resellers to observe fixed prices or margins—by means of refusal of supply or otherwise—is prohibited.

6. GERMANY AND IRELAND

Finally, the attitude of the German and the Irish cartel legislation towards resale price maintenance will be mentioned briefly.

The significant provisions in this respect of the *German* Federal Act against Restraints of Competition (GWB), 1957, will not be discussed in detail here. It may be sufficient to mention that the implication of the general provision in Section 1 of the Act, which declares cartel agreements and cartel decisions in restraint of competition to be invalid, is that *collective* price and margin regulations, whether *vertical* (collective resale prices and margins) or *horizontal*, or *binding* or *recommending*, are also unlawful unless they have been approved expressly by the cartel authorities.

Under Section 15, *individual* price agreements are null and void when they bind a party to the agreement to quote fixed prices when selling to any third party (vertical price binding). The Act makes exemptions from this general prohibition in respect of books and the like, and in respect of branded goods. It is a condition, however, for the validity of such price bindings that they are reported to the authorities. At any time and under certain specified circumstances, the authorities may revoke price bindings of this kind.

The *Irish* Restrictive Trade Practices Act does not contain any special provisions concerning resale price maintenance. But some of the orders directed at individual trades contain prohibitions against both individual and collective resale price maintenance. This is the case, for instance, in respect of radio and television sets and accessories, automobiles, and groceries.

Moreover, the Fair Trade Commission has in its Fair Trading Rules condemned individual as well as collective resale price maintenance in respect of various commodities.* It has not been considered unreasonable, however, that a supplier of certain articles (perambulators, folding-cars, sun-cars, and bicycles) stops supplying to a person who resells at his own purchase price or below, or who advertises or displays

* Rope, cordage and twine; nails and screws; tableware; cutlery, spoons and forks; electric bulbs; sole leather; files and hacksaw blades; dry batteries; carpets, carpeting and floor rugs; household textiles (non-woolen); coal; aluminium hollow-ware, perambulators, folding-cars and sun-cars; pedal bicycles.

the supplier's recommended resale price in close conjunction with his own price.

7. THE NETHERLANDS

The Dutch legislation contains no provisions expressly prohibiting imposed resale prices.

As will appear from the preceding survey of the attitudes taken by the cartel legislation of a number of European countries to the problem topical in all countries about suppliers' fixing and maintenance of minimum resale prices, it is chiefly the *binding* minimum prices which are subject to prohibitions. Only in a few countries—and there in moderated forms—also *recommended* resale prices are forbidden. The fact, however, that recommended resale prices are permitted—either wholly or in part—makes it a natural task for the authorities to inquire into the question of the suggestive power of such prices. In this respect, a Norwegian investigation[13] of the prices of a great number of foodstuffs and common utensils has revealed that the resellers show a considerable "faithfulness" to the recommended resale prices as it was found that 94.5 per cent of all the price observations (totalling 23,799) showed concord between the actual price taken and the recommended resale price. The deviations, 5.5 per cent, distributed themselves as follows:

Price difference in per cent of recommended price	*Retail price lower than recommended price*	*Retail price higher than recommended price*
1–4 per cent	2.1 per cent	0.7 per cent
5–9 per cent	1.1 per cent	0.7 per cent
10 per cent and above	0.7 per cent	0.2 per cent
Total	3.9 per cent	1.6 per cent

Similar inquiries made in Sweden during the years 1955–58 show approximately the same degree of price obedience in the retail trade[14].

In Denmark, on the other hand, there seems to be a tendency towards greater price variations. A recent inquiry, comprising about 10,000 observations of the prices quoted in grocery stores for a number of consumers' branded goods for which recommended resale prices had been fixed, showed an average price obedience of about 80 per cent. Of the deviations, the main part (about 17 per cent) were below the suggested resale price; in most cases the price reductions amounted to more than 5 per cent[15].

It may be safe to doubt, at any rate, whether there is any real reason to take different views of the restrictive effects of the two types of resale prices.

(ii) *Tender Cartels*

Tender cartels may take many forms. That which they all have in common is already expressed in the name which distinguishes them from "sales cartels" (i.e. ordinary horizontal price agreements and decisions, etc.). The existence of tender cartels implies a situation characterized by an invitation to submit tenders, and they are therefore found in Europe mainly in trades connected with the building and construction industry where they are extremely frequent. They may occur as general agreements between a group of entrepreneurs at the same level of economy within the same trade; but they may also have come into existence within the frames of a trade organization, originating from the by-laws of the organization. Besides the general tender cartels, we find also *ad hoc* tender cartels formed exclusively with a view to a concrete invitation to submit tenders. The aim of "pure" tender cartels is either that when working out their tender reply, the parties to the cartel shall follow uniform rules in respect to calculation and terms of delivery, or that when each has worked out his tender—but before the tenders have been submitted—a comparison shall be made of the tender replies for the purpose of a possible regulation (a raising of the lowest tenders in accordance with specific rules, for instance). In addition we usually find rules to the effect that the entrepreneur whose tender has been accepted shall pay a certain percentage of his profit to the other parties to the cartel (as a "compensation") or to a joint relief fund, or the like. Such "pure" tender cartels are comparatively rare, however, for in tender cartels we very often find provisions as to exclusiveness, the reason for which is to be found in considerations for protecting the parties to the cartel against unfair competition from entrepreneurs of an "inferior standard".

Most of the European legislation does not especially prohibit tender cartels, but like the related horizontal price and margin agreements they are, of course, governed by the general provisions of control and intervention laid down by the legislation, including the demand of notification and registration.*

* In some countries, on the other hand, we find special provisions in respect of invitations from the government to submit tenders, and here, for instance, we may find prohibitions against preliminary regulation of the tenders.

The *Swedish* Restraint of Competition Act (1953), however, has a provision (Section 3) under which "an entrepreneur may not without the permission of the Freedom of Commerce Board enter into or carry out an agreement stipulating that consultation or other forms of co-operation shall take place between a number of entrepreneurs before any of them submits a tender reply to a contract to supply a commodity or to render a service...". Violation of this provision involves criminal liability.

As interpreted by the Swedish authorities, this prohibitive provision is applied only to general tender cartels and not to *ad hoc* tender cartels. Exemptions from the prohibition can be granted when a tender cartel may be assumed to have an expense reducing effect or otherwise to work in a way favourable to the public interest (Section 3). As far as is known, no exemptions have been granted yet to tender cartels in pursuance of this provision.

Section 39 of the *Norwegian* Price Act prescribes that entrepreneurs whose tender replies are subject to regulation or control either by an organization or in accordance with restrictive agreements or arrangements shall—when submitting a tender—inform the prospective purchaser inviting the tenders "of the implications of the regulation or control". This means, then, that parties to a tender cartel shall state *pro primo* that such a cartel is in existence and that they are parties to it, and *pro secundo* the contents of the restriction of competition involved, quite regardless of the fact that such restrictions come within the general duty of notification under the law and consequently may already be filed with the public cartel register. But it is not presumed that the provision prescribes any duty on the part of the tenderer to give information as to how the tender regulation or control may have effected his tender reply.

Default in compliance with the duty of giving information is an offence, and may in certain circumstances also make the offender liable to pay damages to the inviter of the tenders.

At present a proposal for the prohibition of tender cartels is being discussed in Norway, and there is reason to expect that the proposal will be carried through.

(b) *The Free and Equal Admission to Trade*

"A restraint of competition shall be deemed to have a harmful effect", states the Swedish Restraint of Competition Act, (Section 5), "if, contrary to the public interest, it ... impedes or prevents the trade of others".

The Danish Monopolies Control Act (Section 11) empowers the authorities to intervene against restrictive practices which "result in, or must be deemed to result in... an unreasonable restriction in the freedom of trade or unreasonable discrimination in respect of the conditions of trading..."

In its Second Schedule the Irish Restrictive Trade Practices Act states as forms of unfair trade practices, inter alia, measures, etc., which "... (b) are in unreasonable restraint of trade, or (c) have or are likely to have the effect of unjustly eliminating a trade competitor..."

As can be readily seen, these provisions touch on a classical and always topical judicial problem, the incompatibility of the two principles: the freedom of trade and the freedom of contract and contracting.

First a few general remarks on this problem.

The Freedom of Trade—as an ideal and a demand formulated by the French physiocrats and adopted by Adam Smith and his school—was one of the clarion calls to the sound of which the great economic revolution and its chain reaction of political upheavals were accomplished at the end of 18th and the beginning of the 19th century.

It is hardly probable that the philosophers' and reformers' concept of the freedom of trade refers to more than the relation between the State and the citizens. A change in this relation was, at any rate, the most immediate demand. Being a part of the program of economic liberalism, the idea was a protest partly against the system of privileges and concessions favoured by absolutism, and partly against the system of compulsory corporations (the guilds) supported by the State in all countries. It is quite natural, therefore, that also in the general understanding of the idea, the freedom of trade first and foremost has come to represent a fundamental civil right protecting the citizens against any attempts on the part of *the state*, to prevent them, directly or indirectly, from carrying out the *trade* they wanted, *where* they wanted and *in the way* they wanted. When in Denmark's first free constitution, The Constitution of 1849, it was enacted that "all restrictions of the free and equal entry to trade, not justified by considerations for the public interest, shall be abolished by law", it was exactly in this meaning, i.e. as a *principle of public law*, that the concept of freedom of trade was adopted.*

* The obligation of the Government under this provision was fulfilled by an Act of 1857, the so-called Trade Act, in pursuance of which the compulsory guild membership was abolished, putting into effect complete freedom of trade and making exceptions

But there is, of course, a reverse side of the medal. Freedom for all implies that all must yield to one another. Between the citizens (the traders) themselves, the Freedom of Trade sets a limit to the activity of the individual person—a limit to his freedom of contract and contracting, a limitation to his freedom of action altogether. This point of view we find for the first time in English Common Law—without any connection with the ideas of the physiocrats and Adam Smith, indeed long before these ideas found wide-spread acknowledgement. Thus, far back in time we find examples in British legal usage of instances where contracts have been declared to be non-binding in law because they were "in restraint of trade". Among these contracts we also find some restricting competition. But as time passed, the criterion "in restraint of trade" was narrowed down considerably—paradoxically in the name of free competition—, and in the 1890's, when private regulations of competition and trading began to make themselves felt in earnest, the development within English law had reached a point where in reality "restraint of trade" no longer in itself constituted an invalidation of a contract, but had been reduced to a mere "label" for competitive methods already unlawful for other reasons (fraud, violence, molestation, etc.)*. If not expressly enacted by Statute, the

only where special consideration of security ("for the common good") made it necessary; and no subsequent trade acts have (of course) deviated from this principle. Although its obligation has been fulfilled, as we have seen, the constitutionel provision in question has remained unchanged through all revisions of the constitution—most recently the one carried through in 1953. It must be understood now as a governmental obligation to preserve the freedom of trade.

* This is expressed especially clearly in a Court of Appeal judgment of 1891 (the "Mogul-Case") where Lord Bowen delivered the following opinion: "What, then, are the limitations which the law imposes on a trader in the conduct of his business as between himself or other traders? There seem to be no burdens or restrictions in law upon a trader which arise merely from the fact that he is a trader, and which are not equally laid on all other subjects of the Crown. His right to trade freely is a right which the law recognises and encourages, but it is one which places him at no special disadvantage compared with others. No man, whether trader or not, can, however, justify damaging another in his commercial business by fraud or misrepresentation. Intimidation, obstruction and molestation are forbidden; so is the intentional procurement of a violation of individual rights, contractual or others, assuming always that there is no just cause for it... But the defendants have been guilty of none of these acts. They have done nothing more against the plaintiffs than pursue to the bitter end a war of competition waged in the interest of their own trade.

...If peaceable and honest combinations of capital for purposes of trade competition are to be struck at, it must, I think, be by legislation, for I do not see that they are under the ban of the Common Law... The substance of my view is this, that competition, however severe and egotistical, if unattended by circumstances of dishonesty, intimidation, molestation or such illegalities as I have above referred to, gives rise to no cause of action at Common Law."[16]

Law Courts would not deprive "peaceable and honest" combinations of capital the freedom to force other peaceable traders out of the market and make themselves dictators of the market*. Thus the legal situation in England had become the same as in other European countries, especially in Germany and Scandinavia where until the latest decades, legal usage in situations where the principles of the Freedom of Trade and the Freedom of Contract were to be weighed against each other always seems to have given preference to the latter principle in cases not governed by Statute.

In the modern cartel acts we have finally obtained what was obviously necessary in order to overcome this inflexible conception of law: positive legislation, legislation which from a social-economic view-point gives the Freedom of Trade renewed actuality and increased weight and scope.

In economic theory it is a common thesis that the larger the supply of a certain commodity made through many (small) independent sellers, the more active the competition. So a disarming or restriction of competition may be brought about by a concentration of the supply on a small number of traders. An instrument very often used for this purpose is *agreements of exclusiveness*, vertical or horizontal, collective or individual—agreements aiming at directing the commodities in question to the market through certain (few) channels excluding other already existing sales outlets—not to speak of new ones. But almost the same effect can be obtained if the manufacturers (or the suppliers of raw materials) pursue a *discriminatory business policy* giving certain resellers a privileged position in respect of supplies, prices, rebates, or the like. In this way unequal conditions of competition are created giving the privileged circle a leading position and consequently a protected market position.

More matter-of-fact and less absolute in its wording, but hardly deviating in its actual contents, is a judgment of 1894 from which we quote the following paragraph:

"The public have an interest in every person's carrying on his trade freely: so has the individual. All interference with individual liberty of action in trading, and all restraints of themselves, if there is nothing more, are contrary to the public policy, and therefore void. That is the general rule. But there are exceptions: restraints of trade and interferences with individual liberty of action may be justified by the special circumstances of a particular case. It is a sufficient justification, and, indeed, it is reasonable—reasonable, that is, in reference to the interests of the parties concerned and reasonable in reference to the interest of the public, so framed and so guarded as to afford adequate protection to the party in whose favour it is imposed, while at the same time it is in no way injurious to the public."[17]

* Cf. the "Mogul-Case" (see previous foot-note).

First and foremost such restrictive business practices are, of course, against the interest of society if they result or may result in unreasonable prices. We have already considered them from this angle under subdivision (a). But also in cases where they cannot have any effect on the prices (because of an active public control and regulation of the price formation, for instance)—or in cases where the probability of having such an effect is remote—restrictive business practices in the form of agreements of exclusiveness and discriminatory business policies may be contrary to the public interest, namely if they mean "an unreasonable restriction in the freedom of trade"*. For the Freedom of Trade is one of the basic conditions of the freedom of competition.

In judging agreements of exclusiveness and discriminatory business policies, however, it is necessary to weigh a number of opposite considerations against each other. The Freedom of Trade, as we have suggested above, is a conception of some ambiguity. On the one hand it means "the free and equal opportunity for all to carry out an independent trade", and on the other hand it means the right of the individual trader to carry out his trade in freedom, i.e. to pursue his own private economic interests. Consequently, within the frames of the legislation, he must have a right to determine himself what and how much he wants to sell, to whom, and on which terms. The question which arises is, then, how to be fair in judging the importance due to the various opposite considerations; and more concretely, what are the limits set by the cartel acts to the freedom of each individual to determine for himself with whom he wants to enter into business and on what conditions?

We will turn to the French Price Ordinance first. As mentioned previously, this Act is based on the principle of prohibition, so it would be natural to expect a clear attitude to the problem just here. A close study of the Act and its application in practice reveals, however, that the problem is so complex that it cannot be solved by any simple formulas.

According to its wording, Article 37, paragraph 1a, of the Act contains a rather far-reaching prohibition against "refus de vente" and discriminatory business terms. The provision dates back to 1945, but has been amended in 1953 (décret no. 53–704) and again in 1958 (décret no. 58–545)**. In the text of the Act itself only three exemptions

* Quotation from the Danish Monopolies Control Act (see page 93).

** Translated, the provision reads as follows: "It shall be deemed to be an illegal practice in connection with prices:

are made from the prohibition against refusal of delivery; delivery may be refused, *if* it would be in contravention of the law or a governmental regulation, *if* the request has "un caractère anormal", or *if* the buyer is not "de bonne foi". As regards discriminatory policies, the Act makes the exemption that the price discrimination shall be legal, if the higher price is warranted by an equivalent increase in the costs. In an administrative circular of 15th February, 1954, contributing to the interpretation of the Decree of 1953, it is stated, however, that "contrats d'exclusivité" are not in contravention of the revised provisions of the Price Ordinance (i.e. Article 37 and the main provision, Article 59 bis,*) as long as they(1) in practice are advantageous to the consumers,(2) do not bring about price increases,(3) do not result in prices being kept at an unreasonably high level, and(4) do not cause such a reduction of the supply that the demand of the market cannot be met. Further, it is stated in the circular that provided these conditions have been fulfilled, especially the following forms of "contrats d'exclusivité" will be outside the scope of the aforementioned provisions of the Price Ordinance and consequently be lawful: (a) agreements (contracts) between only two enterprises, one of which (the manufacturer) reserves his whole production for the other party to the agreement, (b) sole agency contracts when the exclusiveness ensured is countered by certain obligations on the part of the sole agent, for instance that he shall render a certain amount of customer service on the commodity in question (repairs, etc.), that he shall carry a stock of spare parts, that he shall not be entitled to carry other similar commodities, that he shall share the advertising costs, etc.

French jurists[18] and French legal usage[19], however, have gone

1) for any trader, manufacturer or craftsman

a) to refuse to satisfy to the best of his ability and upon the customary trade terms any request for the purchase of goods or the performance of services, which has no abnormal character and is made in good faith, and provided that the sale of such goods or the performance of such services is not forbidden by law or governmental regulation, or habitually to apply discriminatory price increases which are not warranted by an equivalent increase in the costs of production or the costs of performing the services."

* This provision contains a general prohibition against any concerted action, convention, combine, etc., which interferes with full competition (see previous pages 82 and 83).

Under Article 59 ter, however, the provisions of Article 59 bis "shall not apply to any concerted action, convention or combine:

1. ....

2. Whose promoters are able to prove that its effect is to improve and extend the market for their products or to ensure further economic progress by means of rationalization and specialization".

further and have arrived at the conclusion that the prohibition against refusal of supply (Art. 37) does not apply to cases where the party called on to give delivery is contractually bound by a clause of exclusiveness not to sell to any third person. In support of this point of view special importance is attached to the expression "de bonne foi" as it is maintained that a person knowing the trader from whom he demands delivery to be bound by a clause of exclusiveness cannot be considered to be in good faith.* Further, the same jurists have expressed the opinion that a contract between a seller and a purchaser establishing an exclusive business relation cannot be regarded as an "entente" (understanding) and consequently must be outside the scope of the provision of Art. 59 bis—because seller and purchaser are opposite parties ("parties opposées") to the contract.

As a consequence of this it must be assumed that the prohibition of the Act applies primarily to collective arrangements of a horizontal or partly horizontal nature. As an example from practice may be mentioned that an "entente" between a group of leading manufacturers of electric lamps, for the purpose of "normalizing" the market and rationalizing the production, contained provisions, the practicing of which resulted in a discrimination of the manufacturers excluded from the "entente". These provisions, the specific contents of which have not been published, were considered to be in contravention of Article 37, 1a, and the Minister for Economic Affairs called on the members of the "entente" to abolish them[20].

On the basis of the material at our disposal, it has been impossible to draw a more detailed picture of French practice in cases concerning arrangements of exclusiveness and discriminatory business conditions.** We would not be far wrong in saying, however, that as a consequence of the "souplesse" with which the provisions of the French Price Ordinance are now interpreted, French practice follows on the whole the same lines as we find in countries where the legislation does not contain prohibitive provisions corresponding to those found in the French Act. If there is any difference, it may be that in France arrangements of exclusiveness and discriminatory business conditions

* In practice, accordingly, it will be the exception to be or remain in good faith. The parties to an agreement of exclusiveness will be prompted to make the exclusiveness known to the public, by means of labels affixed to the articles, for instance, from which it appears that the articles are sold only through certain specified dealers.

** Publication of the reports from "la Commission Technique des Ententes" was not commenced until January, 1960. Up to the present only reports from the years 1954, 1955, and 1956 have been published.

are accepted to a somewhat greater extent than is the case in other European countries.

We are in this connection thinking of such countries as, for instance, the Netherlands, Denmark, Norway, and Sweden.

In *the Netherlands* the problems of exclusiveness and discrimination have occupied the authorities a good deal. The legislation contains no provisions dealing especially with these problems, but in practice the fundamental view-point is that in general freedom to carry on a trade and to enter the market must not be contested. According to a Dutch author[21], private regulations of the entry into the market—including arrangements directing the use of certain trade channels—are therefore in principle considered to be justifiable only if they are *beneficial* from a social point of view. If this is so, the Dutch legislation operates with a criterion of usefulness as distinct from what is the case in other countries, Denmark and Sweden, for instance, where the legislator asks whether the restrictive practice in question is *detrimental* to the public interest. But Dutch practice, however—under the former Cartel Decree of 1941 *—also seems to show only examples of intervention against arrangements of exclusiveness and discriminatory business conditions which were or could be expected to become contrary to the public interest. An arrangement, for instance, in accordance with which electrotechnical equipment should be sold through specified distribution channels (agents and wholesalers) was declared to be non-binding; the individual manufacturer should be free to decide for himself whether it served his business interests best to sell through agents or otherwise. In several cases also arrangements of exclusiveness serving the purpose of supporting horizontal minimum price agreements have been declared to be non-binding[22].

In a number of instances, the Dutch authorities have found occasion to intervene against *the rules of admission to trade organizations* and against *the conditions stipulated by suppliers for taking on new dealers* ("control of new establishing"). In questions of whether a newly established trader could be admitted as a member of a trade organization, where he belonged according to his trade and where he had a professional interest in being a member, as well as in questions of supply to a new dealer-customer, the authorities have not accepted that it should be taken into account whether the number of the already

* Under the present Act, The Economic Competition Act 1956, which did not come into force until November, 1958, so far no practice worth speaking of has been built up.

established enterprises (dealers) of the trade was sufficient to cover the market ("the criterion of need"). Nor have the authorities approved more extensive demands as to professional qualifications, solvency, etc., than prescribed in the trade legislation, nor accepted that other personal conditions are stipulated leading to purely subjective judgments (questions of "ethics", "good reputation", etc.). Moreover, it is considered inadmissable to keep dealers out of a trade organization or to refuse to give delivery of goods to them because they are dealing also in other goods than those of the trade in question ("horizontal combines") or because they act as wholesalers and retailers simultaneously ("vertical combines"). The cartel authorities have also been opposed to conditions of admission or delivery to the effect that the traders in question are not allowed to enter into business relations with co-operative enterprises, chain stores, one-price stores, and the like. Finally, it is not normally approved that stricter demands as to qualifications, etc., are made on newly established enterprises or applicants to an organization than on those already established in the trade or admitted to the organization[23].

As far as "rationalization" of the distribution is concerned (a phenomenon occupying the Scandinavian cartel authorities a great deal, see below) we have from the Netherlands only one example of intervention. The question concerned was a desire on the part of a group of dairies to simplify the distribution of consumers' milk. The cartel authorities, however, would approve the rationalization only on certain conditions, among them *that* the consumers were ensured the freedom of choice between at least three dealers in the neighbourhood, *that* no dealers were squeezed out of business by the exclusion, and *that* the individual dealer bound up with the system had the opportunity of increasing his sale of milk by means of price competition or better customer service[24].

In Sweden, Norway, and Denmark, the cartel authorities take quite an undogmatic—and rather similar—view of questions of exclusiveness and discriminatory treatment. It is true that both the Swedish and the Danish cartel acts especially emphasize the considerations to be taken to the Freedom of Trade and Commerce (see above, page 93), in which connection the legislator has in mind especially free entry into the market and the opportunity to obtain supplies; but this does not mean that such considerations always will be predominant. Sometimes interests of the suppliers must carry most weight. So we find, in fact, that the questions the Scandinavian authorities ask themselves when judging an agreement of exclusiveness, terms of admission to the organizations, or other discriminatory business practices are consistently the same: Does the practice in question involve a substantial restraint in the Freedom of Trade? And if so, is the practice justified by other considerations of greater consequence?

Among the cases concerning *refusal* or *discontinuation of supply* which have been submitted for authoritative decisions in the Scandinavian countries, we find a number of instances where the authorities have not found occasion to intervene against the refusal or discontinuation of supply for the mere reason that the practice—although not justifiable when considered separately—still could not be deemed to be of any serious disadvantage to those affected by it, because they might be able to buy similar goods (although not of the same brand) from other suppliers, or because the goods in question had never been, or never would be, of any real importance to the trade of the excluded business enterprises. From Danish administrative practice we shall mention a case where a sole agent refused to sell the optical articles he dealt in, mostly spectacle frames of certain makes, to a professional optician, a member of the largest organization of opticians. The reason for the refusal was to be found in the optician's forms of sale (hire-purchase system). Still, the cartel authorities did not find grounds for ordering the agent to give delivery. The reasons stated for the decision were that the optician could buy similar articles of other makes from other wholesalers, and that optical articles—including spectacle frames—are not ordinarily looked upon as branded articles by the purchasing public; it was found, in fact, that it had been possible to build up even large opticians' shops without having to carry the special makes in question[25].

Another example from Danish practice may be of a certain interest. The proprietor of a rather big general store with a special department for hardware and china ware complained that he could not obtain supplies from a large factory of art porcelain and high quality china ware (distinguished by the trade mark of the factory). He referred to the fact that the rural co-operative shops could carry these goods, which they bought through the central organization of the co-operative associations. The factory argued that the reason for its refusal to supply was to be found in a well-founded general business policy. The factory sells direct to retailers, and had—without establishing a sale agent system, and without being bound by any agreements—at its own discretion limited the number of resellers because of its limited possibilities of supply. An additional number of resellers, therefore, might result in difficulties in serving its customers to the usual extent, and a dispersion of the distribution would have a cost increasing effect. When selecting the retailers, the factory took into account the standard and location of the shops, and whether the dealers could achieve a "reasonable" sale of the goods concerned. Apart from the sale to ordinary retailers, the factory had for a long time been selling its goods to the central organization of the co-operative associations; originally, the factory had begun this business relation in order to prevent the co-operative central organization from establishing its own porcelain factory. The central co-operative organization re-distributes the goods to co-operative shops all over the country without discrimination.

The Monopolies Appeal Tribunal, which had the final decision of the case, did not find grounds for complying with the wishes of the appellant by ordering the factory to change the terms it stipulated for applicant resellers. It is true that the Appeal Tribunal found an inequality to exist between the opportunities of the appellant and those of the competing co-operative shops for carrying the goods of the factory, but this circumstance was not found to carry sufficient weight to justify an intervention against the right of the factory to limit its number of dealers in the manner mentioned, based upon reasonable business-like considerations. Further, the Appeal Tribunal attached great importance to the fact that porcelain dealers, even without carrying the goods of the factory—which could not be characterized as ordinary consumers' goods—would be able to satisfy the demand for china ware to a considerable extent [26].

Further, from a Swedish decision concerning a wholesaler's complaint that he could not obtain direct delivery from a chemical plant (X) we shall give the following quotation in illustration of how much is required to establish a case to be harmful from a freedom-of-trade view-point: "In his examination of the case, the Commissioner for Freedom of Commerce has found it to be true that to a certain degree the refusal of supply in question has hampered the wholesaler's trade. However, when the occasion arises, he has a possibility of replenishing his assortment with X's goods (namely by purchase from another wholesaler). The additional expense incurred by procuring the goods in this way must be considered to be slight as compared with his total turnover. Under these circumstances, it is the opinion of the Commissioner that there is no reason to suppose that the refusal of supply should have such a harmful effect on the wholesaler as mentioned in Section 5 of the Restraint of Competition Act..."[27].

In Danish, Norwegian, and Swedish practice, furthermore, we find a number of decisions where the so-called *argument of efficiency* is the decisive factor. The point of view is as follows: A rationalization of the distribution, based upon sound economic and businesslike considerations, and practiced consistently and according to objective criteria, should not be contested even if it is damaging to traders who are dependent on the rationalizing firm in their business. If, on the other hand, the rationalization is marked by inconsistency, it is contrary to the demand of equality, with its bearing on the general sense of justice, and in that case a refusal of delivery should be considered an *undue* restraint of the freedom of trade.

The decisions related to the above problem all concern instances where manufacturers or importers of branded goods in connection with a reorganization of their distributing systems had discontinued their business relations with all or some of their former wholesale customers. The reorganization was to the effect that either the manufacturer or the importer in question began to sell direct to retailers through their own travelling salesmen, or that they introduced a principle of selection in their selling policy, sometimes in the form of sole agency systems based on a geographical division of the market. It is a well-known fact that there may be several causes for such arrangements. By changing to direct sale to retailers, the manufacturer may effect cost savings, namely if the increase of sales and distribution costs amounts to less than what is saved by the disposal of the wholesale allowances. More important to the manufacturer, however, is no doubt the value of a marketing policy creating a direct contact with the retailers, and also in this connection certain advantages as to price policy may be of benefit to the manufacturer (for instance, the fixing of suggested resale prices). Also a change-over to a selective sales system is usually—or we may even say primarily—fostered by a desire for cost savings, but in certain cases also considerations as to competition are taken into account, for instance if it is stipulated in sole agency contracts that the agents must not deal in similar articles of other makes. It is, however, always a delicate question to decide how far one should go in letting such considerations of efficiency justify a notorious restrictive business practice. We will let a few examples speak for themselves.

Example 1: A Danish manufacturer of a widespread branded cosmetic article discontinued his business relations with a number of wholesalers while at the same time he continued to deliver to other wholesalers. The discontinuance of supply was a result of the manufacturer's extension of his own sales organization so that in the future he would be able to book orders directly from the retailers to a greater extent than before. The wholesalers with whom he continued to deal had based their business on direct sale to hairdressers and unspecialized retail shops (general stores, etc.). Retailers of this kind buy only small quantities at a time, and would not be visited by the manufacturer's travelling salesmen. The cartel authorities did not find sufficient grounds for intervention against the new sales arrangement as it was found that in the present case the manufacturer's interest in organizing sales in a way he considered to be the most expedient for him should outweigh any considerations of the interests of the wholesalers[28]. (See for comparison the above mentioned case concerning the porcelain factory).

Example 2: Between the majority of Danish pharmaceutical industries—including all the large ones—an informal agreement ("understanding") existed according to which they would not enter into business relations with new wholesalers. The reasons stated for this agreement were that the number of wholesalers with whom the industries already did business covered the demand of the market completely, and that an additional number of wholesalers would not result in an increase of the trade volume, but would only lead to a rise in the costs of distribution. When one of the pharmaceutical plants then refused to sell its special ready-for-use preparations to a newly established wholesale firm (which had obtained due authorization according to the rules of the legislation concerning pharmaceutical chemists) the question was put before the cartel authorities. They found that this complete exclusion of new wholesalers was unreasonable, and had the arrangement changed so that the manufacturers should instead fix terms of delivery opening up the possibility for new wholesalers to obtain the products of the industries, while at the same time the interest of the manufacturers in avoiding a cost increasing dispersion of sales was protected. The most important of these terms was the one stipulating that, in order to retain his right to continued supplies, a wholesaler should buy a certain minimum quantity within a period of three years[29]. This decision, as will appear, rejects the pure "criterion of need".

Neither is it found to be a sufficient justification for refusal to enter into business with a new dealer that the establishing of a new outlet might detract from the sale to the "old" customers of the enterprise. A *Swedish* decision on this subject states: "...in principle a supplier must be free to decide throught which dealers he wants to have his goods sold; as long as he can state rational reasons for his reluctance to enter into business relations with certain dealers, there is no evidence of harmful effects within the meaning of the law (the Restraint of Competition Act). *If, on the other hand, a supplier permits his attitude to be influenced, directly or indirectly, by competitors of the dealer concerned, the refusal of supply is undue in respect of the public interest*"[30]. The plea that the reason for the refusal of supply is to be found in a selective sales system, organized along sound business lines on rational economic considerations, will, in reality, often be a cover for a pressure from the already existing group of dealers, and in their investigations the authorities are constantly on the alert against such hidden motives. In several Swedish decisions we find examples of this kind[31].

The insistence on "objectivity" is, of course, also found when the question is about terms, collectively or individually fixed, of admission of dealers which stipulate as conditions for entering into business relations with a dealer that he shall meet certain requirements as to professional training, knowledge of the trade, financial standing, location and standard of his shop, as well as requirements as to his purchase of goods (minimum buying quotas, a representative assortment, and a certain constant stock). In Denmark, Norway and Sweden rather comprehensive conditions of this kind are permitted, if only they are adequate and the same for all. What is not permitted on the other hand, is a more or less arbitrary selection. A Danish manufacturing enterprise, occupying a dominating position within the trade, which permitted the adoption of wholesaler connections to take place on an estimate of the "business reputation" and "energy" of the wholesalers, was ordered by the authorities to change its terms of admission in such a way that purchase of a certain minimum quantity became the decisive factor[32].

Terms of admission or delivery stipulating that the dealers should be members of certain trade organizations (terms of "compulsory organization membership") formerly were found very frequently in the Scandinavian countries where powerful trade organizations existed—and still exist—within almost all trades. As a rule, these terms originated in some concerted action within a trade, either in the form of an agreement of exclusiveness between the organizations of the suppliers and the resellers, or in the form of by-laws of a trade organization including traders representing several or all stages of trade. In the Scandinavian countries, such collectively fixed and enforced terms of organization membership for admission to a trade would not be tolerated by the cartel authorities any more, so they are not commonly found. However, one may still come across cases where several traders within the same trade individually practice uniform terms of the character mentioned. In most instances it is a left-over from an abolished agreement or by-law provision on exclusiveness; although officially terminated it continues to live beneath the surface—only as a consequence of habitual thinking, perhaps. But in such cases, of course, the authorities can and will order that delivery be made to the unorganized traders on the same terms as to the members of the organization.

Refusals of entering into business relations with, or discriminatory treatment of enterprises of certain types (such as consumers' co-operative enterprises, chain stores, telephone order shops, self-service shops, and the like) constitute when comprehensive—i.e. when the enterprises concerned are excluded from obtaining important goods—a practice which, in Sweden, Denmark, and Norway, is generally considered to be contrary to the public interest, because these enterprises, on account of their special organization or their untraditional forms of distribution, will often be able to sell at especially low prices. In doing so, they will also have a stimulating effect on price competition in general.

(c) *Obstruction of Technological Progress and Restraint of Production*

One of the arguments for free competition is that it creates the best possible climate for progress. It is maintained that under market conditions characterized by an active and effective competition, ingenuity will be encouraged, and the manufacturing enterprises will vie with one another in securing new inventions that make it possible to improve the quality of the goods or to introduce new goods on the market, or which may lead to a higher efficiency in the manufacturing processes so that production costs may be reduced, resulting in cheaper but not inferior goods. In markets dominated by monopolies, or where competition is neutralized or considerably weakened as a consequence of an extensive cartellization, one does not find the same incentive to hasten development, to open up new avenues, to run the risks involved in costly experiments. Here progress will make slower headway, and, besides, the benefit of such progress that may take place will not—or only to a small extent, at any rate—be reaped by the general public but by the manufacturers in the form of a monopoly profit.*

Against this line of reasoning, however, certain reservations can be made. Firstly, a most important incentive for scientists and technicians to make new inventions is—apart from the never-resting inquiring mind—the prospect of patent rights; and these rights are in fact monopoly creating, although the monopolies in question are legal and limited in time. Secondly, invention comes about only from experimenting, and at the present stage of technical development, technical improvements will in most cases need very comprehensive experiments requiring considerable capital which will be difficult to raise in the ordinary money market. Experiences from the great industrial countries also show that nowadays the experimental work preparatory to a great number of improvements in the industrial arts is carried out under the sponsorship of large industrial enterprises which not only have financial interest in the work but also can afford to pay for it at their own risk. In other words, the best conditions for technical progress may exist where large and financially strong industrial concerns operate. But such large-scale enterprises are to be found rather seldom in markets characterized by strong competition, especially in the small ones. If in such markets a favourable atmosphere is to be created for "a dynamic technology", a certain concentration of the economic forces is required, a collaboration in trade and industry which to some extent must result in a neutralization of competition. In this reasoning we find one of the premises on which this principle statement of the London resolution rests: "that cartels, trusts and other analogous combines are natural phenomena of economic life towards which it is impossible to adopt an entirely negative attitude".

But when this is said, it must at the same time be admitted that we also find some unpleasant examples of efforts on the part of the said powerful cartels and trusts to suppress or delay the exploitation of

* This way of thinking is expressed in a statement made in 1953 by the Danish Minister of Commerce when the bill to the present Danish Monopolies Control Act was introduced into Parliament: "If initiative and enterprise shall be given free scope, we must endeavour to make provisions guaranteeing that monopolies and trusts do not prevent others from carrying on trade by means of unfair methods... *An economic life entangled in a web of agreements and monopolies easily falls in stagnation.* What we need today, more than ever perhaps, is a trade and an industry open to new ideas, ready to explore new avenues, interested in and urged to make continuous improvements. Only in this way the conditions of life can be bettered for the population...".

technical improvement in order to protect their monopolistic interests. To gain this end it has often been possible, unfortunately, for financially strong concerns to use the rules of legal procedure under the patent legislation for a wearing-down and paralysing pettifogging. A characteristic example was revealed by the investigation made in 1944–1946 by the American authorities into the activities of the American patent cartel in the glass container industry, comprising patent rights to various bottle machines, etcetera. A memorandum of 1930, written by one of the controlling members of this cartel (Hartford–Empire Company), gives a very frank outline of the business policy of the cartel stating, inter alia, the main aim to be to block the development of machines which might be designed by other manufacturers for the same purpose by a somewhat different technique, and to obtain patent rights to any improvements of competing machines in order to fence them in and prevent their further development[33]. Such manoeuvres, facilitated by existing restraints of competition and resulting in further restraints of competition, are designs against the public interests which it is the purpose of an anti-trust legislation to protect, and come, therefore, within the scope of such legislation.

This delicate question about the relation between the Patent law and the Cartel legislation was a topical problem in a case which was dealt with in 1955 by the French Commission Technique des Ententes. One of the main points of the case concerned a license agreement containing the clause that the licensee was allowed only to use the products under the license (bars of magnesium alloys) in his own production and was not permitted to resell them in the rough. The licensor (a cartel, see below) pleaded before the Commission *that,* inter alia, the practice in question was in conformity with the patent legislation (which point was not contested), and *that* the patent legislation, on account of its special character ("son caractère absolu") as well as its international ramifications, constituted a self-contained legal field ("un droit autonome") where a special legislation (the cartel legislation) should not interfere. These arguments were supported by the Ministry for Industry and Commerce. The Commission, however, construed the provisions of the patent legislation a well as those of the cartel legislation to the effect that the agreement—in spite of the fact that it was concerned with patent rights—came under the cartel legislation. In its recommendation to the Minister for Economic Affairs, the Commission states, inter alia: "It is not in conformity with the principles of our public law to attribute a special value to a specific legislation excluding its modification by another law, the nature of which is also "une disposition d'ordre public".—". The Commission continues to say that, although it is desirable that the Patent Law, on account of its economic importance and international ramifications, is firmly guaranteed, the considerations of finding the solution best suited to the national economic interests do not permit that the Commission is deprived of the possibility to investigate the practices which, within a cartel agreement, trade on the rights ensuing from the patent legislation.

Also the factual subject matter of the said case is, incidentally, of some interest. The cartel concerned consisted of the company X, the sole manufacturer of magnesium in France, and the company Y, partly owned by X, buying and distributing the whole of X's production. Further, a foundry, Z, was financially combined with X and Y. Five other foundries had license agreements with Y. One of these agreements (with licensee L_1) had the restrictive content as mentioned above, with the obvious purpose of protecting Z. The other licensees, who, due to their individual activities, were not actual competitors to Z, were under their contracts only bound to refrain from selling the raw material (magnesium).

The Commission demonstrated that in actual fact the cartel completely controlled production, distribution, and utilisation of magnesium and certain magnesium alloys, and that this situation of neutralized competition had harmful effects on the national economy in general* and the aircraft industry, important also to the national defense, in particular. For as a consequence of the special clause in L_1's contract of license, manufacturers of aircraft engines simply had to buy the magnesium alloys necessary for their production from Z, meaning the cartel. This situation was apt to disturb the continuity of the production, should the cartel encounter difficulties. Moreover, the lack of competition involved a risk of technical stagnation.

In its recommendation to the Minister for Economic Affairs, the Commission suggested that in the interest of the national defense it should be attempted to establish "une situation concurrentielle" in respect to supplies of the special alloys in question to the aircraft industry, and that the Minister together with the members of the

* While the production of magnesium during the period, 1938–1954 had increased considerably in other countries, it had shown a downward trend in France during the same period (a reduction at about 20 per cent) in spite of the general increase of the economic activity. At the same time, prices were substantially higher in France than in the other countries.

cartel explore the possibilities of setting up a system of price fixing suited to stimulate the activity on the existing markets and rendering it possible to enter new markets.

The Minister accepted the recommendation and insured through negotiations that in the future magnesium alloys for war material would be made and delivered by two foundries in free competition[34].

As a safeguard against *suppression of new inventions*, the patent legislation contains certain provisions which, in the event that within a certain period "a granted patent is not being commercially worked... or is not being so worked to the fullest extent that is reasonably practicable", authorize the patent authorities to order the issuing of a compulsory license under the patent or, as a last resort, to invalidate the patent*. In most cases such phenomena will demand the attention of the cartel authorities, too, and these authorities, especially in countries where the cartel legislation is based upon the principles of control and intervention, will also have ways and means to counteract them, for instance through publication of reports on investigations revealing such practices. When the British Monopolies And Restrictive Practices Commission in 1953 made a general investigation of the conditions prevailing in the match industry, a question of obstruction of the above character was dealt with. During several years the British Match Corporation, which under a system of trading agreements (about, inter alia, market sharing and technical collaboration) had close relations to the Swedish Match Company dominating the world market, had bought up various patents concerning reignitible matches ("continuous matches", "everlasting matches", or "ignition rods"), but when a few years before the Second World War a very modest quantity had been put on the market, production was discontinued. This had started rumours to the effect that the new article had been suppressed by B.M.C. and Swedish Match. The Commission, however, did not find proof of any suppression, but took note of the explanation that the discontinuance of the production was due to the following three factors: failure to arrive at a satisfactory composition (the matches gave off an objectionable smell), the considerable danger of manufacture (danger of explosions), and the impossibility of manufacturing the matches in question at prices which could compete with those of ordinary matches or mechanical lighters[35].

* The text quoted is from The United Kingdom Patent Acts, 1949, Section 37 (2a). Similar provisions are found in patent acts of other European countries.

An intentional incomplete exploitation of the productive capacity within an industry, arranged through *agreements on restriction of production,* is found quite frequently. In some instances, the authorities cannot rightly in the name of the public interest raise any objections against such agreements; as provisional measures of rationalization, at any rate, they may under certain circumstances, be reasonable. In other instances, however, they cannot be tolerated on account of their effects on prices, this being the most frequent cause of intervention. It is but in rare instances that we find the sole or the main reason stated for an intervention against a restriction of production to be under-supply of the market. However, in reports on Dutch administrative practice we have found a case of this kind concerning an agreement on restriction of production between producers of certain foodstuffs within the vegetable trade. By an Order in Council, the agreement was declared to be non-binding for the reason stated above[36].

III

Once more we revert to the London conference in 1930; for we must not forget to mention that the discussions there dealt not only with questions concerning the steps of control and regulation to be taken by the individual countries at home against cartels and trusts, etc., but also with the question of similar measures against international cartels and trusts. In this connection the London resolution declared that as regards international economic combines, cartels, and trusts, a special control was considered necessary, and that the chief instrument lay in the development of publicity, i.e. notification to and registration in an international register managed by the League of Nations or another international body, the duty of which should be to examine the treaties and agreements, to exercise a permanent supervision over all matters concerning cartels and trusts, and, on the basis of the experience gained, to make proposals for the further international regulation in this field.

As is well-known, the League of Nations never succeeded in taking on this task. But after World War II, in connection with the intensified international collaboration on political, economic, and social problems, the endeavours to counter restrictive business practices within the world trade were resumed. There is certainly no lack in broad concordance in resolutions as regards aims and principles. Take, for instance, the Havana Charter of 1948, which directed the states to combat private restrictive business practices restraining competition to the detriment of production and trade, restricting access to markets, or fostering monopolistic control[37].* We may also mention the draft prepared by a United Nations' committee about international collaboration in counteracting abuses of international restraints of competition (March, 1953)[38]. This draft suggests that a special international organization be empowered to investigate and judge—on the basis of motivated complaints—international restrictive business practices, and the procedure proposed may be characterized by the keywords negotiation, recommendation, and publicity; but the draft was shelved, for the time being, by the United Nations' Economic And Social Council (ECOSOC).

In 1954, the Governments of Denmark, Norway, and Sweden suggested that provisions as to restrictive business practices affecting international trade be inserted into the *General Agreement on Tariffs and Trade* (GATT). They proposed taking the provisions of the above draft of the ECOSOC committee as models. At nearly the same time the Government of the Federal Republic of Germany made a proposal of similar content differing, however, from the ECOSOC draft in certain points relating to the rules of procedure. These proposals as well as alternative ones have been discussed at the sessions of the GATT organization up to the present, but so far it has not been possible to arrive at an agreement as to the solution of the problems[39].

Within smaller international market areas, however, the idea of supranational control of and intervention against restrictive business practices has been realized. What we have in mind here are the provisions to this effect which are laid down in the treaties of the *European Coal and Steel Community* (E.C.S.C.) and within the so-called Common Market, the *European Economic Community* (E.E.C.). As far as these organizations are concerned, however, we shall refer to the respective essays on these subjects found elsewhere in this volume.

* The Havana Charter was signed by representatives from 54 countries, but was ratified by only a minority of these countries.

NOTES

1. Union Interparlementaire, *Compte rendu de la XXVIe Conférence*, Génève: Payot et Cie, 1931, pp. 33–34.
2. The text of the Act (English translation) is to be found in *Guide to Legislation on Restrictive Business Practices, Europe and North America*, (hereafter called: *Guide*), Paris: The European Productivity Agency (E.P.A.) of the Organization for European Economic Co-operation (O.E.E.C.), 1960, vol. II, Section Norway, para. 1.0.
3. TORSTEIN ECKHOFF and ØYSTEIN GJELSVIK, *Prisloven* (The Price Act), Oslo: Grundt Tanum, 1955, p. 37.

4. *Guide*, vol. I, Section Denmark, para. 1.0.
5. *Ibid.*, vol. II, Section Sweden, paras. 1.0 and 1.1.
6. *Ibid.*, vol. II, Section The Netherlands, para. 1.0.
7. *Ibid.*, vol. I, Section Ireland, para. 1.0.
8. *Ibid.*, vol. I, Section France, paras. 1.0, 1.1 and 1.2.
9. *Den nya pris- och kartellagstiftningen* (The New Price and Cartel Legislation), Stockholm: Statens Pris- och Kartellnämnd (State Price and Cartel Office), 1958, p. 14.
10. *Konkurrensbegränsning* (Restraints of Competition), Stockholm: Swedish Ministry of Trade and Commerce, 1951, p. 517.
11. Adam Smith, *Wealth of Nations*, Book I, ch. X, Part II.
12. Søren Gammelgaard, *Resale Price Maintenance*, Paris: E.P.A. (O.E.E.C.), 1958, pp. 13 and 17–18. This work is the source of some more details given in our paragraph "Imposed Resale Prices".
13. *Pristidende* (bulletin), Oslo: Price Directorate, October 30, 1959, No. 17, pp. 470–505.
14. *Näringsfrihetsfrågor* (bulletin), Stockholm: Statens Pris- och Kartellnämnd, 1955, No. 6, Section II, pp. 1–11; *Ibid.*, 1956, No. 4, Section II pp. 31–33 (photo-articles); *Pris- och Kartellfrågor* (bulletin), Stockholm: Statens Pris- och Kartellnämnd, 1959, No. 4, pp. 275–84 (woolen ready-made clothing) and pp. 285–92 (footwear).
15. *Meddelelser fra Monopoltilsynet* (bulletin), Copenhagen: Monopoltilsynet (the Monopolies Control Authority), 1960, No. 10, pp. 153–173.
16. William Sanderson, *Restraint of Trade in English Law*, London: Sweet & Maxwell, 1926, pp. 104–07.
17. *Ibid.*, pp. 5–6.
18. R. Plaisant and J. Lassier, *Les ententes industrielles* (formules), Paris: Librairies techniques, 1957, p. 7.
19. Giannantoni Guglielmetti, "Les exclusivités de vente", *La libre concurrence dans les pays du Marché Commun* (supplement to the Revue du Marché Commun), Langres, 1959, p. 39.
20. *Journal Officiel: Documents Administratifs*, Paris: 1960, No. 2, p. 22.
21. P. J. van Leeuwe, "La législation aux Pays-Bas", *La libre concurrence dans les pays du Marché Commun* (see note 20) p. 22 (II).
22. *Ibid.*, pp. 22 and 24–28.
23. *Ibid.*, p. 22.
24. *Ibid.*, p. 23.
25. *Meddelelser fra Monopoltilsynet* (see note 15), 1957, No. 7, p. 110.
26. *Ibid.*, 1957, No. 9, pp. 148–52.
27. *Pris- och Kartellfrågor* (see note 15), 1959, No. 7, pp. 458–59.
28. *Meddelelser fra Monopoltilsynet* (see note 15), 1957, No. 4, pp. 57–58.
29. *Ibid.*, 1957, No. 9, pp. 153–54; *Ibid.*, 1958, No. 2, pp. 20–24.
30. *Pris- och Kartellfrågor*, (see note 15), 1957, No. 9, pp. 545–46.
31. *Ibid.*, pp. 549–56; *Ibid.*, 1958, No. 9, pp. 607–08; No. 10, pp. 637–39.
32. *Meddelelser fra Monopoltilsynet* (see note 15), 1957, No. 4, p. 57.
33. Frederik Neumeyer, *Patentkarteller*, Stockholm: Kooperativa Förbundets Bokförlag, 1947, p. 40.
34. *Journal Officiel: Documents Administratifs*, 1960, No. 1, pp. 10–12.
35. *Report on the Supply and Export of Matches... etc.*, London: The Monopolies and Restrictive Practices Commission, H.M.S.O., 1953, pp. 46–51.
36. Van Leeuwe, *op. cit.* (see note 21), p. 23.
37. *Restrictive Business Practices*, Génève: GATT, 1959, pp. 69 et seq.
38. *Ibid.*, pp. 76 et seq.
39. *Ibid.*, pp. 97–98.

CHAPTER 4

RESTRICTIVE PRACTICES

THOMAS WILSON

University of Glasgow, United Kingdom

I

Among economists in both America and Britain, the weight of opinion has always been strongly hostile to such practices as the fixing of producers' prices, the regulation of output, restrictive agreements with distributors and all the many devices by which newcomers may be kept out of an industry. It is true that there have been some dissentient voices. Schumpeter was prepared to argue that the greater security of a monopolistic position would be favourable to innovation,[2] and such security could presumably be obtained not only by achieving a dominating position in a market but also by forming a restrictive agreement between a number of independent concerns. In Britain, the work of the Monopolies Commission was criticized with some force by the late Sir Henry Clay[3] who was convinced that some of the practices generally held to be in restraint of trade were beneficial both to the industry concerned and to the economy as a whole. These views have won little support. There appears to be less difference of opinion among economists about cartels than there has been about monopolistic control by a single concern. A firm that accounts for a high proportion of an industry's output may admittedly have swollen profits but it is often conceded that it may also offer some compensation from the economies of scale. A cartel may also restrict and exploit, but in this case there is held to be no cost-reducing concentration of effort; on the contrary, a cartel may prevent such a development from taking place.

This is the verdict that has, I think, been fairly generally accepted. It can be regarded as a broad practical judgment which owes surprisingly little to the detailed analytical studies of "imperfectly competitive" or "monopolistically competitive" markets. Restrictive agreements have not been altogether ignored in these theories but have received little more than passing mention. This neglect is a serious inconvenience but would not in itself be so harmful if it were at least the case that some clear and practicable criteria had emerged from the analysis that could serve to guide legislators and lawyers in determining where "the public interest" should be deemed to lie. Is it reasonable to suppose that competition is generally favourable to the public interest? Should any exceptions or qualifications be made? What conditions are likely to ensure that prices and output will be appropriately determined and industrial progress fostered? Such questions are also part of the subject matter of welfare economics and it would be only reasonable to suppose that there had been much fruitful co-operation between lawyers and economists. That there has been some is no doubt true but only to a limited degree, at least in Britain. Part of the explanation may be found in the somewhat confused condition to which welfare economics has now been reduced. The exaggerated claims once made for a deceptively precise analysis have been demolished and replaced by extreme iconoclasm—not unmixed with boredom. But a negative attitude is, in its way, as unrealistic as the over-ambitious claims once confidently advanced on behalf of the Marginal Rule and the like. Decisions must somehow be made and action must be taken. Bland agnosticism is a luxury reserved for dons.

In fact the agnosticism on the more rarefied analytical plane has not prevented economists from discussing cartels in more general terms and proffering advice; but the thinness of the analytical treatment has undoubtedly been a handicap. Nor have the facts about restrictive agreements been at all easy to obtain. When restrictive agreements are held to be illegal *per se,* the lack of detailed information is not surprising. The opinion of the Supreme Court as delivered by Mr. Justice Stone in *United States v. Trenton Potteries Co.* may be quoted here:

> "The aim and result of every price fixing agreement, if effective, is the elimination of one form of competition. The power to fix prices, whether reasonably exercised or not, involves arbitrary and unreasonable prices. The reasonable price fixed today may through economic and business changes become the unreasonable price of to-morrow. Once established, it may be maintained unchanged because of the absence of competition secured by the agreement for a price reasonable when fixed. Agreements which create such potential power may well be held to be in themselves unreasonable or unlawful restraints, without the necessity of minute inquiry whether a particular price is reasonable or unreasonable as fixed and without placing on the government in

enforcing the Sherman Law the burden of ascertaining from day to day whether it has become unreasonable through the mere variation of economic conditions."[4]

No doubt it is true that some *per se* prohibitions are indispensable if any effective action is to be taken against the practices held to be restrictive. So much was conceded by the British Parliament insofar as it prohibited collective resale price maintenance in the Restrictive Trade Practices Act of 1956. An incidental consequence may be a subsequent lack of detailed information about the effect of the practice deemed to be illegal *per se*. Not only may such practices become less common but, in so far as they tend, in one form or another, to survive for a time, it should suffice for the prosecution to establish their existence. Thus if a price-fixing agreement were brought before a U.S. court it would be unnecessary to prove detriment and the detailed inquiry that such proof might require, would be redundant. In Britain restrictive practices were commonplace for many years and, with some exceptions, were both legal and enforceable at law. There were, therefore, plenty of instances to investigate, but the very immunity from interference by the state that permitted their existence, also made investigation less probable. Two official inquiries of a general nature were held between the Wars which threw some light on the extent of restrictions without affording much detailed information about their modes of operation. There were also some official surveys of particular industries, such as steel and road transport, and there were, of course, some private studies. In 1948 the position was changed by the appointment of the Monopolies and Restrictive Practices Commission, which was charged to carry out investigations at the request of the Board of Trade and to make recommendations. This was an admirable arrangement from the point of view of any academic economist who simply wished to learn something about the operations of cartels: the law was not changed and the restrictive agreements remained legal except in so far as specific action was taken after the Commission had reported;* these practices were studied in a detail never before attempted in Britain and the Commission was required to assess the consequences for the public interest. The defect even from this academic viewpoint was the slow rate of progress: when the Act of 1956 removed responsibility for restrictive practices from the Monop-

* The only instance was the official Order issued by the Board of Trade in 1951 after the report on Dental Goods. In several other cases undertakings to desist were given by the industries concerned.

olies Commission * to the new Restrictive Practices Court, reports had been published on only 18 industries. As already indicated the Restrictive Trade Practices Act introduced a strong ruling in favour of competition: the collective enforcement of resale price maintenance became unconditionally illegal while price agreements between producers and most other restrictions could be defended only on narrowly specified grounds.** As a consequence a substantial proportion of the agreements registered under the Act were abandoned without defence by the participants; of the remainder, only a small number have come before the court at the time of writing. From the point of view of our enquiry, it is fortunate that the exceptions permitted by the Act, although deemed by the Court to be so narrow as to make a favourable verdict difficult, have at least permitted some general discussion of the agreements and their probable consequences. In the United States itself, the *per se* ruling has not been applied so unequivocally to so comprehensive a range of practices as to eliminate debate and to make inquiry unnecessary: one need only refer, by way of example, to the treatment of retail price maintenance under the Miller-Tydings Amendment of 1937 or to the debate about the basing-point system in 1948.

The discussion that follows falls into several parts. Section 2 will consist of a brief review of the analytical treatment of competition and two questions will be asked. What criteria, if any, can be derived from economic analysis that will be of help in practical judgments about the public interest? How could firms be expected to behave if restrictive practices were genuinely abandoned? The third part will survey some of the fragmentary information available about the ways in which cartels fix their prices, regulate output and the like. In this section the empirical evidence will be mainly British although some incidental references will be made to the United States and other countries. In the fourth section reference will be made to quotas, the restriction of entry and similar practices. The fifth section will record some of the arguments advanced in defence of restrictive practices and will indicate the extent to which such arguments have been conceded in the form of tentative exceptions under the British Act of 1956. A general summing up will then be attempted in the sixth section.

* The Monopolies Commission remains reponsible for the investigation of the existence and effects of monopolies of scale. Such a monopoly is deemed to exist when one firm (or group) provides about one-third or more of the supply of a commodity in the U.K.

** See Appendix.

II

In the theory of monopolistic competition it is usually supposed that firms are acting independently, and the upshot of the analysis is all the more discouraging because it starts from this apparently optimistic assumption. For it appears to be the case that the market suffers from inherent defects that would cause a misallocation of resources and an undesirable distribution of income, even if all cartels were to be swept away and "conscious parallelism" were unknown. Some people may indeed believe that, without any so-called restrictive agreements, conditions would be worse in some respects, rather than better.

(a) The first criterion we shall consider is that, in equilibrium, profits should not be "abnormally high"; in other words the price at which a product is sold should not exceed what would be its long-run supply price on a free market. This is a ruling that has been generally accepted in formulating policy and it is clearly right that it should be so. The real difficulties arise in trying to determine whether the profits actually being earned by a particular firm are abnormal or not. First of all, methods of accounting may not be standardised and the border-line between "profits" and "costs" may not always be drawn at the same place. Secondly, overhead costs will often be on a historical basis and irrelevant divergences may thus appear in the figures for "profits". Thirdly, even in equilibrium, profits are unlikely to accrue at the same rate to different firms within an industry because special rents will be included in them, notably the rent of superior managerial ability. The final reason is that the firms under examination are unlikely to be in long-run equilibrium. Abnormal profits (or losses) must not then be regarded as improper: on the contrary, it is by means of such abnormal receipts that change is brought about. As the Monopolies Commission observed, "high profits are not in themselves against the public interest provided they are earned in open competition as the reward of efficiency".[5]

Faced with such difficulties an investigating body can do no more than make a rough practical judgment. If the general level of profits in an industry is high in comparison with those in other industries that are not obviously less risky or less progressive, then there is a *prima facie* reason for supposing that profits are "abnormal". A more indirect approach is to inquire whether there are any restrictive practices, such as obstacles to new entrants, that would protect abnormal profits from competition. (The Monopolies Commission has relied heavily upon indirect inferences of this kind.) It must be observed that such practices do not in themselves afford indirect proof that profits actually are abnormally high but indicate rather that, should such abnormality occur, it may be protected. If there is further evidence that the more efficient firms would expand their output but for the restraints imposed by a cartel, the right inference may be that the *price* is too high, although it may be true that *profits* would be just as large if these firms with their lower costs were not so hampered.

(b) Although free entry may eliminate abnormal profits, it may do so only at the cost of unexploited economies of scale. This is the disconcerting conclusion of the theories of monopolistic and imperfect competition, and it affords, perhaps, some explanation of the comparative neglect in analytical works of the activities of cartels. For, if the theory is right, the market suffers from inherent defects that would merely show themselves in different ways if all restrictive agreements were abolished and every kind of informal collusion abandoned. With sloping demand curves and U-shaped cost curves, an unsatisfactory choice has apparently to be made: on the one hand, freedom of entry might ensure that profits were normal, but costs and prices would be "too high" because each firm was operating at less than its optimum scale; on the other hand, a restrictive agreement might imply fewer firms and greater economies, but these firms would be able to extract abnormal profits.

In recent years this theory has been subjected to damaging criticism and few economists would presumably wish to defend it in the form in which it was originally propounded.* The objections to it can be only briefly mentioned here. (i) "Perfect competition" is not a norm and the fact that it has been taken as one is a remarkable example of the way in which we can mislead ourselves with our own emotive terminology. Indeed the expression "perfect competition" has probably done more to darken counsel than any other in modern economic literature, and its use should now be discontinued; it would be wiser to rest

* Unfortunately something like this theory is still presented as the central account of competition in many text-books with all the old jargon that has caused so much confusion—"perfect competition", "imperfect competition" and the like. Is there any other subject where the student is led so far astray in his undergraduate work on the implicit understanding that, if he carries on long enough, he may be put right later?

Admittedly the supplementary assumptions sometimes made of complete mobility and unclouded knowledge may suggest more genuine aspects of social perfection, though scarcely attainable ones!

content with a colourless reference to infinite elasticities. "Pure" competition is only slightly less confusing. (ii) As soon as it is realised that the "perfection" of "perfect competition" relates primarily to the elasticity of the curves and does not necessarily imply any sort of social perfection, it becomes clear that production at minimum average cost should not be regarded as a satisfactory criterion merely on the ground that this is the position reached in long-term equilibrium with "perfect" competition. Obviously it is desirable to produce as cheaply as possible but, if the market for a commodity is not large enough to permit full economies, there is insufficient reason to infer that resources are badly distributed. Before such a verdict could be accepted, it would be necessary to have proved that preferences were faulty in the sense that consumers could be expected to opt for less variety and greater cheapness if they were more cognizant of the facts and less confused by the blandishments of the advertisers. That ignorance and bad advice may bring loss is obvious enough, although it is not at all obvious that preferences will be biased in favour of "too much" diversity. It is surely a little strange that, in this theory, advertising should always be associated with the differentiation of the product whereas in fact it is associated with mass production for large markets. The attachment of consumers to a few well-known brands is as familiar a feature of their behaviour as an exaggerated preference for variety. If, as a consequence, the loss of economies of scale is less likely, the newcomer may not find it easy to attract custom even when he can offer genuine innovations of product or process.

Views will differ about the importance of these conflicting considerations, but it will suffice here to observe that the argument has now changed its character. It is no longer suggested that the inherent wastefulness of the market can be demonstrated conclusively by means of a little geometry. The waste is no more than a possibility admitted on general grounds; empirical evidence is needed to establish its presence and its importance in any particular situation.

(c) For some years the central propositions of welfare theory have been a number of marginal rules of which, in this brief survey, one will be made the centre of discussion as representative of them all: this is the rule that in order to obtain the best allocation of resources, output should be expanded to the point where marginal cost is equal to price. This position will not in fact be reached by profit-seeking firms if the curves fall as steeply as the familiar diagrams suggest, and it follows, once more, that the removal of restrictive practices would leave the market in what was still a sorry condition. The proper answer is then held to be the transfer to public ownership of all firms that would be operating with falling costs at the optimum position; these firms should be run deliberately at a loss which would be met from public funds. If this is really the right diagnosis, then it would be somewhat pointless to devote much attention to the removal of restrictive practices; it would be better to proceed at once with widespread nationalization.

On the face of it, the remedy seems a little desperate, and one can scarcely consider it seriously without taking account of all sorts of dynamic considerations excluded from the static welfare analysis.[6] How would the publicly-owned firms be organised and controlled? What would be the effect of nationalization on managerial efficiency, industrial relations and so on? Apart from any general effect on management of the transfer to public ownership, the subsequent decision to run the firms deliberately at a loss would have repercussions of a kind that would almost certainly be harmful. First of all, it would be extremely difficult to ascertain how far a loss reflected the application of the Marginal Rule and how far it was a consequence of inefficiency. It would certainly be difficult to convince managers of the need to reduce costs by better methods if they were also informed that total costs need not, and indeed should not, be covered. A subsidy per unit of output of a size specified in advance would still leave some restraint and some incentive; but the blank cheque recommended by the marginal theory might be disastrous. Secondly, it would not be easy to estimate whether new investment was justified if firms were not in fact selling at prices anywhere near those required to cover total costs and were therefore ignorant of how much consumers would pay if obliged to do so. There is the further more general objection that the losses would have to be met from taxation with the implication that the consumers of different commodities were being subsidized in varying degree as determined, not by special social considerations, but simply by the slope of the cost curves and the demand curves. Such an arrangement could be regarded as inequitable on the ground that consumers should pay in each case for what they get unless there are reasons less adventitious than elasticities for granting subsidies or imposing taxes. (Moreover taxation in itself offends some of the other marginal principles.)

In reply to such criticism it is sometimes maintained that it is better to follow a sound principle in face of the greatest practical difficulties than to compromise so much that all principles are destroyed and mere confusion results. From the opposite extreme in this debate it is often objected that the Marginal Rule "is all right in theory but hopeless in practice". Both of these conflicting statements must be rejected, the former as not strictly applicable, the latter as an example of a confused use of terms. The Marginal Rule is unacceptable because it is a bad *theory*. All theories abstract from reality but the part of reality excluded in the usual formulations of the Marginal Rule is far too important. Moreover, even as an exercise in analysis, the reasoning is somewhat faulty. The proposition that output should be expanded as long as the marginal cost is less than the price has strong *a priori* force only on the condition that marginal cost represents all the marginal sacrifices involved and price all the gain. To proceed from a general *a priori* statement to static analysis and then to try to derive conclusions immediately applicable to policy would not be "all right in theory"; it would be all wrong. In this case there is a special complication in that the *position* of the cost curves cannot be taken as independent of the application of the Rule: if the prescribed expansion of output can be carried out only by running at a loss and undermining managerial efficiency, then the cost curves will move upwards.

Is it then the case that a loss of social benefit must be accepted, if not on one count then on another? Although the Marginal Rule is not so unequivocally right as has often been suggested, it retains some validity. Must this be disregarded or the gain bought at high cost in other directions? The answer will depend partly upon the slope of the demand curves and the cost curves. Fortunately the precipitous descents usually represented in the diagrams are rarely based on empirical evidence; they reflect little more than the convenience of teachers who have to draw on blackboards and printers who have to make blocks! The long-run cost curves may fall sharply for a time but thereafter the decline is likely to be much more gradual, if it continues at all. Until recent years the demand curve received comparatively little attention in this apparently elaborate analysis: it seemed enough to say that few firms were likely to be confronted with an infinitely elastic demand curve in order to draw a curve for a "typical" firm that was very steep. But the demand curve, as well as the cost curve, will change its slope over time as customers learn more about alternatives and make new arrangements. It is not sufficient to say that many firms could raise their prices without losing all their custom; a few faithfuls whose loyalty will tolerate a higher price will be inadequate compensation for a large loss of more sensitive customers. That this loss may be swift as well as substantial, even in the case of well-known branded goods, seems to be indicated by certain case studies.[7] Moreover one must distinguish between the demand curves for a firm's output as it actually is, if one could ascertain the facts, and the assumptions about demand on which the firm's policy is based. There is a good deal of evidence to indicate that firms often take a long view and place much emphasis on good-will even at the expense of short-run profits. Although they may not think in terms of a curve at all, their attitude may be such as would be consistent with fairly elastic curves. If this is indeed the case, marginal cost is not likely to diverge so much from price over a wide range of industry as the orthodox diagrammatic analysis would suggest. For the same reason the loss of economies of scale will be less serious. Thus, in the absence of restrictive agreements, the operation of the market—as judged simply by the marginal criterion—may be less unsatisfactory after all.

There are two further points that must be made before leaving this discussion of the marginal analysis. The first is that in those firms where costs appear to be falling sharply in the long-run, there is a case for expanding production as much as may be consistent with the covering of costs by the firm. It follows that price discrimination of one form or another, including the use of two-part tariffs, appears to be justified on welfare grounds. It may be noted in passing that this use of the word "discrimination" differs somewhat from the use to which it is put in most discussions of restrictive practices. The second point is that it is wrong to allow bygones to influence policy. This general proposition of the theory of opportunity costs has come to be somehow peculiarly associated with the marginal analysis and may even seem to afford a justification for the Marginal Rule. In fact, the two propositions do not really come to the same thing. Perhaps the source of the confusion is the belief that whereas in the short-run, with certain factors fixed, a distinction may be made between average costs and marginal costs, no such distinction can hold in the long-run when "all costs are marginal"; although it is true to say that in the long-run all costs will be *represented* in a marginal curve, it is not true to say that a distinction between the average and the marginal will therefore disappear. It follows from this that one can think of average cost in a forward-looking or *ex ante* sense just as one thinks of marginal cost as *ex ante*. It is pretty clear that costs as a guide to action should be *ex ante* because it is only the alternatives still open that are relevant. Historical costs should not be the basis of action. Admittedly it may be necessary, *faute de mieux,* to use historical costs as some sort of guide to forward-looking costs; but it is only to this extent, and on this ground, that the use of historical costs can be justified.

(d) So far we have retained implicitly the conventional assumption that profit-seeking firms will try to equate marginal cost with marginal revenue. This assumption has come under heavy fire from two sources in recent years:[8] first, it has been criticized on the ground that the widespread presence of oligopoly makes the marginal analysis indeterminate; secondly, empirical work has shown that firms in many industries do not seem to behave in a way that, even after translation into academic jargon, seems to correspond to the marginal pattern. These firms seem to base their prices on some estimate of costs, and are price-makers rather than price-takers. The various theories of costed or administered prices can be regarded both as answers to the problems of oligopoly and as attempts to meet what empirical investigation seems, at least at first glance, to require. It is necessary to pay particular attention to this theory in the context of the present chapter, because one must anticipate that in many cases the market would be an oligopolistic one if restrictive practices were abandoned. Would this be a reasonably satisfactory state of affairs? Can it plausibly be supposed that it would represent any great improvement on the arrangements that prevail when restrictive practices are in force?

The calculation of a costed price appears to begin with an estimate of the prime cost per unit of the commodity in terms of direct labour, raw materials and bought-in components. Presumably the calculation is based upon past experience but with some allowance for probable changes in the prices of these factors or their productivity; the estimate may, therefore, be regarded as *ex ante*. An estimate of actual overheads will be made, largely in the form of historical costs, and this may then be turned into a figure for overheads per unit by assuming that the firm will, in fact, be operating at something like the capacity for which its plant and equipment were designed. The figure for costs, so determined, will thus be a combination of forward-looking prime costs and historical overheads. How will overhead costs be divided if the firm is producing a number of commodities with some costs in common? What allowance should be made for net profits? What will happen if demand at the costed price differs markedly from the supply the firm is offering? If the price is too low, the management may be content to carry on with waiting lists until production can be adjusted, although it may be apprehensive of retaliation if the price is significantly below that of its competitors. If the price is too high, its sales may fall sharply. On general grounds we would expect the firm to make some allowance for the state of demand even although it did not envisage a demand curve, and discussions with firms about the procedure they adopt tends to confirm this observation. Crude full-costing is not, therefore, a very convincing explanation of how matters are determined. The margin for profits will clearly take some account of what other firms in the industry are likely to be doing and will also allow for the possibility that new firms may enter the industry if the price is too high.[9] (Such newcomers may, of course, be well-established concerns although new to this particular line of production.) Can it then be inferred that the costing procedure is nothing more than an empty ritual? If it is the case that the price has to be adjusted in order to allow in some way for the competitiveness of the market, is there any point in going through the whole procedure of costing? I do not think that, in fact, the ritual is an empty one. The calculations provide the firm not only with an indication of its own capabilities, but also afford some sort of pointer to what its rivals can be expected to do.[10] It is true that the firm may make mistakes at this point and may underestimate, or conceivably overestimate, what other firms will be able to achieve. But the costing procedure at least provides a starting point; it narrows the range of possibilities. Such a procedure does not imply the abandonment of the maximisation of profits. It is necessary to stress this point because it is frequently assumed that administered prices are somehow inconsistent with the assumption that firms wish to maximise their gains. Surely it is rather the case that this method of fixing prices is one way of trying to get as large profits as possible, and it is a way that is believed to be adapted to the circumstances in which these firms find themselves. They have not the knowledge of the marginal curves usually implied in the formal textbooks, and they are also likely to be bemused by oligopolistic uncertainties. In such conditions, profit maximisation may well begin with some costing as a check on prices.

With this general reasoning in mind, we can now consider the proposition that oligopoly is inconsistent with price competition. If this proposition were really valid, the implications for policy would be far-reaching. Thus the Monopolies Commission has held that "it is generally true that price competition provides the keenest stimulus of all to the pursuit of efficiency."[11] But oligopoly, though not perhaps as universal as is sometimes suggested, is sufficiently widespread to suggest some doubts about the possibility of reviving price competition by abolishing restrictive agreements. Of course, if price competition and oligopoly were after all to appear consistent, then the prospect would be more hopeful. It is clearly necessary to examine in a little more detail the manner in which the competitive process is supposed to operate.

Now uniformity of prices has sometimes been regarded as evidence of the damage done to the public interest by a cartel; in the absence of a cartel such uniformity has sometimes been deemed to indicate informal collusion. The reasoning appears to be that where costs differ from one producer to another, the prices should also differ. What implicit assumption is being made about the formation of prices in competitive markets? If competition were atomistic and each firm were a price-taker, then a uniform price would prevail. The low-cost firms would not reduce their prices below the prevailing level in order to attract custom; it would be futile for them to do so. Their right course would be to expand production so long as their marginal costs remained below the market price and, if the rise in output from these firms as a group was significant, the price would then begin to fall. But there would still be only one price at any time for all producers—apart from transport costs, tariffs and the like. Thus the uniformity which appears to follow from the activities of trade associations, is also a feature of so-called "perfect" competition. Is it then under conditions of competitive oligopoly that differences in prices can be anticipated? It is just in such circumstances that prices are often said to be rigid because the fear of mutual retaliation prevents sellers from indulging in this form of competition. It is not, therefore, altogether clear what competitive model is being contrasted with the state of affairs that results from the activities of a cartel. It may be that contracting should be regarded in a somewhat different light from the production of goods that are produced and put on the market at fixed prices. Where such work consists of large new buildings, power plants, dams and the like, it is bespoke. One contract is different from any other and prices have to be specially calculated accordingly. In the absence of explicit agreement or secret collusion, one would certainly expect differences in the prices at which contractors offer to undertake work of such a kind. Here is a case where the more efficient firm would presumably be putting in lower tenders provided it had sufficient capacity to undertake additional work; but fears of retaliation might still enjoin some caution.

Let us now suppose that we are dealing with a small group of firms producing the same commodity. We shall further suppose that no single firm is so large and powerful as to be able to dominate the others completely, and that there is no collusion between the firms. Each concern will then, by means of its costings, try to form some sort of idea as to what is the "right" price. Some measure of competition will therefore be present: it will be felt at the point where the price is itself being fixed. Thus it would be untrue to suggest that there is no price competition in such circumstances. Suppose, however, that a price has, in fact, come to be accepted; the price may be a little higher than would be the case but for oligopolistic fears, but will in some degree reflect competitive pressures. Let us then assume that some firm makes marked improvements in its methods of production so that it can now produce more cheaply; it will want, as always, to expand its sales and it would be feasible to reduce its price in order to attract custom. But a cut might provoke a price war that could be damaging even if the more efficient firm was able to hold its relative position. In fact it might suffer severely because, notwithstanding its efficiency, it may not be a large and strong concern. Efficiency and dominating size do not always go together. It may, therefore, be more prudent to avoid the provocation of a cut price, but the more efficient firm will still be able to expand relatively to the others, though more slowly. At a given price its profits will be larger, it will acquire greater financial strength and it will be better able to invest. When the product is changed as well as the process, there will be more scope for making what in effect amounts to a reduction in price; a better article can now be offered without ostensibly cutting the price and, even if the other firms seek to retaliate, they will not be in such a strong position to do so if their products are obsolescent.

Next let us consider the case of a firm that is falling behind the general level of efficiency in its industry. If it is tendering for contracts at prices that would give it a reasonable profit, it will fail to get them unless demand is so much in excess of supply that competition has lost its edge. If it is selling a manufactured consumers' product and has advertised a price that is proving to be too high, it will find itself in an embarrassing position. An immediate reduction in price would be a confession that too much had been asked: goodwill might be damaged and the quality of the article might even become suspect. It may be better to carry on for a time with rising stocks until more indirect ways of selling at a discount, perhaps through special distributive channels, can be exploited. Meanwhile it will be under a powerful incentive both to lower its costs and to substitute another product at a better price.

It is, in my view, a somewhat confusing use of language to maintain that, in oligopolistic circumstances of the kind envisaged, there is no price competition. The level of prices *is* influenced by competitive forces, but the operation of these forces will vary in some measure with the structure of the market and the manner in which prices are determined. It cannot surely be claimed that price competition is unknown in, for example, the motor-car industries of either the United States or Britain; if it is so claimed, then price competition is being defined implicitly in a somewhat special way. Perhaps the conditions in which competition of this special kind could be anticipated are those corresponding to Professor Chamberlin's "large group" where (i) firms set increased sales against lower prices in a way that would be inappropriate if demand were infinitely elastic, but (ii) they need not be troubled by any fear of retaliation. It is now generally agreed, however, that the "large-group" is not a particularly relevant model.

The danger of retaliation may make an oligopolist hesitate to cut his price in order to enlarge his share of the market, but much will depend upon the state of demand for the output of the industry. In a period of recession, whether the recession is widespread or peculiar to the industry, there may be a strong temptation to lower the price below the level that would only be appropriate if output were running at a figure for which the plant were designed; at the same time, however, the fear of retaliation will be greatly intensified and even modest changes feared lest they give rise to widespread and mutually ruinous reductions. This is the cut-throat competition to be discussed in a later section. On a rising market, however, a firm may be able to expand its sales to an extent consistent with increased capacity without leaving its rivals with a large amount of unused capacity. The latter may cut their prices too but not so sharply as to cause serious embarrassment to the original price cutter for, if prices were reduced very severely, demand in the industry would exceed supply. The further point may be noted that under conditions of general inflation what are, in effect, competitive reductions of price may be made more confidently: that is to say prices for some products may not be advanced as much as factor prices. (Electric lamps are a good example in Britain.)

It was assumed above that each firm produced only one product. The analysis becomes more complicated when we suppose, realistically, that each firm produces a wide range of products. Not only does this make industry vastly more competitive because new entry is then greatly facilitated, but it also creates additional uncertainty about the fixing of prices because the allocation of common costs between different products is liable to be arbitrary. Perhaps some kind of formula —floor space or the like—may be generally adopted by all the firms concerned. But it is now going to be more difficult for them to hit upon a reasonable price that all will be able to accept. One firm may put a larger part of its common costs on to one product and less on to another than is regarded as appropriate by a second firm, and so on. A combination of oligopoly with joint production is one of the situations in which firms may be particularly inclined to form a cartel and determine their prices in a co-operative way. The temptation to do so will be all the stronger when overheads are a large part of total costs and when demand is highly unstable.

III

When a number of firms combine in order to fix prices, it is obvious that they intend to restrict competition, but it may not be their wish to abolish it altogether. Such an association is similar to an alliance between a group of nations who may be prepared to sacrifice some degree of independence in face of a common peril without abandoning completely their separate interests. The instability of alliances is a familiar theme of political history as rivalries revive and countries try to assert their claims at the expense of their allies. Cartels are likely to experience strains of a similar nature. That internal competition often continues is freely admitted by the cartels themselves, but it is usually indicated that it takes the form of improving the quality of the product, providing better ancillary services and so on. We shall have more to say later about these methods of competing, but the more immediate question is to ask whether competition in price is really eliminated by an agreement to sell only at common rates. In one sense the answer is so clearly in the affirmative that the question may appear to be pointless: if firms stick to the agreement and sell only at the prescribed rates, then those producing at lower cost will not be able to offer potential customers better value and thus attract their trade. But competition may make itself felt at the time when the common price is being fixed: the level chosen may then be lower than some members of the ring would wish. Now there is only a small amount of detailed information available about the manner in which these prices are determined by cartels and one can usually do no more than imagine the debates that presumably take place before a compromise is achieved. As we have already seen, however, in discussing oligopoly without collusion, price competition may take place without price cutting of this kind. With collusion, the force of competition will still affect the level at which the cartel sets its price.

On general grounds one would suppose this price to be set at a higher level with collusion than without, but allowance must be made for any greater stability that results from the cartel's activities. For the fixed price will be a maximum as well as a minimum and may, at certain times, be less than the market would bear. It seems to be the case, however, that oligopolists acting without collusion may also sometimes hold down their prices below those that equate supply and demand. (Moreover the consequent shortages and waiting lists are not always socially preferable to higher prices.) Even if it is the case that the cartel's price level will tend on average to be high, one must regard with some suspicion the familiar claim that it will be so high as to allow even its most inefficient members to make a comfortable profit. No doubt these firms will often be able to exert a significant influence and may sometimes succeed in having their way to an indefensible extent. But it would be surprising if, as a general rule, the worst firms were able to dominate policy. Suppose, for example, that the governing committee of the cartel sets itself to choose the most profitable price in much the same way as if it were the board of management of a unitary monopoly; the answer will not necessarily be a price so high as to be comfortable for the least efficient members. (In the same way, a company created by several mergers would not feel obliged to allow its price to be determined by the costs of its weakest establishments.) After all, the more efficient firms within the cartel will not be averse to expanding at the expense of their fellow members and will be more likely to do so at a lower common price. The fact that the price is common will, of course, determine the manner of their expansion: although they will not be able to tempt customers by offering lower prices, they can make profits and acquire funds for expansion and modernisation at a price which may gradually reduce their rivals' share or even force some of them out of the trade. The better firms will, however, be prepared to sacrifice their inclinations to some extent if, on balance, they consider that the cartel offers them certain advantages: they will then compromise and accept a somewhat higher price than they might otherwise wish. They may be the more inclined to do so if they fear a price war with one or two large firms that dominate the cartel without being its most efficient members—for the evidence of the Monopolies Commission confirms that size and efficiency do not always go together.[12]

With these general considerations in mind let us now turn to some of the information available about the way in which prices have been fixed by British cartels. This information is not only incomplete in that the number of industries covered is small but it is also, in many cases, inadequate and confusing not withstanding the efforts of the Monopolies Commission to ascertain the relationship between costs and prices in each of the industries it investigated.

In general the Monopolies Commission was dissatisfied with the arrangements adopted by cartels for relating prices to costs, and much criticism is contained in its reports. Sometimes the trouble arose from inadequate accounting, sometimes from a lack of comparability between the accounts of different companies. As might be expected special difficulties were caused by the spreading of common costs when there was joint production. Moreover, apart from any such defects in the estimates of costs, it was frequently suggested that prices were not properly related to the calculations of costs. For example, in the case of *semi-manufactures of copper*, the Commission complained that "the individual costs which are averaged are themselves unsatisfactory and, further, the prices fixed by the associations do not in fact bear any close relation to that unsatisfactory average. It follows that the relationship between the price which an individual member is required to charge for particular goods, and his own costs of producing those goods is remote."[13] In the case of *cast-iron rainwater goods* it was found to be difficult to get a clear picture of costs because each foundry produced so many other goods, and it was not easy to separate the costs attributable to rainwater goods.[14] The same problem arose in the case of *calico printing*. Here it was pointed out that the printers generally undertook work other then printing on commission, and that they could not, in most cases, distinguish the costs incurred by the printing. It would appear that the prices fixed by the Federation of Calico Printers were, therefore, somewhat arbitrary. These prices were, of course, adjusted from time to time in order to take account of changes in the cost of the raw materials and of labour. Moreover attempts were made to adjust the relationship between prices of different kinds of calico-printing to the types of material used, the weight and value of the cloth, the number of rollers, and so on; this, however, was only a very incomplete way of calculating a price for each particular type of cloth that would reflect the costs of the firms producing it.

The procedure adopted by some cartels was to calculate a weighted average of the costs of its members. Something like this appears to have been done in the *linoleum industry* where a weighted average was obtained for the more important products. The costs, however, were not based on a standard system of accounting and the Linoleum Manufacturers' Association appeared to use the average only as a rough guide in fixing prices; indeed, it was explained that they had no formula for arriving exactly at a price from the weighted average of costs.[15] The *Metal Windows Association* obtained a weighted average of costs by a somewhat complicated formula and added a target rate of profit ranging from 7½ to 10 per cent. for popular types of window.[16] *The Tyre Manufacturers' Conference* also made use of a weighted average in preparing the prices it recommended for the sale of tyres for replacement; in this case the average was much affected by changes in the costs of the largest producer, the Dunlop Rubber Company.[17] *The Scottish Bakers,* whose agreement came before the new Restrictive Practices Court, arranged for a weighted average of costs to be prepared and an allowance for target profit was then added. It should be noted that, as in most cases, the costs were submitted to an outside person, usually an accountant, who prepared the average in some agreed way. The Association, which was itself subsequently responsible for fixing the price, had before it this weighted average but not as a rule the costs of its individual members nor even a proper indication of the spread of these costs.[18]

The *yarn spinners,* investigated by the Restrictive Practices Court in 1959, had a way of fixing prices that is of some analytical interest. The first step was to estimate the cost of the raw material and for this purpose a notional figure was taken that was supposed to indicate replacement cost. In principle, this appears to be the right *ex ante* approach but it will be appreciated that the estimate might reflect varying degrees of optimism or pessimism and, in fact, diverge from what was really justified as much as a crude *ex post* average. To this figure was added a margin for spinning cost derived from returns submitted by a representative number of mills. The highest one-third of these costs was ignored and the median of the remainder taken as a guide. An addition was then made for depreciation and interest "based on the area, layout, building, plant, machinery and equipment which would be required to establish, separately, seven representative modern freehold ring-spinning mills of the most economical size and operating methods..."[19] Thus an *ex ante* ingredient was again added to this somewhat strange cocktail. Mr. Justice Devlin observed that some of the machinery and equipment in the industry was old. "If they were bought at pre-war prices and if their value has already been largely written off, a figure for interest and depreciation calculated on post-war values may easily provide a big enough margin to absorb the higher operational cost and provide a profit." There would, of course, be no reason to object to such a profit if the *price* were at a "proper" level—in the sense that the competitive pressure of the more efficient firms was not inhibited—and in considering this level it is irrelevant whether capital has been written off or not. But it is clear that the price of yarn, as determined by this formula, was not right. In considering whether new capital should be installed it is customary to say that the annual running costs on the old should be compared with the annual total costs on the new. What was remarkable, in my view, about the yarn spinners' formula was the combination of running costs on the old with capital costs on the new. In principle such a procedure could scarcely be justified and was likely to be a deterrent to innovation. It is only fair to add that the resulting price was made less extravagant by (i) eliminating the highest one-third of the running costs and (ii) by allowing for only a modest return on the new hypothetical capital. Nevertheless, in Mr. Justice Devlin's view: "One way or another the minimum price appears to insure a reasonable return all the time for the majority of spinners."[20]

We have already referred to the complications that arise in the case of contracting. The *London Builders' Conference* operated for some years what was called a Fair Price Scheme.[21] The chairman of the conference determined the Fair Price for a particular job on the basis of preliminary prices that had been quoted to him. If he considered that all the tenders were "genuine and economic", he chose the lowest price as the fair one, subject to the addition of a Tenad, a sum to be divided among the unsuccessful tenderers. The reason for this addition was that tendering is an expensive business and unsuccessful tenderers should be compensated in some way. (Alternatively the compensation might presumably be obtained on the average from the actual prices.) If the chairman considered the tender to be in some respect uneconomic he averaged the lowest two-thirds of the prices quoted and then calculated a sum to be added to the lowest price quoted in order to bring it up to this average. This surcharge was called the Conad; once more the Tenad was included.

The *Watertube Boilermakers' Association* had an arrangement by which the cartel simply allocated a particular contract to one of its members; all the others then quoted higher prices.[22] This arrangement was abandoned at the beginning of 1957 when it was recognised that it would be a restriction within the meaning of the Act of the previous year. Another scheme was then introduced which came before the Restrictive Practices Court in 1959. The object of the new scheme was to spread the work among the members of the Association according to their respective needs to secure contracts in those cases where more than one firm had received an inquiry. A somewhat curious formula was devised by which a firm's trading results over the previous five years was compared with its percentage of trade in the relevant area over the years 1947 to 1956. If the previous five years' trade represented a decline as compared with its "basic" average, the company was in a strong position to claim to be awarded the new contract, although other considerations might be taken into account as well. The cartel then nominated a firm to do the job without at this stage paying any regard whatsoever to the prices at which various members of the Association were prepared to undertake it. These prices would have been previously submitted in confidence to the director who managed the scheme and he would now reveal them. The selected member to whom the contract had been awarded by the Association would then be free to adjust his own tendered price down to the lowest price tendered by any other member, although he would not be obliged to act in this way. Some statistics presented to the Court deserve mention at this point in order to ensure that the importance of this restrictive arrangement be seen in perspective. Out of 1048 inquiries from February 1957 to December 1958, 688 were addressed to only one of the British firms within the scheme which was therefore irrelevant in the majority of cases. Out of the remaining 360 cases the scheme was applied to 83. Of the 83, the selected member had quoted the lowest price in 43 cases, in the remaining 40 cases, the selected member reduced his price to some extent on 25 occasions.

The prices of the commodities that come within the purview of a cartel are sometimes determined primarily by the views of one of its members; price leadership can exist within such an association as well as in an industry without a cartel. This was the procedure in the case of *matches* where the price adopted was that of Brymay, the largest producer in the Association and also as it happened the highest cost producer;[23] admittedly the situation was greatly complicated in this case by the fact that the various concerns were subsidiaries of a holding company, the British Match Corporation. In the case of *electric lamps*, the changes in prices were usually taken on the initiative of two of the largest members of the Electric Lamp Manufacturers Association, i.e. the General Electrical Company and Associated Electrical Industries. According to the Monopolies Commission, the first step taken by either of these firms would be to consult the other. Information about costs would then be exchanged and the next step would be to consult a third producer, Siemens, a firm that has subsequently been included in the A.E.I. group. The proposed change in price would then be put before the Council of the cartel and would generally be adopted. The Association itself explained that "the selling price for all is fixed by reference to the yardsticks established by the two largest and most experienced companies".[24] In the case of *rubber tyres*,[25] the price was determined mainly by the biggest of the British tyre manufacturers, the Dunlop Rubber Company. It has already been indicated that the costs of this company were of particular importance in affecting the weighted average used in working out the price for tyres sold for replacement. For tyres sold as original equipment and for exports, a weighted average was not constructed, but Dunlop's leadership was implicitly accepted. It is worth noting in passing that although the Dunlop Rubber Company was the largest producer its costs were by no means the lowest. It may be that price leadership will be accepted with less strain and embarrassment when the price leader itself is a medium-cost producer.

Although the Monopolies Commission had good reason to complain about the inadequacy of the information on costs and the lack, in so many cases, of comparability between the figures, it nevertheless succeeded in obtaining sufficient information to show that costs and profits varied widely between producers in many of the industries examined. Not only were there frequent instances of profits so low as to be trivial, but there were a good many cases of losses being made on particular lines of production. Such figures scarcely support the view that cartels always fix their prices at levels that allow even the least efficient producers to cover their costs and earn a comfortable profit. That particular charge may, I think, be dismissed. It is, however, interesting to ask why firms so often continue to produce at very small profit or, even more strikingly, at a loss. In some cases perhaps the firms may have been unaware that profits were not being made on particular lines of production until the costing investigation had been forced upon them. (If this is so, serious doubt is cast on the more rigid versions of the full-cost theory.) In other cases the losses may have simply reflected the somewhat arbitrary nature of the accounting procedures adopted by multi-product firms. In yet other cases, the firms may have been in process of winding up their unprofitable production: the industry, that is to say, may not have been in a state of equilibrium. This was clearly true of the manufacture of *television tubes and valves:* large losses were being made by some of the producers and it is of interest to note that some firms went out of production over the course of the two or three years after the Monopolies Commission had made its inquiry.[26]

What conclusion can be drawn, in the light of British experience, about the manner in which cartels affect the determination of prices? Is the effect much less than is sometimes supposed? Consider the case of tyres. Here price leadership was exercised by a large concern but this was unsupported by formal commitments to accept a particular price, even in the case of tyres sold for replacement where a weighted average of costs was calculated. May it not be true that the abolition of the Tyre Manufacturers' Conference would leave the situation largely unchanged because price leadership would be the natural outcome in an oligopolistic market of this kind? Indeed it is sometimes suggested that price leadership would be more widespread if cartels were abolished because it could be regarded as the alternative to the widespread price cutting and confusion that might otherwise occur in an unorganized oligopolistic market. Or consider the case of commodities such as metal windows and doors for which the prices were determined by the cartel with reference to a weighted average. If it is assumed that uniform prices can be expected for each commodity, is it then reasonable to suggest that the prices fixed with reference to such an average by the cartel would be fairly close to those that might emerge on a more competitive market? After all there is no warrant in economic theory for supposing that prices will be determined under competition by the most efficient firm, any more than that they will be determined by the least efficient. It is true that, as we have seen, some of the British cartels fixed their prices without any particular relationship to costs at all; this was the case especially when joint production made it difficult to isolate costs. But, even if no collusion took place, a somewhat arbitrary figure might emerge on a market where joint production together with oligopoly gave rise to a grave danger of instability.

The line of defence taken by the Council for the Yarn Spinners was that: "Low cost producers can only be held in the scheme if prices are sufficiently low to penalize the high cost producers and that requirement is satisfied by the Association's method of fixing margins based on the median of the lowest two-thirds of cost return."[27] It is, of course, one thing to concede that the cartel's price will not always be a comfortable one for the least efficient producers but a very different matter to suggest that the price will be as low as it would be under more competitive conditions. If it were just as low, the activities of the cartel would in some respects appear redundant. There are moreover sufficient pieces of information about the way in which prices are fixed to indicate that the cartel's price will, at least in the short run, usually be higher. Apart from these specific items of information relating to the way in which prices are fixed, the effect of the organisation of the market, for example with regard to new entry, is likely to leave prices at a higher level.

Even when an average of costs was calculated, it did not by any means follow that the final price would be related in any clear way to this average. It was so related in the case of *metal windows and doors*, but there were many instances where this was not so. To begin with, a margin for profits had to be added and this margin might be high or low according to views held about the pressure of competition outside the cartel. (For example, it is interesting to note that the prices of the lower grades of *linoleum* which encountered more outside competition were fixed rather lower relatively to costs than those of the higher grades.) Some cartels aimed at a particular percentage for profits but did not always adhere strictly to this figure. For example the *Scottish Bakers* had additional receipts for wrapping and slicing, flour rebates and cash discounts; indeed these additional sources of profit were nearly as large over the period examined as the baking margin.[28]

In the *linoleum industry* there was a ceiling clause which provided that any member could ask for the price to be reduced if it were 20 per cent. above his costs. This ceiling clause would appear to allow some flexibility in the arrangements, but in fact it had rarely been invoked when the Monopolies Commission made its investigation although, in 1954, nearly half of the total sales of the industry were above the ceiling. It is difficult to believe that the price would have stood as high as this even in an oligopolistic market if there had been no explicit price-fixing agreement.

IV

The extent to which prices are held above the competitive level by a cartel will depend not only upon the nature of the price agreement but upon the extent to which it is buttressed by other agreements. Of these the first we shall consider is the sharing of output by the different members of the cartel.

Such arrangements were not uncommon before the war but appear to have been less frequent subsequently than price-fixing agreements alone. Perhaps it is because a combination of fixed prices and quotas is so much more restrictive that such arrangements have been less popular at a time of booming trade. We have already dismissed the view that a cartel consists of a happy band of brothers who have laid aside their rivalries in order to unite in the common exploitation of the consumer, and have suggested that it should often be regarded as an uneasy alliance held together by compromise and requiring some degree of flexibility. The fixing of common prices may not, in itself, prevent the relative growth of the more efficient firms, although their growth may be retarded; quotas may, however, be a severe handicap. The more progressive firms will be restless, except perhaps during a general recession, if the restraints imposed upon them are very severe; such restraints may also endanger the position of the cartel if it is at all possible for new firms to enter the industry or for reasonable substitutes to be produced elsewhere.

In the United States the fixing of quotas is industry was ruled to be illegal *per se* as long ago as 1898 in *United States* versus *Addyston Pipe and Steel Company;* in United States agriculture, however, the state has adopted a very different attitude and restrictions have at times been officially imposed on what might otherwise have been an atomistically competitive industry—and have been cheerfully accepted. In Britain, the classical example also involved official action: in 1930, the Coal Mines Act provided for the determination of quotas for each colliery with penalties for production in excess and rewards for deficient production. In his recent essay on the coal industry, Professor Arthur Beacham observes: "It seems almost certain, therefore, that the general inefficiency of the industry in 1939 was partly the outcome of the 1930 Act."[29] It was hoped at the time that amalgamations would absorb many of the smaller units, and quotas were transferable; this hope, however, was largely disappointed.

To what extent, if any, can competitive pressures affect the determination of quotas? What provision is made for flexibility? Is the pattern of the industry allowed to change?

The quota allocated to a firm is usually based on its share of production in some selected historical period. Thus in the case of the *calico printers*, it is necessary to go back to the wartime arrangement for the concentration of the industry in 1941. Each firm was then allocated a quota based largely on its share of the market in the year ended June 1940—a year that appeared somewhat remote and scarcely "normal" when the industry was investigated in 1954. There was admittedly some provision for adapting the war-time proportions: a firm that exceeded its quota by, say, 10 per cent in one year, would be able to claim in the next year a quota larger by one-tenth of the previous excess i.e. by 1 per cent in the example taken. It could scarcely be said that such cautious adjustments provided scope for rapid expansion, although a little additional flexibility was introduced by a provision for the sale of quotas. The penalty for exceeding the prescribed output was a fine equal to 20 per cent of the excess turnover, while a deficiency was correspondingly rewarded.[30] This fine was held by the cartel not to be penal in the sense that it would not remove all the profit on marginal output, but it must surely have been a serious deterrent in an industry where the *average* profit on turnover was not greatly in excess of this figure.

The other illustration we shall take is the system of quotas for the sale of *electric lamps* which had its origin in the international Phoebus agreement of 1924.[31] Territorial quotas were then determined by reference to sales in a basic period and penalties were prescribed on an ascending scale of severity according to the extent to which a quota had been exceeded; once again, deficiencies were rewarded. The British Group had a single quota, which it had then to allocate among its members. This international agreement, revived after the war on a somewhat more limited scale, was the foundation of the system as investigated by the Monopolies Commission in 1951. The penalties had, however, been substantially reduced in 1948 and an upper limit was placed on the compensation for not producing. On the internal side, the scheme had been adjusted in various way after 1924 in order to allow another firm (Crompton) to come in and to provide supplementary quotas to two firms outside the Electric Lamp Manufacturers' Association. The Association did not in fact succeed in eliminating all independent competition in the types of lamp covered by the Phoebus Agreement, and was also threatened by competition from lower quality lamps; controlled companies, formally outside the cartel, were used to meet it.

A quota system of this kind seems more surprising in a modern growing industry, such as that producing electric lamps, than in an older industry, such as calico printing. In defence, it was urged by ELMA that the fines for "excessive" production, as revised in 1948, were not a serious hindrance: "since the manufacturer retains a substantial proportion of the (marginal) profit, there remains an adequate incentive to increase his share of the market". If so, the Monopolies Commission appears to have been justified in concluding that an elaborate and unnecessary piece of administrative machinery is being maintained.[31] In so far, however, as the fines were a real deterrent, the public interest was likely to be damaged.

In some cases where the Monopolies Commission did not recommend the abolition of price-fixing by the cartel, it proposed that other types of restrictive practices should be abandoned. For example, price-fixing might continue for electric lamps and for cables but quotas, exclusive dealing and discriminatory rebates were to go and, in the case of lamps, restrictions on patents and the use of fighting companies were also condemned. In justification of such recommendations, it is a reasonable presumption that the cartel will fix its prices at a lower level if the efficient firms are not hampered by quotas and new entry is not restricted. A similar consideration applies where the abandonment of the price agreement would in itself appear to leave the form of the market basically unchanged. So much was indicated by the Monopolies Commission in its *Report on the Supply and Export of Pneumatic Tyres.* It was conceded, in effect, that the market was oligopolistic and price leadership was to be expected in the various parts of the market if the restrictive agreements, formal and informal, were to be dropped. The prices charged by different firms might continue to be more or less identical, but something would have been gained because "the general level of prices would be different."[32] In fixing his prices, the leader must have regard to the possibility that his position may be challenged by competitors inside the industry or by potential newcomers; if these rivals can be rendered harmless or at all events seriously handicapped by various restrictions, the leader's prices may be set at different levels from those that would be chosen in an oligopolistic, but unrestricted, market. Such considerations suggest that the Monopolies Commission was right in laying so much stress on freedom of entry as a way of ensuring that prices are reasonable whether or not the prices themselves are determined by agreement among the producers.

In this connection a distinction must be drawn between collective and individual resale price maintenance. Both have the effect of reducing competition within the retail trade but their effect on manufacturing industry may be by no means the same. Collective resale price maintenance allows the more efficient manufacturer to pass on the benefits of his economies only to the extent that the association as a whole is prepared to sanction the change; the penalties may be such as to deny the offender an outlet. Individual resale price maintenance need not imply restriction of this kind and it may, moreover, facilitate new entry. A manufacturer who wants to persuade a retailer to stock his products may naturally encounter some reluctance if his firm is little known or if he is trying to enter what is for him a new market. It will probably be easier to overcome this reluctance if he can offer a definite margin that will not be threatened by price-cutting on the part of other retailers. It may be suggested that such price-cutting would be a way of extending the sales of the new commodity but this is not necessarily so. Such cuts might well be taken as proof that the commodity, already viewed with some reserve on account of its newness, had proved to be such a failure that it had to be sold off cheaply.* (It is, of course, desirable that the price initially announced should be low—a very different matter).

The evidence put forward in this section does not lend much support to the view that price-fixing, the control of production, exclusive dealing and the like are socially justifiable. The suggestion that individual resale price maintenance may sometimes assist new entry has been the only favourable mark so far. The next step is to consider more fully and explicitly the arguments in favour of restrictive practices and to ask whether these outweigh the disadvantage of higher prices that the evidence of the present section appears to have established.

* This is only one of the many considerations that are relevant in assessing the effects of resale price maintenance, though it is not the most familiar. More attention is usually given to the alleged danger that in the absence of resale price maintenance some popular commodities may be used as "loss leaders" which would cause uncertainty for the manufacturer. This is not, I think, an important contention. Loss leaders might do little harm and might not, in any case, appear. In Canada, r.p.m. was prohibited in 1952 on the recommendation of the MacQuarrie Committee. Three years later a special inquiry by the Restrictive Trade Practices Commission revealed that serious cases of the use of a loss leader had been rare. (See the chapter on Canada by W. Gordon Blair in *Anti-Trust Laws*, ed. by W. Friedmann. London, Stevens & Sons Ltd., 1956.)

V

The arguments in favour of restrictive practices will now be considered. It will be convenient at the outset to summarise these arguments under a number of headings which will serve to indicate the lay-out of this section. Restrictive practices may be thought desirable, from a social as well as a private viewpoint, in order:

(I) to prevent cut-throat competition and to ensure reasonable stability of prices;
(II) to protect the consumer from a deterioration of quality and service in general and, more particularly, to protect him against a deterioration that may affect his safety;
(III) to obtain from receipts a surplus that can be used to finance some other product or some desirable objective such as research and development;
(IV) to encourage firms to share their trade secrets and to make more feasible the joint planning of new investment in such a way as to avoid waste and duplication;
(V) to preserve the level of employment;
(VI) to foster exports or to protect the domestic economy against imports;
(VII) to cope with those problems that may now be conveniently brought together under the label "countervailing power";
(VIII) to prevent excessive concentration in an industry.

Some of these considerations that may be advanced in favour of cartels have in fact been accepted as possible grounds of defence under Section 21 of the British Restrictive Practices Act of 1956 which is set out in the Appendix.[33]

(I) The need to prevent cut-throat competition has been one of the considerations most frequently put forward in defence of cartels to the Monopolies Commission and to the Restrictive Practices Court. It was held that unless some form of agreement were in existence, producers would engage in the most extravagant price-cutting which would lower prices well below costs and prove to be mutually ruinous to the competitors. Nor would they alone be the sufferers. The consumer himself—so the argument runs—could scarcely hope to benefit in the end from such price-cutting even if he had initially a deceptive and transient gain. In a famous judgment of 1914 Lord Chief Justice Haldane presented the argument in the following words: "Unquestionably the combination in question was one the purpose of which was to regulate supply and to keep up prices. But an ill-regulated supply and unremunerative price may, in point of fact, be disadvantageous to the public. Such a state of things may, if it is not controlled, drive manufacturers out of business, or lower wages, and so cause unemployment and labour disturbance."[34] It is not perhaps surprising that such considerations should be strongly pressed in defence of restrictive agreements in declining industries where a large amount of excess capacity is in existence. What is more surprising is to find the same argument presented by industries that are in a technologically favourable position and can expect their sales to grow with rising national income.

Let us first, however, consider the case of the declining industry. Is it reasonable that even in this case prices should be fixed by agreement between the producers? How in this situation will price-fixing help? Indeed it is very likely that price-fixing will not prove to be workable unless it is strengthened by output quotas which will share the limited amount of work among the firms. It can scarcely be claimed that such a situation is one that should be perpetuated indefinitely. The industry is clearly out of equilibrium but nothing will be done to remedy the position if the shrinking volume of sales is merely distributed among the given number of firms. No doubt the number of firms will gradually contract as managements decide not to replace capital and leave the industry. As the Restrictive Practices Court observed: "Excess capacity in any industry means short-time working and idle plant. It is in the public interest that labour and capital should be employed as productively as possible, and we consider, therefore, that the excess capacity in the cotton industry is a public detriment."[35] It may be held that the existence of excess capacity has the further disadvantage of discouraging new investment, but it is not clear that new investment would be desirable in such circumstances. If the existing plant permits production at prices lower than those at which it would be possible with new plants, then the old should continue to be used.

If it is assumed, as we have done, that the industry must contract, the question is how the contraction can be brought about most quickly and smoothly with the least damage and the least hardship. Competition by means of price cutting is obviously not the worst way. It is true that prices may be driven below average costs even in the most efficient of the plants. But this is not necessarily wrong. The consumer will derive the benefit of cheap production even if prices do little more than cover running costs. The plant is already in existence and bygones are bygones. Some firms will go bankrupt but it would be a sorry comment on the present state of private enterprise if bankruptcy as a way of reducing the size of an industry were held to be almost intolerable. So much may be conceded, but it may be argued that the producers in a declining industry, such as cotton, may prove to be extremely obstinate and inclined to hang on a very long time. Thus the contraction of the industry will be a slow process and it will fail during this period to attract both new and able management and labour of good quality. This argument, too, is not altogether convincing. The fixing of prices and the allocation of quotas will scarcely put the industry in a position where it will be attractive to dynamic managers: on the contrary it will then be so organised as to make a vigorous new manager more or less impotent. More weight may, perhaps, be given to the consideration that it is not always the efficient who will survive a spell of price cutting: some firms that are now less efficient may still have larger liquid reserves on which they can survive. Price competition may not therefore yield the desired results in all cases, but it remains to find a method that is, on balance, preferable. One alternative is a scheme for deliberately reducing the number of establishments in the industry by administrative means. This is what was meant by the term "rationalisation" that was so generally current before the war. If the process of rationalisation is left to the industry itself to organise, it will be necessary for its planning committee to select what it regards as the most appropriate units for closing down. The selection will not be an easy matter, even if it is done in the most public-spirited way. It may be that competition by means of prices would in the end select the victims more efficiently. At all events in the classical case in Britain, that of *shipbuilding* between the wars, the scheme organised by the industry resulted in the closing down of some of the more suitably sited shipyards on the Clyde and the preservation of others at places where the river was narrow and unsuitable for the launching of large ships. There can be little doubt that the efficiency of the industry has suffered, and continues to suffer, from this "rationalisation". On the other hand, the political reluctance to allow the price system to do its work is obviously very marked. Shortly after the Restrictive Practices Court ruled that the arrangements for fixing prices of *cotton yarn* were contrary to the Act, the Government itself introduced a new scheme for concentration and reorganisation. One would perhaps not be going too far if one were to say that in the eyes of legislators, competition that is "workable" does not include atomistic competition in a depressed industry.

The fear of cut-throat competition has been expressed by several industries that can in no sense be described as declining, such as branches of the *electrical and allied trades*. It was, however, represented to the Monopolies Commission that these industries were subject to sharp fluctuations in activity, that capital costs formed a high part of their total outgoings and that there would be a danger of mutually wasteful price-cutting during recessions unless agreements were allowed to persist.[36] This argument was presented as follows by the *Council of the Water-tube Boilermakers:* "If there were a shortage of capacity the arrangement would be unnecessary, and if there were any permanent surplus capacity it would be undesirable. But where there is a temporary surplus capacity which will be required in the future, any arrangements tending to preserve that capacity, if it would otherwise be lost, is in the public interest." It is not altogether clear how such capacity would be lost in such circumstances. Even if there were violent competition and one or two firms in an oligopolistic industry went bankrupt, their capacity would not necessarily be scrapped but might very well be bought up by new firms or taken over by some of their competitors. It became clear in this case, however, that what the industry had in mind was not physical capacity but highly skilled employees who might be dismissed. In this form the argument was even less convincing and it was also difficult to attach much plausibility to the further contention that research would suffer because the industry would be unable to finance it during a recession. The industry consisted of a few large strong well-established firms and it seemed inconceivable that they would be incapable of taking a reasonably long view apart from any explicit arrangement to prevent price competition.[37] The most effective rejoinder to arguments of this kind is that many industries where there are no price agreements manage nevertheless to survive recessions without the disasters so vividly described. In America where agreements of this type would be deemed illegal *per se*, industry somehow manages to survive and progress! In Britain itself the motor car industry is scarcely free from booms and recessions, but it does not indulge in frantic spells of price cutting when trade is somewhat depressed. It is true, however, that an industry that has been accustomed to an explicit agreement may indulge in a severe spell of price cutting, if the agreement is removed at a time of poor trade. This is what in fact happened in the case of the *cable* industry.* After an investigation by the Monopolies Commission, certain quota schemes and arrangements for exclusive dealing and rebates were abandoned "by voluntary agreement" in 1954. An arrangement for common prices was replaced by one for minimum prices subject to Government review. This arrangement was in turn abandoned after the new Act came into force. Then, after a brief spell of cut prices, which seems to have done the industry no very serious harm although embarrassment might have been caused had it continued much longer, price leadership took the place of the old system of prices fixed by a cartel. The price leader is British Insulated Callender's Cables which accounts for something like two-fifths of the total production of main cables. This part of the industry is fairly highly concentrated but in the part that produces wire for general purposes there are still about forty producers. Here, too, price leadership has emerged under B.I.C.C., although it came rather more slowly and appears to be less firmly and completely established.[38] It is, of course, impossible to give any clear and unequivocal answer to the question whether the level of prices that is emerging with price leadership is different from what would have emerged had the cartel been allowed to continue undisturbed. On general grounds, however, one can make a reasonably favourable assumption that prices will be somewhat lower as a consequence of the greater competitiveness following upon the abolition of quota schemes, exclusive dealing and rebates.

The contention that agreements were needed in order to prevent violent price cutting and instability was sometimes supported by arguments so extravagant as to be fanciful. For example the *Association of Dental Manufacturers and Traders* claimed that without resale price maintenance, collectively enforced prices would be cut so much that traders would not find it economic to carry stocks, with the result that there would be shortages and the unfortunate consumer would be left toothless.[39]

(II) One of the most frequent arguments advanced by the defenders of price agreements was the beneficial effect they would have on the quality of the product.[40] First of all, there would be a positive gain because competition, diverted from price, would manifest itself in attempts to provide the consumer with a better product; secondly, in addition to this positive gain, there would be the negative advantage

* I am informed by Mr. J. B. Heath that the prices fixed by the association were in any case under pressure, and reductions might well have occurred even if the agreement had remained in force.

of preventing the deterioration of quality below existing standards that would occur if price competition were resumed. It is always a little puzzling to find that firms do not seem to be concerned about the danger of cut-throat competition in the improvement of quality or even in advertising. Yet the offer of a better product for the same price could be regarded as merely a roundabout way of reducing the price level itself. Is it not therefore conceivable that firms might carry such competition too far in the circumstances in which they might also carry price-cutting too far? For some reason, however, this possibility is rarely mentioned. A similar danger arises in the case of advertising including the giving of presents to purchasers of the products. Why is it that cut-throat advertising is not feared as well as cut-throat pricing?[41] Perhaps the explanation is that competition by advertising, or by innovation and change of product, will require additional outlay whereas prices can be cut without any such extra expenditure by the firms concerned; therefore, at a time of really serious depression the temptation to cut prices may be more attractive than the temptation to compete in ways that would also involve additional expenditure. In less depressed conditions, however, the fear of extravagant price competition may be no more justified than would be fears of excessive non-price competition. (Indeed, excessive advertising may be a stronger probability.)

Competition in the form of improved quality may undoubtedly take place although a cartel prevents competition by price-cutting. In much the same way there may be an incentive in an oligopolistic market without collusion to change the product rather than simply to lower the price of the product already available. The fear of retaliation may be somewhat less in the former case. It is probably true to say that, whether the fruit of collusion or not, uniform prices for a given type and quality of product tend to afford a strong inducement to change the product as well as the process of manufacture. There may therefore be some effect on the form that technological advance takes. At all events it may be conceded that the consumer will benefit from this competition in quality. What cannot be so readily conceded is that he should be obliged to take the benefits of progress simply in this way. Why should he not have the choice between existing products at lower prices and new products at different prices? His range of choice appears to be unreasonably narrowed by the activities of cartels.

In some cases the manufacturers have maintained that it would be improper to allow the consumer this freedom because he is so incapable of judging what is best. Thus the makers of *tyres* claimed that collective resale price maintenance was necessary in order to ensure that proper services were provided by the garages without which the danger of accidents would be increased. The Dunlop Rubber Company went so far as to say: "The only way to make buyers use this service is to make them pay for it, in the expectation that, having paid for it, they will use it."[42] Under the Restrictive Practices Act of 1956, the first of the grounds on which an exception might be made to the general prohibition of restrictive practices, is that such practices are necessary in order to protect the public from some injury. It is interesting to observe, however, that when a plea was made under this heading by the *Chemists' Federation*,[43] on the ground that only qualified chemists should be allowed to sell a wide range of proprietary drugs, the Court rejected the contention. That there is a need to protect the public from bad quality and deceptive advertising will be very generally recognised. But it is not obvious that collective resale price maintenance together with a wide range of other restrictive devices represents the best way of achieving this end. A further reason why it is difficult to accept at face value the arguments for restrictive practices on grounds of safety, is that there are other industries where such restrictions do not exist, apparently without disastrous results. It is not clear, for example, why restrictions should be necessary in the tyre industry, whereas the assembly of the motor cars themselves can be carried out without the necessity of restrictive practices in order to ensure that proper regard be paid to safety.

In assessing the likelihood of deteriorated quality one must recall that a large part of output will be sold not to ignorant consumers but to expert buyers who would not readily be deceived. Mr. P. W. S. Andrews has very rightly laid considerable stress on this fact in order to dispel the exaggeration in the theories of monopolistic competition about the way in which product differentiation may mislead the consumer.[44] By the same token, the fears expressed by the cartels must also be viewed with some scepticism. Consider, for example, the case of the manufacturers of *cables*. It seems unlikely that a major electrical undertaking or an undertaking responsible for telegraphic communications would grasp eagerly at a lower price and pay no attention to a fall in quality. Nor can one attach much credence to the suggestion of the *dental manufacturers* that the quality of artificial teeth would deteriorate without their elaborate system of regulation. The manufacturers of *water-tube boilers* tried to persuade the Restrictive Practices Court that in their case, too, quality would decline although the bulk of their output for the domestic market was sold to the Central Electricity Authority; their argument was dismissed by the judge in his summing up. A similar contention was advanced by the manufacturers of *heavy electrical machinery* when they were cross-examined by the Monopolies Commission. It does not seem unfair to conclude that the argument about a deterioration of quality is often quite perfunctory and is advanced simply as a matter of routine without any attempt to ask whether it is relevant in the circumstances.

In discussions of resale price maintenance, a good deal has been said about the possible effect of its abolition on the quality of the services supplied by the shopkeepers: it is often predicted that the shopkeepers would be less attentive, the shops would be less attractive, delivery would not then be provided, there would be inadequate arrangements for the repair and maintenance of goods where this was relevant and so on. It is probably true to say that the shops that cut their prices very tightly would not be able to offer these services on quite such an elaborate scale. Once more, however, it may be rejoined that purchasers should be given the freedom to choose between the not very pleasant low-price shop and the more attractive and more convenient shop where prices were slightly higher. (There may, of course, be other reasons for preserving resale price maintenance, as already indicated.)

(III) In discussing some of the services which may go with the supply of a commodity we have already begun to touch on the difficult problem of spreading common costs and discrimination. The term discrimination is a highly ambiguous one. It may mean the charging of discriminatory prices in favour of members of an association or the provision on specially favourable terms of raw materials, components or services. It was in this sense that the term was used by the Monopolies Commission in its report on *Collective Discrimination*.[45] Sometimes what is intended is a difference in charges that reflects differences in costs: this is what is meant by "permissible discrimination" under the Clayton Act. In analytical works discrimination often means that the same commodity is sold at different prices to different purchasers, not because some are and some are not members of an association, but rather because their demands vary in intensity and they are treated accordingly. Thus a higher price would be charged to the purchasers with an inelastic demand than is charged to those with a more elastic demand. The feasibility of doing so depends of course on the possibility of separating the different groups of purchasers so as to prevent sales between them. A related meaning of discrimination concerns the treatment of common costs; for example, on the railways the differences in charges do not simply reflect differences in attributable costs but are rather based on some estimate of what the market will bear—or should be so based, if the job is being done efficiently. The service supplied to each purchaser is not the same but the differences in charges do not correspond in any way to differences in costs. In yet other cases the services may be quite distinct, for example, the supply of new motor cars and of repair facilities. The demand is nevertheless to some extent a joint demand and what is often done is to make one service help to meet the cost of another.

An example sometimes quoted is that of gramophone records. The more popular records earn high profits while the more highbrow records are sold at very little profit or even at a loss. It is held that there is a social advantage in having the highbrow records subsidized in this way. A somewhat similar argument is sometimes advanced in defence of the British "net book agreement". It is held that by maintaining the prices of books a sufficient margin is earned on the more popular works to allow booksellers to stock other works on a scale that would otherwise be impossible. Were it not for this type of arrangement the popular books would be sold at lower prices by department stores, drug stores and the like, which do not and would not undertake to sell books with a slower turnover; thus the real booksellers would be deprived of the more profitable part of their trade and would not be able to maintain their function of supplying the more highbrow works. The argument here is a cultural one. It is admitted that some discrimination takes place, but this is defended on the ground that it is right for the vulgar to be made to subsidize the learned. In reply it may be urged that if some subsidization is necessary the issue ought to be determined by Parliament and open subsidy given through the Budget. A rejoinder would be that in fact Parliament would be unlikely to behave in this way, or, if it did, very difficult issues would be raised in selecting the beneficiaries for public aid. We should apply a pragmatic test and thus be prepared to acquit a private arrangement that works reasonably well in practice. There are, of course, many other cases where no such argument would be advanced. A particularly interesting one in Britain was the case of television tubes and radio valves.[46] The market here may be divided into the supply of such goods for initial equipment and the supply for replacement. In the case of initial equipment there is no price agreement between the producing firms. Each firm is free to compete although the relations between valvemakers and assemblers are so technical and involve so much research that they are likely to remain fairly stable for a considerable period except in so far as mergers take place between the valve companies themselves. The prices of the valves sold for replacement, however, were collectively maintained by the British Valvemakers Association at what were extremely high levels. These prices were not worked out with any close regard to costs and it was not denied that the profit was large except in the case of the less efficient firms. The large profit earned in this way made it possible to sell the valves for initial equipment rather more cheaply than they might otherwise have been sold. Why should this arrangement have been made? It can perhaps be argued that there is a case for selling the commodity cheaply in order to keep down the initial price of a television set or a radio because in this way purchasers can be attracted. Once the set has been bought, however, the owner will want to keep it in working order and can, therefore, be made to pay much higher prices for replacements.

A similar procedure was adopted by the manufacturers of components for the motor-car industry.[47] It seems doubtful whether discrimination of this kind could be brought within the provisional defence of discrimination that has been derived from the Marginal Rule. Here it is not a case of charging different persons different prices according to the varying elasticities of their demand curves but rather of charging the same people different prices at different times. What it implies, in fact, is the attempted exploitation of short-sightedness. (The attempt may not always succeed: an enterprising rival may offer cheap components for replacement as a special attraction to initial purchasers.)

A more important argument in favour of discrimination is that the prices of certain established commodities should be held at a sufficiently high level to finance research and development on some other commodities. The price of gramophone records, for example, should yield profits above the "normal" level required for their production in order to provide funds for costly experiments with computers, navigators and the like, within multi-product firms. It will be appreciated that this argument is also different from the one based on the Marginal Rule; it is dynamic whereas the latter is static.

"Abnormal" profits, made possible by restrictive agreements, may thus be defended on the ground that innovation will be fostered thereby. If it is suggested that the funds required could be obtained from outside the firm, it may be replied that lower profits would not only reduce the supply of internal finance but would also make it more difficult to resort to the capital market. Investors, it may be argued, will risk their capital only if they are satisfied with realised results; they cannot be expected to finance expenditure on esoteric projects of which the outcome must remain unknown for several years. If it were further objected that it is arbitrary and unfair to "tax" the consumers of one commodity in order to foster the development of another, the rejoinder might be that such discriminatory practices are commonplace even when explicit restrictions do not exist; the object of the restrictions is to arrive at a more generally accepted and rational procedure.* Discrimination may of course be possible without an agreement but an agreement will provide protection against "pirates". A group of responsibly minded firms may be prepared to keep up the price of such bread-and-butter lines as television receivers in order to finance the development of quite new products, but there is always the danger that their markets may be threatened by firms prepared to sell such receivers more cheaply because they make no attempt to contribute to industrial innovation and are content to imitate others when products have been sufficiently established to become profitable.[48] Restrictive agreements may keep such pirates out.

It must, I think, be conceded that these arguments in defence of restrictive agreements have some validity. Just as expenditure by the state may foster research and development (e.g. in the aircraft industry), so may discriminatory pricing by private firms. The question is whether there is sufficient substance in the argument to out-weigh the disadvantages. The first reason for doubt is that although abnormal profits are sometimes used in this manner, they need not be. Although it has become common practice in Britain to refer to the assistance given to research by restrictive agreements, there have been many such cases where research appears to be conducted on only a

* A striking example of discrimination was afforded by the Monopolies Commission's investigation of the Electric Lamp Industry. It was reported that "only about 10 per cent. of the total capital employed by the E.L.M.A. members in the whole of their undertakings is employed in their home lamp business but that, immediately before the war, the estimated distributed profits on this business were nearly 30 per cent. of the distributed profits on the whole of their undertakings. This fact appears to us to explain to some extent the very large amount of care and attention which has been devoted by E.L.M.A. members, over a large number of years, to regulating the trade in electric lamps" (*Report*, para. 255). How far the abnormal profits on lamps helped innovation is not clear.

very modest scale. For example the counsel defending the *Scottish Bakers* before the Restrictive Practices Court "very wisely conceded that he could not substantiate his claim in respect of research".[49] The *Blanket Manufacturers* also failed to convince the Court. The manufacturers of *Water-Tube Boilers* referred to their collective expenditure on research but the sum was trivial; their individual expenditure may have been more substantial but the Court was of the opinion that, if such research were desirable, it would be made even if there were no agreement. If restrictive agreements help innovation by swelling undistributed profits and giving a greater sense of security, they also retard somewhat the growth of the more efficient firms and, for the others, weaken the sting of competition that might disturb their lethargy. For example, little progress was made for years in raising the efficiency of conventional power-stations notwithstanding the restrictive agreements among the suppliers of the equipment; it was the impending competition of nuclear power that provided the stimulus to advance.

The possible harm done by "pirates" may be conceded but the desirable solution may appear to be more adequate protection by patents. The strength of the argument in favour of other restrictions partly rests on the extent to which patents cannot be made really effective. Even then it may be wiser, on balance, to risk the harm rather than regiment the industry. Finally some doubt must be cast on the assumption that investors will not finance highly uncertain innovations with the result that the firm must rely on abnormal profits earned on other lines. The enthusiasm in both Britain and the United States for "growth stocks" in the electronics industry and the like, is scarcely consistent with this assumption. Very small innovating firms may be handicapped, it is true, but will have little say, in any case, in shaping restrictive agreements. Finance corporations of one kind or another would seem to be the more appropriate answer.

(IV) The Monopolies Commission appears to have been impressed in a numbers of cases by the argument that a price agreement could facilitate technical co-operation. Thus, in commenting on the Electrical Lamp Manufacturers' Agreement, the Commission observed: "We see considerable advantage in the exchange of technical knowledge within the industry and much force in the argument that it could not continue if there were price competition between the companies concerned."[50] Largely for this reason they recommended that, subject to certain conditions, price fixing might be allowed to continue. At a later date, however, in reporting on *Electrical and Allied Machinery and Plant*, the Commission observed: "The progress of the industry has probably been assisted by technical collaboration between the manufacturers, but we do not believe that the elimination of price competition is a necessary prerequisite to other and more desirable forms of co-operation."[51]

The argument that agreements are necessary to encourage the sharing of trade secrets seems inconsistent with the argument that restrictions are necessary to protect the innovators. At all events it is not easy to see how both arguments could be logically advanced in the same set of circumstances. Nor is it by any means clear that a restrictive agreement will persuade progressive firms to share secrets that could otherwise be kept. Unless the agreement is so rigid as to retard their relative expansion, they may want to keep the fruits of their research, as far as may be, to themselves; if it is as rigid as this, the harm done may outweigh the gain from any sharing that takes place. Of course innovating firms may often want to exchange their secrets among themselves, but a patent pool can be formed and operated effectively without any agreement to fix the prices of the final products or to share the market. (The British radio industry affords a clear example.)

An agreement to fix prices is sometimes held to be a necessary condition for the co-operative planning of investment such as takes place in the British iron and steel industry. Unfortunately the reasoning is not always very explicit, but much emphasis is usually placed on the large size of the additional units of investment required and the need to avoid both duplication in some directions and too little expansion in others. Clearly a firm will want to find out what it can about the intentions of other firms, but the relevance of price fixing is more difficult to see. Is it implied that firm A will agree to forego a certain project for expansion while firm B goes ahead on the understanding that B will not damage A by lowering prices to the extent it might otherwise be able to do with its new and more efficient plant? Would it not be more sensible for A to invest too and scrap his old plant? What assumptions are being made about the equation of supply and demand and about over-capacity or under-capacity in the industry?

On reflection it is not obvious that the planning of investment, if this is achieved, can always be regarded as a compensating advantage that follows from price-fixing. It may rather be a further disadvantage. As we have seen the fixing of prices by a cartel tends to retard rather than halt the growth of the more efficient firms, but the restrictive effect will be much more severe if output is also allocated between the producers. Now the planning of investment may amount, in effect, to a scheme for sharing the market.

It is interesting to note that whereas largeness of scale is the reason given for co-operatively planned investment in the iron and steel industry, smallness of scale has been held to require restrictions in the case of *road transport*. Here competitors were believed to be too optimistic and entry to be too easy because the unit of investment was so modest (i.e. a lorry). It was inferred that over-investment would occur without some restriction on entry, and the state, therefore, enforced an elaborate system of licensing in Britain in the thirties. In a recent analysis of the evidence, Mr. P. E. Hart[52] has cast serious doubt on the validity of the case, but the official restrictions remain in force unaffected by the new attitude to restrictive practices in other industries.

Co-operation may be more clearly advantageous in achieving a reasonable standardisation of components. In the theory of monopolistic competition much stress is laid on the wastes arising from "product differentiation"; on closer inspection the argument would seem to be either that people *should* prefer cheapness to variety or that they *would* do so if they were not misled by advertisers. A less dubious case for standardisation can be made by pointing out that much diversity may be accidental, and relates to components and could be reduced without any loss of diversity among final products that any consumer would regret or even notice. (For example there was no need to have about fifty sizes of headlamp for British cars before the War.) Trade associations have performed a useful function in achieving greater standardisation, but there is no presumption that in order to do so they must also fix prices.* Standardisation may undoubtedly make it

* In the British radio industry, for example, there has been a great deal of work on standardisation without any accompanying price fixing. Nor have the international efforts to standardize necessitated price agreements in this industry.

The Central Electricity Authority complained to the Monopolies Commission as follows: "In their experience the manufacturers [of electrical equipment] have been very ready to have standard or rationalized practices established, but the artificial nature of some of the price relationships in the case of machines in class (a) in particular has presented obstacles to the arrival at the forms indicated by natural engineering economics to be the most appropriate, and in some cases have operated to give little or no incentive to the Authority to establish such practices." *Report on the Supply and Exports of Electrical and Allied Machinery and Plant*, para. 675. That is to say the fixing of prices handicapped standardization instead of helping it.

It should be noted that, in determining whether an agreement should be registered, the Act of 1956 rules in section 7(3) that "no account shall be taken of any term by which easier to fix prices if, on other grounds, firms wish to do so. That, however, is a different matter.

(v) In a country as much committed to full employment as Britain, it was perhaps natural that, in selecting certain grounds on which restrictive pratices might be justified, an adverse effect on employment should have been included in the Act of 1956. (See Appendix.) But it is necessary to consider whether there really are any circumstances in which a restrictive agreement can plausibly be expected to contribute to what, in other contexts, is understood to be a policy for full employment. In the first place, it must be conceded that if the restrictions hamper imports from abroad, employment in the industry may benefit; whether employment in the country as a whole will benefit is more doubtful and the standard of living may, of course, suffer. The usual arguments about protective tariffs apply. Secondly, if the restriction slows down the relative growth of the efficient firms, the industry's total sales, at home and abroad, may be less and so may the level of employment. An exception must be made in the case of an industry where (a) there is little scope for introducing new products or improving the existing ones and (b) the elasticity of demand is so low that more efficient processes with consequently lower prices would have little effect on sales. If competition eliminated some of the less efficient firms, an unchanged output might be produced with less man-hours and some labour might be redundant. It is doubtful, however, whether higher productivity could be convincingly opposed on such grounds. Thirdly, a reorganization of the industry brought about by competition—or in any other way—might well involve an expansion of employment in the efficient firms and contractions elsewhere. Some frictional unemployment might then appear in the short period, but frictional unemployment has never been regarded as inconsistent with a full employment policy. Special measures may, indeed, be taken to improve mobility, but it has been repeatedly emphasized that "full employment" does not mean, and cannot mean, the guarantee of a particular job in a particular factory, office, or shop.

The Restrictive Practices Court decided that serious local unemployment would probably follow from the abolition of the agreements in the *cotton spinning industry*, largely because of the high proportion of female and elderly workers.[53] It concluded, however, that the disadvantage would be outweighed by the gain in other directions and

the parties... agree to comply with... standards of dimension, design or quality for the time being approved by the British Standards Institution."

the agreements were held to be, on balance, contrary to the public interest. In the event the unemployment proved to be much less serious than was anticipated.

(VI) The Restrictive Practices Court has interpreted the new legislation more severely than was predicted in some quarters when the Act of 1956 was passed. A favourable verdict was, however, given on the agreement of the manufacturers of *Water-Tube Boilers*, some features of which have been described above. Although many of the pleas advanced by the defendants were rejected, the Court decided that the benefit to the export trade outweighed the other considerations. It was felt that, by co-operative tendering, the industry could secure more overseas business.[54] The verdict was a puzzling one. Admittedly, by acting together like a national monopoly, firms may strike a harder bargain, but an advantage of this kind would be difficult to justify on more general welfare grounds. (Nor is it clear that this is the consideration the Court really had in mind.) Even if viewed nationalistically, the benefit to the export trade could not be decided by reference to bargaining power alone: account should also be taken of the effect of the agreement on the general efficiency of the industry and a balance struck. A further reference was made by the Court to the fact that some of the firms had offices abroad, and it predicted that some of these might be closed if the restriction were removed and "valuable local contacts lost". No reason was given for this belief. Why should contacts be sacrified if they were really valuable?

A restrictive agreement may be so designed as to keep out imports. For example, this was one object behind the elaborate arrangements for collective resale price maintenance and exclusive dealing enforced by the British Radio Valve Makers Associations. The usual arguments for and against protection then become relevant once more, but there is the further consideration that the final verdict should rest with the state, not with the industry concerned. Privately organized protection is familiar enough—not only in Britain—and can be an intractable and unpredictable complication in international efforts to achieve freer trade.

(VII) The Theory of Countervailing Power has been reflected in both the reports of the Monopolies Commission and in the Act of 1956.[55] The reasoning has followed two separate lines. First, it has been held that a cartel, however dangerous in other circumstances, will not be able to do much harm if it has to deal with a sufficiently powerful buyer or seller; secondly, the existence of such a buyer or seller has been regarded as a possible justification for the existence of a cartel. The first argument was advanced by the Monopolies Commission in one of its earliest reports, that on *Insulin*.[56] Although the producers of insulin were tightly organized, most of their output was sold to the nationalized health authorities who were invited to exercise "in the future such supervision as may appear to them to be necessary". The Commission's verdict on countervailing power was less optimistic in the case of *Electrical Machinery and Plant*. It was reported that the Central Electricity Authority had tried to obtain "either a justification of the common prices on the basis of disclosed costs or a measure of price competition. Having met initial resistance on the question of obtaining costs, the Authority has taken every opportunity open to it to foster price competition, and it contends that this has had some effect, not only on the level of prices but also in inducing the manufacturers to make some disclosure of their costs".[57]

The same report on electrical equipment also records that the second argument about countervailing power was advanced by the manufacturers[58] but failed to convince the Commission. The Central Electricity Authority, for its part, declared that it did "not wish to encourage anything in the nature of "cut-throat competition" and that if, as a result of price competition, tenderers made offers which were consistently substantially below those of their competitors it would wish to be assured that they were genuine offers carrying a fair expectation of reasonable profit to the tenderer..."[59] This disclaimer can probably be accepted, not so much because the undertaking is nationalized but rather because no responsible buyer will want to ruin suppliers on whom he must continue to depend. Subsequently, the Act of 1956 laid it down that the need for countervailing power could be a permissible defence of a restrictive practice, and an appeal was made to this clause by the makers of *water-tube boilers*. The Court exonerated the Electricity Board but went on to rule that the paragraph does not require "proof of the existence of a preponderant buyer who is likely to try to enforce unfair terms." It would, apparently, be enough to show that the sellers might tender at uneconomic prices, and the Court then tried to contend, in a still more bewildering paragraph, that that might happen in this industry.[60] After conceding so much, the Court then ruled that the defence under this clause could not be accepted because the restriction applied not only to sales to the preponderant buyer but to all sales (i.e. to exports as well as to sales at home.)

The whole argument rests on the assumption that firms with preponderant power will exploit their customers in a ruthless and short-sighted way. If this is plausible, then it constitutes a strong argument against monopoly. The Act of 1956 would then have been more logical in structure if it had contained some provisions for preventing such preponderance from arising except in cases of natural monopoly. This, however, was not done.[61]

(VIII) The view that the removal of restrictions will lead to a greater concentration of industry cannot be examined in detail without raising many issues that belong more properly to another chapter. It may be recorded, however, that such a claim was advanced by the *yarn spinners* and the *Scottish bakers* and was dismissed in both cases by the Court. The possibility of greater concentration has, however, become a topic of debate and the mergers that occurred in the few years after the passage of the Act have sometimes been attributed to it, although the causal link has not been very explicitly established. It is then concluded either that the attack on restrictive practices is mistaken or that the Act should be so amended as to allow action to be taken against excessive concentration.[62]

If any greater concentration following the removal of a restriction reflected the expansion of a more efficient producer, then the change might well be thought desirable, or there would, at all events, be some gain to set against possible loss. This might be regarded as a case where monopoly offered the economies of larger size while the restrictive agreement offered no such compensation; it is on this ground that trusts have often been held to be preferable to cartels.[63] In recording this argument I do not wish to endorse the assumption that it is simply, or even mainly, a question of economies of scale, important though these may sometimes be. It may often be rather a question of the quality of management—only homogeneous in static theory! The ending of a restriction may allow a firm that is already efficient to obtain a larger share of the market apart from any economies of scale. The emphasis on such economies should not be allowed to obscure the importance of personality although any gain from greater scale may possibly be more enduring.*

* The vigorous personalities may tire or die or move elsewhere and the efficiency of the firm, if not the firm itself, may decay like the trees of Marshall's forest. The view that such considerations apply only to small firms is simply contrary to the facts. Personality is immensely important in large firms—and in government departments. Modern economics, in its desire to be impersonally "scientific", tends to be so unscientific as to ignore this fact.

Now we have already seen that a price-fixing agreement does not by itself eliminate competition, although it will tend to blunt its force. The efficient may, therefore, win ground gradually within a cartel but, by the same token, the cartel may not be such an effective barrier to concentration. The evidence produced by the Monopolies Commission showed that this was often, in fact, the case. Cartels that imposed a real halt to concentration, perhaps by coupling price-fixing with the control of output, would probably do so only by hampering the lower-cost producers. It can scarcely be held that we have here a very impressive defence of restrictive practices. Moreover, although such practices sometimes keep a larger number of existing producers in existence, it is generally one of their aims to restrict new entry. In so far as this aim is achieved, it will be easier for one or two large units to extend their control over the industry.

So far it has been implied that the process of concentration always means the relative growth of the more efficient firms, but this may sometimes be an over-optimistic assumption. Mergers, in particular, are liable to take place for less satisfactory reasons. The removal of restrictions on prices, output and the like may well induce some of the firms affected to band together, but the objective need not simply be greater efficiency. It may rather be to avoid the effect of competition on profits or to escape disturbance and uncertainty. Once again, however, it would be somewhat unconvincing to defend such restrictions as a way of keeping down the degree of concentration. The proper moral may rather be that a policy directed against restrictive practices should be accompanied by action to prevent or discourage mergers and, perhaps, to break up firms already swollen beyond a reasonable size.*

Finally, it is of some interest to compare the degree of concentration in the United States with that in the United Kingdom. After the initial attack on the trusts, United States efforts were largely concentrated upon the avoidance of restrictive practices until the Clayton Act was amended in 1950; in practice, the policy was therefore lop-sided in much the same way as British policy under the Act of 1956. Over these years little or no action was taken against either trusts or cartels in Britain. If, then, cartels tend to discourage concentration, American

* Cf. JOHN JEWKES, "British Monopoly Policy 1944–56", *The Journal of Law and Economics*, October, 1958, p. 18: "In fact, in the ten reports in which the Commission has provided evidence of the relative costs and profits of different sized firms, there is only one, that relating to electronic valves and cathode ray tubes, where it was found that the largest producer showed the lowest costs". (Although there may have been some ambiguities in the accounting, the broad conclusion can scarcely be challenged.)

industry should have become more highly concentrated than British, but the statistics do not indicate any great difference.[64] Such evidence, of course, is far from conclusive when other things are by no means equal, but it is of some interest in that it does not afford any clear positive evidence in favour of the proposition under discussion.

VI

It is more difficult to reach a conclusion about the effect restrictive practices may have on innovation and growth than it is about their effect on pricing. The difficulty is undeniably increased by the confused and unconvincing way in which the defenders of these agreements so often present their arguments. Thus time is wasted while industries that spend little or nothing on research claim that price agreements are necessary to finance it; impatience and boredom follow from the now predictable reiteration of the prophecy that quality will sharply deteriorate if pricing is freed; and so on. With a defence often so lame that those responsible can scarcely be supposed to believe what they are saying, there is a strong temptation to conclude that no defence is possible and to reach a hostile verdict without feeling that the investigation needs to be pushed further. That some more serious defence can be offered is, I think, the case. First of all, the negative point may be made that restrictive practices do less harm than is often supposed. The authors of a recent study of innovation, C. F. Carter and B. R. Williams, conclude that "the dangers to technical progress set by restrictive agreements are limited and to some extent theoretical: they are dangers which might reasonably be expected to occur, rather than dangers which can be proved to have occurred". They also hold the view that "there is no striking evidence of a deliberate suppression of new knowledge".[65]

Some competitive industries have been stagnant while some less competitive ones have been progressive. There is thus no simple correlation between competition and innovation, but it is only fair to add that, with other things far from equal, it would be too much to expect any such correlation; the question is whether, on balance, restrictive practices are likely to be helpful or harmful. Moreover, even if it is the case that their effect for good or ill is small, this is scarcely an adequate defence; unless there is a significantly favourable effect under this heading, the verdict, on other counts, must be hostile. Some positive arguments in their favour can, of course, be advanced. As

Schumpeter has maintained, the greater security they afford may be favourable to investment and we may add that the force of this argument is likely to be stronger when taxation is high. Discriminatory pricing may also help research and development, as we have seen above, although it may not always be so used.

On the other side, it can be argued that progress will be more rapid when vigorous managements within an industry, or enterprising newcomers, are able to go ahead unhampered by artificial restraints. It is also true that many of the alleged benefits of restrictive practices could be provided in other ways with less accompanying danger and more certainty of effect. If research and development need to be fostered, there are all sorts of ways of doing so apart from permitting cartels: tax concessions, development contracts, special finance corporations for small firms, educational efforts of all kinds, and so on. A sound patent system should give the reasonable security and reward that is needed without imposing too much restraint. When we turn to price fixing, it seems clear that the benefits of greater efficiency will affect prices more favourably if the market is free. It is true that "open price agreements" may follow the abolition of the more formal arrangements of a cartel,[66] but it would be rash to infer that nothing will therefore have been accomplished. Not only may the "open" price agreements be looser and less binding than the price structure explicitly determined by a cartel, but the other possible restrictive activities may have disappeared or been greatly weakened, in particular the allocation of quotas for output and the restriction of new entry. We have already seen that a cartel itself will probably have a lower and more sensitive price structure if these other arrangements are absent, and the same should be true, *a fortiori*, of "open" agreements. No doubt the latter can be extended in some measure to other activities, but the difficulties will be formidable unless the competitive spirit is completely dead within the industry, an unusual state of affairs. Indeed one can go so far as to say that the exchange of information about prices that leads to an "open" agreement may have certain merits provided other shackles on competition from newcomers have gone. As has already been stressed, great uncertainty may be experienced in an oligopolistic industry of multi-product firms where overheads are heavy and demand is unstable. One must take care that these complications, so inadequately treated in economic theory, are not allowed to drop out of sight in passing judgment on such devices as "open" price agreements.

How can one balance these favourable and unfavourable arguments, some of them apparently little more than rival hunches? At the outset we denied ourselves any academic indulgence in agnosticism. We must also regard with some scepticism the view that "each case has to be judged on its merits": overwhelmingly conclusive evidence will not always be obtainable even if a case is studied in detail "on its merits", and such a procedure is too slow. The real question is whether one feels that a general presumption against restrictive practices is reasonable. It is difficult to believe that the British Act of 1956, with its saving clauses,* goes too far in this respect.

This is the first conclusion. Is it possible to go beyond this and recommend a strengthening of the legislation? Should some of the "gateways" be closed if the Act were being amended? Would it be wise to extend the *per se* condemnation of collective resale price maintenance to some or all of the agreements that have to be registered —the fixing of producers' prices or conditions of sale, the allocation of output quotas, the control of processes and exclusive dealing? Would any harm be done thereby? In attempting to reach a definite conclusion in face of somewhat conflicting evidence, one must remember that, even if a wider range of practices were proscribed, firms could still protect themselves by means of price leadership, open-price competition and the like, against some of the more extreme uncertainties of oligopolistic competition. Moreover collective agreements made under the supervision of an official committee, such as the Iron and Steel Board, would, of course, continue to be permitted. On balance, there is much to be said for the view that, unless they are under public supervision, restrictive agreements of the kinds indicated should be made illegal *per se*. Neither the evidence so far presented to the Restrictive Practices Court nor the experience over many more years of the U.S.A. would suggest that much harm would be done if the legislation were simplified in this way. The simplification would be a genuine gain although it is only fair to add that, if the Act continues to be interpreted by the Court as it has been in some of its first leading cases, it should provide an effective, if somewhat slower, way of removing undesirable restraints on the forces of competition.

* See Appendix, pp. 164–65

Appendix

PRESUMPTION AS TO THE PUBLIC INTEREST—SECTION 21 OF THE ACT OF 1956

"(1) For the purposes of any proceedings before the Court under the last foregoing section, a restriction accepted in pursuance of any agreement shall be deemed to be contrary to the public interest unless the Court is satisfied by any one or more of the following circumstances, that is to say

(a) that the restriction is reasonably necessary having regard to the character of the goods to which it applies, to protect the public against injury (whether to persons or to premises) in connection with the consumption, installation or use of these goods;

(b) that the removal of the restriction would deny to the public as purchasers, consumers or users of any goods other specific and substantial benefits or advantages enjoyed or likely to be enjoyed by them as such, whether by virtue of the restriction itself or of any arrangements or operations resulting therefrom;

(c) that the restriction is reasonably necessary to counteract measures taken by any one person not party to the agreement with a view to preventing or restricting competition in or in relation to the trade or business in which the persons party thereto are engaged;

(d) that the restriction is reasonably necessary to enable the persons party to the agreement to negotiate fair terms for the supply of goods to, or the acquisition of goods from, any one person not party thereto who controls a preponderant part of the trade or business of acquiring or supplying such goods, or for the supply of goods to any person not party to the agreement and not carrying on such a trade or business who, either alone or in combination with any other such person, controls a preponderant part of the market for such goods;

(e) that, having regard to the conditions actually obtaining or reasonably foreseen at the time of the application, the removal of the restriction would be likely to have a serious and persistent adverse effect on the general level of unemployment in an area, or in areas taken together, in which a substantial proportion of the trade or industry to which the agreement relates is situated;

(f) that, having regard to the conditions actually obtaining or reasonably foreseen at the time of the application, the removal of the restriction would be likely to cause a reduction in the volume or earnings of the export business which is substantial either in relation to the whole export business of the United Kingdom or in relation to the whole business (including export business) of the said trade or industry; or

(g) that the restriction is reasonably required for purposes connected with the maintenance of any other restriction accepted by the parties, whether under the same agreement or under any other agreement between them, being a restriction which is found by the Court not to be contrary to the public interest upon grounds other than those specified in this paragraph, or has been so found in previous proceedings before the Court and is further satisfied (in any such case) that the restriction is not unreasonable having regard to the balance between those circumstances and any detriment to the public or to persons not parties to the agreement (being purchasers, consumers or users of goods produced or sold by such parties, or persons engaged or seeking to become engaged in the trade or business of selling such goods or of producing or selling similar goods) resulting or likely to result from the operation of the restriction.

(2) In this section "purchasers", "consumers" and "users" include persons purchasing, consuming or using for the purpose or in course of trade or business or for public purposes; and references in this section to any one person include references to any two or more persons being inter-connected bodies corporate or individuals carrying on business in partnership with each other."

These possible exceptions to the general prohibition are less wide than they may at first sight appear: the drafting of the Act was such as to impose a considerable onus of proof. Even (b) has not proved to be a wide "gateway" in the rulings of the Court.

Mr. R. L. Sich, the registrar, gave the following figures in "Progress under the Restrictive Practices Act, 1956", *Yorkshire Bulletin*, December, 1959: 2,200 agreements had been registered by August 7, 1959, of which 600 had been abandoned; only a few agreements had, at that time, come before the Court but 130 cases were being prepared or the initial steps had been taken; of the remainder, over 1000 were likely to depend upon agreements in other cases. Thus about 400 were not accounted for, but it was possible that about 200 might be removed from the register.

NOTES

1. The author is indebted to Professors Arthur Beacham, S. R. Dennison and Mr. J. B. Heath who have read and commented on this article, and to Mrs. D. J. Wilson who has checked the references. For any errors that remain he alone is responsible.
2. JOSEPH SCHUMPETER, *Capitalism, Socialism and Democracy*, London: George Allen & Unwin, ch. 7.
3. Sir HENRY CLAY, "The Campaign against Monopoly and Restrictive Practices," *Lloyds Bank Review*, April, 1952.
4. LOUIS B. SCHWARTZ, *Free Enterprise and Economic Organization: Legal and Related Matters*, New York: Foundation Press, 1952, pp. 391 et seq.
5. *Report on the Supply and Export of Certain Semi-Manufactures of Copper and Copper-based Alloys*, H.M.S.O., 1955, p. 97.
6. What follows is largely a summary of the points made in my article, "The Inadequacy of the Theory of the Firm as a Branch of Welfare Economics," *Oxford Economic Papers*, vol. 4, February, 1952, pp. 18–45.
7. Cf. R. B. TENNANT, *The American Cigarette Industry*, New Haven: Yale, 1950; T. WILSON, "The Electronics Industry" in *The Structure of British Industry*, ed. by Duncan Burn, Cambridge: Cambridge University Press, 1958, vol. 2, p. 151.
8. Both lines of argument are to be found in the pioneering article by R. L. HALL and C. J. HITCH, "Price Theory and Business Behaviour," *Oxford Economic Papers*, May, 1939, pp. 12–46; the article is reprinted in *Oxford Studies in the Price Mechanism*, edited by T. Wilson and P. W. S. Andrews, Oxford: Clarendon Press, 1951.
9. This is, I think, the gist of the theory of the "right price" as developed in Britain by P. W. S. ANDREWS—who is often wrongly described as an exponent of full-cost pricing. See his *Manufacturing Business*, London: Macmillan, 1949, "Industrial Analysis in Economics," in *Oxford Studies in the Price Mechanism*, and "Competition in the Modern Economy" in *Competitive Aspects of Oil Operations*, London: The Institute of Petroleum, 1958, edited by George Sell. See, too, the survey by ELIZABETH BRUNNER, "Competition and the Theory of the Firm," *Economica Internationale*, vol. 10, August, 1952, pp. 509–27.
10. Cf. R. F. HARROD, "Imperfect Competition Revisited," *Economic Essays*, London: Harcourt Brace, 1952.
11. *Report on the Process of Calico-Printing*, H.M.S.O., 1954, p. 71.
12. Cf. DONALD DEWEY, *Monopoly in Economics and Law*, New York: Rand McNally Company, 1959, ch. 8.
13. *Report on the Supply and Export of Certain Semi-Manufactures of Copper and Copper-based Alloys*, H.M.S.O., July, 1955, para. 305.
14. *Report on the Supply of Cast-Iron Rainwater Goods*, H.M.S.O., 1951, and *Report on the Process of Calico-Printing*, H.M.S.O., 1954, paras. 72–78 and ch. 6.
15. *Report on the Supply of Linoleum*, H.M.S.O., 1956, ch. 12 and para. 192.
16. *Report on the Supply of Standard Metal Windows and Doors*, H.M.S.O., 1956, ch. 7.
17. *Report on the Supply and Export of Pneumatic Tyres*, H.M.S.O., 1955, ch. 11.
18. Restrictive Practices Court, *Reports of Restrictive Practices Cases*, London: The Incorporated Council of Law Reporting for England and Wales, March, 1960, vol. 1, part 6, pp. 348 and 373 *et seq.* (These law reports will be referred to hereafter by the abbreviation, L.R. I R.P.).
19. *Ibid.*, pp. 131–32, 180–82.
20. *Ibid.*, p. 183.
21. *Report on the Supply of Buildings in The Greater London Area*, H.M.S.O., 1954, ch. 3.
22. L.R. I R.P., p. 329 ff.
23. *Report on the Supply and Export of Matches and the Supply of Matchmaking Machinery*, H.M.S.O., 1953, ch. 10.

24. *Report on the Supply of Electric Lamps,* H.M.S.O., 1950, para. 203.
25. *Report on the Supply and Export of Pneumatic Tyres,* H.M.S.O., 1955, chs. 9, 10, 21 and 24.
26. *Report on the Supply of Electronic Valves and Cathode Ray Tubes,* H.M.S.O., 1956, ch. 9.
27. L.R. I R.P., p. 153.
28. L.R. I R.P., p. 348.
29. D. BURN, ed., *op. cit.*, pp. 137–38.
30. *Report on the Process of Calico Printing*, paras. 59, 92–98, 197, 201–03.
31. *Report on the Supply of Electric Lamps,* ch. 6 and para. 278–79.
32. *Report on the Supply and Export of Pneumatic Tyres,* para. 486. See also ALEX HUNTER, "The Monopolies Commission and Price Fixing," *Economic Journal,* vol. 57, December, 1956, pp. 587–603.
33. For a detailed survey of the Act, see R. A. WILBERFORCE, A. CAMPBELL and N. P. M. ELLIS, *Restrictive Trade Practices and Monopolies,* London: Sweet and Maxwell, 1957; M. ALBERY and C. F. FLETCHER, *Monopolies and Restrictive Trade Practices,* London: Stevens, 1956. A review of the decisions of the Court under the various headings is given in two articles in the *Yorkshire Bulletin,* vol. 11, December, 1959, by R. L. SICH and S. R. DENNISON. (The former is Registrar and the latter has been one of the economic witnesses.) See, too, J. B. HEATH, "The Restrictive Practices Court on Competition and Price Restriction," *Manchester School,* vol. 28, January, 1960, pp. 1–19.
34. Quoted by W. A. LEWIS, *Overhead Costs,* London: George Allen and Unwin, Ltd., 1949, p. 161.
35. L.R. I R.P., p. 196.
36. *Report on the Supply and Export of Electrical and Allied Machinery and Plant,* Monopolies Commission, H.M.S.O., 1957.
37. This was the view taken by the Court. "The directors realize perfectly well that if they are to remain in business, they must retain these personnel; they will do so". L.R. I R.P., vol. 1, Part 6, p. 337.
38. *Economist,* London: February 6, 1960.
39. *Report on the Supply of Dental Goods,* H.M.S.O., 1950, paras. 197–98.
40. The argument was advanced to the Restrictive Practices Court in four cases: Yarn Spinning, Blankets, Water-Tube Boilers, and Scottish Bread. In all four it was rejected. The Monopolies Commission had been somewhat less sceptical.
41. There was an example of cut-throat advertising in the British soap industry before the war which caused so much embarrassment that a halt had to be called. See CHARLES WILSON, *History of Unilever,* London: Cassell, 1954, ch. 6, vol. 1. Some associations have agreements restricting non-price competition. Cf. N. CUTHBERT and W. BLACK, "Restrictive Practices in the Food Trades," *Journal of Industrial Economics,* vol. 8, October, 1959, pp. 45–46.
42. *Report on Pneumatic Tyres,* p. 103.
43. L.R. I R.P., p. 43.
44. P. W. S. ANDREWS, *Manufacturing Business.*
45. Monopolies Commission, *Collective Discrimination,* H.M.S.O., 1955.
46. See the Monopolies Commission's *Report on the Supply of Electronic Valves and Cathode Ray Tubes,* H.M.S.O., 1956; and T. WILSON, "The Electronics Industry," D. BURN, ed., *op. cit.*, pp. 162 *et. seq.*
47. See AUBREY SILBERTSON, "The Motor Industry," D. Burn, ed., *op. cit.*, vol. 2, pp. 1–44.
48. I have heard this complaint made by some firms in the British radio industry that were unprotected by price agreements.
49. L.R. I R.P., p. 385.

50. *Report on Electric Lamps*, para. 262.
51. *Report on Electrical and Allied Machinery and Plant*, para. 761.
52. P. E. HART, "The Restriction of Road Haulage," *Scottish Journal of Political Economy*, vol. VI, June, 1959, pp. 116–39.
53. L. R. I R.P., pp. 191–195.
54. L.R. I R.P., pp. 343–46. Price agreements have, of course, been defended on the ground that they allow exports to be sold at less than full cost because high profits are being made on the home market. Cf., e.g., *The Report on Electrical and Allied Machinery and Plant*, para. 705. There is some evidence relating to the same industry which suggests that foreign buyers may resent price agreements by exporters even to the extent of rejecting a tender. *Ibid.*, paras. 661–67.
55. Cf. ALEX HUNTER, "The Monopolies Commission and Economic Welfare," *Manchester School*, vol. 13, January, 1955, p. 32. Although it is convenient to use Professor Galbraith's label, I do not suggest that the arguments advanced have always been those set out in his book, *American Capitalism*, Boston: Houghton Mifflin, 1952.
56. *Report on the Supply of Insulin*, H.M.S.O., 1952, para. 98.
57. *Report on Electrical Allied Machinery and Plant*, para. 772. (One large and efficient producer—Parsons—left the ring.)
58. *Ibid.*, para. 684.
59. *Ibid.*, para. 772.
60. L.R. I R.P., pp. 340–42. Cf., too, an article by the Registrar, R. L. SICH, "Progress under the Restrictive Practices Act," *Yorkshire Bulletin*, vol. 11, December, 1959, p. 123.
61. It is interesting to note in passing that the restrictive agreements have sometimes been directed against large groups of small buyers rather than preponderant buyers. The makers of electronic valves and motor-car components had elaborate arrangements governing sales for replacement but not governing sales to large buyers of initial equipment.
62. As it is, the problems raised by concentration and monopoly may be investigated by the Monopolies Commission in its truncated form, but this is liable to be a slow procedure and there is no general guiding presumption that action against monopoly will be subsequently taken by the Board of Trade. As compared with the American legislation, the British is lop-sided.
63. See page 114 above.
64. Cf. P. SARGANT FLORENCE: "The facts show an amazingly similar picture in both countries." *The Logic of British and American Industry*, London: Kegan Paul, 1953, p. 132. Reference should also be made to a more recent review of the evidence by W. GEOFFREY SHEPHERD, "A Comparison of Industrial Concentration in the United States and Britain," *Review of Economics and Statistics*, vol. XLIII, No. 1, February, 1961.
65. C. F. CARTER and B. R. WILLIAMS, *Industry and Technical Progress*, London: Oxford University Press, 1957, pp. 167–68. See, also, the report on pp. 20–21 of an inquiry into the possibility that industry has neglected or suppressed new ideas. Cf., B. R. WILLIAMS, "Some Conditions of Useful Competition," *Yorkshire Bulletin*, vol. 11, December, 1959, pp. 71–79.
66. An interesting account of "open price agreements" in Britain is given in a paper by J. B. HEATH, "Some Economic Consequences," *Economic Journal*, vol. 70, September, 1960.

CHAPTER 5

GERMAN EXPERIENCE WITH CARTELS AND THEIR CONTROL DURING PRE-WAR AND POST-WAR PERIODS

FRITZ VOIGT

University of Hamburg, Germany

During the past century cartels of different types, behavior and potential have flourished in Germany in response to changes in economic and political conditions. The study of the German experience with cartels, therefore, is very useful for an understanding of the nature and development of cartels and of the potentiality of various types of government policy. There have been long periods in which German cartels could evolve without any government control or intervention by government authorities. There have been other periods when the government could intervene in various ways with the behavior and development of cartels if they threatened to abuse their power. And while in one decade a special independent court controlled the activities of cartels, in another period the highest economic authority bore the principal responsibility for control. Moreover, there have been periods in which cartels were tools of state policy, and others in which they were generally prohibited.

When studying the cartels in Germany we note that certain types could easily be influenced, directed or even dissolved by state policy, but that others could hardly be dealt with effectively by the state, so that they survived even when prohibited.

I. The Period of Governmental Non-interference (1860–1923)

In the epoch of liberalism in which economic theory and parliament were of the opinion that economic processes would lead to an optimal order if left to themselves, i.e. if state intervention was eliminated, cartels were viewed as private associations towards which the state should remain neutral. Prior to World War I there were no particular norms regulating cartels as private legal and economic agreements controlling market conditions for a particular product. They were subsumed under the general laws concerning business organizations and other associations. As long as cartels operated within the bounds of these laws, the state did not interfere. Until 1923 the formation and operation of cartels in the German Reich were completely free from state intervention and state control.

1. Period of industrialization until 1914

Forerunners of cartels existed in Germany in earlier centuries. The modern cartel, however, is a product of liberalism, a reaction of enterprisers to the opportunities inherent in a free market economy, but also a safeguard against the adverse effects of business cycles inherent in the process of industrial growth.

The distinguishing characteristics of cartels were already clear in the tin plate cartel of Cologne in 1862: it was the result of temporary overproduction which, in turn, was caused by the pressure of fixed costs. Its scope was limited to contractual engagements legally possible and enforceable at the time. Sombart estimates that there were four cartels in 1865. According to Philippovich there were eight cartels in 1875. Attempts to establish market agreements as protective measures against price collapses in the course of a depression became more frequent following the "promoters' crisis" (Gründerkrise) of 1873 and the adoption of protective tariffs in 1875. The first cartels in an industry were usually a "product of necessity." However, once enterprisers became accustomed to this type of private economic co-operation cartels were formed at an increasing rate in the course of industrial growth, the objective being to realize the economic advantages of collective monopolies and to shift the total demand curve further to their advantage. An estimate by Philippovich gives 70 cartels for the year 1887 and 106 for 1889. Sombart counts 250 cartels for 1896. Although in the course of industrial growth the cartels varied in strength, life span and duration of effect, a certain pattern of development became increasingly apparent. In this development relatively weak agreements controlling the conditions of sale under the civil law were predominant (term-fixing cartels). Only in the basic industries and in some sectors producing semi-finished and finished goods, private arrangements developed of varying effectiveness depending on the degree to which the products involved could be defined in precise legal terms. Some of these cartels proved to be lasting and achieved the position of a collective monopoly. Thus, cartels in the coal, steel, potash, nitrogen, and gas and coke industries, which employed the selling syndicate system, succeeded in setting up relatively rigorous agreements. The strength of a cartel increased as the cost curves of its members became more uniform in shape and position, as fewer firms operated in the market and as more and more of the competitors within the industry were included in the cartel. Since these conditions could be fulfilled completely only in a few industries, the duration of cartels, with few exceptions, was strikingly short. The more dissimilar the cost curves of the members became as economic conditions changed, the more rapidly the cartels collapsed. Only a few effective agreements lasted for a longer period of time, as for instance the Rhenish-Westphalian Coal Syndicate of 1893,[1] the Steel Mill Federation and the salt,[2] linoleum[3] and woodscrew cartels.[4]

In the course of industrialization the cartel movement developed a peculiar rhythm which can be well observed in the cement industry[5] as well as in other industries. Inasmuch as cartels were only private legal and economic agreements, their effect, in contrast to trusts, was limited by the extent to which market regulations for a product could be formulated and protected under the provisions of the Civil Code and to which the observance of the cartel statutes by the participating firms could be controlled. This can be formulated in the following way: the market arrangements were effective only to the degree to which the "parameter of action"* of the members as to market objectives, prices and quantity coincided; particularly, they were dependent upon a similarity in shape and position of the members' cost curves during the various phases of the business cycle. If a cartel succeeded in raising prices for its members in accordance with the "Cournot Point," new firms entered the industry as a result of the attractive marginal efficiency of capital in that industry. Owing to the fixed cartel prices, these firms were able to obtain through price cuts a substantial portion of the business. The greater the pressure of fixed costs, the more rapidly the cartel collapsed as a result of the decreased output, caused by the activity of outsiders whose volume of business was dependent

* "Parameter of action" refers to those areas in which an acting person (such as an enterpriser or a civil servant) or an institution (such as a parliament or a state) can make free decisions. In making a decision the person or body equipped with the right or power to do so must reckon with certain given facts (e.g. basic ethical principles, customs, compulsory laws, unchangeable human behavior, foreign power positions, etc.). The ability to make decisions is thus narrowed by data which are beyond control of the deciding person or body. The parameter of action comprises only those areas in which free decisions can be made.

upon the elasticity of demand and the extent to which they could cut prices. After a period of cut-throat competition following the cartel termination, a new tendency toward agreements emerged in which the previous outsiders, through compromises, were included. The new cartel sought to compensate for the losses sustained during the period of cut-throat competiton, thus raising prices and, once again, attempting to reach the Cournot Point. New firms began to enter the market as a reaction to the increasing return on investments in that industry. Operating as outsiders these firms again prompted the collapse of the cartel. Thus, a characteristic rhythmic movement developed as these phenomena reoccurred with great regularity save in a few industries where it was possible to impede entry of new firms effectively through superior patents, through obstructing the access to raw materials or through other measures. This "rhythm" had a significant bearing on the growth rate of the economy: as long as the cartel was in operation its members seized the opportunity for plowing back earnings in order to finance new investments and technological improvements internally and thus to prepare for the tough competitive struggle which was surely to be expected following the collapse of the cartel. The price collapse caused by the dissolution of the cartel meant decreasing profitability, decreasing marginal efficiency of capital, decreasing possibilities for self-financing and for obtaining loans. The volume of investments began to drop considerably. Thus, the "cartel rhythm" gained influence upon the general economic growth process.

In its decisions around the turn of the century the German Supreme Court (Reichsgericht)[6] was faced with the question as to whether or not cartels were consistent with the freedom of trade as proclaimed in paragraph 1 of the Industrial Code (Gewerbeordnung) passed in 1869. At that time this Court was not yet in a position to recognize the characteristic effects of cartels upon economic growth, and their significance with respect to the vitality of a market economy. It did not sufficiently realize that the development of a free economy is largely determined by the prevailing form of competition. The Court upheld the legality of cartels under the Civil Code and Commercial Code. In the following decades this ruling was the decisive determinant in the attitude of the courts towards cartels.

The Supreme Court, under the liberalistic rule of law then prevailing, could not have acted differently. The guarantee of the freedom of trade of 1869 was exclusively directed against the state. A paragraph in the

Industrial Code of 1869 which provided every citizen with the right to operate a business and which constituted the basic law of the liberal economic order was exclusively designed to rule out any state interference with the individual freedom of the citizen. The legislature was not yet cognizant of the fact that the freedom of the individual had to be protected also against collective practices by business men designed to restrict competition. Furthermore, the Industrial Code established the right of coalition for labor, thus permitting collective restrictive practices in wage negotiations (the positive right of coalition). Only the old compulsory rights exercised by the guilds and formerly sanctioned by the state were abolished. Convinced that the self-regulating market forces would assure the free and unrestrained functioning of natural tendencies if the state did not interfere, neither the public nor the legislature understood to what large degree the development of the market economy in the 19th and 20th centuries was influenced by the principle of non-interference by the state. Laws, once passed, develop a certain tradition and thereby continue to exist even if the interests to be protected have changed.

The first step of a governmental policy was taken as late as 1909–10, and then in favor of rather than against cartels: when the potash syndicate,[7] operating on a voluntary basis, collapsed, it was transformed into a compulsory cartel. One of the reasons for this intervention was that the government held an interest in some of the enterprises participating in the cartel. Prior to World War I German firms held a relatively important oligopolistic position in the international potash industry.

Debates on cartels were conducted in German parliaments only sporadically, as for instance in 1879–81 on the bid-submission cartels in the railroad locomotive and railroad car industries. During a debate on price increases in the coal industry in 1900–01, the National-Liberal representative Heil in Parliament brought forward a motion to establish governmental control over those cartels and syndicates whose operations showed demonstrable monopolistic characteristics.[8] Various bills introduced in the Reichstag demanded tariff measures as a means of governmental policy against cartels. The advocates of free trade in the 19th century held that without protective tariffs cartels would have never been formed and that the rise of many of them was made possible only through the tariffs adopted in 1879.[9]

The Government of the Reich, for the purpose of obtaining insight into the cartel situation, initiated a survey which was conducted from

1902 to 1905.[10] A total of 395 cartels were counted, distributed among the following industries;

Coal industry	19
Iron ,,	62
Other metal industries	11
Chemical industry	46
Textile ,,	31
Brick ,,	132[11]

After the turn of the century the social sciences began to deal more intensively with the problems imposed by cartels. At the 26th convention of jurists in 1902 suitable measures for the legal treatment of cartels were examined.[12] At the 27th convention in 1904 legal recognition of cartels was held to be necessary. However, governmental intervention in case of unfair and economically unjustified price increases as well as equal freedom of coalition for employers and employees was demanded. The German Economic Association (Verein für Socialpolitik) dealt with questions and problems involved in cartels at the convention of Mannheim in 1905. Schmoller pointed out that cartels represented one of the most important and fundamental changes in the economic structure since 1860. He particularly emphasized that the recognized principles of the market economy were in the process of change. He asserted that cartels lead directly to a socialistic state since free competition would vanish.

In March of 1908 an active governmental cartel policy was demanded by almost all political parties represented in Parliament. Already at that time the establishment of a cartel authority, publication of cartel agreements and maintenance of a cartel register were urged. However, no legal measures were taken prior to World War I. The government continued its policy of non-interference since greater damages or intolerable situations did not become known to, or were not realized by, the public. Further measures supporting an active public cartel policy were introduced after the end of World War I,[13] but proved to be unsuccessful.

2. Influence of the war economy and the revolution after World War I

A war-time economy always has long-range effects upon postwar economic development. World War I influenced economic trends particularly in those industries which were characterized by the existence of effective and continuing cartels. At the same time governmental policy towards cartels changed in a certain way.

The first mild governmental intervention as to the relations between cartels and consumers took place at the beginning of World War I in the textile industry. In August of 1914 the Prussian Minister of Commerce and Trade (Minister für Handel und Gewerbe) demanded cancellation of certain price increases. The cartels consented.

As the first signs of a collapse of the monarchy appeared in the wake of the defeat, new attempts were made towards economic self-regulation in those industrial sections in which particularly strong cartels prevailed. In the revolutionary wave after the war—and, at the same time, as a result of the experiences with the war-time economy as well as a reaction to emerging socialistic tendencies—self-regulative bodies such as the "Reichskohlenrat" and "Reichskalirat" were created. In other words, market regulations were set up on the basis of self-control in those branches of industry which were characterized by effective private economic cartel agreements. These self-regulating bodies, constituting an antithesis of the private economy,[14] were designed to represent all segments of the public which had an interest in the productive process: employers, employees, the trades, consumers, scientists, and government representatives. The idea of economic self-regulation arose as a reaction to the planned economy during the war and the demands for nationalization of the key industries by the revolutionary labor parties. The cartels of the pre-war period as well as the compulsory syndicates set up in the war served as a model. No longer should the self-interest of the individual or the state be dominant, but "the central will of an organism motivated by a sense of self-awareness," whereby the initiative and responsibility of the individual was to be maintained, supported by the common cause. In this way the task of public economic policy was to be carried out, equivalent to the principles of communal self-government.[15] Undersecretary of State von Möllendorff and Minister of Economics Wissel hoped in May of 1919 to achieve these objectives through a special type of planned economy: an economy operating under a plan, controlled by the public and based on the tendencies towards unification of the working population. The basic idea was to incorporate enterprises, associations and cartels in a social-economic system on the basis of the public law. The task of self-regulation was to be carried out by a special parliament including such organizations as the Reich Coal Council (Reichskohlenrat), Reich Potash Council (Reichskalirat), Full Assembly of the Iron Industry (Vollversammlung des Eisenwirtschaftbundes), Association of the Tar Industry (Teerwirtschaftsverband), Sulfuric Acid Committee (Ausschuss für Schwefelsäure), etc. supervised by the Reich Economic Council (Reichswirtschaftsrat).[16]

The Möllendorff plan was temporarily realized in some sections of the economy.[17] Thus, compulsory syndicates and supervisory committees were set up in the shoe and soap industries, first as war-time organizations through decrees and proclamations of March 17, 1917, June 9, 1917, and July 26, 1917.[18] Similar compulsory cartels were formed in the textile industry by Decree on the Economic Measures for the Transition Economy in the Textile Industry in June 27, 1918.[19]

Except for the coal and potash industries, these plans failed.[20] However, the economic development of these two industries was deeply influenced by this period for the next two decades and even until today. Regional compulsory syndicates and a uniform gas syndicate were organized under the coal law.[21] They were controlled by the Coal Board of the Reich in which employers, employees, consumers, the coal trades and the interested states (Länder) were represented. It was the task of the Federation to supervise the policy and price structure of the syndicates. The Reichskalirat exercised a similar control over the potash syndicate until 1933.[22]

At about the same time the central employer associations united as a response to the attempted nationalization during the revolution of 1918–19, and began to operate in those sections of the economy which were not controlled by the government. The Federation of the German Industry (Reichsverband der Deutschen Industrie) formed a cartel division in 1920 under the direction of Max Metzner whose function it was to serve as a link between government and industry and to prevent the abuse of cartels. The division set up a cartel register, collected cartel charters and maintained cartel archives.[23] Also at that time, a cartel advisory board was formed and attached to the Ministry of Economics.

II. Governmental Cartel Policy; Supervision of Abuses

From 1923 to 1933 German governmental cartel policy pursued the "abuse principle" (Mißbrauchsprinzip), which recognized basically the legality of cartels, but which, through the establishment of special legal norms set certain limits to the use of cartels beyond which all arrangements and cartel decisions were null and void. The primary aim of the legislation was to give cartel members the freedom to cancel their membership under certain circumstances.

1. Period until the great depression (1923–1929)

The first decisive steps with respect to cartels were taken by the German Legislature in 1923 when the Decree against the Abuse of Economic Power Positions (Verordnung gegen Missbrauch wirtschaftlicher Machtstellungen) was issued on November 2, 1923. Only a short time before the Decree was issued the Minister of Economics (Reichswirtschaftsminister) had declared on November 30, 1921, that there was no intention to curb the economic freedom of the individual in this particular respect.[24] The steps taken by the Legislature towards an active cartel policy grew out of the emergency situation caused by the complete collapse of the German currency during the Great Inflation and was, therefore, a rather impulsive reaction.[25] Based on the Empowering Act of October 13, 1923, (Ermächtigungsgesetz) one of the then short-lived governments issued this decree which in the following years influenced the entire cartel policy, although its analysis of the cause of the collapse of the economy was at least partly wrong. The decree did not reflect the definition of cartels as generally advanced in economic theory, but, in order to prevent any circumvention of the norms, was kept in broader and less precise terms. Basically, cartels were considered legal and, consequently, were given legal protection. However, such legal protection ceased in case of cartel abuse. In order to facilitate enforcement of the decree, written cartel agreements were required. Any verbal agreements were null and void. The decree applied only to contracts and agreements between at least two economically and legally independent enterprises. Thus, consolidated firms did not come within the meaning of the decree since the contractual relationship among the consolidated parts of such firms were substantially different from that among cartel members.

The Cartel Decree (Kartellverordnung) was designed as an instrument for state intervention in case a cartel agreement or cartel decision was found to threaten the economy as a whole or the public welfare. According to paragraph 4, such a threat was posed if production or distribution were "restricted in a manner unjustifiable from an overall economic viewpoint, if prices were increased or kept high, or if, in addition to price increases necessitated by inflationary trends, surcharges for risks were included, or if the economic freedom was unreasonably impaired through boycotts of suppliers or customers or through discrimination as to prices or terms."

The decree set limits only to the civil-legal validity of obligations imposed by cartel agreements. If cartels continued to operate despite being declared null and void by the State, criminal codes could not be applied. In consequence, the protection afforded by paragraph 18 was insufficient. Disciplinary penalties which could be imposed represented an inadequate instrument for effective intervention by the courts or the State. Thus, the Minister of Economics, who was the responsible authority for the governmental cartel policy, possessed no decisive power to pursue an active policy against cartels. He had merely the right to issue orders to the effect that each firm participating in a cartel or cartel decision could withdraw or ignore any cartel decision if the economy as a whole or the public welfare were endangered. However, if no member withdrew from the cartel, the Minister could only file a request with the Cartel Court to nullify it in a formal proceeding. If the firms involved continued, nevertheless, to adhere to the nullified agreements, no further means of intervention were available. Here becomes evident the much too optimistic attitude then prevailing that self-regulation of the economy will insure optimal economic behavior of the individual if only freedom of decision is preserved.

A special Cartel Court was formed under the auspices of the Federal Court of Economics (Reichswirtschaftsgericht). Its decisions were made by a chairman and four assessors. It was stipulated that the chairman and his deputy had to be qualified for the office of a judge. An attempt was made in staffing the highest cartel authority to recognize both the democratic and self-regulative principles. Thus, two of the assessors were to be appointed "under consideration of the opposing economic interests" while the third one was to be chosen as "representative of the public interest."

The effect of the legislation based on the abuse principle was small.[26] The Cartel Court nullified agreements as requested by the Minister of Economics only sparingly and in minor cases.

As already indicated, the decree provided an opportunity for cartel members to withdraw or to consider a joint decision non-binding for "important reason." This stipulation was more significant in that no proof of a threat to the economy as a whole or the public welfare had to be established. A cartel member could cancel his membership without court proceedings or governmental action. The Cartel Court examined the justification for such cancellation only upon request by a cartel participant. Unreasonable restriction of economic freedom of the cancelling member with respect to production, distribution or prices was recognized as an "important reason." Here again, the law-makers believed that the termination of legal restrictions would automatically lead to the elimination of monopolistic market positions as a result of the self-regulating forces inherent in economic processes. This was an erroneous belief as the law-makers failed to recognize under which "parameter of action" of the participating firms collective agreements were considered either valuable or burdensome. Thus, they did not strike at the urgent cases of abuse where economic power was employed, but chiefly exercised pressure on those cartels which were and would have remained relatively insignificant because of too many participants and dissimilarities in the shape of the members' cost curves. Nevertheless, relatively frequent use was made of this provision for the purpose of withdrawal and dissolution of the cartel. Prior to the establishment of a cartel almost all firms which are in competition with each other have an interest in collective agreements with respect to price increases or other improvements of market conditions, even if the cost curves of such firms are of different shape and position. But once the cartel is formed, the behavior of the parties towards the agreement usually undergoes changes if, as is normally the case, in the various phases of the business cycle the different shapes and positions of the cost curves begin to work varyingly to the advantage of some members and to the disadvantage of others. As demand declines, modernly equipped firms with high fixed costs seek to reduce cartel prices in order to alleviate the burden of the fixed costs through increased output, while enterprises with low fixed but high variable costs aim at higher prices as a result of their differently shaped marginal cost curves.

In other words, the greater the dissimilarities in the historical and technological development of the firms within an industry the sooner, after the establishment of a cartel, will there be a disparity in the parameters of action of the cartelized firms as market conditions change. This is due to dissimilarities in the cost curves of the participating firms which, as a result of the cartelization, create varying advantages for some members and disadvantages for others.[27] Firms with high fixed costs are particularly pressed to withdraw from the cartel in the hope that, as demand declines, they can increase their proportionate share of the market as outsiders by way of price cuts, i.e., by better adjustment of prices and output to the intersection of their marginal cost and marginal revenue curves. Thus, these firms are able to make better and more efficient use of their capacity and to distribute fixed costs over a larger output than would be possible if they remained in the cartel. The more modern one of the members' production facilities and the higher the percentage of old and inefficient firms in the same cartel, the faster do they collapse in face of the constantly changing phases in the business cycle. Here the Government, by giving cartel members the opportunity to terminate their membership without notice, succeeded in increasing the inherent tendency of cartels to collapse.

Many proceedings were instituted at the Cartel Court as a result of the imposition of restrictive penalties and of fines payable from the security deposits made by cartel members. Paragraph 9 of the Cartel Decree of 1923 required the consent of the chairman of the Cartel Court to the application of such sanctions by cartels as a means of forcing outsiders to join and of compelling members to adhere to the agreements.

The opposition existing between cartels and cooperatives in the years 1922 to 1923 played an important role in the movement for creating a cartel law. Various cartels, by means of mutual agreements and exclusive contracts between producers and wholesalers, had succeeded in restricting supply through cooperatives.

The Cartel Decree of 1923 was very much influenced by the antagonistic relationship which prevailed between cartels and cooperatives. In subsequent years, however, this situation changed, particularly during the Great Depression as cooperatives were able to maintain a larger sales volume than the wholesale trade. The Cartel Decree of 1923 also provided cancellation rights for trusts. However, this provision was never used as such combinations are characterized by a common capital basis, united ownership, etc. rather than contractual agreements among firms under separate ownership with respect to prices, output, and related matters. Moreover, the Minister of Economics issued a decree which gave interested persons the right to file a request with the Cartel Court for the issuance of an injunction concerning the use of certain terms of sale and certain types of price calculations by monopolistic enterprises or trusts, if economic power was used and the economy as a whole or the public welfare were threatened. As a result of the formal and unwieldy procedure involved, however, little or no use was made of this measure.

Another special decree was issued in 1923[28] which imposed an obligation on all business enterprises to disclose upon request certain information to both Federal and State authorities, who could also conduct inspections. The use of this decree became part of the cartel policy.

The proceedings under the Cartel Decree of 1923 were much too rigid and inflexible for an active and systematic governmental cartel policy. The tendency towards concentration continued unchecked. Throughout this period only a few cases of interference pursuant to paragraph 4 (lines 1–2) occurred,[29] and the formation of cartels was insignificantly affected by governmental policy. Its main effect was in further shortening the duration of the already short-lived cartels. It was characteristic during this period that a large number of such cartels existed for only a few months and that time and again breakdowns occurred, followed by the establishment of new collective agreements.

By the year 1929 the number of cartels had increased to more than 1800.[30] The basic industries were regulated by a few strongly organized cartels; the industries producing semi-finished goods were largely cartelized, and in the finished goods industries a similar situation prevailed, although only a few cartels proved to be effective and were able to survive. Thus, the development of the German economy was decisively influenced by cartels and the peculiar cartel "rhythm" inherent in them. By and large, the State was unable to interfere effectively with the cartel development: it lacked adequate legislation.

2. Cartel policy during the great depression (1930–1933)

The Great Depression, which stirred up substantial political passions in large sections of the German population as a result of the millions of unemployed workers and a temporary loss of confidence in the self-regulating forces of the economy, led to a change in governmental policy. This was a development comparable to that in the United States. As demand declined sharply and prices collapsed, only the cartelized industries were, despite heavy cuts in their profits, in the position of keeping their markets in relatively good order. Thus, the government, which in the absence of sufficient majorities in Parliament was forced increasingly to resort to emergency decrees and to take steps against deflation and the collapse of business firms, adopted cartels as a measure of relief. Compulsory cartels were designed for the support of industries which became particularly vulnerable in the Great Depression and which were characterized by a large number of bankruptcies at that time. Thus, the use of cartels began to constitute a part of governmental crisis policy. The first compulsory cartels were formed in the agricultural sector where private cartel agreements had never been established as a result of the large number of operating units. These cartels embraced such commodities as milk,[31] sugar and potato starch.[32]

The Great Depression had far reaching structural effects on the shipping industry which for some forms of enterprise proved to be downright catastrophic, as for instance in the case of the "bargees." These people possessed only one barge on which they lived with their families and on which their entire existence was based. The bargees did not maintain their own feeder service for freight to be shipped. Larger manufacturers with regular shipping needs had built up their own fleets during the boom years and employed the bargees only if their shipping requirements exceeded their capacity. Therefore, the livelihood of the bargees became particularly endangered in the Great Depression. The government intervened and established market regulations which, in essence, are still in existence today: the bargees were combined in a compulsory cartel and guaranteed a predetermined portion of the total shipping volume as well as predetermined prices. Here the government employed compulsory cartels in favor of the bargees also as part of its social policy.[33]

The attitude of the State towards cartels, however, was not always consistent during the depression. On the one hand, it recognized the stabilizing effects of cartels on those industries which were in distress, while on the other hand it viewed them, in accordance with the doctrines of Keynes, as being partly responsible for the loss of flexibility and adaptability of firms to changing economic conditions, and believed that this was the reason why the long expected upswing still did not materialize. Therefore, a special cartel emergency decree was issued during the depression by the government for the purpose of preventing and destroying "uneconomic price fixing," as the law-makers called it.[34] It was at this point that the Reich Government, for the first time in German cartel history, obtained the power to outlaw certain price cartels and to bring resale price fixing by manufacturers under state supervision.[35] Thus, under the impact of the depression, the Reich Minister of Economics became the most important agent of state cartel policy, replacing in this respect the Cartel Court set up under the Decree of 1923. The government was now in a position to nullify cartel agreements and decisions and to prohibit the application of cartel terms. Even price recommendations became subject to state supervision. Cartel members had to terminate their membership upon order by the government. Moreover, the government considered reductions or the elimination of tariffs as a measure directed against cartels, but little was actually done in this respect.

On August 30, 1930, a regulatory statute was issued by which the Minister of Economics was authorized to eliminate sales schemes set up by manufacturers using their economic power to require customers not only to maintain the resale prices for the goods they manufactured, but also for other manufacturers' goods or services.

As the effects of the depression became more and more drastic and unemployment continued to increase, it still was the prevailing view among economists that the bottom of the slump was not yet reached as a result of the widespread price fixing. Consequently, the government issued a decree on January 16, 1931 (RGBl I, p. 12) by which a general price decrease of 10% was ordered for all branded goods for which price agreements existed. Nine months later a new emergency decree followed, providing for another 10% decrease. However, no significant results were achieved. Total employment continued to decline, gradually creating a politically dangerous atmosphere.

At the same time the office of a state Price Commissioner (Preiskommissar) was established, an action which proved to be more significant than any other previous governmental cartel measure.

The new legal instruments of the government devised during the depression served to abolish in 1931 the Central German Brown Coal Syndicate of 1927, to dissolve a cartel agreement in the pencil manufacturing industry, to interfere with the Dextrine Sales Association and to intervene in the strike in the automotive parts industry. The state government attacked the Kiel Combine of Brickyards and Brownstoneyards.[36] But still, measured by the total number of the then existing cartels, the effects of the new governmental policy were relatively weak.

Legislation was passed on July 15, 1933, by which the cartel control function was finally passed from a judicial authority to a political authority. The Reich Minister of Economics was now equipped with the power to nullify collective agreements and decisions inconsistent with the public welfare. It was only through this change that paragraph 4 (lines 1–3) of the Cartel Decree of 1923 became a usable and effective instrument of an active cartel control.

A look at the cartel situation in Germany at the beginning of the year 1933 may serve for the purpose of evaluating the effectiveness of the government policy. With a few exceptions all raw materials and semi-finished goods produced in Germany were cartelized. Approximately one-fourth to one-third of the production of finished goods was within the influence of cartel agreements.

These cartels, most of which were only short-lived, gave the economic processes and developments a peculiar rhythm. If they succeeded in raising prices, new firms entered the industry, operating as outsiders which led to a decline in sales by the cartel members; the cartel collapsed and a price war set in until, as a result of the destructive competitive struggle, a new cartel emerged and the next round began. The short-lived nature of the cartels forced the members to undertake high investments during the existence of the cartel with its good opportunities for self-financing in order to be prepared for the competitive warfare following the breakdown of the cartel. Thus, investments were noticeably high in times of high market prices, and technological advances were rapidly adopted by the cartelized firms.

Only the longer-lived well organized cartels in the basic industries or those cartels that were based on certain patents behaved in the way that was frequently suggested by economic theory. They curbed production of the cartelized products and showed, as a result of their secure market position, no interest in technological progress. But cartels of this type were the exception in Germany. Nevertheless, studies of individual cases clearly indicate the typical market behavior of these cartels which was altogether different from that of the usual short-lived type of cartel. Even the increasingly drastic governmental policy could not disturb the awareness by these firms of their secured position in the market. Thus, entirely different secondary processes can be noticed in the longer-lived cartels as compared with those which were always threatened by outsiders and collapse. With respect to dividends, however, no difference in behavior is noticeable: neither in the short-lived nor in the longer-lived cartels were the high profits which resulted from the price agreements used to benefit the shareholders. The firms belonging to the small group of well organized cartels used the increased profits to build vertical and conglomerate trusts, adding to their operations production units which had a marginal efficiency of capital higher than their own.

III. Cartels as Integral Part of the Planned Economy[37] (1933–1943)[38]

As in other countries, the experience in Germany during the Great Depression showed that cartels could serve under certain conditions as effective instruments of economic control by the state. The repeated attempts made in the years of the depression encouraged the Government of the German Reich to issue general cartel rules. Accordingly, a law on the formation of compulsory cartels was promulgated on July 15, 1933 (RGBl I, p. 488). While in previous years governmental policy with respect to cartels was legally limited to interventions in cases of proven abuses, inconsistent with the interest of the public and the economy as a whole, and to restrictions of compulsory membership, it now became possible for the government actually to employ cartels in the pursuit of its economic policy. Whereas previously the formation of compulsory cartels always required special legislation, the law of 1933 gave the Reich Minister of Economics general authority to combine firms into syndicates or other cartels or to include outsiders in such combines, if the interest of the firms, the public or the economy as a whole required such action (par. 1).

When the law was enacted, it was emphasized in the official commentary that its provisions were to be used only in exceptional circumstances and with utmost discretion, and that compulsory cartels were to be formed only after private industry had failed to resolve existing problems by its own initiative and self-regulation. Under no circumstances was the economic system, based upon the initiative and responsibility of the individual entrepreneur, to be changed. Moreover, it was pointed out that the provisions were of transitory nature, to be abolished immediately after the economic situation resulting from the world depression should have improved.

A law, once it is passed, frequently develops its own dynamics. The 1933 act, originally devised as an emergency measure, became permanent legislation and, at the same time, served National Socialism (Nationalsozialismus) as an instrument for its economic policy which differed basically from the policy under previous governments. Paragraph 5 of the measure provided that the Reich Minister of Economics could temporarily prohibit the establishment of new firms or the expansion of already existing enterprises in distressed industries. Furthermore, the Minister could make investment decisions of private industry subject to governmental approval, issue investment stop orders or demand that investments be undertaken. With the passage of the four-year plan legislation the Minister received the authority to require or to forbid the utilization of certain raw materials or semi-finished products.

Governmental interventions based on the Compulsory Cartel Law increased from year to year. The validity of each intervening measure was generally short-termed. Certain stop orders with respect to investments, for instance, were ordinarily limited to several months. Unlimited compulsory cartels, extending over several years, were the exception. Upon expiration of the intervention period, the government was to examine the structure and the economic condition of the industry involved and to intervene again if a change in that structure was deemed necessary under the current objectives of public economic policy. The compulsory cartel law was applied in the following instances: cartelization of industries in which no cartels existed, continuation of cartels which had collapsed or were about to collapse, compulsory inclusion of outsiders, investment orders or investment bans with respect to the installation of certain machines, expansion bans, group protection and plant relocation bans. These "bans" made all relevant decisions by private industry subject to governmental approval. Thus the state could control and shape the economy in accordance with its objectives. The compulsory cartel law became to an increasing degree a tool of public economic control until Germany finally switched to a wartime economy.[39]

In 1936 again a Price Commissioner was installed in office whose price control authority was subsequently increased, as evidenced by a change in title to "Price Formation Commissioner" (Reichskommissar für Preisbildung). Prices throughout the economy were not to exceed the 1936 level. This measure curtailed the scope of the price cartels and other collective agreements to a large degree.

The Minister of Economics issued a decree on November 12, 1936, which provided for participation in the cartel supervision by the industrial organizations. By placing cartels under the self-regulation of the industrial organizations[40] and by transferring governmental control functions to private business and trade associations, all cartels—and not only the compulsory cartels—came under direct control of the Ministry of Economics as the authority responsible for public economic policy.

The most important functions of the Cartel Court being changed, a law was issued on February 25, 1938, providing for its combination with the Reich Court of Economics. During the war the court was absorbed by the newly established Reich Court of Administration (Reichsverwaltungsgericht).

Immediately prior to World War II and during the first phases of the war, when the market economy became more and more controlled by the four-year plans, cartels remained formally in existence, but their activities stagnated in the face of high employment and favorable prices. As the rigidity of the centralized control over the war-time economy increased, the cartels were less and less in a position to fulfill their tasks and achieve their objectives.

Finally, on January 29, 1943, the Minister of Economics issued an order by which all quota cartels were prohibited in order to eliminate any limitations on production during the years of war. This was followed by the issuance of a cartel adjustment decree on May 20, 1943, which provided for a transfer of all regulating functions to the Organization of Trade and Industry (Organization der Gewerblichen Wirtschaft) which included the newly formed Reich Associations (Reichsvereinigungen).

Syndicates remained in existence as a result of their distribution functions within the war-time economy. At the end of the war the total number of cartels had declined to 650, a larger number of which were nothing more than mere shells.

IV. Period of Cartel Prohibition

1. Cartel prohibition by the occupying powers (1945–1956)

The decartelization and deconcentration of trusts by the occupying powers was undoubtedly one of the greatest experiments undertaken by political forces in a market economy.

After the allied policy had been determined in section B-12 of the Declaration of Potsdam, decartelization laws were issued in the three western zones: Law No. 56 for the US Zone and Ordinance No. 78 for the British Zone, both on December 2, 1947, as well as Decree No. 96 for the French Zone, issued on October 6, 1947. All agreements limiting competition were forbidden.[41]

Thus, all cartels were prohibited. German administrative authorities and courts unconditionally recognized these measures. Occasional exemptions from the general prohibition of cartels were granted by the occupying powers, although no uniform policy and procedure with respect to such exemptions evolved.

Unfortunately, in retrospect, it must be stated that the decartelization and deconcentration policy was a failure. To be sure, the interventions by the occupying authorities, which particularly disregarded property rights in connection with the deconcentration, had far reaching effects. But market economic processes which continuously emerges as a result of decreasing marginal costs, inelastic demand and elastic supply curves cannot be reversed entirely by legal prohibitions and orders. A successful policy in this field would have required other means.

Despite the cartel prohibition uniform market behavior began to appear in those industries which had previously been characterized by the existence of strong cartels. The economic effects of this uniform behavior did not differ from those exercised earlier by the cartels. The only contrast existed in the fact that such behavior lacked a legal foundation and enforcement. The uniform type of price formation, production agreements and general business terms continued to prevail in the industries which were previously strongly cartelized. Only in industries where under the regime of free cartelization reluctant firms had to be forced to adhere to collective agreements did uniformity in economic behavior fail to emerge under the regime of general cartel prohibition. However, when we analyzed the length of time that cartel agreements lasted, we recognized that this group of cartels was characterized by short-lived agreements since the divergent cost curves determined the parameter of action and since the mere contractual arrangements did not prevent the termination of cartel membership.

This period of cartel policy demonstrated particularly the great significance for the behavior of competing enterprises in a market economy of the shape and position of their cost curves as well as the demand and supply elasticities. Moreover, this period showed how relatively secondary legal norms are in such a market structure.[42] Even the most rigid prohibitions are effective only if the state authorities are in a position to oversee and control the economic processes or to change cost curves and demand and supply elasticities. Ordinarily, state authorities lack adequate means of gaining insight into business and its constantly changing phenomena within a market economy.[43]

2. Cartel policy in the European Coal and Steel Community and the European Economic Community

The 1951 Treaty of the European Coal and Steel Community (of which Belgium, Germany, France, Italy, Luxemburg and the Netherlands are members) provides cartel prohibition for the industries which come within its scope, although exemptions from the general cartel prohibition may be granted by the High Commission under certain conditions. The following actions are unlawful:

1) Restriction of market entry (article 3b).
2) Actions or practices which lead to a discrimination of producers, sellers or consumers, particularly with respect to prices and terms

of delivery (article 4b), and which are aimed at a division of markets (article 4d).

The High Commission may permit agreements on certain products, if it is convinced that such agreements will contribute to an improvement in production or distribution and if such agreements do not create possibilities within the common market area to fix prices or to control production or distribution.

The disputed dissolution of central national coal sales agencies may serve as an illustration of the effectiveness and limitation of these provisions. In Germany the Joint Ruhr Coal Organization which possessed the character of a syndicate, ceased its operations on March 31, 1956, in order to comply with the cartel provisions. This was followed by the formation of three, about equally sized, joint sales agencies. In France and Belgium, on the other hand, central coal sales and import agencies remained in existence. As a result of the experiences during the coal crisis, the Ruhr coal industry again plans the establishment of a central sales organization and submitted to the High Commission a corresponding proposal which was rejected at first, although examinations regarding its legality under the provisions of the Treaty are not yet concluded.

When the pithead stock of the Ruhr coal enterprises, after years of prosperity, began to pile up as a result of the competition of oil and of coal from overseas, a coal-oil cartel, set up with the assistance of the state, failed to bring about the uniform market behavior of the competing firms which was a prerequisite for lessening the crisis in the coal industry. Particularly the emergence of outsiders led to a quick collapse of the cartel. Subsequently, the Ruhr coal industry attempted on its own to form a rationalization cartel by organizing the Action Group of the Ruhr Mining Industry (Aktionsgemeinschaft Ruhrbergbau). It was the objective of this organization to make mines, coke plants and other operations of the mining firms more efficient, to shut down high cost mines and to pay cash compensation for the transfer of their business to the more efficient mines. The High Commission, however, raised doubts as to the legality of this program under the provisions of the Coal and Steel Treaty.

The Treaty of the European Economic Community also contains legally binding provisions with respect to competitive relations within the Common Market. Although primarily regulating supra-national commerce in the Common Market Area, the Treaty may also be applied to governmental measures within any one country, if restrictive agreements among firms controlling the national market show evidence of uniform market behavior.

Thus far, the effects of these provisions have been insignificant.

3. Cartel policy based on the law against limitations on competition since 1957 (prohibition legislation)

(a) *Basic features of the law*

The discussions of the bill against limitations on competition during the preparatory stage of the new German cartel legislation gave rise to dissenting opinions among economists and politicians. The controversy ultimately concentrated on the issue of "prohibition legislation" vs. "abuse legislation." Should cartels be generally forbidden? Or should they, in accordance with general legal norms, be valid, if set up and operated in compliance with applicable laws, and become illegal only in case of an abuse of economic power? Both the German experience in the previous years and the cartel legislation in most other European countries show that the difference between these two alternatives is not as great as it appeared to be at the time when anti-cartel legislation was proposed by the German administration. Countries which basically accepted the prohibition principle built a number of exemptions into their legislation against cartels and restrictive business practices. It is only with respect to the burden of proof that the difference between the two principles gains significance.

The Neo-Liberals, grouped chiefly around the Freiburg School,[44] demanded of the state an active intervention policy in order to prevent the formation of collective market power, detrimental to the restoration of maximum competitive conditions. The group of economists favoring the abuse principles,[45] on the other hand, called for a general permissibility of cartels, subject to a thorough control of their abuse and administrative supervision. Although differences of opinion with respect to details existed, there was no economist of any authority in Germany who advocated unlimited freedom for cartels.

The Law against Limitations on Competition (Gesetz gegen Wettbewerbsbeschränkungen) was expressly conceived as the Magna Charta of economic freedom. In the bill which was finally passed as a compromise after seven years of deliberations on July 7, 1957 (RGBl, I, p. 1081) the prohibition principle was adopted. However, many exemptions from the general prohibition of cartels were provided. As far as these exemptions are concerned, a distinction has to be made between

"Widerspruchskartelle" (i.e. cartels which will generally come into existence after registration, unless the Federal Cartel Office in charge rejects the application, owing to special reasons outlined in par. 12) and "Erlaubniskartelle" (those cartels which are in want of a special approval of the Federal Cartel Office and are not allowed to start their activities before the Federal Cartel Office has made its decision). The former type comprises term-fixing cartels (par. 2), rebate cartels (par. 3), cartels which were founded to support specialization and standardization (par. 5,1 and 5,4), and export cartels on condition that their activities do not encroach upon internal market conditions (par. 6,1). Structural crisis cartels (par. 4), rationalization cartels (par. 5, 2, 3), import cartels (par. 7), and export cartels (if their activities encroach upon internal market conditions), however, belong to the "Erlaubniskartelle". Furthermore the law gives the Minister of Economics authority to permit cartels if in exceptional circumstances limitations on competition become necessary in the interest of the economy as a whole or the public welfare (par. 8 sec. 1).

Thus, the German law allows rationalization cartels and term-fixing cartels[46] which are not permitted in United States antitrust legislation. Under the Law against Limitations on Competition the responsible administrative agency is authorized either to approve or to forbid cartel agreements and decisions which regulate production or market conditions. This is quite in contrast to the antitrust laws in the United States, where the industry must make decisions at its own risk with respect to cartel agreements as no antitrust enforcement agency has the authority to grant permissions.

When the bill was debated special attention was given to the problem of resale price maintenance. The provisions of the law, which were finally accepted as a compromise, make agreements on non-branded products void, if a party to such an agreement is restricted in the formation of prices and other terms of sale (par. 15). In other words, the vertical fixing of prices and other business terms are generally void. However, vertical price fixing of branded goods[47] and products of the publishing industry are exempted (par. 16)[48]. Agricultural products despite their natural fluctuations in quality are, nevertheless, treated as branded goods. In order to prevent abuse, permissible resale price maintenance contracts are subject to the filing of a registration statement with the cartel authority. Horizontal agreements on the introduction of vertical price maintenance contracts[49] are in any case unlawful. Thus, the German law generally permits resale price maintenance by the individual manufacturer, but makes its legal effectiveness subject to registration with and written confirmation by the cartel authority. It was the intention of the law makers to equip the cartel office in this way with a means of intervention in the matter of resale price maintenance under certain conditions. Here again, we find a procedure foreign to United States antitrust legislation.

Although agreements among agricultural enterprises and associations are subject to registration, such agreements become legally effective even if no registration is undertaken, provided that no price fixing is involved. Agreements on uniform methods of contract specifications and break down of prices, if no price fixing is involved, are treated by the law in the same way.

The following arrangements are legally effective without registration, but subject to a supervision of abuse by the Federal Cartel Office.[50]

Agreements among shipping lines and airlines covering routings beyond national borders.

Vertical price agreements in the publishing industry.

Agreements in forestry, providing that no price fixing is involved.

Certain contracts among public utilities.

Contractual limitations on the utilization of products.

Exclusive dealership contracts, distribution agreements and obligations with respect to tie-in deals.

Tie-in deals which are set up through the use of economic power by market controlling firms and by which increased prices or less favorable contract terms are imposed.

Relatively large sections of the economy are generally exempted from the anticartel provisions of the Law against Limitations on Competition. This general exemption includes:

The Federal Railway.

The Federal Postal Service.

Certain other contracts in the field of transportation.[51]

Agriculture, forestry, the banking and credit institutions and the insurance industry, particularly the German Federal Bank and the Reconstruction Loan Corporation (par. 101 No. 1).

The liquor and match monopolies[52].

The law does not prohibit industrial and trade organizations from rejecting firms which apply for membership. However, the cartel authority may order the acceptance of an applicant for membership if the rejection represents an unjustified and unequal treatment, resulting in unfair competitive disadvantages for the applying firm. The same regulation applies to quality-mark associations (par. 27).

The German law provides that each member of a cartel, regardless of its type and regardless of the provisions under which it may be permitted, has the irrevocable right to terminate his membership without notice "for important reason." No consultation with the Cartel Office is required for the effectiveness of a membership termination. The term "important reason" is based on the definition given in the Cartel Decree of 1923; for example, the economic freedom of the terminating member must be unduly restricted. The termination of a membership is further facilitated by the stipulation that an objection to such termination in the form of a suit on the grounds of insufficient reason must be raised within four weeks following the receipt of the termination notice. In addition to facilitating the termination of a cartel membership the framers of the anticartel legislation sought to shorten the life even of the permitted cartels as much as possible.

Under the German law fines may be imposed in case of violations. This again is in contrast to American antitrust legislation which permits both civil and criminal prosecution and the imposition of fines as well as imprisonment.

(b) *Cartel Authorities*

The German Law against Limitations on Competition provides for a decentralized cartel administration. The Federal Cartel Office (Bundeskartellamt), an independent agency in Berlin, is charged with the essential tasks and authority with regard to governmental cartel policy. Its independence is emphasized by the fact that it does not come within the budget of the Minister of Economics and that the scope of its functions is legislatively insured. However, as a result of the administrative organization, the Cartel Office is still placed under the supervision of the Ministry of Economics, although the latter authority cannot issue specific directives in individual cases. In emergency situations the Minister of Economics may take active part in the work of the Cartel Office. Under the above mentioned general clause (par. 8) he has the authority to grant special approval to cartel objectives or cartel decisions otherwise prohibited, if a restraint of competition becomes necessary in the interest of the economy as a whole or the public welfare.

Decisions affecting an individual state fall within the competence of the supreme authorities of that state (state cartel offices). Cooperation between state and federal authorities is insured by a mutual obligation to exchange information and by participation in anti-cartel proceedings (par. 51, sec. 3). The cartel authorities may collect information and conduct examinations as well as investigations (par. 54ff).

The framers of the Law against Limitations on Competition placed emphasis upon subjecting the Federal Cartel Office as well as the Federal Minister of Economics, if acting under the general clause of paragraph 8, to a legislatively insured control by providing certain remedies (objection and complaint). Complaints must be filed with the Regional Court of Appeal (Oberlandesgericht), i.e., a court of civil law, having jurisdiction over the case. This court, in its rulings, may exercise judicial discretion. Only the "appraisal of condition and development of the economy as a whole" is beyond the competence of the court. Thus, the lawmakers recognized that the measure deeply interferes with the freedom of contract and that the administrative decisions of the Cartel Office do not differ substantially from the exercise of judicial functions.

The Federal Cartel Office is headed by a President and a Vice-President and consists of the following departments: 5 departments with decisional functions; 1 appeal department; 1 department for economic surveys, also exercising investigatory functions; 1 judicial department; 1 administrative department. In December of 1960, 170 persons were employed by the Cartel Office (68 civil servants, 102 clerks and other workers).

(c) *Past activity of the federal cartel office* [53]

Since the effective date of the Law against Limitations on Competition (January 1, 1958) up to December 1960, 189 motions for registration or approval were received by the Federal Cartel Office. The largest group contains 54 motions for registration of export cartels. It is succeeded by 39 motions for approval of rationalization cartels, 26 motions for registration of term-fixing cartels and 23 of rebate cartels, 16 motions for approval of export cartels with regulation of the inland-market. Twenty-three of these motions were withdrawn.

In Holland 1600 export cartels were counted for 1960, while in England 2500 export cartels were registered. Thus, the number of German cartels of this type is relatively small.[54]

Up to December 1960, 191,762 resale price maintenance contracts were registered with the Federal Cartel Office. Of these, 85,175 contracts cover spare parts in the automobile industry. The absolute number of contracts has not changed substiantially since 1959 because new registrations and cancellations of contracts nearly equalled one another. The Federal Cartel Office intends to examine systematically all registered contracts with regard to possible abuses. However, up to the present time, this agency has conducted such examinations only in individual cases.

Up to December 1960, 87 cartel contracts belonging to the field of "Widerspruchskartelle" had come into existence. Furthermore, 13 cartels in want of a special approval have obtained the incontestable approval of the Federal Cartel Office in the same way as 27 so-called "Überläuferkartelle" (i.e. cartels which were in existence before 1945, and continued their activities with the permission of the respective Military Government). That means that most of the decisions of the Federal Cartel Office were favorable to the cartels. Clearly unfavorable decisions were made in only three cases: one refusal of registration, and two rejections of approval.

An application for a pipe-connector cartel was rejected. Further, a structural crisis cartel for shoe materials (soles, heels, etc.) was not granted approval. The Cartel Office stated in its opinion that the members had refused to present a plan for the elimination of excess manufacturing capacity. Also rejected in the first instance was an application by the "Stove Market Association" (Marktgemeinschaft Öfen). It was the objective of this cartel to insure effective price competition, based on efficiency, through elimination of an alleged cut-throat policy followed in that industry with respect to rebates and general business terms.

A mill cartel—representing an unusually branched out cartel, consisting of three main and nine regional conventions—applied for permission to continue in the form of a structural crisis cartel certain restrictive agreements set up in 1955. However, the examination of the legal and economic problems involved had not yet been concluded. This cartel suffered rather severely from the activities of outsiders and time and again was in danger of collapse.[55]

The 39 syndicates[56] which were registered with the Cartel Office had already been in existence when the law became effective, and, for the present, may probably continue to operate. Their effect upon the market as well as their actual market behavior has thus far been neither limited nor examined by the cartel authority.

On the basis of the empowering clause contained in the German law, the Federal Cartel Office gave approval to two syndicates: the Stoneware syndicate (Steinzeugsyndikat)[57] and the Association of German Potash Producers (Gemeinschaft deutscher Kalierzeuger), representing a continuation of the Potash Syndicate which dates back to 1876, with its Sales Association of German Potash Mines (Verkaufsgemeinschaft deutscher Kaliwerke GmbH) in Hannover. Permission was granted for three years. In its support of the latter cartel, whose predecessors had already been exempted from the cartel prohibition imposed by the Allied Forces, the Cartel Office pointed out that this cartel was suitable for a reduction in the number of different potash grades and an improvement in the product quality. It was moreover argued that the syndicate would provide a continuous supervision over the various potash qualities.

The cartel members are obligated to notify the Cartel Office with respect to any participations in enterprises engaged in the distribution of fertilizers. This provision is designed to preclude an extension of the syndicate's market power from the production level to the distribution level. Since the Ministry of Economics set a price ceiling for cartels in this industry, the cartel authority reserved the right to revoke the cartel permission in case of a change or elimination of the governmental price regulation.

Up to December 1960 the Federal Cartel Office instituted 1398 proceedings in connection with possible violations of the law.

Exercise of the abuse supervision with which the cartel authority is charged, led to 535 proceedings in the first three years. The majority of these cases concerned resale price maintenance on branded goods and restrictive agreements under the exemption clauses. Forty-two proceedings were discontinued after the abuses were remedied. Two hundred and thirty-two cases were discontinued for other reasons. In addition, quite a number of adequate proceedings were registered with the State Cartel Authorities (Landeskartellbehörden).

Thus far, little use has been made of the provisions of the law under which legal proceedings may be instituted in regular courts.

(d) *Self-Dynamics of the Cartel Policy*

As with other governmental organizations, the Federal Cartel Office, shortly after its foundation, began to develop dynamics of its own which went beyond legislative design. Perhaps unintentionally, the Office continuously broadened the scope of its decisions related to the administrative construction of the measure. Let us look at a few of the many illustrative cases.

When the Stoneware Syndicate filed its registration statement, the Cartel Office attempted to secure continuous control over the syndicate by ordering its members to file annual balance sheets with the Office. The three-year permission was tied in with a stipulation by which the syndicate's joint sales organization in Hannover was obligated to notify the Cartel Office promptly with respect to all changes in prices, rebates and terms of sale and payment. Copies of the minutes of all advisory committee meetings, the text of all membership decisions as well as the reports required by the syndicate under its statutes from the members must be filed with the Office. On the basis of the balance sheets and profit and loss statements the Cartel Office intends to determine whether the expected gains in efficiency were actually achieved.[58]

The electrical installation industry maintained a price reporting system which, in its opinion, was beyond the scope of the law. The Cartel Office intervened, and the firms agreed upon the registration of a sales volume rebate cartel.

The Cartel Office urged the Association of German Electrical Technicians (Verband Deutscher Elektrotechniker, "VDE") to report with respect to the effects upon the manufacturers and dealers of "Schuko" two-way plugs as a result of the withdrawal of the "VDE" quality mark for that item. The association, a voluntary organization for quality tests of electrical products, had withdrawn its quality mark for the plug after it was established in court that accidents had occurred in connection with its use.[59] The Cartel Office obviously suspected that cartel-like agreements might be hidden in the withdrawal.

The Office, as a rule, demanded changes in the cartel agreements filed for registration. In this way, governmental cartel policy is confined to a petty regimentation of business in those industries which happened to trigger actions by the Office through the registration of cartel agreements. Let us give some examples.

In connection with a term-fixing cartel covering supplies to barber shops an objection by the Cartel Office was dropped only after a clause which prohibited the supply of consignment stock had been eliminated, thus limiting the agreement to the direct supply of materials consumed by the barber shops.

The term-fixing cartel of the Association of German Lining Weavers (Verband Deutscher Futterstoffwebereien) and the Convention of German Silk and Velvet Manufacturers (Konvention der deutschen Seidenstoff- und Samtfabrikanten) became effective in the summer of 1959 only after the Cartel Office had demanded and obtained a number of changes. Thus, a provision had to be eliminated by which sales were to be made only at definite prices.

A term-fixing cartel covering fabrics and dress materials as well as hair and other elastic linings (Deutsche Tuch- und Kleiderstoffkonvention) was also changed and supplemented by the Cartel Office. Thus, avoidance of terms of payment and delivery, particularly through consignment orders, was held unlawful. Here also the definite-price clause was stricken.

In the registration statement of a term-fixing cartel of German dyers and dry cleaners (vol. no. 189 of February 10, 1959) the Cartel Office changed the terms of delivery.

The Office also exercised influence on those cartels requiring only notification by setting relatively high fees and by causing considerable costs. It erected innumerable procedural barriers. Requests for comments from other sectors of business, as for instance from the retail trade or large buyers, resulted at times in side effects which were undesirable for the registrants.

The provisions of the law requiring either approval or registration of cartels have caused relatively great expenditures since the formation of the Cartel Office as a result of a heavy volume of questionnaires, examinations, and discussions. The Office established norms for the appraisal of cartels requiring registration. Thus, cartels which are subject only to registration are treated almost like cartels requiring approval. Registration statements are usually answered by various requests for further information. Objections are raised and interviews are requested.

The governmental machine necessary for processing and supervising the cartel agreements gradually exceeds in size the administrative apparatus of all cartels taken together. At the same time, the authorities are swamped with mounting trivialities.

Rebate and term-fixing cartels take such a large part of the Cartel

Office's work load that the urgent problems remain untackled. The time limit provided by the law for raising objections requires immediate processing of all cartel registrations.

The incomparably more important concentration movement, which takes place constantly, as well as the competitive restraints exercised by great power concentrations slip by the Cartel Office completely and thus escape from the law. Term-fixing cartels which are of no great significance for the over-all economic development have always been formed—even in times of total cartel freedom—by enterprises of small and medium size. These firms, as a result of the large number of participants and the existing dissimilarities in shape and position of their cost curves, were unable to reach stronger cartel agreements and, consequently, greater market power. Thus, the Cartel Office drastically interferes with relatively unimportant market agreements in those industries which had been equally unable in earlier periods to form strong and long lasting cartels as a result of types of products which do not lend themselves to cartelization and as a result of other unfavorable conditions.[60] However, in industries with uniform cost curves, elastic demand and inelastic supply curves—industries which in earlier periods had strong and effective cartel agreements—the firms (which are becoming increasingly concentrated) are today induced to follow uniform market behavior even in the absence of agreements. The new law prohibiting such explicit agreements and the activities of the Cartel Office have little impact on the market behavior and parameters of action of business firms in those sections of the economy which are characterized by constantly narrowing competitive conditions.

(e) *Impact of the Law on the General Concentration Movement*

Combinations of enterprises, as for instance in the form of mergers, are generally permitted and legally valid. Such combinations are not even subject to supervision of abuse.

The bill introduced by the Government required special advance approval of combinations in the form of mergers or trusts, if the total market share of the firms involved exceeded 20%. But the Government was unable to achieve passage of this bill by Parliament. The law now only requires notification if a market share of 20% is reached as a result of a combination. The lawmakers argued that the development of firms towards an optimal size should not be impeded. This provision actually means that the law can hardly interfere with concentration in the form of control over share capital. The legal implications of the notification procedure are highly inadequate; the law requires written explanations by the enterprises involved or verbal discussions with the Cartel Office.

The President of the Cartel Office himself stated on various occasions that he regarded the instruments provided by the law against economic concentration as inadequate.

Market controlling firms, however, are subject to supervision of abuse. This section of the law shows in particular the weaknesses of an insufficiently considered and hastily passed compromise. The Cartel Office is authorized to issue cease and desist orders to market controlling firms in case of abusive market behavior and to nullify certain agreements. However, this compromise will prove as ineffective as the Cartel Decree of 1923 and the Decree for the Supervision of Markets of 1942 when the government was unable to establish a conceptual framework for its position towards economic developments as well as for specific economic interventions, and when it lacked adequate power to influence the parameter of action and the parameter of expectation* of large enterprises producing a multitude of different goods.

V. Summary and Conclusions

The behavior and economic effects of cartels as well as the possibilities, effects and limitations of governmental intervention can be well studied in the German cartel history which saw almost all theoretically possible forms of governmental cartel policy and regulation, including periods of cartel freedom, total cartel prohibition and the present period of general cartel prohibition with specified exemptions.

1. Let us again outline in what areas of the economy and in what form cartels may emerge, provided that a policy of complete freedom for cartels is granted. Long-term, effective and strong cartels arose only when the following conditions existed in an optimal combination: a small number of manufacturers, products whose nature and quality lent themselves to precise legal definitions, a lack of buyer preferences, uniform cost curves, ability to control each cartel member's market behavior, and effective restrictions of entry. Only in a few cases were

* The "parameter of expectation" refers to that area within which the actor expects the consequences of his acts to be encompassed. Each act of a person, a political party, a state, an enterprise, or a cartel is dependent on the resulting reactions of those persons toward whom the action is directed and the actor must also reckon with the changes brought about by the countermeasures of third parties.

all these conditions fulfilled. Therefore, short-lived cartels predominated, characterized by a constant "rhythm" of cartel formation, appearance of outsiders, cartel collapse, cut-throat competition and new cartel formation. Capital investments, the application of technological improvements and even over-all economic developments reflected the impact of this "rhythm."

As a result of the varying degrees to which the specified conditions were fulfilled, the significance and strength of cartels varied typically from industry to industry, ranging from powerful, market-controlling cartels to almost ineffectual collective agreements covering certain optional provisions of the Civil Law (term-fixing cartels).

Grouped by industries, the following picture presents itself: the strongest cartels were formed in the mining industry, where almost all products were covered by cartel agreements. In the basic industries the "Roheisenverband" and later the "Stahlwerksverband," the "Rohstahlgemeinschaft," the "Rheinisch-Westfälische Kohlensyndikat," the "Oberschlesische Kohlenkonvention," the "Rheinische Braunkohlensyndikat" and the "Stickstoff- und Gaskokssyndikat" were some of the most rigid cartels ever in existence. In contrast, cartels became weaker in subsequent production stages (as for instance the loose price cartel for small motors), with the exception of a few large trusts which were able to obtain patents with similar effects, giving them approximately equal market positions as for instance in the electric bulb syndicate (Glühlampensyndikat).

The iron and steel processing industries also formed numerous cartels especially in the mass-production goods. The same holds for the machine manufacturing industry, although here cartels were less complete and possessed less market influence. In the metal-goods industries syndicates and quota cartels were rare. Term-fixing and rebate cartels emerged in areas where the finished goods were geared to individual tastes and needs.

A typical situation existed in the precision instrument and optical industries. Mass products, such as low-priced wrist and pocket watches, were cartelized: here a few large concerns with great capital resources exercised considerable influence on the market, so that the continued effectiveness of the cartel agreements was relatively well insured. However, firms producing specialized watches were, like other specialities manufacturers, unable to form any cartels. The cable industry and the low-voltage electric bulb industry, on the other hand, were characterized by a narrow range of product types and few enterprises operating in the market, with consequently effective and long lasting cartels. As the number of manufacturers increased, as more product types were marketed and individual taste increasingly became a determining factor in a product's marketability, the number of effective cartels decreased. The textile industry, where term-fixing cartels prevailed, is a case in point: relatively small capital expenditures required for new production facilities as well as free accessibility to raw materials resulted in a continuous establishment of new small and medium-sized enterprises, so that there never existed the small, "closed" group of firms which was one of the prerequisites for the formation of strong cartels. In agriculture, cartels were never formed in face of a large number of relatively small enterprises which operated independently in a free market. Such conditions did not permit any cartel agreements. In particular a mutual control of the farmer's market behavior, which is a decisive factor in the successful operation of cartels, proved to be impossible. A similar situation existed in the handicraft industry: occasionally weak cartel agreements were set up on a local level. In the glass blowing industry, musical instrument industry, soap industry, tie-fabric industry, to name only a few examples, market agreements were entirely absent.

We find only a very few cases in German cartel history where firms achieved by means of cartel agreements a pure monopoly position in the market. Considerable tension and discord usually existed among the cartelized firms as new outsiders continually entered the market; the result was recurring breakdowns of cartels and the formation of new agreements. Thus, most cartels were short-lived. Since the cartelized firms retained their legal and economic independence—cartels being only contracts of Civil Law—each member attempted to push its sales volume to the intersection of marginal revenue and marginal cost curves. The more the parameters of action and expectation of the participants varied, the faster the cartel collapsed. If consensus was reached among the cartel members to raise prices substantially, outsiders appeared in the market and began to undercut prices. As output of the cartelized members fell, the outsiders' market position improved. Thus, the cartel was forced to reduce prices, attempting at the same time to include the outsiders in the collective agreements. But even if the cartel succeeded in either compelling or persuading the outsiders by great concessions to become members, the re-establishment of prices in accordance with the Cournot Point only served as an inducement for still other firms to enter the market. This process is well illustrated by the development in the cement industry in Germany. The strained relationships among the cartel members and the continuous fight against outsiders led to peculiar cycles of economic growth in the cartelized industries.

2. During the period of supervision of cartel abuses the effects of federal legislation upon the dynamics of cartels were small. However, governmental authorities exercised a substantial and valuable influence upon the type and fairness of competition, in which the required publicity of cartel agreements and cartel decisions were of particular importance. Cartels had little reason at that time to conceal their measures as it became customary later when they were prohibited.

Particularly during the period in which interventions were restricted by court decisions, governmental cartel supervision was confined to instituting a handful of formal court proceedings which dealt with strikingly unimportant cases and not with those which we, from our historical perspective, would regard as significant restraints on competitive market conditions. The State was too little aware of existing situations in the economy which warranted intervention. Too large an administrative machinery would have been required for comprehensive analysis and appraisal of business opportunities and of restrictions in the various sections of the economy.

It was only after the self-administrating business organizations were employed in the supervision of cartels that the government gained more complete insight into what it considered unhealthy developments resulting from the multitude of business relations in the economy.

Cartels as well as other types of business combinations are quick to circumvent regulations which are in conflict with their objectives. This is particularly so if the number of participating firms is small and the participants' cost curves show a great degree of conformity. Only in this way can the astounding fact be explained that during the periods of stiff cartel prohibition the well organized and effective cartels were hardly affected by government policy. They continued to operate almost undisturbed. They circumvented the probibitions while still complying with the law and brought about the same economic effects through other means. Given a similarity in the cost curves of the firms which operate in an industry and given the same parameters of action and expectation for such firms, there is little need for the legal formulation of contracts, or, if such contracts exist, for their legal enforcement.

Thus, in times of strict cartel prohibition, there indeed existed no compelling legal cartel contracts. However, the economic effects of uniform economic market behavior were the same as those achieved through strictly enforced cartel agreements during the periods of cartel freedom. From a legal point of view, it is correct to speak of an effective cartel prohibition after World War II. However, any critical analysis cannot overlook the fact that, in terms of economic effects, cartels continue to exist.

Only the many relatively weak cartels were drastically affected by the cartel prohibition. But these cartels were able to operate only intermittently anyway because of the many participating firms, the differences in their cost structures and cost curves, and the difficulties in forcing members to adhere to their contractual commitments.

Another important fact deserves emphasis in a critical analysis of cartels and their economic effects throughout the various historical periods: at no other time was the movement toward concentration of economic power and the emergence of industrial giants so pronounced as during the periods of strict cartel prohibition. In their over-all effects, cartels served to a considerable degree as a protective device for the small and medium-sized business firm in the market economy. Thus, predominant market positions of individual enterprises could not emerge as easily as in a market without any agreements limiting competition.

3. Despite the fact that only little time has elapsed since the passage of the Law against Limitations on Competition in 1957, it may be said that experiences with the measure have not in every respect been constructive. The law has quite a few weaknesses and in some areas of the economy cannot produce the effects which the legislature originally expected. On the other hand, it cannot be denied that the new legislation also brought about some noteworthy favorable results. Thus, it may be assumed that, without the existence of the Federal Cartel Office, market manipulations with undesirable consequences for the economic growth process would have again been undertaken in various sections of the economy. The legislation as well as the establishment of the Federal Cartel Office guaranteed in many industries a fairness of competition and a certain freedom of decision.

Even in those areas of the economy where the effects of the legislation were generally small it nevertheless exercised an influence on the construction of cartel agreements as well as on the character of competition through the mere existence of state supervisory authorities. The Market Association of Furnace Manufacturers (Marktgemeinschaft

Öfen), for instance, intended in 1959 to form a term-fixing cartel. Of course, even without governmental cartel supervision this industry would not have been in a position to set up a firmer and more effective cartel in the light of the divergent parameters of action for the furnace producers and the heterogenous cost structure in that industry. The new legislation did not have any effect upon the basic structure of the industry or upon the supply curves for furnaces. However, since the new law provides other interested business groups with an opportunity to intervene, the Association was more or less forced to satisfy such groups in order to avoid lengthy Cartel Court proceedings. Thus, the Association granted preferential rebates to specialized dealers. However, the building industries and cooperatives regarded such preferential treatment as discriminatory and unlawful under the new legislation. As a result, the Association modified its contracts so as to elimitate beforehand any possible objections by the Cartel Office.

The formulation of general business terms by other industries was influenced by similar considerations. Thus, the mere existence of a state supervisory authority affected the market behavior of business firms.

The experience thus far with the legislation of 1957 indicates that the provisions pertaining to resale price maintenance for branded goods tends to overburden the Federal Cartel Office with work. Each resale price maintenance contract must be registered with the cartel authority. Since its establishment, the Cartel Office has been flooded with such registrations, which have far exceeded its capacity to handle them.

Thus, it is rather discouraging to see the Cartel Office burdened with an excess of time consuming minor cases which tie up a considerable part of its staff, while significant restraints of competition and concentration movements in important sectors of the economy are not covered.

The German Law against Limitations on Competition places too much emphasis on securing competitive conditions in the non-branded goods areas of the economy, although these sectors are no longer a very decisive factor in the development of the modern economy.

As the branded product became more and more predominant in the course of industrial development, the traditional type of price competition, which today is oftentimes overemphasized by economic theory, was replaced by other forms of competition, such as sales promotion on the basis of the goodwill of a firm, types of business organizations which create the impression of sales and deliveries at reduced prices, customer service, etc. The consumer, usually equipped with little technical knowledge, is seldom in a position to compare prices of complicated technical devices and appliances with varying components and of varying quality and durability. Frequently, such comparisons are possible only after years or even decades of use. A survey conducted by the Federal Ministery of Economics in the summer of 1958 revealed that an unexpectedly large number of consumers was no longer able to determine if and when a price might be considered reasonable and what price differences exist between competitive manufacturers.

In the formation of trusts and in the establishment of power positions by means of patents we find today more drastic and more comprehensive restraints of competition than the Federal Cartel Office, in its sacrificing and exhausting work, is able to cover. Where the theory of market organization speaks of price leadership, we often find abuses of market power which are of far greater significance than those exercised by cartels. Competition based on efficiency, which still plays an important role in economic theory, is today overshadowed by competition based on capital resources. A firm with substantial capital resources that is able to sell successfully a large number of products may easily distribute some of these products at an initial loss in order to drive out of business weaker competitors who cannot shift indirect and other types of costs to other products as a means of market strategy. The use of capital resources to such ends can hardly be prevented through legal norms. A prohibition of sales of goods below manufacturing costs has been tried at various times in Germany. But who is to define "below manufacturing costs"? The Decree on Competition of December 21, 1934 (RGBl I, p. 1280), provided penalties for firms that offered, to the damage of the State or of the firms' employees or creditors, products below cost and below the requirements of an orderly economy. But such penalty was effective only after a firm became insolvent. Now, from a business point of view, a sale of goods below cost may be quite justified in order, for example, to avoid larger losses, to increase working capital, to add another profitable product line or to introduce a product into the market. Long-term market strategy of this type followed by trusts and other large multi-product enterprises in the course of their growth process cannot be curbed by any law effectively. This also explains why only little use has been made by the public of the provision of the new law under which observations of competitive restraints or unfair competition should be reported to the Cartel Office.

The Cartel Office will undoubtedly continue to face many cases in industries where German cartel history indicates that, even without any restrictions on cartels, no effective long-term collective market agreements would have been formed: for instance, those attempts to regulate markets which, as a result of divergent cost curves and divergent parameters of action as well as too large a number of participating firms, were unsuccessful unless based on legal contracts. But even then there were always some members who soon began to resent such contracts and who endeavoured to escape from their contractual commitments. However, if there is agreement among the participating firms, if their cost curves and parameters of action are approximately identical, then, today as in the past, competition can easily and effectively be eliminated, while the government, the legislature, or any cartel authority is unable to interfere with such market behavior or even to follow and observe the economic processes that take place in this area.

4. Let us add up the results of the general cartel prohibition with specified exemptions which have governed the cartel policy of the Federal Republic of Germany since World War II.

In the basic industries there continue to be many cases of uniform market behavior which are beyond the reach of the law, although the economic effects of such uniform behavior do not differ much from those exercised by a cartel.

If, in such situations of uniform market behavior, rebate cartels or freight basing points are established, such cartels must be regarded as being only ancillary to an otherwise quite effective market control exercised by the manufacturers.

In the petroleum industry, for example, price leadership is not known. Nevertheless, price movements take place, even in times of general market disturbances such as in the early parts of 1960, with a uniformity that could not be exceeded by any cartel. The Federal Cartel Office made several attempts to investigate this phenomenon in accordance with the cartel philosophy expressed in the new law. These attempts, however, ended in the assembly of more or less meaningless, formal data, without providing a basis of possible influence by the Cartel Office.

Steel pipes, radio tubes, radio and television sets, automobiles and automobile tires offer further examples of market controls beyond the reach of the Cartel Office. Only rebate cartels or resale price maintenance agreements were registered by the manufacturers involved.

The most important syndicates are the sales associations for hard coal, coal derivatives (tar and phenol), fertilizers and building materials (cement, natural stones and slaked lime). The production of fertilizers (superphosphate and lime) is almost entirely cartelized.

The agricultural industry as well as the transportation industry including the automobile liability insurance business is governed by a system of state market regulations. In many other industries, such as the handicrafts, which are free of any governmental regulation, uniform market behavior that is beyond the reach of the Law against Limitations on Competition plays a significant role. Finally, the retail business is characterized by tens of thousands of retail price maintenance contracts for branded products.

NOTES

1. Cartels in the Coal Industry
   - 1878 Conventions of mine operators, production cartels
   - 1887 Price cartels among Rhenish-Westphalian firms
   - 1890–1891 Sales associations
   - 1893 Foundation of the Rheinisch-Westfälische Kohlensyndikat A.G. (Rhenish Westphalian Coal Syndicate, Inc.)
   - 1903 Establishment of other sales associations
   - 1915 Forced termination of the Rhenish-Westphalian syndicate contracts. Prolongation until 1917, later prolonged until 1922
   - 1919 Reorganization of the coal industry by the State. Sozialisierungsgesetz, Gesetz übeı die Regelung der Kohlenwirtschaft, Ausführungsbestimmungen (Socialization Act, Regulatory Statute for the Coal Industry)
   - 1920 Formation of the Reichskohlenrat (Reich Coal Council) and the Reichskohlenverband (Reich Coal Association)
   - 1930 The last outsiders are absorbed by the Rhenish-Westphalian Coal Syndicate
2. Cartels in the Salt Industry
   - 1868 Agreements among the salt works
   - 1875 Verein deutscher Salinen e.V. München (Association of German Salt Works Munich). 33 members
   - 1888 Mitteldeutscher Salinenverein (Association of Central German Salt Works) and others until 1928
   - 1928 Norddeutsches Siedesalzsyndikat GmbH, Berlin (North German Salt Syndicate, Ltd.)
   - 1930 Deutsche Steinsalzsyndikate GmbH, Berlin (German Mineral Salt Syndicates, Ltd.)
3. Cartels in the Linoleum Industry
   - 1900 Loose collective price agreements. 1898 Verband der Teppich-, Linoleum- und Möbelstoff-Händler Deutschlands (1898 Association of German Carpet-, Linoleum- and Furniture Fabric Dealers)
   - 1901 Discontinuance of agreements and merger movement (Acquisition of firms)
   - 1909 New price agreements

1910 Verband der deutschen Linoleumfabriken (Association of German Linoleum Works)
1911 Fixing of discounts and minimum prices
1912 Verband deutscher Linoleumhändler (Association of German Linoleum Dealers)
1913 Production quota cartel, existing for less than one year
1914 Continuation of the price cartel
1915 Verband deutscher Linoleumfabriken GmbH in Liquidation (Association of German Linoleum Works in liquidation)
1921–1923 Strengthening of the linoleum dealer association. Introduction of price lists on a national level
1927 New price cartel and merger movement

4. Cartels in the Woodscrew Industry
1853 Manufacturers in Elberfeld (Westphalia) set up the first collective agreement
1887 Six manufacturers form a term-fixing cartel. Members were assessed or compensated for over- or under-deliveries.
1905 Eleven firms set up a sales syndicate, Verkaufsstelle Deutscher Holzschraubenfabrikanten, Köln (Sales Bureau of German Woodscrew Manufacturers, Cologne), which continued to operate until 1945

5. Cartels in the Cement Industry
1880–1885 Acquisitions of firms for the purpose of shutting them down. Price agreements
1888–1894 Acquisition of firms for the purpose of shutting them down. Price agreements
1893–1895 Price- and quota cartels
1901 Termination of the Nordwest-Mitteldeutsches Zement Syndikat (Northwest-Central German Cement Syndicate)
1903–1905 Syndicate formation on a regional basis (24 firms)
1910 New competitive warfare. Termination of the syndicate in Central Germany and in Hannover
1916 Plant restriction decrees
1917 Governmental influence on prices until 1923
1924 Formation of four homogeneous large-scale associations following lengthy preparations
1925 Prolongation for ten years
1926 Cartel agreement among the four large associations

6. Decisions of June 25, 1890 (*RGZ* 28, 238) and of February 4, 1897 (*RGZ* 38, 155)

7. Cartels in the Potash Industry
1860 Loose price agreements
1875 Price agreements among the raw salt works
1876 Loose cartel agreement
1879 Quota cartel for the Kainit Syndicate
1880 Inclusion of Karnallit
Oct. 1, 1883 Collapse as a result of outsider activities. Karnallit-producers withdraw
Oct. 21, 1883 Formation of a new syndicate for both minerals
1888 Prolongation for ten years
1898 Prolongation for three years
1901 Prolongation for three years
1904 Prolongation for five years
1909 Collapse due to dissention among members as to production quotas
1910 Passage of the Reichskaligesetz (Reich Potash Act), formation of a new syndicate

1919–1921 Passage of a new measure resulting in the formation of the Deutsche Kalisyndikat GmbH (German Potash Syndicate, Ltd.)

8. *Reichsdrucksache* (Governmental Release) No. 94, 1901.
9. W. Rosenberg in *Zeitschrift für Staats- und Volkswirtschaft*, vol. IV, No. 17; Ludwig Pohle, *Die Kartelle der gewerblichen Unternehmer*, Leipzig, 1898, p. 68.
10. *Denkschrift über das Kartellwesen. Reichstagsdrucksache*, No. 4, 351, 1905–06; *Reichstagsdrucksache*, No. 255, 1907; *Reichstagdrucksache*, No. 1019, 1907–09; Debates in the Reichstag: *Kontradiktorische Verhandlungen über deutsche Kartelle*, Berlin, 1903–06, 5 vols.
11. This figure indicates particularly that the mere number of cartels is relatively meaningless in terms of their economic significance. The Association of Steel Mills, which controlled the national market for rolling mill products, could influence the market mechanism much more effectively than the 132 cartels in the brick industry, which operated mostly on a local level. The large number of cartels in this industry was due to the ubiquitous character of the raw material and the high transportation costs which limited the market for each individual firm.
12. Report by H. Waentig and I. Landsberger. Both experts regarded an intervention by the State as desirable. They particularly advocated public administration, possibly nationalization, but at least governmental supervision and a public cartel register.
13. *Drucksache des vorläufigen Reichswirtschaftsrates* (Release by the Provisional Reich Economic Council), No. 28, p. 34; Debates in the Reichstag, 1st election period 1920, *Drucksachen*, No. 1958, Session of the Reichstag on June 16, 1921, Session of the Reichstag of July 7, 1921; debates in the Reichstag, 1st election period 1920, *Drucksachen*, No. 2455, *Bericht des Ausschusses für Volkswirtschaft des Reichstags* of January 16, 1923. *Reichstagdrucksachen*, No. 5478.
14. Based on the concept of self-government, through which Freiherr vom Stein led, with surprisingly great success, the citizenry to political responsibility following the collapse of the Prussian State (*Steinsche Städteordnung* of November 19, 1808). See F. Voigt, *Die Selbstverwaltung als Rechtsbegriff und juristische Erscheinung*. Leipziger Rechtswissenschaftliche Studien, Leipziger Juristische Fakultät, Leipzig, 1938.
15. Wichard von Möllendorff, *Deutsche Gemeinschaft*, Berlin, 1916; *Denkschrift des Reichswirtschaftsministeriums* of May 7, 1919. (Memorandum by the Reich Ministry of Economics).
16. In the Weimar Republic only a provisional Reich Economic Council was set up. (Act of May 4, 1920, April 5, 1933. Termination on March 23, 1934).
17. Gesetz über die Regelung der Kaliwirtschaft (Regulatory Statute for the Potash Industry) of April 24, 1919, *RGBl*, p. 413. Executory Ordinance of July 18, 1919, *RGBl*, p. 663; Gesetz über die Regelung der Kohlenwirtschaft (Regulatory Statute for the Coal Industry) of March 23, 1919, *RGBi*, p. 1449; Gesetz über die Sozialisierung der Elektrizitätswirtschaft (Act on the Nationalization of the Electricity Works) of December 31, 1919, *RGBl*, p. 19, 1920.
18. Dissolved by official notices of August 27, 1919 and June 3, 1921.
19. Dissolved by official notice of March 29, 1922. Also in this category: the Wirtschaftsverband für Rohteer und Teererzeugnisse (Association for Raw Tar and Tar Products), based on the decree of June 7, 1920 and dissolved by official notice of January 12, 1924 as well as the Schwefelsäureausschuss (Sulphuric Acid Committee), based on the decree of May 31, 1920 and dissolved by official notice of June 19, 1923.
20. R. Wissel and Striemer, *Ohne Planwirtschaft kein Aufbau*, Stuttgart, 1921; Georg Gotheim, *Planwirtschaft*, Berlin, 1919; Friedrich Glum, *Selbstverwaltung der Wirtschaft*, Berlin, 1926.
21. Law of March 23, 1919, *RGBl*, p. 342. Law of August 20, 1919, *RGBl*, p. 1447;

Decree of June 5, 1931, sec. 7, ch. VII, *RGBl* I, pp. 279, 313; and Law of April 21, 1933, *RGBl* I, p. 203.

22. Gesetz über die Regelung der Kaliwirtschaft (Regulatory Statute for the Potash Industry) of April 24, 1919, *RGBl*, p. 413; Law of April 21, 1933, *RGBl* I, p. 205; Kaliwirtschaftsgesetz (Potash Law) of December 18, 1933, *RGBl* II, p. 1027.
23. Max Metzner, *Die Kartelpolitik in Deutschland*, in Jahn-Junckerstorff, *Internationales Handbuch der Kartellpolitik*, Berlin, 1958, p. 89ff.
24. Despite a resolution by the Reichstag of June 5, 1921 which demanded a continuous observation of the cartel activities.
25. The equivalent of one dollar was:

July 1, 1914	4,20	Mark
Dec. 31, 1918	8,00	,,
End of December 1921	184,00	,,
End of December 1922	7.350,00	,,
June 30, 1923	154.500,00	,,
Nov. 15, 1923	4200 billion	,,

26. Compare Fritz Voigt, *Unternehmungszusammenschlüsse* III, *Staatliche Politik*, in *Handwörterbuch der Sozialwissenschaften*, vol. 10, Stuttgart-Tübingen-Göttingen, 1959, p. 565ff.
27. Compare Fritz Voigt, *Verhaltensweise und Entwicklungsmöglichkeiten der Kartelle*, Köln-Opladen, 1961.
28. Basis: Verordnung über Auskunftspflicht (Decree on the Obligation to give Information) of July 12, 1917, April 11, 1918; Verordnung zur Ausführung des Art. VI des Notgesetzes (executory Ordinance to Article VI of the Emergency Act) of July 13, 1923.
29. 1924: proceedings for the cancellation of price-fixing agreements by a wholesale association.
    1925: several proceedings for the elimination of the so-called value clause. Proceedings against the Halle'scher Verkaufsverein für Ziegelfabrikate AG (Halle Sales Association for Brick Products, Inc.).
    1926: proceedings against the Vereiniging der Kohlenhändler Lübecks e.V. (Association of Coal Dealers of Lübeck).
    1928: proceedings against the Rohstahlgemeinschaft (Raw Steel Association).
30. Metzner, then chief of the cartel department of the Reichsverband der deutschen Industrie (Reich Association of German Industry), reports 1500 cartels for the year 1925.
31. Milchgesetz (Milk Law) of July 31, 1930, *RGBl* I, p. 421. Remained in effect until new measures for the regulation of the agricultural markets were issued on March 27, 1934.
32. Verordnung über den Zusammenschluss der Zuckerindustrie (Decree on the combination of the Sugar Industry) of March 27, 1931, *RGBl* I, p. 86, of November 19, 1931, *RGBl* I, 687; Verordnung über den Zusammenschluss der Feuchtstärkeindustrie (Decree on the combination of the Starch Industry) of April 30, 1932, *RGBl* I, p. 188; Verordnung über den Zusammenschluss der Kartoffelstärkeindustrie (Decree on the combination of the Potato Starch Industry) of June 12, 1931, *RBGl* I, p. 339.
33. Verordnung des Reichspräsidenten (Decree by the Reich President) betreffend Schifferbetriebsverbände des Elbe-Oder-Gebietes, of December 23, 1931, *RGBl* I, pp. 779, 783. (Associations of Shipping Companies of the Elbe-Oder Area), Decree of March 23, 1932, *Reichsanzeiger* No. 74; Schifferbetriebsverband für die ostpreussischen-Wasserstrassen (Shipping Firm Association for East-Prussian Waterways), Decree of April 25, 1932, *Reichsanzeiger* No. 99; Grossschifferverbände für Elbe-Berg, Elbe-Tal und Elbe-Hafenverkehr (Associations of Large Shipping Firms for the Elbe

Upstream, Elbe Downstream and Elbe Harbour), Decree of July 12, 1932, *Reichsanzeiger* No. 136.

34. Verordnung des Reichspräsidenten auf grund des Artikels 48 der Weimarer Reichsverfassung zur Behebung finanzieller, wirtschaftlicher und sozialer Notstände (Decree by the Reich President on the Basis of Article 48 of the Weimar Reich Constitution for the Overcoming of Financial, Economic and Social Crises) of July 26, 1930, Section 5; Verhütung unwirtschaftlicher Preisbindungen (Prevention of uneconomic price fixings), *RGBl* I, 1930, pp. 311, 382.
35. Resale price maintenance by the manufacturer, which the Cartel Decree of 1923 did not cover, is defined as an arrangement under which the manufacturer, legally or through use of economic pressure, forces the buyers of his branded products to resell only at certain prices or to impose on subsequent distributors the same conditions, all the way down to the last retailer.
36. For details compare Horst Wagenführ, *Kartellrundschau*, 31. Jahrgang, 1933, p. 1ff.
37. For further details and a systematic representation compare Fritz Voigt, *Die Wandlungen der Marktordnungsverbände vom liberalen zum autoritären Staat*, Stuttgart und Berlin, 1943.
38. In the course of the war economy, and particularly after the year of 1942, most of the cartels found themselves unable to carry on their operations. Thus, either by silent consent or officially, they were dissolved for lack of tasks. Only sales syndicates, export cartels and international cartels remained in existence until the end of the war as these organizations exercised, by governmental authorization, certain self-regulating functions in connection with the war-time control of distribution and commerce. This is why we use the year 1943 rather than 1945.
39. For details compare Fritz Voigt, *Die Wandlungen der Marktordnungsverbände vom liberalen zum autoritären Staat*, Stuttgart und Berlin, 1943.
40. The Organization of Trade and Industry was initially conceived as a provisional setup within a planned organization of industry and commerce by trades and professions following the year of 1933. Although some efforts were made towards realization of these objectives (Formation of the Reichsnährstand and the Reichsstand des deutschen Handwerks), the plan proved to be unsuccessful and was dropped. The Organization of Trade and Industry became an instrument of public economic policy.
41. The preambles of Military Government Law No. 56 for the US Zone and Ordinance No. 78 for the British Zone, both of February 28, 1947, posed the following objectives:

    i) To prevent Germany from endangering the safety of her neighbors and again constituting a threat to international peace, ii) to destroy Germany's economic potential to wage war, iii) to insure that measures taken for Germany's reconstruction are consistent with peaceful and democratic purposes, iv) to lay the groundwork for building a healthy and democratic German economy.

    To this end it is desirable that the German economy be reorganized and that concentrations of economic power as exemplified, in particular, by cartels, syndicates, trusts, combines, and other types of monopolistic or restrictive arrangements which could be used by Germany as instruments of political or economic aggression, be eliminated at the earliest practicable date. It is likewise desirable to prevent Germany from using international cartels and similar international arrangements in the same manner.
42. Compare Fritz Voigt, *Verhaltensweise und Entwicklungsmöglichkeiten der Kartelle*, Köln-Opladen, 1961.
43. Compare Fritz Voigt, *Unternehmungszusammenschlüsse*, III Staatliche Politik, in *Handwörterbuch der Sozialwissenschaften*, Stuttgart-Tübingen-Göttingen, 1959, vol. 10, p. 565 ff.

44. Eucken, Müller-Armack, Rüstow, Roepke, Böhm, v. Hayek.
45. Herbert v. Beckerath, Schumpeter, Vershofen, Wagemann.
46. Term-fixing cartels, rebate cartels and rationalization cartels are only 'conditionally effective'. They are subject to registration. If no objections are raised by the cartel authorities within three months following registration, they become fully effective.
47. Branded goods are defined as goods whose constant and uniform quality is guaranteed by the price-fixing manufacturer.
48. Moreover, the general prohibition does not apply to certain contracts involving agricultural products, certain factual situations in the credit and loan business (par. 102) as well as in the insurance business and public utilities (par. 103). Contracts which exclude the public supply of energy or water are null and void.
49. I.e. cartel agreements among several manufacturers in the same production stage on price fixings in subsequent production stages.
50. For details see Hans von Müller-Henneberg and Gustav Schwartz (editors), *Gesetz über Wettbewerbsbeschränkungen*, Berlin, 1958, p. 128 ff.
51. Under the prerequisites of par. 99 of the Law against Limitations on Competition.
52. Under the prerequisites of par. 101, No. 2.
53. *Bericht des Bundeskartellamtes über seine Tätigkeit im Jahre 1960, sowie über Lage und Entwicklung auf seinem Aufgabengebiet* (Activity report of the Federal Cartel Office for 1960), Deutscher Bundestag, 3. Wahlperiode, *Drucksache* 2734; *Geschäftsbericht für das Jahr 1960* (Activity report for 1960).
54. Source: releases of the Federal Cartel Office; speech by its president, Dr. Eberhard Günter, before the Chamber of Industry and Commerce in Braunschweig.
55. It was repeatedly cancelled, for example on September 30, 1959. However, this cancellation was withdrawn.
56. Syndicates are defined as cartels which secure their agreements by a centralization of all sales and eventually all purchases by the membership. Each cartel member gives up direct entry into the market and discontinues all sales activities. The central sales agency negotiates contracts on a principal or agency basis. At the same time a syndicate performs always the functions of a price-, term-fixing- and quota cartel.
57. In existence since 1927; since 1958 operated as a rationalization cartel.
58. No such obligations were imposed upon the potash syndicate which shows similar features.
59. Compare Ralf Stecklum, *Die Entwicklung zum Prüfzwang in der Elektrotechnik*, Nürnberger Dissertation, 1959.
60. Compare Fritz Voigt, *Die Wandlungen der Marktordnungsverbände*, Stuttgart und Berlin, 1943, p. 50 ff; also *Verhaltensweise und Entwicklungsmöglichkeiten der Kartelle*, Köln-Opladen, 1961.

CHAPTER 6

ANTITRUST POLICY: THE UNITED STATES EXPERIENCE[1]

JOHN PERRY MILLER
Yale University, New Haven, Conn., U.S.A.

I. Introduction

Antitrust policies in the United States reflect as much a deep seated and persisting suspicion of the social and political consequence of positions of unchecked economic power as they do a belief in the economic beneficence of competition.[2] The Sherman Antitrust Act of 1890 followed a quarter century of discussion of the abuses of the growing large scale firms of the Post-Civil War period. Prior to the Civil War industry had been predominantly local in character. Corporate charters were granted sparingly, if increasingly, first by individual acts of the state legislatures and later under state enabling statutes providing for the grant of corporate charters to limited classes of industries.[3] The behavior of business firms was limited and regulated, often very substantially, by the state legislatures and sometimes by the corporate charter itself.[4] It was not until the Post-Civil War period that easy incorporation became freely available under state laws to any group who would go through simple routine procedures. With the passage of general incorporation statutes by the several states the corporate charter served less and less as an instrument of regulation. The growth of large firms engaged in business transcending the boundaries of a single state substantially weakened the effectiveness of state efforts to control business activities and led to a shift from state to federal controls over business. The development of large trusts, often controlling a substantial share of their respective markets, raised a challenge to deeply ingrained concepts of democracy, to the American preference for a dispersion of power, to the prevailing belief in equality of opportunity and to the contemporary sense of fair play.[5] The growth of large firms had often been accomplished at the expense of small, "independent" firms. In some cases such firms had been merged or consolidated with the large firms voluntarily and on terms favorable to the former owners. But often the "independent" was eliminated by the use of competitive tactics which shocked the public conscience. In any event the trusts were believed to have power of life or death over their competitors, whether actual or potential, and substantial power over the consumer and laborer as well.

The proponents of antitrust legislation had no sophisticated economic concepts of monopoly or competition. Academic economists played little role in the discussion preceding the legislation. In fact, most leading economists doubted the wisdom of the attack on the trusts.[6] The beneficence of free enterprise as it had developed in the Anglo-American tradition—the freedom of individual enterprise and contract subject to the limitation that freedom be used not in "restraint of trade" or "to monopolize"—was undoubtedly the assumption, whether articulate or inarticulate, of sponsors of antitrust. But this implied no clear concept of the nature of the market situations which might result. The proponents were against the abuse of economic power which had been documented in many studies by legislative bodies, private parties and numerous judicial proceedings. These trusts were seen to have bankrupted their competitors, exploited the consumer, oppressed labor, made and broken communities, and corrupted legislatures and the courts.[7] Whatever the contribution of the trusts may have been to the growth of the economy, the prevailing view was that many had abused their power economically, socially and politically. This fear of the abuse of power by big business has persisted, with varying intensity.[8] And although public opinion has come to have increasing respect for the efficiency and economic contribution of big business, the opinion persists widely that the performance of big business socially, politically and morally has been significantly wanting.[9] While economists have been more concerned with the economic effects of big business, its effects on the allocation of resources, efficiency, stability and growth, it has been a wider concern with the social, political and moral effects of big business which has provided the drive to develop and enforce antitrust policy. The American ideology is imprecise, often difficult to apply and certainly imperfectly realized. But it has played an important part along with the self-interest of politically powerful groups in welding together a shifting coalition which has supported antitrust with increasing vigor for seventy years. Some of the apparent inconsistencies of the law, such as policies with respect to discrimination and resale price maintenance, and some exemptions from the law, such as those for labor and agricultural associations, can be understood only in terms of the relation between ideology, self-interest and the requirements for successful coalition. While the strength and composition of the coalition has varied with economic conditions and the climate of opinion, at most times it has been pervasive enough to weigh heavily in the political strategy of the major political parties. Today a strong antitrust policy is supported vigorously by articulate and influential persons among both academic economists and men of affairs in business, labor and government.

II. Statutory Basis of Policy

The legislative basis of antitrust policy is to be found in three basic statutes and their amendments: the Sherman Antitrust Act of 1890, the Clayton Act 1914 and the Federal Trade Commission Act of 1914. This Federal legislation applies only to business in interstate commerce and not to purely intrastate activities. Many firms engaged in the service industries, retail or wholesale trade, the construction industries and purely local finance and real estate do not come within the purview of this legislation. Most states have antitrust statutes applicable to intrastate trade, but in only a few states is there much effort to enforce this legislation.[10]

THE SHERMAN ACT

The Sherman Act creates two types of offenses long recognized in the common law: (1) restraint of trade and (2) monopolizing or attempts to monopolize trade.[11] The interpretation placed upon these offenses will be developed in more detail below. But four aspects of policy should be emphasized at once. First, the proscribed offenses had long been recognized at common law in England and in the individual states. In fact, one interpretation of the intent of the Sherman Act was that it would extend to interstate commerce the standards of conduct previously applicable to intrastate commerce under common law. Second, the act is negative in its approach, *proscribing* certain behavior but *not prescribing* specific market structures or behavior. "Competition" is not mentioned; at no point does the statute require firms to "compete". Third, the act is on its face concerned with business behavior. It is concerned not with monopoly or size *per se* but with "restraint of trade" or "monopolizing". As will appear below, the Sherman Act has been concerned with the dynamic effects of behavior on structure and the development of positions of economic power rather than with market structures and market power *per se*.[12] Finally, the prohibitions of the statute are unqualified. No finding need be made in a particular case of adverse effects of the behavior or of a public interest in its prohibition. The statute itself makes no distinction between restraints of trade or acts of monopolizing which are "good" and those which are "bad". It makes no explicit provision for exceptions. Such limitations as have been placed on the seemingly sweeping prohibitions of the act arise from the judicial interpretation of the concepts of "restraint of trade" and "monopolizing", which have been interpreted as concepts subject to a "rule of reason".[13]

Initiative in the enforcement of the Sherman Act rests primarily with the Assistant Attorney General in charge of the Antitrust Division of the Department of Justice, who may bring either criminal prosecutions or civil suits in equity when he has reason to believe there is violation of the law.[14] Moreover, any person or firm injured by reason of violation of the act may bring an action for treble damages against the violator. This latter remedy was, however, not frequently invoked before World War II. More recently the private suit for treble damages has been resorted to successfully with greater frequency.[15] Action initiated by the Department of Justice is often settled without litigation by a consent decree, i.e. by a voluntary agreement in which the alleged violator agrees to certain changes in his behavior or to divestiture or other arrangements. Such a decree has substantially the same effect as a decree in litigated cases except that it is not accepted as *prima facie* evidence of violation of the act in private damage suits.[16]

LEGISTATION OF 1914

Twenty years experience with the Sherman Act, despite the famous decisions of the Supreme Court in 1911 which led to the dissolution of the Standard Oil and American Tobacco trusts,[17] convinced many that antitrust policy needed strengthening in several respects.[18] There was a widely held view that the growth of monopoly, except in the case of such natural monopolies as railroads and public utilities, was due primarily to the use of unfair competitive practices and that enforcement of antitrust policy would be facilitated by specifically proscribing such unfair practices. It was also believed that enforcement would be more effective if it were entrusted to an expert body with power to initiate action against alleged violators and with authority and competence to investigate and report on conditions and practices in industry which might warrant public attention. Accordingly Congress established the Federal Trade Commission with authority to undertake general investigations of industry, to initiate proceedings against firms alleged to be engaged in unfair practices as specified in the Clayton and Federal Trade Commission Acts and to issue cease and desist orders against those found to be in violation.[19]

The Clayton Act[20] prohibited four general classes of trade practices where their effect may be to lessen competition substantially or tend to create a monopoly. These include discrimination (section 2), tying and exclusive dealing arrangements (section 3), mergers (section 7) and interlocking directorates (section 8). The restrictions on discrimination were elaborated in considerable detail by the Robinson-Patman Act of 1936.[21] The purpose of these amendments was in large part to protect the traditional channels of distribution from the increasing inroads of mass-distributors, a trend which had been already evident in the 1920's and which provoked Congressional action when the depression of the 1930's aggravated the plight of the traditional channels. Many believed that the success of the mass distributors depended in large part not on their efficiency, but upon their power to exact discriminatory concessions from manufacturers in the form of lower prices, special discounts, advertising allowances or brokerage fees. Section 7 of the Clayton Act concerned with mergers, which had been narrowly interpreted by the courts, was amended by the Celler Antimerger Act of 1950 to cover explicitly the acquisition of the assets of as well as acquisition of a stock interest in another firm and implicitly to cover vertical and conglomerate as well as horizontal mergers, where the effect might be substantially to lessen competition or to tend to create a monopoly in any line of commerce in any part of the country.* [22]

In addition to the four classes of unfair practices specifically forbidden by the Clayton Act, section 5 of the Federal Trade Commission Act forbade all "unfair methods of competition," a provision designed to enable the Commission to proceed against unconscionable competitive practices in whatever form they might appear. It was intended to enable the Commission to extend the range of proscribed practices in light of its cummulative experience and of the development of new business practices. This provision was amended by the Wheeler-Lea

* The original section 7 had been interpreted to apply only to the acquisition of stock holdings in another firm. The acquisition of the assets of another firm before proceedings were instituted by the Federal Trade Commission was not covered. It was widely assumed that the act applied only to horizontal mergers until the Du Pont-General Motors decision. See pp. 231 and 235-36.

Act of 1937 to prohibit "unfair methods of competition in commerce, and unfair and deceptive acts and practices."* [23] Section 5 was interpreted to cover among other practices a wide variety of unethical or "unfair" practices which had been illegal under the common law of "unfair competition" but which have generally little relation to the monopoly problem, such as misrepresentation, misleading advertising, defamation of competitors and industrial espionage. For these practices, section 5 often provides a more effective procedure for protection of "fair" competitors than the civil procedures of the common law.[24] Much of the energies of the Commission is concerned with eliminating such unfair or deceptive practices; important though this activity is we shall not pursue this matter further.[25] Since section 5 was also interpreted to include many practices covered by the concept of "restraint of trade" and "monopolizing" under the Sherman Act, there is considerable overlap between the enforcement activities of the Commission and the Antitrust Division. The antitrust laws were amended subsequently first by the Miller-Tydings Act and later by the McGuire-Keogh Act to permit resale price maintenance under certain limited circumstances.[26]

FOREIGN COMMERCE

The Sherman Act applies not only to interstate commerce but to trade or commerce with foreign nations as well. The objectives of this provision were apparently to foster domestic competition by preventing restraints upon imports and to prevent evasion of the Sherman Act by firms operating from a foreign jurisdiction. Section 5 of the Federal Trade Commission Act also applies to commerce with foreign nations. But sections 2 and 3 of the Clayton Act apply only to sale of goods for use or consumption in the United States or its territories or possessions. Section 7 of the Clayton Act may apply to acquisitions abroad if the acquisition affects substantially the alternatives open to United States consumers or export opportunities open to United States firms.[27] The Webb-Pomerene Act of 1918 exempts associations engaged solely

* The courts had interpreted the original section 5 to require a showing that the alleged violator was guilty not simply of a particular unfair *act*, but had adopted the unfair conduct as a customary practice, that he had competitors and that these competitors were hurt. The requirement of a showing of injury was costly and time consuming. Moreover, if all or most competitors were engaged in the practice, a showing of injury to competitors was difficult if not impossible. The Wheeler-Lea Amendment was designed to eliminate the need for a showing of injury and to enable the Commission to proceed against individual unfair or deceptive acts.

in the export trade provided the association does not restrain trade within the United States or the export trade of any domestic competitor.[28] Such associations must be registered with the Federal Trade Commission. As of June 1958 there were 37 such associations registered with the Commission including 468 American firms. Exports by such associations in 1957 were approximately $930 milion.[29] The business advantages of export associations are clear in bargaining with foreign lawyers or governments over prices or import quotas, in raising prices on foreign sales or in achieving economies of joint selling abroad. The fact that so few associations are in existence indicates, however, that in many industries firms believe they have more to gain by independent than by joint action.

Although the United States long showed a lack of concern with foreign activities of domestic firms, there has been greater concern with these matters since the approach of war in 1939, first, as a part of the program of economic warfare and, since the war, as a part of a program of promoting both exports and economic development abroad. In a series of cases the courts have circumscribed the participation of United States firms in foreign cartels where there were direct effects on United States markets through territorial division of markets[30] or where dominant domestic firms engaged in joint foreign investments which might reduce competition among these firms in exports.[31] Enforcement policy appears to be moving in the direction of exempting activities which have no direct adverse effects upon domestic competition or upon freedom to export and of permitting joint activities whose primary and direct affect are upon foreign markets. In doing so many jurisdictional questions have arisen involving the interests not only of United States firms but of foreign firms and governments as well.

EXEMPTIONS

There are extensive exemptions from the antitrust laws other than those affecting foreign commerce.[32] Thus, the Clayton Act exempts "labor, agricultural and horticultural organizations instituted, for the purposes of mutual help and not... conducted for profit."[33] Many activities of the regulated industries are also exempted, including railroads, motor carriers, water carriers, the communications industries, public utilities, insurance companies, crude oil and gas producers, and anthracite coal producers. However, these exemptions are not complete in all cases. Thus, the exemption for labor is limited and does not extend to the use of labor unions to effect commercial restraints or the combination of labor and business to restrain a product or service market. Kaysen and Turner estimate that in 1954, 18.4 per cent of the national income originated in sectors of the economy exempt from the antitrust laws.

III. Process of Policy Formation and Administration

An understanding of the legislative, administrative and judicial processes by which antitrust policies are effected is crucial. Congressional legislation has necessarily been cast in quite general terms. Responsibility for determining the meaning of the legislation rests with the federal courts, although they may give weight to Congressional reports and debates as evidence of Congressional intent. And if Congress is dissatisfied with the courts' interpretation, it may enact new legislation. But between the Congress and the courts are the administrative agencies, which exercise wide discretion in selecting cases and pressing them to a conclusion. It is with the Antitrust Division of the Department of Justice and the Federal Trade Commission that principal responsibility lies for initiating action to clarify the "gray" areas of antitrust legislation and to enforce the laws. But administrative initiative can be either stimulated or retarded in many ways. The Attorney General may defer to the opinions of the State Department, the National Security Council or other agencies in possible proceedings affecting industries with which they are concerned. The relations between the administrative agencies and the Congress are several and often subtle. Not the least important is the movement of staff between Congressional Committees and the enforcement agencies. Also Congress through its control over appropriations may influence both the direction and extent of enforcement. Other avenues of influence are available, such as Congressional investigations and the Senate's responsibility to approve the nominations for the posts of Assistant Attorney General in charge of antitrust enforcement and Federal Trade Commissioners. There is, consequently, considerable scope for public opinion and interested parties to bring their views to bear on the administrative process through Congress as well as through the executive branch of the government.

The courts are relatively immune from such influences. Not that the judges' decisions are uninfluenced by their economic, political and social philosophies. To the contrary. But judges are appointed for life and their attitudes on antitrust matters are at the most only one of several factors influencing their selection. On matters where there are clear precedents, interpretation is relatively stable. But these are not the kinds of cases that are normally taken before the courts. In proceedings calling for the clarification of the law, the philosophy of individual judges may make a difference.

In short, there is on the one hand a legislative-administrative process which provides a degree of flexibility in detailed application of the law in the face of different situations and changing attitudes, and on the other hand a judicial process which provides for substantial consistency and continuity in broad principles. This combination of flexibility in detailed enforcement and continuity in broad principles has contributed to and gained strength from the broad public support of the principles of antitrust. Without these there would not have been the stability of statutory laws on which the administrative and judicial agencies have built.

IV. Collective Agreements

It is in the area of collective agreements in restraint of trade that success of the antitrust laws has been greatest and least controversial. In this area, the courts early delineated a series of *per se* violations—i.e., acts which are in themselves unreasonable restraints of trade. And it is in this area that enforcement policy has been the least ambiguous and judicial interpretation most consistent.

All collective agreements fixing prices,[34] limiting sales or production,[35] allocating markets,[36] or providing for a boycott of particular sources of supply or customers[37]—i.e., all collective agreements on matters central to competition—are illegal *per se*. The illegality of collective horizontal price-fixing and division of the market by bid-pooling was established in 1898 in the *Addyston Pipe and Steel Company* decision. This was reaffirmed in *Trenton Potteries* in 1927 when respondents manufacturing and distributing 82 per cent of the vitreous pottery fixtures produced in the United States were found guilty of combination (1) to fix and maintain uniform prices and (2) to limit sales to a special group of "legitimate jobbers." In its opinion, the court said, "The aim and result of every price-fixing agreement, if effective, is the elimination of one form of competition. The power to fix prices, whether reasonably exercised or not, involves power to control the market and to fix arbitrary and unreasonable prices... Agreements which create such potential power may well be held to be in themselves unreasonable or unlawful restraints, without the necessity of minute inquiry whether a particular price is reasonable or unreasonable as fixed..." Reviewing the history of previous decisions, it concluded that "it has since often been decided and always assumed that uniform price-fixing by those controlling in any substantial manner a trade or business in interstate commerce is prohibited by the Sherman Law, despite the reasonableness of the particular prices agreed upon."[38]

The *Appalachian Coal* decision of 1933 raised some question concerning this doctrine.[39] This involved a joint-selling agency established by 137 producers of bituminous coal producing about 12 per cent of the total output east of the Mississippi and 54 per cent of the production in the so-called Appalachian area (64 percent excluding the output of "captive" mines). The opinion in this case gave much attention to the plight of the bituminous coal industry, which had been depressed even in the prosperous 1920's, and seemed to look with favor upon joint efforts to reduce "ruinous" competition in the industry. But the view that this decision represented a fundamental change in policy proved unfounded as was indicated in *Socony-Vacuum* in 1940. The Appalachian case must be interpreted at the most as permitting joint-selling agencies where they do not have the power to "fix" prices even though they may affect them. It may also be interpreted as representing a response of the courts to a serious social problem. Shortly thereafter, Congress responded to this problem with the NRA and subsequently with special legislation providing minimum price-fixing for bituminous coal. These together with the development of strong industry-wide labor unions and economic recovery did much to mitigate the industry's problems.[40] *Socony-Vacuum Oil Company* involved a regional program of price stabilization by a group of major oil companies through the purchase of "distress" oil designed to affect the level of prices in the "spot" market, to which other prices were tied by contract or convention. The program, started during the NRA period, had continued after the NRA was declared unconstitutional. The scheme was found to be illegal as a case of price-fixing. "Under the Sherman Act, a combination formed for the purpose and with the effect of raising, depressing, fixing, pegging, or stabilizing the price of a commodity in interstate or foreign commerce is illegal per se."[41]

The prohibition of collective price-fixing arrangements was interpreted by the courts to include resale price maintenance arrangements whether by formal contracts or by a system of suggested resale prices which are enforced by elaborate policing arrangements combined with refusal to sell to uncooperative dealers.[42] The effect of this early interpretation of the law was subsequently weakened by amendments which permit resale price maintenance under state laws.[43]

Collective boycott arrangements have been found illegal in numerous cases. In *Fashion Originators' Guild*[44] and *Millinery Creators' Guild*[45] the court found arrangements by which the "style creators" tried to prevent "style piracy" to be illegal. The "style creators" had arrangements with manufacturers by which the latter agreed not to supply textiles to "style pirates" and agreed among themselves to boycott retailers who sold products of the "style pirates." These arrangements were found to be illegal under the Sherman Act and under section 3 of the Clayton Act. In another interesting case restrictive practices of the Associated Press were found to violate the Sherman Act.[46] The by-laws of the AP, a cooperative news gathering agency of some 1200 newspapers and the chief single source of news for the American press, forbade members to furnish news to non-members and reserved to each member the right to protest admission of new papers which served the same area as it served.

These prohibitions leave a wide range of matters on which collective agreement may be undertaken. They include agreements providing for limitations on the hours of work,[47] limiting conditions for accepting returned merchandise, systems for grading and labelling merchandise, cooperative advertising, standardization of product, a central selling agency,[48] and the collection and dissemination of statistics. Such practices may quite generally be permitted unless they are found to be ancillary to other agreements which control matters central to competition.

The distinction between what is permitted and what is not is perhaps best illustrated by the series of cases involving the statistical reporting activities of trade associations. In two of the earlier cases, *American Column and Lumber*[49] and *American Linseed Oil*,[50] the statistical reporting activities were found to be illegal because of the evidence of an intent and agreement to restrict production or increase prices. This was based in part on discussion at industry meeting and activities of the staff of the trade associations.

In *Maple Flooring Manufacturers Association*[51] and *Cement Manufacturers Protective Association*[52] in 1925, the activities of the trade associations in circulating price and other statistics and freight rate books were found to be legal because of an absence of evidence that their necessary effect was to control prices or output or that they had been so used. In *Sugar Institute*[53] in 1936, however, many activities of the association in connection with an open price-filing plan were held to be illegal including meetings to discuss business conditions and attempts to control prices and various ancillary terms of trade. The dangers of such activities in an oligopoly market producing a standardized product are clear. Again, in *Cement Institute*[54] in 1948, the basing-point system was held in the particular circumstances to be a collective device for eliminating price competition and achieving uniform delivered prices and terms of sale. As such, it was found to violate section 5 of the Federal Trade Commission Act and section 2 of the Clayton Act.

The logic of the policy with respect to collective agreements is clear.* As regards boycotts and the selection of customers, it is designed to protect the freedom of entry or access of suppliers and customers to various markets. Elimination of artificial barriers to entry is central to a policy of competition. Restriction on entry increases the market power of those favored by the arrangement and is often an obstacle to innovation in product, service, distributive methods or production techniques. At the best, restriction increases the cost of innovation; at the worst, it prevents or delays innovation. The logic of the prohibition of collective agreements on prices, output or sales is simply that on matters central to competition, decisions should be made independently. This does not insure competition whether perfect, pure or workable. But it increases its likelihood. Where numbers are large, this is clearly so. But even in oligopolistic markets the prohibition of collective agreements has similar effects. It permits and even encourages heterogeneity in market conditions and behavior which in turn encourages conflicting strategies rather than joint-maximizing strategies in such markets. Oligopolists, being unable to reduce uncertainty and insecurity by agreements with their competitors, must divert their energies into other directions in order to insure their survival and growth. Each oligopolist must seek its security through strengthening its individual

* The recent indictments in the electrical equipment manufacturing industry involving 29 companies and 20 different products illustrate vividly the importance of public policy in respect to market-allocating and price-fixing arrangements. These cases were all settled without a prolonged trial reflecting the unambiguous evidence and the clear cut legal precedents. In this case fines of $1,924,500 were imposed; seven officers of the companies were given jail sentences of 30 days, and twenty-three others were given suspended sentences. It is anticipated that customers, including some twenty Federal agencies and one hundred and seventy local communities, will bring suits to cover damages. These indictments together with the penalties imposed have evidently led many industries to check carefully their pricing behavior.

market position—by reducing costs, improving products or service, better sales promotion, etc. While the magnitude of this effect cannot be measured, its reality seems clear.

It is with respect to collective agreements for statistical reporting or controlling the ancillary terms of trade that the effectiveness of the law concerning collective agreements is open to question. Where the number of sellers is large, present interpretation is adequate. The same is true in oligopolistic markets where product is varied or subject to change, innovation is frequent and entry is relatively easy. But in oligopolistic markets with standardized product, similar costs, no or infrequent innovation and barriers to entry, the present interpretation of the law is unsatisfactory. The classic example is the American cigarette industry.[55] It is in such situations that oligopoly is most likely to tend toward some qualified maximization of joint profits[56]—i.e towards a monopolistic rather than a competitive result. In such circumstances, a public policy designed to promote competition will seek to encourage uncertainty and heterogeneity of product and sales policies. An economic case can be made for a more restrictive policy toward group activities or the activities of trade associations in such markets, especially where entry is difficult.[57] Variety, change and uncertainty are the enemies of "tacit collusion" or "conscious parallelism" and as such are to be fostered, not eliminated, by joint agreements in oligopolistic or concentrated industries.[58]

V. Monopoly, Oligopoly and Large Size

Policy toward the growth of large business and its practices has not shown the same degree of consistency and clarity as policy toward collective agreements. This is not surprising since the law itself does not define any *per se* violations, and simple unambiguous measures of monopoly are difficult to come by. This is particularly true in many situations where there are elements of legal monopoly or where economies of scale create substantial imperfections in the market. In such cases the problem becomes one of the use to which monopoly power is put, although this has been seldom recognized.

The approach to the problem of monopoly and oligopoly has been twofold: (1) through section 2 of the Sherman Act, which prohibits monopolizing or attempts to monopolize, and (2) the Clayton and Federal Trade Commission Acts, which provide for control of business practices believed to lessen competition or to tend to create monopoly.

In view of the admitted ambiguities in the concept of monopolizing and lessening of competition, it is understandable that the courts in developing their policies, especially under section 2 of the Sherman Act, have erred on the side of conservatism, thereby respecting the freedom of business decision when in doubt as to monopolistic effects. This has been especially true where the remedy might have been dissolution of or divestiture by a going concern.[59]

At the risk of oversimplification it may be said that monopolizing under section 2 of the Sherman Act means essentially the possession of unreasonable power to fix prices or exclude competition, combined with a purpose to acquire and preserve this power. The requirement that the power be "unreasonable," first clearly enunciated in the *Standard Oil* opinion in 1911,[60] follows from the consideration that not all elements of "monopoly" in the economic sense can or should be eliminated. The courts have made it clear that neither large size nor a preponderant share of the market is illegal *per se.* This doctrine has been clearly enunciated by the courts even in the *Alcoa* case where although the company was found to supply 90 per cent of the relevant market and thereby to be characterized as a "monopoly", the court was at considerable pains to demonstrate that the defendant had consciously sought to acquire and maintain its position.[61] While size or dominant market position are not illegal *per se,* it appears that the courts will be less tolerant of certain business practices when engaged in by firms with large size or dominant market position than otherwise.

It is likewise clear that "conscious parallel action" and price leadership are not illegal *per se,* although in several cases evidence of conscious parallelism has been considered relevant in a finding of conspiracy.[62] The present position of the court was perhaps best summarized in the opinion in the *Theatre Enterprise* case:

> The crucial question is whether respondents' conduct toward petitioner stemmed from independent decision or from an agreement, tacit or express. To be sure, business behavior is admissible circumstantial evidence from which the fact finder may infer agreement... But this Court has never held that proof of parallel business behavior conclusively establishes agreement or, phrased differently, that such behavior itself constitutes a Sherman Act offense. Circumstantial evidence of consciously parallel behavior may have made heavy inroads into the traditional judicial attitude toward conspiracy; but "conscious parallelism" has not yet read conspiracy out of the Sherman Act entirely.[63]

Granted that concentrated or oligopolistic industry structures are not in themselves illegal, the present position of the courts appears to be economically and legally sound. Where the number of firms are few and product is standardized, one must expect a large degree of parallelism of action because of high cross-elasticity of substitution between brands. Whether this leads to the exercise of monopoly power in an economic sense depends upon the levels of price and output around which parallel action takes place.

In the early cases involving monopolization the courts placed considerable emphasis upon the "intent" to monopolize. In the *Standard Oil*[64] and *American Tobacco*[65] cases of 1911, involving trusts with an overwhelming predominance of position in the market, the courts placed considerable emphasis upon the predatory and exclusive practices by which the trusts acquired and defended their positions. These practices together with a record of mergers and collusive agreements were considered to indicate a purpose or intent to monopolize. In both of these cases the emphasis on an intent to exclude and the destruction of potential competition were given major attention.

In the *United States Steel*[66] case, on the contrary, the absence of exclusive or predatory practices was an important factor in finding that the merger was not in violation of the law. The courts found that while the combination had been formed with an intent to monopolize, this intent had not been realized. Evidence of attempts at price-fixing by the device of "Gary" dinners and similar behavior, was taken as an indication of United States Steel's failure to achieve power to fix prices. Since these collusive practices had been abandoned and the combination did not have the power to fix prices, the court refused to order dissolution. The decision has been widely criticized on the grounds that in fact United States Steel had acquired power over price through the exercise of price leadership under the basing-point practice. But on the court's interpretation of the facts the decision is not out of line with previous decisions or with regnant economic opinions.[67]

There were several early decisions involving the combination or merger of competing railroads or other bottleneck situations in which the courts found the intent to monopolize and the fact of monopolizing sufficient reason for declaring the combination illegal even though there were no exclusive or predatory practices.[68] But in these cases the technical characteristics of the market made the "potentiality" of competition from new or other firms minimal, so that consolidation which reduced the number of independent rivals gave power over price. In the *Terminal Railroad Association* case there was an association controlling all the terminal facilities, access to which was vital to the 24 railroad companies converging upon St. Louis.[69] This the court found to violate the Sherman Act, although instead of dissolution it proposed a decree which, while providing for continuation of the association, insured access to the facilities by all transportation lines on fair and equal terms. In the *Northern Securities* case the court forced dissolution of a holding company which had acquired stock control in two competing railroads serving the Pacific Northwest.[70] In a series of cases involving various combinations between railroads and anthracite coal companies the courts also forced dissolution in situations where the access of owners of anthracite coal mines to markets might be interfered with by the combinations.[71] In these "bottleneck" cases the courts were clearly concerned with the power of the combinations to exclude others from the market in situations where entry, whether of new railroads or new coal mines, was limited by technical factors. While predatory practices did not play a role in these cases, exclusion of the "potentiality" of competition based on the technical situation was crucial.

Since 1940 several decisions have pointed in the direction of more rigorous interpretation of the Sherman Act. In 1945, Judge Learned Hand, speaking for a court of last resort, found Alcoa guilty of monopolizing under section 2 of the Sherman Act in a decision which stands as an important landmark in the interpretation of the antitrust laws.[72] Although the court found little evidence of predatory practices on the part of Alcoa, it found the company not only had a position of monopoly (control of 90 per cent of virgin ingot available in the United States) but had consciously sought to retain this position by expanding its facilities in anticipation of increasing demand so that competitors were excluded, thereby becoming guilty of "monopolizing." In an interesting but not binding dictum the Judge found that ninety per cent "is enough to constitute a monopoly; it is doubtful whether sixty or sixty-four per cent would be enough; and certainly thirty-three per cent is not."[73] This, it should be noticed, refers to tests of what constitutes a monopoly. "Monopolizing" is something else again. Firms with smaller percentages may be guilty of this by adopting collusive or predatory practices. In view of the fact that aluminum capacity had been greatly expanded during the war and much of this capacity was owned by the government, the court delayed issuing a decree until after disposition of the government facilities. Since they were disposed of so as to establish two new aluminum producers, whom the court found to be effective competitors, Alcoa avoided dissolution. The court did, however, require major shareholders of Alcoa who held stock in Aluminium Ltd. of Canada to dispose of their holdings in one of the firms in order to insure that the latter would function as an independent firm in the United States.

The implications of the Alcoa decision were articulated further by Judge Wyzanski in the *United Shoe Machinery* decision in 1953.[74] An earlier attempt to dissolve the company under the Sherman Act had been unsuccessful despite evidence that by merger and control of patents the company had come to dominate the industry.[75] In subsequent action, however, the company was found to violate section 3 of the Clayton Act because of various clauses in the contracts by which machinery was leased to shoe manufacturers.[76] In the decision in 1953 Judge Wyzanski found that the company's continued dominance of the market was based on its original structure, approved by the Court in 1918, its superior product and service and its practices and methods which though not "predatory, immoral nor, on their face, discriminatory... have operated as barriers to competition."[77] The Judge emphasized that

> The facts show that 1) defendant has, and exercises, such overwhelming strength in the shoe machinery market that it controls that market, 2) this strength excludes some potential, and limits some actual, competition, and 3) this strength is not attributable solely to defendant's ability, economies of scale, research, natural advantages, and adaptation to inevitable economic laws.[78]

Such monopolistic power deliberately acquired was found to violate the Sherman Act. The Judge sought to reestablish competition not by dissolution but primarily by providing that the company must agree to sell its machines when shoe manufacturers wished to buy rather than lease, by limiting conditions in leases and by requiring the company to grant non-exclusive licenses under existing patents to any applicant at a reasonable royalty.

The *American Tobacco* case of 1946 was interpreted by some as representing an important turning point in policy toward oligopolistic industries with uniform prices and price leadership.[79] This involved the cigarette industry, in which three firms had been responsible for between 68 per cent and 90 per cent of sales during the interwar period and in which there was considerable evidence of uniformity of prices and virtual simultaneity of price changes. The jury found a conspiracy to fix prices and exclude competitors and the Supreme Court sustained the finding. "Where the circumstances are such as to warrant a jury in finding that the conspirators had a unity of purpose or a common design and understanding, or a meeting of minds in an unlawful arrangement, the conclusion that a conspiracy is established is justified."[80] But careful study of the record by two economists[81] has led them to conclude that the behavior of the industry is explicable without any assumption of overt collusion but as the rational behavior of oligopolists acting "consciously parallel" in light of their interdependence. Nevertheless, the essence of the legal position was the finding of a "conspiracy"; and the present view is that while conscious parallel action may be evidence relevant to a finding of a conspiracy, such action is not illegal *per se*. The government after winning the case was hard pressed to find any effective remedy since, in view of the structure of the market, instructing the firms not to conspire is of little significance.[82]

The legal status of vertical integration has been raised in several suits particularly since World War II. The incentives to vertical integration may be many including efficiency in production or distribution, the protection of sources of supply or market outlets, and the foreclosure of sources of supply or market outlets to competitors.[83] It has been demonstrated that in a static market situation rational vertical integration, though it eliminates an independent firm, leads to no restriction of output and raising of price, in fact; often the reverse will be the case.[84] But the effects of vertical integration on the opportunities and incentives to innovation, to establishing new firms and to growth are more serious. The dangers of vertical integration are to be found in its possible effects on the dynamics of market structure. Although the courts have on the whole been deferential to business decisions with respect to vertical integration, in recent years they have forced vertical disintegration in several cases where there appeared to be some significant element of arbitrary foreclosure of the market. Thus, in the *Du Pont-General Motors* case, Du Pont was found to have violated section 7 of the Clayton Act by holding 23 per cent of the common stock of General Motors. The court argued that this constituted a vertical relation which gave Du Pont a preferential position in the market for auto finishes and fabrics, thereby foreclosing a section of the market to potential competitors.[85]

Equally significant was the *Paramount Pictures* case in which the court found that the defendants, five major producer-exhibitors of motion pictures along with two other producers and a distributor, had through a series of agreements and trade practices acquired a monopolistic position in the industry of exhibiting films. The court ordered divestiture of exhibition from the production and distribution of moving picture films. The majority of the court rejected the view that vertical integration in the producing, distributing and exhibiting of motion pictures is illegal *per se*; "... the legality of vertical integration under the Sherman Act turns on 1) the purpose or intent with which it was conceived, or 2) the power it creates and the attendant purpose or intent. First, it runs afoul of the Sherman Act if it was a calculated scheme to gain control over an appreciable segment of the market and to restrain or suppress competition, rather than an expansion to meet legitimate business needs... Second, a vertically integrated enterprise... will constitute monopoly which, though unexercised, violates the Sherman Act provided a power to exclude competition is coupled with a purpose or intent to do so."[86] It is clear that vertical relationships are open to question where not based on "legitimate needs," and it may well be that the Celler Antimerger Act will be so interpreted as to discourage vertical mergers.* Nevertheless, it appears that the courts will not interfere with vertical relations based unambiguously on considerations of efficiency.

VI. Mergers**

The Celler Antimerger Act of 1950[87] was designed as a preventive measure to avoid further concentration of industry by preventing mergers whose effects might be to lessen competition or tend to create a monopoly in any line of commerce in any part of the country. Although there have not been many decisions under the law, and consequently, it is too early to predict the long run effects on the structure and functioning of industry, present indications are that it will stop many mergers which might otherwise have been undertaken.

Mergers have played an important role in the development of the contemporary structure of industry in the United States. While the merger process has been continuous, there have been three major bursts

* See pp.. 218, 235–36.

** Throughout this chapter we follow popular usage and include under the term "mergers" consolidations and holding companies as well as mergers in the narrow legal sense of the term.

of merger activity, 1898–1902, 1926–1930, and the post-World War II period, 1946–1956.[88] The first wave of mergers led to substantial concentration in many industries and left an imprint on United States industry to this day. The second wave represented in part concentration in some new industries which had developed after the turn of the century, e.g. automobiles. The merger movement after World War II has been less sharp than the previous waves and has probably not had as great an effect on market concentration. It is, however, significant to note that of the 100 largest manufacturing corporations in 1955 ranked by asset size, 37 had never experienced a significant merger.[89]

Attempts to explain the bursts of merger activity in the United States have not been conclusive. A recent attempt to explain the merger wave at the turn of the century concludes that "such factors as the rate of industrial growth, the rise of technological innovation, and the growth of interregional transportation... were not likely to have been important immediate factors in the merger wave. The leading factors of immediate importance appeared to be the newly achieved development of a broad and strong capital market and the existence of institutions which enable the organizers of mergers to utilize this market... This in turn permitted the centralization, in one corporate structure, of control of a large part of an industry, and made possible a more effective rationalization of industry output by business leaders."[90]

The reasons for mergers are many, most of them based on greater profitability. That a merger is a device for acquiring market power is clear. This undoubtedly played a significant role in the early merger movement. In other cases, a merger is the means to exploit a preferred production function. Thus, merger often represents a way of effecting economies in production, purchasing or distribution. In other situations it is a device by which a firm gains access to the management, funds or markets necessary for its survival or growth. Sometimes a merger is a device for diversifying risk. In other cases a merger may be motivated by tax consideration or estate planning. It has been estimated, for example, that between 1940 and 1947 tax considerations were of major importance for something less than one-tenth of all mergers of manufacturing and mining companies and a little over one-fourth of the total assets involved in such mergers, and one-third of the assets of companies with assets of over $1 million involved in such mergers.[91] Sale through merger is one way by which the individual owner of a small firm may insure continuity of management, in case of retirement or death, and liquidity for his estate. The estate tax and the relatively high income tax rates combined with low capital gains tax rates work in this direction. Moreover, tax considerations may motivate purchasers in view of the loss carry-back provisions of the corporate income tax and the excess profits credit under the wartime excess profits tax. When security prices are low, merger may represent the cheapest way of acquiring facilities desired for expansion and may have the added advantage of not immediately intensifying competition as much as would the building of new facilities. Finally, during periods of comprehensive price control such as during World War II, special incentives may arise for forward or backward integration in order to insure supply of raw materials or to gain the advantages of the larger rates of profits available at one stage of production than at another.

The very diversity of circumstances under which mergers may be undertaken and of their effect has complicated the problem of developing a rational public policy. At an early date mergers, whether by the consolidation of several firms, by the merger of one or more firms into another, or by the acquisition of stock ownership by one firm in another, were found to violate the Sherman Act if they led to a monopolizing or an attempt to monopolize trade. As early as 1904 the Supreme Court found the combination of the Great Northern Railroad Company and the Northern Pacific Railway Company by a holding company device to be in violation of the law.[92] Other cases such as the *Standard Oil* case and the *American Tobacco* cases of 1911 also involved mergers. However, the showing of illegality in the case of mergers under the Sherman Act has, in general, been a difficult one. As indicated above, to prove monopolizing under section 2 of the Sherman Act it is not enough to show that the firms are large or that they have a substantial control of the market. Size *per se* is not illegal. Generally during the first fifty years of antitrust policy in cases involving manufacturing or trade, the courts have insisted upon a showing of an intent to monopolize, especially as evidenced by certain exclusive practices. It was only in the railroad and bottleneck cases that a merger of firms having a dominant position in the market was found to violate the act in the absence of predatory or exclusive practices of some sort.[93] The steel industry is perhaps the classical case of development of a substantial degree of concentration through mergers and in which until recently the law has failed to put any stop to the process.[94] Many students of antitrust policy have been highly critical of the *United States Steel* decision of 1920[95] and also of the decision of the court in *Columbia*

Steel in 1948.[96] In fact, the record of mergers by the United States Steel Company, Bethlehem Steel Company and others played an important part in the Congressional deliberations leading to the Celler amendments to section 7 of the Clayton Act in 1950.[97] While the Sherman Act did not prevent substantial concentration in many industries, it is probable that it did discourage mergers which would have engrossed all or a substantial part of a market.

The original section 7 of the Clayton Act was of very limited effectiveness in retarding the merger movement because the courts interpreted it to prohibit only stock holdings by one company in another company and not to prohibit the purchase of assets.[98] Moreover, it was assumed to apply only to horizontal mergers until the decision in *Du Pont-General Motors* in 1957. The Celler Antimerger Act of 1950 was intended to correct the defects of the original section 7 in several respects. It was designed in the first place to apply to mergers by the acquisition of assets as well as by the acquisition of stock holdings. Secondly, it was designed to apply to vertical and conglomerate mergers as well as horizontal mergers. Thirdly, it states specifically that such mergers shall be illegal if their effect may be substantially to lessen competition or tend to create a monopoly in any line of commerce in any part of the country. The test of a lessening of competition or tendency to create a monopoly was intended to require a less substantial anticompetitive effect than is required to show "monopolizing or attempt to monopolize" under the Sherman Act. Thereby, it was hoped to stop in its incipiency a merger or series of mergers which in its initial phases might not have any clear monopolistic effect but the cumulative effects of which might be serious.

As indicated above a recent decision held that the Du Pont Company had violated the original section 7 of the Clayton Act by its purchase of a 23 per cent stock interest in the General Motors Corporation in the years 1917–1919.[99] The question at issue was whether Du Pont's commanding position as a supplier to General Motors of automotive finishes and fabrics was achieved on its competitive merit alone or because of the stock acquisition. In arriving at its decision the court decided that the market for automotive finishes and fabrics had sufficiently peculiar characteristics to constitute a line of commerce within the meaning of the act. Du Pont had been supplying about 70 per cent of General Motors' needs for automotive finishes and 40 per cent to 50 per cent of its automobile fabric needs. Since General Motors itself was the dominant firm in the automotive field, these percentages, of course, represented a substantial part of the total purchases of these types of products. This case suggests that the court may apply a very rigorous test in the case of vertical relations based upon security holdings at least where two "large" firms are involved. Whether the test would be so rigorous in the case of a vertical arrangement based on an asset purchase or involving firms of lesser size is, of course, not certain.

A second case which evoked considerable interest is that of the proposed merger of the Bethlehem and Youngstown Steel Companies, which are respectively the second and fifth largest integrated steel companies in the United States. Although the two companies sold many products in common, they argued that they were not selling most products in the same market, and that, in any event, there was a substantial amount of competition in major markets. The court, however, concluded that "the proposed merger would eliminate the present substantial competition between Bethlehem and Youngstown in substantial relevant markets. It would eliminate substantial potential competition between them. It would eliminate a substantial independent alternative source of supply for all steel consumers. It would eliminate Youngstown as a vital source of supply for independent fabricators who are in competition with Bethlehem in the sale of certain fabricated steel products. It would eliminate Youngstown as a substantial buyer of certain fabricated steel products."[100] The companies had urged that the purpose of the merger was to make it possible for the Bethlehem Steel Company to invade the Chicago market by establishing a new heavy structural steel mill in a market where the only supplier of the largest sizes of structural steel shapes was the United States Steel Corporation. The companies argued that it would not be feasible for the Youngstown Company to undertake this expansion itself because of lack of financial resources and know-how, and that for Bethlehem Steel to undertake it by building a brand new mill would be substantially more costly than by expanding Youngstown's facilities. The Judge made it clear that while he was not persuaded that the companies' arguments concerning the necessity for a merger in order to undertake this expansion were correct, even so "if the merger offends the statute in a relevant market then good motives and even demonstrable benefits are irrelevant and afford no defense."[101]

The Department of Justice and Federal Trade Commission have instituted numerous cases in order to establish the controlling principles under the new amended section 7.* The precise line between legal and illegal mergers is not clear at this time, but it seems probable that the tests, as applied by the court, will be quite severe. It is clear that where the court finds a substantial lessening of competition in any market in any part of the country, a merger will be prohibited even though there may be demonstrable benefits in other markets. This means, in the case of many large diversified firms, that opportunities for mergers which will not run afoul of the law will be limited.

VII. Business Practices

INTRODUCTION

While antitrust policy with respect to collective agreements is quite clear and consistent, policy with respect to the business practices of individual firms is less clear and uncertainty concerning the boundaries of legal behavior is substantial. In empowering the Federal Trade Commission to proceed against unfair methods of competition and declaring such practices as tying and exclusive dealing arrangements and discrimination to be illegal where they may tend to lessen competition substantially or to create a monopoly, Congress intended to prevent in their incipiency practices which may be used to create, expand or defend monopoly positions. The purpose of this legislation was represented as preserving competition and preventing monopoly. But in economics as well as in law this is an oversimplification of the problem. The classical and popular dichotomy between monopoly and competition does not do justice to the reality of contemporary markets in free societies. Each of the practices in question presupposes the existence of some element of monopoly power or some serious imperfection in the market. These are practices of "oligopolistic" or "monopolistic" competition, not of atomistic markets for staple products. While these practices may be used to exploit an element of market power more fully or to increase this power, antitrust policy must generally reckon with a substantial residual of legal monopoly power based on such factors as economies of scale, advertising, copyright, trademarks, patents or perhaps simply imperfect information. The failure to recognize the preexistence of monopolistic elements in these cases has often served to confuse the issue. Where the element of monopoly power cannot be or is not eliminated, the alternative to the

* By May 1960 the Federal Trade Commission had initiated 32 cases and the Department of Justice, 30 cases. They had, of course, investigated many more mergers.

"monopolistic" behavior in question is not "purely" or "perfectly" competitive behavior, but a different type of "monopolistic" behavior. The problem is one of regulating the use of monopoly power, i.e. regulating the practices or competitive methods of firms with a degree of "monopoly" power in the economic sense of the word. That the courts and administrative agencies enforcing the law have had difficulty in developing clear and consistent criteria of "a substantial lessening of competition" or "a tendency to monopoly" is not surprising in view of the failure of economists to develop a consensus concerning measures of the degree of competition or monopoly which are both meaningful and operational.[102]

The problem of public policy is to distinguish between those alternative actions which are permissible and those which are not. In a free private enterprise economy, the presumption favors the freedom of the firm to adopt its market policies to its own situation and interest except in so far as there is some overriding public interest to the contrary. It is one of the purposes of antitrust policy to develop the relevant criteria of public interest. One criterion is to promote competitive rather than monopolistic behavior whenever possible. The problem here is that mentioned above, the lack of agreement concerning meaningful and operational tests and the suspicion, not without some justification, of *a priori* reasoning based on simple models of competition and monopoly. A second criterion is to protect competitors from the many unfair practices involving deceit, misrepresentation, espionage, defamation, etc.—practices characteristic not of markets for staple products but rather of markets involving "heterogeneous" competition[103] or "competition among the few." A third but less explicit criterion is the protection of the small competitor against the large competitor.

In general the center of attention in the regulation of business practices has been not on the structure of the industry *per se*, nor on the efficient allocation of resources, but on the foreseeable effects of various practices on competitors and especially on the freedom of entry or exclusion. In this respect, policy has been concerned with the dynamics of market structures, rather than with economic statics.

TYING CONTRACTS

The tying contract, by which the sale or lease of one product or service, the "tying product", is conditioned upon the purchase or lease of one or more other products or services, the "tied product", is a device which is feasible only where at least one of the products has a strong monopoly position or is the subject of contrived scarcity. Typically the tying product is protected by patent, copyright or trademark.* The purpose of the tying contract is to increase the monopoly profit accruing to the firm.[104] The additional profit may arise from any of several factors: a savings in cost; the usurpation of some consumers' surplus; an increase in sales by the firm of a tied product selling at a monopoly profit, some of which would otherwise be purchased from rivals. In some situations a tying arrangement may serve as a counting device which will facilitate the charging of discriminatory prices for the tying product based upon its use. While the tying arrangement will lead to some redistribution of income in favor of the owner of the tying product, it need not and generally will not affect the allocation of resources adversely. Its principal effect is one of exclusion by raising a barrier to entry: competitors are excluded from a part of the market for the tied products unless they succeed in developing a substitute for the tying product. Over the long run, by increasing the barriers to entry, tying arrangements may impede competitive innovation and entry of new firms to the market for the tying product as well.

A fair number of cases involving tying arrangements have been litigated under both the Sherman and Clayton Acts. In early cases under the Sherman Act the Supreme Court had permitted tying clauses to stand.[105] Perhaps the most notorious use of tying contracts and full-line forcing was that involving the United Shoe Machinery Corporation, which had acquired control over practically all the patents under which various types of shoe machinery were manufactured. In the acquisition and preservation of its dominant position it had made extensive use of exclusive leasing arrangements by which lessees agreed to use only United Shoe machines. A suit under the Sherman Act to dissolve the company and to find these lease arrangements illegal was denied.[106] However, subsequently these tying clauses were condemned under the Clayton Act in view of the dominant position of the company in supplying shoe machinery.[107] In *International Salt,* tying arrangements by which lessees of International's patented salt dispensing machines agreed to purchase their requirements of salt from

* But tying sales are also found when prices of a commodity are fixed by law or custom below the price which will clear the market. In this case the tied product is some product whose price is not controlled or the supply of which exceeds demand at the controlled price.

International were held to be invalid on the ground that "patents confer no right to restrain use of, or trade in, unpatented salt... It is unreasonable, *per se*, to foreclose competitors from any substantial market... The volume of business affected by these contracts cannot be said to be insignificant or insubstantial..."[108] At an earlier time arrangements by which an oil refiner leased equipment to service stations on the condition that the equipment be used only to dispense the refiner's gasoline were permitted as a device auxiliary to the protection of the refiner's goodwill.[109] But the goodwill exemption has been narrowly defined. For example, in *International Business Machines* involving the lease of business machines on condition that the lessee purchase his punch cards from IBM, the court held that while IBM might protect its goodwill by insisting that lessees use cards meeting reasonable specifications, it could not prevent use of rivals' cards which met such specifications.[110]

The current position of the court is that tying arrangements are illegal if the supplier has a monopolistic position in the tying product or if a substantial volume of commerce in the tied product is foreclosed.[111] This amounts in effect to finding tying arrangements illegal *per se*. Such a policy is not only law but also good economic policy. It is difficult to see any harm done by this rule except so far as it limits the value of the patent grant. Whether the policy makes much difference, it is difficult to say. But by preventing foreclosure and reducing barriers to entry the policy favors the survival of efficient competitors and favors competitive innovation.

EXCLUSIVE DEALING AND REQUIREMENTS CONTRACTS

Exclusive dealing contracts are one among several merchandizing devices by which a seller may seek to enhance or defend his market position.[112] Alternative devices involve agency systems, forward integration or greater reliance on advertising and other forms of selling effort. A firm with a strong monopoly position, i.e. selling a product for which there is no close substitute, has no incentive to use exclusive dealing; a firm selling in a purely competitive market has neither incentive nor ability to use exclusive dealing.

The types of exclusive arrangements vary. Typically a manufacturer enters agreements with distributors by which the latter agree not to handle substitute products. In some cases the manufacturer in turn will agree to limit the number of its distributors in any market. In the case of complicated machinery and similar products, the manufacturer may also insist that the distributor maintain service facilities of certain types and quality. Frequently, exclusive dealing is combined with full-line forcing, thus involving in effect a tying arrangement as well. The purpose of exclusive dealing is to enhance a manufacturer's market position by enlisting the sale efforts of distributors or by precluding rivals from access to the market.

Requirements contracts involve arrangements with customers, usually final users of a product, by which the latter agree to purchase all their needs for a given product from one seller. Such requirements contracts may serve purposes similar to exclusive arrangements. But they may also serve to increase certainty and reduce risks in markets where demand and supply varies widely, e.g. the market for tin cans.

The danger in these practices lies in their possible effects upon competition through their effects upon entry. Where the numbers on each side of the market are large or where entry is easy, the effects of exclusive dealing or requirements contracts will not be serious. But these are the situations where the incentives for exclusive dealing are small. Where the distributors are few and entry into distribution costly, exclusive dealing by foreclosing existing channels to new or growing firms increases the cost of entry and thereby reduces one important avenue of competition. Likewise, where sellers are few, requirements contracts, if of substantial duration, may have similar effects. It is clear, then, that the effects of exclusive dealing and of requirements contracts depends on the market structure in question.

Congress and the courts have recognized the need to act selectively with respect to these practices.[113] A *per se* prohibition of such practices would in some cases interfere with arrangements which promote generally efficient operations and in others might lead to alternative merchandising techniques which would promote less rather than more competitive conditions.[114] In several of the early cases where the courts sustained orders of the Federal Trade Commission enjoining exclusive arrangements, the courts stressed especially the dominant position of the seller.[115] In several cases where the degree of concentration was substantially less, the court found in favor of the seller's right to insist on exclusive dealing. The *Standard Stations* case figures prominantly in the recent development of policy.[116] This case involved contracts by which service stations agreed to take their full requirements of gasoline, and in some cases accessories as well, from Standard Oil of California. Such contracts covered 23 per cent of total gasoline gallonage in the western area and 16 per cent of existing gasoline outlets.The Supreme

Court sustained the lower court in invalidating the contracts on the grounds that even though the supplier did not have a dominant market position, the exclusive arrangements foreclosed "competition... in a substantial share of the line of commerce affected," which it deemed sufficient to satisfy the test of section 3 of the Clayton Act without further showing of harm to competitors or competition. While it was thought by some that this decision meant that exclusive dealing is illegal provided it covers a "quantitatively substantial" line of commerce, subsequent orders of the Federal Trade Commission and decisions by the courts have not relied upon a "quantitative substantiality" test. The Commission has instead proceeded in exclusive dealing cases to a more detailed finding of injury to competition or injury to competitors through foreclosure.[117] While the line between legal and illegal exclusive dealing arrangements is not clear, it appears that in oligopolistic industries where entry is difficult, efforts to tie up a substantial share of the best distributors' outlets by exclusive arrangements are illegal.[118]

RESALE PRICE MAINTENANCE

The vacillation in policy with respect to resale price maintenance illustrates well the conflicting economic, political and social forces impinging upon antitrust policy in the United States.[119] In the context of United States policy resale price maintenance refers to the policy of a single manufacturer of a branded or trademarked product establishing a minimum or fixed price for the resale of his product by a distributor, whether jobber, wholesaler or retailer. That a manufacturer may legally fix the sale price of a distributor acting as his agent is clear. The problem arises only where the manufacturer tries to limit the resale price after ownership of the goods has passed to another. It should be emphasized that horizontal agreements between manufacturers or wholesalers to enforce resale prices for their respective products have always been illegal. The relative ineffectiveness of resale price maintenance in the United States, even when permitted, in contrast with experience in Great Britain and elsewhere, is to be explained in large part by this prohibition of collective agreements to enforce such policies.

As early as 1911 in the *Dr. Miles Medical Co.*[120] decision the courts held that a system of resale price maintenance by contracts was illegal under section 1 of the Sherman Act, arguing that the system has the same effects as would a system of agreements to fix prices between the distributors themselves. Resale price maintenance was subsequently found to be illegal as an unfair method of competition under section 5 of the Federal Trade Commission Act. Moreover, in the *Beech-Nut Packing*[121] decision it was decided that although it is not illegal *per se* to announce suggested resale prices and to refuse to sell to those who do not abide by such prices, an agreement, whether formal or informal, to abide by such prices is illegal especially if conformance is insured by cooperative efforts at detection of price-cutters. But the revolution in the distribution system by which the mass distributors replaced the traditional distributive channels gave rise to efforts at protecting the traditional channels in several ways including the legalizing of resale price maintenance. Beginning with California in 1931 many states passed enabling legislation permitting resale price maintenance in *intrastate* commerce by a seller of a trademarked or branded product "which is in free and open competition with commodities of the same general class produced by others." The legality of these state laws was established in *Old Dearborn Distributing Company v. Seagram Distillers Corporation.*[122] The court's decision was based primarily on the interest of the manufacturer in protecting the goodwill in his trademark or brand name. In 1937 the Sherman Law was amended by passage of the Miller-Tyding Act to exempt from section 1 contracts in interstate commerce on identified products which are in free and open competition with other goods of the same general class provided the contracts are legal under the law of the state in which this resale is made.[123]

By 1941 some 45 states had legalized resale price maintenance and had included generally a "non-signers" clause which made resale prices, embodied in contracts signed with one or more distributors within a state, applicable to sales by all distributors within the state. This non-signers clause, which was designed to facilitate the enforcement of resale prices, was subsequently declared to be unconstitutional by the Supreme Court in the *Schwegmann* decision.[124] Subsequently, Congress in the McGuire-Keogh Fair Trade Enabling Act of 1952[125] overruled the Schwegmann decision and legalized the non-signers clause on sales in interstate commerce where state laws permitted.

Despite this there has been a gradual decline in the effectiveness of resale price maintenance as a result of decisions of many state courts which have declared the state laws unconstitutional, especially the non-signers clauses. Moreover, various devices have been found for selling in "fair-trade" states at cut-prices despite resale contracts. Thus, in *General Electric Co. v. Masters Mail Order Co.*,[126] the courts refused to enjoin Masters, a mail-order house in the District of Columbia which does not permit resale price maintenance, from selling and shipping electrical equipment to customers in New York at less than the prices required of retailers in New York, who were operating under legal resale price maintenance contracts. The court argued that the sale was made in the District of Columbia, which does not permit resale price maintenance, and consequently the New York law did not apply.

The limits placed on manufacturers' enforcement of resale price maintenance are illustrated by two other cases. In *Eastman Kodak*[127] a manufacturer of color film was enjoined from adopting resale price maintenance because he was the sole producer of the good in question, which was, therefore, not in "fair and open competition with commodities of the same general class." And in *McKesson & Robbins*[128] the defendants were enjoined from entering fair trade contracts with independent wholesalers since the company itself competed with these wholesalers through its own wholesale operations.

While pressure for effective resale price maintenance by various retail and other groups remains strong, it seems probable that the movement is on the wane. Although traditional channels still play a role in the distribution of many products, mass distributors of various sorts are well established in most lines of products in areas with large consumer income. The variety of channels of distribution and the different price sensitivities of various markets encourage manufacturers to adopt varied merchandising strategies. This heterogeneity of market conditions and merchandising strategies together with various possibilities for evasion of state laws limits seriously the incentives and ability of many manufacturers to enforce resale price maintenance. The problems faced by retail druggists, who have been among the principal proponents of "fair trade," illustrate well the effective market limits to enforcement of the policy. The last few decades have seen increasing sale of drugs and toiletries by department stores, chain variety stores and the mass food distributors. It is doubtful whether as much as 10 per cent of all retail sales is covered by resale price arrangements, and the coverage appears to be declining.[129]

DISCRIMINATION

Discrimination as a device for developing and protecting monopoly positions has figured in antitrust discussions from the beginning. Local price cutting was alleged to be one device by which some early trusts acquired their dominant market positions. Local discrimination was one of the predatory practices considered to be evidence of illegal intent under section 2 of the Sherman Act.[130] Section 2 of the Clayton Act, which was designed to prevent discrimination which might lead to the development of monopoly, was on the whole not very effective. Of the thirteen orders issued by 1936, two were directed at simple discrimination between customers, one involved simple local price discrimination, one was directed at local price discrimination incident to a basing-point system, eight involved discrimination between customers who had been classified arbitrarily according to trade status, and one involved discrimination between a mail-order house and independent distributors.[131] In several cases the courts interpreted the act as applying only to the lessening of competition between a seller and his competitors thereby excluding from the terms of the act discrimination which might lessen competition between customers of the seller.[132] The courts subsequently reversed themselves on this point.[133] But they also held that if the discrimination was made in good faith because of differences in grade, quality or quantity, the law placed no limit on the price differential.[134] It was against this background that the Robinson-Patman Act was passed.

The Robinson-Patman Act, as it is interpreted and enforced, is an excellent example of the conflicting objectives of antitrust policy and of the social and political forces influencing antitrust.[135] This act was designed to protect the traditional channels of distribution against the inroads of the mass distributor. It was not designed to eliminate discrimination in an economic sense in order to promote efficient use of resources, but rather to change the bargaining relations between the large buyers and manufacturers. The act sought to do this in several ways. It forbids the payment of brokerage or any equivalent thereof to the person on the other side of the transaction or to his agent. This was designed to protect the traditional broker and to prevent large buyers from benefiting through receipt of brokerage allowances directly or indirectly. The act also prohibits a seller from making payments to a customer for services rendered or from providing sales services to his customers unless such payments or sales services are available to all competing customers on proportionally equal terms. Moreover, the act prohibits discrimination "in price between different purchasers of like grade and quality" where either transaction is in interstate commerce, and where the effect "may be substantially to lessen competition or tend to create a monopoly in any line of commerce, or to injure, destroy, or prevent competition" with either the person who grants or receives the benefit or with customers of either.

The act permits, but does not require, differentials which make only due allowance for differences in the cost of manufacture, sale or delivery resulting from the differing methods or quantities in which goods are sold or delivered. However, the Federal Trade Commission is authorized to fix quantity limits for a particular commodity, despite cost differences, where it finds that the number of purchasers buying large quantities are so few that a price differential for such quantities would be "unjustly discriminatory or promotive of monopoly." A seller may rebut a *prima-facie* case of discrimination by showing that his lower price or his furnishing of services or facilities to a customer "was made in good faith to meet an equally low price of a competitor."

The impact of the act on the competitive position of the various channels of distribution, upon business behavior and on the over-all efficiency of the distributive process is difficult to assess. While it has undoubtedly forced the large buyers to change their buying practices and reduced some of their buying advantage, there is evidence that it has been of less advantage to the traditional channels than might have been supposed since the large buyers have often found other legal ways of gaining an advantage such as manufacturing for their own supply or developing of their private brands. It appears also that the act has served to deter the growth of voluntary chains in rivalry with the corporate chains.[136] Moreover, there is evidence that the act promotes inefficiency in distribution, not solely by discouraging the growth of new channels of distribution but in other ways as well. For example, large corporate chains, denied brokerage payments, appear often to purchase smaller quantities and to demand more services than they would otherwise. And the requirement that the payment for services or the supply of services to customers be available on proportionally equal terms to all has served not only to foreclose one indirect form of price concession to large buyers, but in some cases has also forced the manufacturer either to abandon promising selective promotional programs or to incur the greater cost of proportionally equal programs. The provisions with reference to brokerage and proportionality illustrate dramatically a dilemma of antitrust. When, as in these cases, the rules are simple requiring no showing of monopolistic effects, they are relatively easy to enforce; but their impact may be very arbitrary and often unintended.

The price discrimination provisions of the Robinson-Patman Act, so far as they have been effective in eliminating price differences, have also reduced the competitive pressures to efficiency.[137] Moreover, in markets where secret price concessions or other secret consessions are the instrument of competition, the elimination of such practices, often initiated by the more skilled buyers, reduces the competitive forces in the market. The act without a doubt has reduced short run price competition in many oligopolistic markets. By failing to distinguish between temporary unsystematic price differences incidental to competition and persisting systematic discrimination, the act has gone beyond the objective of limiting the abuse of monopoly power and has become an instrument in restraint of competition. It is doubtful whether the mass distributors often have a significant degree of monopoly power beyond advantages arising from their greater efficiency, or that they have often abused such power as they have. The Robinson-Patman Act is the product of depression psychology—of anticompetitive policies born of depression superimposed on a long run change in the character of distributive channels. The act has probably done little to stem the decline of the traditional channels, but it has probably on balance reduced the efficiency of distribution, impeded experimentation and reduced the pressures of price competition.

BASING-POINT PRICING

The development of policy with respect to basing-point pricing has been one of the more controversial and significant chapters in the history of the Federal Trade Commission's efforts to regulate business practices.[138] The basing-point system is a form of delivered pricing in which the price for any destination is arrived at by adding a standard transportation charge (normally the published railroad rate) to the "base-price" for some designated "basing-point mill." Its essence is a common formula for pricing by all or several members of a market. Industries which have used the system extensively have generally had several characteristics: a highly standardized product, freight costs which are an important element in the delivered price, and either a high concentration of sales in a few firms or a strong trade association engaged in attempts to control price competition. Where there is a single basing-point, the delivered price from the base-mill is the effective one for all sellers and buyers no matter where located. If there are several basing-points, or if all mills are basing-points, the effective price charged by all sellers for delivery at any destination is the lowest of the delivered prices calculated for the various basing-points.

One effect of this method of pricing is that except for sales by a base-mill within its "natural market", i.e. the area within which its delivered prices are lower than others, sellers experience non-uniform net mill prices, a form of price discrimination.* Thus, under a single basing-point system any mill not located at the base will have non-uniform net mill prices for sales to different destinations. Under a multiple basing-point system, any firm which absorbs freight, i.e. sells outside its "natural market", by meeting the lower prices of another basing-point, will have non-uniform net mill prices. These discriminatory effects of a basing-point system deny to some consumers the natural advantages of their location and may lead in some industries to an uneconomic location of facilities, including both mills producing the product concerned and fabricating firms which use the product.

While the practice has some incidental discriminatory effects which may interfere with a rational location of firms, its principal significance is as a device facilitating identical delivered prices, whether through agreement or the conscious parallel action of oligopolistic firms. By formula pricing, competitors are able to achieve identical prices at all points provided only that they all abide by the formula. Where the product is standardized, this can often be achieved by simply publishing price lists. Such a system serves to reduce short run price competition at the very least and, if there are barriers to entry, may serve to restrict long run investment and output.

The basing-point system may have other incidental though not necessarily inconsequential effects. By requiring the buyer to pay a delivered price based on rail rates, it eliminates any cost incentives to take delivery at the mill or to use less expensive forms of transportation where they are available. Moreover, by providing a uniform price for delivery at any point from any source, the system eliminates all cost incentives to purchase from the nearest mills, thus inducing unnecessary crosshauling. The general thrust of these incidental effects is to encourage inefficient use of transport facilities.

Although since 1948 the legal status of the practice has been relatively clear, the development of public policy under the antitrust laws was a long and at times acrimonious process. The initial step was taken in 1924 when the Federal Trade Commission ordered the United States Steel Corporation to cease quoting prices "upon any other basing-

* It is common under a basing-point system for firms to sell outside their "natural" market as defined above through absorbing freight to meet the price of a more favorably situated supplier.

point than that where the products are manufactured or from which they are shipped."[139] Although the steel industry changed to a multiple basing-point system and increased the number of basing-points from time to time, the industry did not abandon the practice until after the Supreme Court's decision in the *Cement Institute* case in 1948.

In 1945 the Supreme Court upheld two orders of the Commission which found the use of a single basing-point system in the glucose industry to violate section 2a of the Clayton Act because it involved discrimination injurious to competition.[140] Lower courts also upheld orders which found a basing-point system and a zone pricing system to violate section 5 of the Federal Trade Commission Act as well as the Clayton Act.[141] The *Cement Institute* case represents the climax in the development of policy.[142] Here a multiple basing-point system, in use for many years, was found to violate section 5 of the Federal Trade Commission Act, thereby sustaining the Commission's finding that "concerted maintenance of the basing-point delivered price system is an unfair method of competition" and also section 2a of the Clayton Act, because it involved discrimination which substantially lessened competition between the cement manufacturers and was not made in good faith to meet a competitor's price. This decision was interpreted by some as outlawing not only the concerted use of a basing-point system, but all freight absorption as well. Unsuccessful efforts were made to pass legislation which would specifically permit freight absorption by sellers acting independently. The present consensus is, however, that freight absorption is not illegal *per se,* and the Commission has made clear that its current policy is to proceed against the practice as a collusive policy violating the Sherman and Federal Trade Commission Acts rather than under the Clayton Act because of the incidental discrimination.

Since the *Cement* decision, the formal basing-point system has been abandoned in cement, steel and other industries.[143] In cement and steel sales are now made on an f.o.b. mill basis and although freight absorption by individual firms is not uncommon, it appears that there is less absorption than before. Moreover, there has been a substantial increase in the use of truck rather than rail transport. The abandonment of the basing-point system has on balance increased efficiency in various ways. But the industries concerned are generally oligopolistic in their structure and it is questionable whether the abandonment of the system has increased competition substantially in the industries affected if at all.[144]

VIII. Patents and Antitrust

The problem of patents and antitrust policy is the subject of chapter 8.[145] It is sufficient to note here that properly conceived, a patent is designed to promote economic welfare by providing an incentive to innovation and to facilitate the eventual diffusion of new knowledge after the expiration of the patent grant through public disclosure. Its purpose is to provide competition by providing new alternatives. But a patent does represent a temporary grant of monopoly power and may be used in various ways for a further restriction of competition. The general thrust of antitrust policy has been to narrow the scope of the patent grant by preventing its use to foreclose entry to other markets or its use to facilitate price-fixing, market-sharing, etc. in a market beyond that for the product or process on which the patent is granted. This represents a retreat from earlier policy where the emphasis was upon the protection of the monopoly reward of the patent owner.[146] The *Ethyl Gasoline* decision illustrates well present policy. The Ethyl Gasoline Corporation had licensed major oil refiners to manufacture gasoline containing ethyl fluid on which it held both product and process patents on the condition that they sell only to jobbers who had been licensed by it to sell ethyl gasoline. But the Ethyl Gasoline Corporation had adopted the policy of licensing only those jobbers who abided by the marketing policies and prices of the major integrated companies in their area. In effect, the licensing system was being used to stabilize prices and distributive practices in accordance with the wishes of the major integrated companies, including Standard Oil of New Jersey, which owned one-half of the capital stock of Ethyl Gasoline Corporation. This the court found to be an unlawful extension of the patent right.[147]

The development of a restrictive policy towards the patent grant through carefully limiting the right of a patentee to extend his power to other products represents an important development of antitrust policy in the last twenty years. Moreover, in many decrees where the courts have found a violation of the antitrust laws and in many consent decrees, there has been provision for compulsory licensing of all responsible applicants at reasonable royalties or even royalty free. Such arrangements have played an important part in the settlement of the Alcoa and the United Shoe Machinery cases among others.

IX. Summary and Conclusions

Antitrust policy initiated after a period of rapid growth of large and often dominant business firms was conceived as part of the American vision of a pluralistic and mobile society. The problem is to a large extent to develop a policy with respect to oligopoly or monopolistic competition. The alternatives are three: to alter the market structure, to change the behavior by changing the horizons and attitudes of management, or to change behavior by developing a code of business practices. While there has undoubtedly been some change in management's horizons and attitudes affected in part indirectly by antitrust policy, until very recently the direct concern of antitrust policy has been principally with business practices. There has been considerable deference and respect for business success acquired by fair means even though a firm grows to have a dominant position in its market. In this regard the emphasis has been upon the freedom of enterprise. The principal thrust of policy has been to prevent collusive behavior and arbitrary restraints upon entry. In recent cases involving large or dominant firms, the emphasis has been on the power and purpose to fix prices or exclude competitors. While both such powers are evidence of monopoly in law, and of monopoly or oligopoly in economics, we lack consensus concerning unambiguous, meaningful and operational tests of such power in both law and economics. But market position acquired via the path of merger is more suspect and under recent legislation is more likely to be found illegal where it leads to a significant growth in market concentration.

It should be emphasized that antitrust policy is only one part of United States policy with respect to competition. The patent laws are conceived as a competitive device through their incentives to enterprise, though it is clear that the line between patents which promote competition in the long run and those which prevent it is difficult to draw. There is considerable legislation designed to promote small business by preferential tax treatment, special provision for financial resources, educational services and other means. It must also be pointed out that certain government policies serve in various ways to promote concentration or reduce the factors making for competitive behavior. These include some tax laws, licensing provisions, tariff and import quota restrictions, government purchasing policies, agricultural legislation, and some aspects of collective bargaining of labor.

EXTENT AND TREND OF MONOPOLY

Some efforts have been made at the measurement of the extent and trend of monopoly in the United States economy. Studies by George Stigler[148] and Warren Nutter[149] on the extent of monopoly in 1939 suggest that about 20 per cent of the national income may be produced under conditions of private monopoly. Nutter's study suggests that there was no clear cut increase in the extent of monopoly from 1899 to 1939. A study by Morris Adelman[150] on the extent of concentration in the United States economy indicates that there has been no increase during the period 1901 to 1950. The significance of these studies is, of course, limited for several reasons, more especially because of the heavy reliance upon indexes of concentration as a measure of monopoly power. That such indexes have limited economic meaning is generally conceded. It is highly probable that the development of new products, new distributive methods, better transportation and improved information has increased the number of effective alternatives for most buyers. This is one aspect of competition. It is not unreasonable to conclude that on balance monopolistic power may have decreased during this century. But this is at best a personal and tentative conclusion.

ADMINISTRATION

The United States in contrast with most other countries depends heavily upon the judicial process for clarification and enforcement of antitrust law. Many of the "big" cases and much of the initiative in the clarification of the law have come from the Department of Justice, working through the courts to establish the facts and to clarify the law. In establishing the Federal Trade Commission as an independent regulatory body specializing in the study and regulation of industry, it was intended to provide an agency which would develop special competence in this field and serve both as an innovating and judicial body. But its orders are also subject to appeal to the courts. The Commission has not fulfilled the hopes of its proponents. Although it continues to do much good enforcement work, the Department of Justice has shown more initiative and imagination.[151]

The predominant opinion appears to favor the continuation of this dual system for the enforcement of antitrust.[152] Although it is recognized that the judicial process is not the ideal method for determining facts, most informed observers favor continued reliance upon the courts, subject to some improvement in procedures, rather than the development of special tribunals for the regulation of industry. United States experience with independent agencies has not been altogether favorable. It has often been difficult after the initial period to maintain high quality in either the Commissioners or the staff. Moreover, such agencies often run the risk of becoming captives of the interests they are designed to regulate. But if a more logical policy is to be developed and if cases are to be handled more judiciously, improvements in the practices of the antitrust division of the Department of Justice, Federal Trade Commission and the courts are in order. More careful selection of cases based on a prior study of the economics of the industry and of the importance of the industry in question would yield high returns. More effective use of pre-trial procedures for developing the facts is also appropriate. Proposals have also been made for the establishment of a special constitutional court to handle "big" cases and more especially those in which divestiture is sought. Without question, improvements in existing procedures can do much to speed up the handling of cases and to develop a more consistent body of law.

EFFECTIVENESS OF ANTITRUST

The effectiveness of antitrust policy in the United States is difficult to assess. While there is a good deal of *a priori* opinion and informed judgment, carefully analyzed evidence on the matter is not substantial. The record of the number of cases initiated or of the cases won in the courts is not a good test. The significance of antitrust is to be found in the change in business behavior or in the structure of industry resulting from the existence of the law. A large number of cases initiated may merely show energy in its enforcement. The cases which eventually get to court tend to be cases which are in the "gray" areas of antitrust policy and because of the uncertainty of these areas, one must expect reversals. The initiation of cases is important but of more importance are the changes in business behavior resulting from the mere existence of the law and the content and effect of the decrees entered as a consequence of antitrust actions. Because of the failure to follow up on many of these decrees and because of the lack of study of changes in behavior resulting from the law, little can be said on these matters.

No extensive use has been made of divestiture and dissolution as a remedy in antitrust proceedings. Dr. Simon Whitney, reporting on his study of 20 basic industries, notes that while dissolution proved beneficial in the oil, tobacco and explosive industries, the "failure to dissolve four other big trusts (tin cans, steel, farm machinery, aluminum) did not prevent these industries from developing in about the same way..."[153] He concludes that "a dominant firm is not likely—if an industry's technology is free—to retain its original share of the market even if it is not dissolved by antitrust action."[154] The failure of competitors to develop in the shoe machinery industry he attributes to the United Shoe Machinery's control over the whole technology of the industry. While he believes that divorcement in anthracite coal, pullman cars and motion pictures has made for a more open market, he doubts that the practical benefits have been impressive. He notes that the corn refining, farm machinery and meat industries have developed in a competitive fashion even though the divestitures in these industries were modest. He concludes, "dissolution under the antitrust laws has, then, served a useful function in some instances, by shortening the period needed for competition to assert itself against an original near-monopoly; but it has not achieved, and has not seemed likely to achieve, valuable results when used in oligopoly situations."[155] Although some critics believe that the remedies of dissolution and divestiture should be used more frequently,[156] it is clear that courts are reluctant to use such remedies. This reluctance is in itself a sign of the deference shown to successful enterprise. While dissolution and divestiture have been used sparingly, it seems probable that the antitrust laws have deterred the development of dominant firms through growth or merger such as was characteristic of the late 19th and early 20th centuries. Recent antimerger legislation is likely to be an even more effective deterrent.

The effects of the control of business behavior is even more difficult to assess. The prevention of collusive action and insistence upon independence of decision probably serve to promote uncertainty, heterogeneity in market structures and conflicting market strategies. In typical oligopolistic markets this should encourage the market results which are characteristic of competition rather than monopoly. It is also probable that rather than seeking to insure their survival and profits through collusion, firms turn in other directions such as cost reduction, product development and sales effort. The Robinson-Patman Act and to a lesser extent the encouragement given resale price maintenance have probably on balance reduced the effectiveness of competition somewhat in some areas. But the prevention of predatory practices and of artificial attempts to foreclose the market thereby reducing the barriers to entry has probably reduced the effective monopoly power of dominant firms. The net effect of antitrust has probably been to increase the competitive pressures and reduce the extent of monopoly power even though in some cases encouraging concentration.

Antitrust policy in the United States, which has wide support in principle, represents a constructive attempt to promote competition in the private industrial sector so as to reconcile private enterprise with broad concepts of the public interest. Clearly this policy is not without contradictions and has not been able to cope in a completely satisfactory way with all problems of modern industry. But more energetic enforcement and further effort at cooperation between economists and lawyers should lead to better results. The policy is deeply embedded in the political-social system of the United States and under the prevailing climate of opinion is likely to become increasingly effective.

NOTES

1. The author is indebted to Paul MacAvoy of the University of Chicago, Richard C. Carr of Yale University and Gordon Pierson of the University of Washington, Seattle, for assistance in the research on which this essay is based.
2. For detailed analysis of the background of the Sherman Act, see Hans B. THORELLI, *The Federal Antitrust Policy: Origination of an American Tradition*, Stockholm: Kungl. Boktryckeriet P. A. Norstedt and Sons, 1954; WILLIAM LETWIN, "Congress and the Sherman Antitrust Law: 1887–1890," *University of Chicago Law Review*, vol. *23*, Winter, 1956, pp. 221–58. See also JOHN D. CLARK, *The Federal Trust Policy*, Baltimore: The Johns Hopkins Press, 1931, especially chapter 5 on the prevailing opinions of contemporary economists. For the changing political background out of which antitrust policies grew, see RICHARD HOFSTADTER, *The Age of Reform; from Bryan to F.D.R.*, New York: Alfred A. Knopf, 1955; ARTHUR SCHLESINGER, Jr., *The Age of Roosevelt Vol. I: Crisis of the Old Order, 1919–1933*, Boston: Houghton Mifflin, 1957.
3. For the early development of the corporation in the United States, see E. MERRICK DODD, *American Business Corporation until 1860: with Special Reference to Massachusetts*, Cambridge: Harvard University Press, 1954; JOSEPH S. DAVIS, *Essays in the Earlier History of American Corporations*, 2 vols., Cambridge: Harvard University Press, 1917.
4. For a study of the role of state regulation of economic affairs in the pre-Civil War period see OSCAR HANDLIN and MARY F. HANDLIN, *Commonwealth, A Study of the Role of Government in the American Economy: Massachusetts, 1774–1861*, New York: New York University Press, 1947; LOUIS HARTZ, *Economic Policy and Democratic Thought: Pennsylvania, 1776–1860*, Cambridge: Harvard University Press, 1948; MILTON S. HEATH, *Constructive Liberalism: The Role of the State in Economic Development in Georgia to 1860*, Cambridge: Harvard University Press, 1954.
5. For a recent summary of American value-orientations, see ROBBIN M. WILLIAMS, Jr., *American Society; A Sociological Interpretation*, New York: Alfred A. Knopf, 1951, pp. 388–442. Williams suggests several elements in the American value system which reinforce an antitrust policy: e.g., emphasis on "achievement" and "success" and on the importance of "activity" and "work"; a moral outlook; an emphasis on efficiency, progress and material comfort; an avowal of equality,

especially of opportunity, and of freedom and democracy; an emphasis on applied science and secular rationality; the cult of individual personality. These value-orientations all serve to reinforce a vigorous economy. The potential conflicts among these, e.g., the potential conflict between freedom and equality of opportunity or between individualism and efficiency, are reflected in the fabric of antitrust policy. See also ROBERT S. LYND, *Knowledge for what?* Princeton: Princeton University Press, 1939, ch. 3, and RALPH B. PERRY, *Characteristically American*, New York: Alfred A. Knopf, 1949.

6. See J. D. CLARK, *op. cit.*
7. For history of some of the early trusts see ELIOT JONES, *The Trust Problem in the United States*, New York: MacMillan, 1923. HENRY R. SEAGER and CHARLES A. GULICK, *Trust and Corporation Problems*, New York: Harper, 1929.
8. For various facets of this concern, see the essays in EDWARD S. MASON, editor, *The Corporation in Modern Society*, Cambridge: Harvard University Press, 1959; also J. D. GLOVER, *The Attack on Big Business*, Boston: The Plimpton Press, 1954.
9. GLOVER, *op. cit.*, p. 107. ELMO ROPER, "The Public Looks at Business," *Harvard Business Review*, vol. 27, March, 1949, pp. 170–72. BURTON R. FISHER and STEPHEN B. WITHEY, *Big Business as the People See It*, The Survey Research Center, Institute for Social Research, University of Michigan, December, 1951.
10. VERNON MUND, *Government and Business*, New York: Harper, 2nd edition, 1955, ch. 20. For compilation of state statutes, see United States Department of Commerce, *Marketing Laws Survey: State Antitrust Laws*, 3 vols., Washington, D.C.: Government Printing Office, 1940.
11. Sherman Antitrust Act, 26 Stat. 209, 15 U.S.C.A., §§ 1–7 (1890). For detailed studies of the antitrust laws see: Attorney General's National Committee to Study the Antitrust Laws, *Report*, Washington, D. C.: Government Printing office, 1955 (hereafter cited as Attorney General's Committee); CORWIN D. EDWARDS, *Maintaining Competition: Requisities of a Governmental Policy*, New York: McGraw Hill, 1949; CARL KAYSEN and DONALD F. TURNER, *Antitrust Policy: An Economic and Legal Analysis*, Cambridge: Harvard University Press, 1959: FRITZ MACHLUP, *The Political Economy of Monopoly: Business, Labor and Government Policies*, Baltimore: Johns Hopkins Press, 1952; GEORGE W. STOCKING and MYRON W. WATKINS, *Monopoly and Free Enterprise*, New York: The Twentieth Century Fund, 1951; CLAIR WILCOX, *Public Policies Toward Business*, revised edition, Homewood: Richard D. Irwin, 1960. For a study of the effects of antitrust policy in some twenty industries, see SIMON N. WHITNEY, *Antitrust Policies: American Experience in Twenty Industries*, 2 vols., New York: The Twentieth Century Fund, 1958. For a foreign view of the United States experience, see A. D. NEALE, *The Antitrust Laws of the United States of America: A Study of Competition Enforced by Law*, Cambridge: Cambridge University Press, 1960.
12. "Since the existing law is primarily oriented toward conduct, it does not effectively deal—or at least has not effectively dealt in the past—with undue market power that cannot be associated with bad or unduly restrictive conduct." KAYSEN and TURNER, *op. cit.*, p. 44. See also EDWARD S. MASON, *Economic Concentration and the Monopoly Problem*, Cambridge: Harvard Univeristy Press, 1957, especially chs. 15, 16 and 19 for discussion of changing emphasis in antitrust interpretation; JOHN PERRY MILLER, *Unfair Competition: A Study in Criteria for the Control of Trade Practices*, Cambridge: Harvard University Press, 1941, chs. 2–3; Attorney General's Committee, *op. cit.*, p. 11.
13. On the "rule of reason" see the opinion by Justice White in *Standard Oil Co. of N. J. v. U. S.*, 221 U. S. 1 (1911). See also Attorney General's Committee, *op. cit.*, pp. 5–12.
14. For discussion of the administration and enforcement of antitrust laws, see

Attorney General's Committee, *op. cit.*, ch. 8; Walton Hamilton, *Antitrust in Action*, Temporary National Economic Committee, Monograph No. 16, Washington, D. C.: Government Printing Office, 1940, section 2; Kaysen and Turner, *op. cit.*, ch. 8.

15. Attorney General's Committee, *op. cit.*, pp. 378–85.
16. For a critique of the consent decree procedures, see Antitrust Subcommittee of the Committee on the Judiciary of the House of Representatives, 86th Congress, 1st Sess, *Report on Consent Decree Program of the Department of Justice*, Washington, D. C.: Government Printing Office, 1959.
17. *Standard Oil Co. of N. J. v. U. S.*, 221 U. S. 1 (1911); *U. S. v. American Tobacco Co.*, 221 *U. S.* 106 (1911).
18. For background of the 1914 legislation, see Miller, *Unfair Competition*, ch. 4, and John Perry Miller, "Woodrow Wilson's Contributions to Antitrust Policies," *The Philosophy and Policies of Woodrow Wilson*, Earl Latham, editor, Chicago: University of Chicago Press, 1958.
19. Federal Trade Commission Act, 38 Stat. 717, 15 U. S. C. A., § § 41–51 (1914).
20. Clayton Act, 38 Stat. 730, 15 U.S.C.A., §§ 12–27 (1914).
21. Robinson-Patman Act, 49 Stat. 1526, 15 U.S.C.A., § 13 (1936). For critique of the Robinson-Patman Act see: Corwin D. Edwards, *The Price Discrimination Law: A Review of Experience*, Washington D.C.: The Brookings Institution, 1959; M. A. Adelman, "The Consistency of the Robinson-Patman Act," *Stanford Law Review*, vol. 6, December, 1953, pp. 3–22; Joel B. Dirlam and Alfred E. Kahn, *Fair Competition: The Law and Economics of Antitrust Policy*, Ithaca: Cornell University Press, 1954, ch. 4.
22. Celler Anti-Merger Act, 64 Stat. 1125, 15 U.S.C.A., §§ 18 and 21 (1950). U.S. Congress, House Committee on the Judiciary, *House Report No. 1191*, August 4, 1949, 81st Congress, 1st Sess.; U.S. Congress, Senate Committee on the Judiciary, *Senate Report No. 1775*, June 2, 1950, 81st Congress, 2nd Sess.
23. Wheeler-Lea Act, 52 Stat. 114, 15 U.S.C.A., §§ 52–58 (1938); Miller. *Unfair Competition*, pp. 101–03.
24. *Ibid.*, pp. 15–22. For an extended discussion of the common law of unfair competition, see Milton Handler, "Unfair Competition," *Iowa Law Review*, vol. 21, January, 1936, pp. 175–262. (Reprinted in American Economic Association, *Readings in the Social Control of Industry*, Philadelphia: Blakiston Press, 1942, Edgar M. Hoover, Jr. and Joel Dean, editors).
25. While big business is not completely guiltless of such behavior, these are primarily the practices of small-scale and aggressively competitive industries. See Edwin H. Sutherland, *White Collar Crime*, New York: Dryden Press, 1949.
26. Miller-Tydings Act, 50 Stat. 693, 15 U.S.C.A., § 1 (1937); McGuire-Keogh Fair Trade Enabling Act, 66 Stat. 632; U.S. Code 15 U.S.C.A., § 45 (1952).
27. For an excellent and detailed study of the applicability of antitrust to foreign commerce, including foreign investment, joint ventures and licensing arrangements see Kingman Brewster, Jr., *Antitrust and American Business Abroad*, New York: McGraw Hill, 1958. See also Attorney General's Committee, *op. cit.*, ch. 2.
28. 40 Stat 516, 15 U.S.C.A., §§ 61–65 (1918).
29. Federal Trade Commission, *Annual Report 1958*, Washington, D.C.: Government Printing Office, pp. 62–63.
30. *U.S. v. National Lead Co.*, 63 F. Supp. 513 (S.D.N.Y. 1945); *U.S. v. Imperial Chemical Industries, Ltd.*, 100 F. Supp. 504 (S.D.N.Y. 1951); *U.S. v. General Electric Co.*, 82 F. Supp. 753 (D.N.J. 1949); *U.S. v. Timken Roller Bearing Co.*, 83 F. Supp. 284 (N.D. Ohio 1949).
31. *U.S. v. Minnesota Mining and Mfg. Co.*, 92 F. Supp. 947 (D. Mass. 1950).

32. See Attorney General's Committee, *op. cit.*, ch. 6; KAYSEN and TURNER, *op. cit.*, pp. 41–43.
33. 38 Stat. 731, 15 U.S.C.A., § 17 (1914).
34. *U.S. v. Addyston Pipe and Steel Company*, 85 F. 271 (1898); *U.S. v. Trenton Potteries Co*, 273 U.S. 392 (1927); *U.S. v. Socony-Vacuum Oil Company*, 310 U.S. 150 (1940).
35. *American Column and Lumber Company v. U.S.*, 257 U.S. 377 (1921).
36. *U.S. v. Addyston Pipe and Steel Company*, 85 F. 271 (1898); *U.S. v. National Lead Company*, 332 U.S. 319 (1947); *U.S. v. U.S. Alkali Export Association*, 86 F. Supp. 59 (S.D.N.Y. 1949). *Timken Roller Bearing Company v. U.S.*, 341 U.S. 593 (1951), condemning the allocation of territories between a dominant American producer and British and French firms, the latter owned jointly by Timken and the British company.
37. *Fashion Originators' Guild of America, Inc. v. F.T.C.*, 312 U.S. 457 (1941); *Millinery Creators' Guild Inc. v. F.T.C.*, 312 U.S. 469 (1941); *Associated Press v. U.S.*, 326 U.S. 1 (1945).
38. 273 U.S. 397–98 (1927).
39. *Appalachian Coals, Inc. v. U.S.*, 288 U.S. 344 (1933).
40. JOHN PERRY MILLER, "The Pricing in the Bituminous Coal Industry: Some International Comparisons," in *Public Policy*, C. J. FRIEDRICH and E. S. MASON, editors, Cambridge: Harvard University Press, 1940, pp. 144–175.
41. 310 U.S. 223 (1940).
42. *Dr. Miles Medical Co. v. John D. Park and Sons Co.*, 220 U.S. 373 (1911): *F.T.C. v. Beech-Nut Packing Co.*, 257 U.S. 441 (1922).
43. See below, pp. 242-44.
44. 312 U.S. 457 (1941).
45. 312 U.S. 469 (1941).
46. 326 U.S. 1 (1945).
47. See *Chicago Board of Trade v. U.S.*, 246 U.S. 231 (1918) where the court sustained the "call" rule prohibiting members from purchasing or offering to purchase grain at a price other than the closing bid at the call, during the period between the close of the call and the opening of the session on the next business day.
48. *Appalachian Coals, Inc. v. U.S.*, 288 U.S. 344 (1933).
49. *American Column and Lumber Co. v. U.S.* 257 U.S. 377 (1921).
50. *U.S. v. American Linseed Oil Co.*, 262 U.S. 371 (1923).
51. *Maple Flooring Manufacturers Association v. U.S.*, 268 U.S. 563 (1925).
52. *Cement Manufacturers Protective Association v. U.S.*, 268 U.S. 588 (1925).
53. *Sugar Institute, Inc. v. U.S.*, 297 U.S. 553 (1936).
54. *Federal Trade Commission v. Cement Institute*, 333 U.S. 683 (1948). Concerning the basing-point system see FRITZ MACHLUP, *The Basing Point System: An Economic Analysis of a Controversial Pricing Practice*, Philadelphia: Blakiston Press, 1949.
55. RICHARD B. TENNANT, *The American Cigarette Industry: A Study in Economic Analysis and Public Policy*, New Haven; Yale University Press, 1950; WILLIAM H. NICHOLLS, *Price Policies in the Cigarette Industry: A Study of "Concerted Action" and Its Social Control, 1911–50*, Nashville: Vanderbilt University Press, 1951.
56. WILLIAM FELLNER, *Competition Among the Few: Oligopoly and Similar Market Structures*, New York: Alfred A. Knopf, 1949, chs. 4–8.
57. For a discussion of the problem of entry, see JOE BAIN, *Barriers to New Competition: Their Character and Consequences in Manufacturing Industries*, Cambridge: Harvard University Press, 1956, and a review by RICHARD B. HEFLEBOWER, *American Economic Review*, vol 47, June, 1957, pp. 363–71.
58. KAYSEN and TURNER have argued similarly, *op. cit.*, pp. 46–47, 148–52.
59. WALTER ADAMS, "Dissolution, Divorcement, Divestiture: the Pyrrhic Victories

of Antitrust," *Indiana Law Journal*, vol. 27, Fall, 1951, pp. 1–37; MACHLUP, *Political Economy of Monopoly*, pp. 232–33.

60. 221 U.S. 1 (1911).
61. *U.S. v. Aluminum Co. of America*, 148 F. 2d 416 (1945).
62. See Attorney General's Committee, *op. cit.*, pp. 36–42; *Interstate Circuit, Inc. v. U.S.*, 306 U.S. 208 (1939); *F.T.C. v. A.E. Staley Mfg. Co.*, 324 U.S. 746 (1945); *American Tobacco Co. v. U.S.*, 328 U.S. 781 (1946); *F.T.C. v. Cement Institute*, 333 U.S. 683 (1948); *Theatre Enterprises, Inc. v. Paramount Film Distributing Corp.*, 346 U.S. 537 (1954).
63. 346 U.S. 540–41 (1954).
64. 221 U.S. 1 (1911).
65. 221 U.S. 106 (1911).
66. 251 U.S. 417 (1920).
67. For criticism of the decision see Attorney General's Committee, *op. cit.*, pp. 50–52; KAYSEN and TURNER, *op. cit.*, p. 242; MACHLUP, *Political Economy of Monopoly*, p. 232; GEORGE W. STOCKING, "The Rule of Reason, Workable Competition, and Monopoly," *Yale Law Journal*, vol. 64, July, 1955, pp. 1129–36.
68. MILTON HANDLER, *Construction of the Antitrust Laws*, Temporary National Economic Committee, Monograph No. 38, Washington, D.C.: Government Printing Office, 1941, pp. 49 *et seq.*
69. *U.S. v. Terminal R.R. Ass'n*, 224 U.S. 383 (1912).
70. *Northern Securities Co. v. U.S.*, 193 U.S. 197 (1904).
71. *U.S. v. Reading Co.*, 226 U.S. 324 (1912); *U.S. v. Reading Co.*, 253 U.S. 26 (1920); *U.S. v. Lehigh Valley R.R. Co.*, 254 U.S. 255 (1920).
72. *U.S. v. Aluminum Co. of America*, 148 F. 2d 416 (1945); 91 F. Supp. 333 (1950). For comments on Alcoa decision see WALTER ADAMS, "The Aluminum Case: Legal Victory-Economic Defeat," *American Economic Review*, vol. 41, December, 1951, pp. 915–22.
73. 148 F. 2d 424 (1945).
74. *U.S. v. United Shoe Machinery Corp.*, 110 F. Supp. 295 (1953). For discussion of the case by an economist who served as clerk to the Judge see CARL KAYSEN, *United States v. United Shoe Machinery Corp.*, Cambridge: Harvard University Press, 1956.
75. *U.S. v. United Shoe Machinery Co. of N.J.*, 247 U.S. 32 (1918).
76. *United Shoe Machinery Corp. v. U.S.*, 258 U.S. 451 (1922).
77. 110 F. Supp. 297 (1953).
78. *Ibid.*, p. 343.
79. *American Tobacco Co. et al. v. U.S.*, 328 U.S. 781 (1946). See Eugene V. Rostow, "The New Sherman Act: A Positive Instrument of Progress," *University of Chicago Law Review*, vol. 14, June, 1947, pp. 567–600.
80. 328 U.S. 810 (1946).
81. Nicholls, *op cit.*; Tennant, *op. cit.*
82. WHITNEY, *op. cit.*, vol. 2, pp. 38–41.
83. ARTHUR R. BURNS, *The Decline of Competition*, New York: McGraw Hill, 1936, pp. 421–45; M. A. ADELMAN, "Concept and Statistical Measurement of Vertical Integration," in *Business Concentration and Price Policy*, National Bureau of Economic Research, Princeton: Princeton University Press, 1955, pp. 281–322.
84. JOSEPH J. SPENGLER, "Vertical Integration and Antitrust Policy," *The Journal of Political Economy*, vol. 58, August, 1950, pp. 346–52; ROBERT BORK, "Vertical Integration and the Sherman Act: The Legal History of an Economic Misconception," *University of Chicago Law Review*, vol 22, Autumn, 1954, pp. 157–201. For study of vertical integration in petroleum see MELVIN G. DE CHAZEAU and

ALFRED E. KAHN, *Integration and Competition in the Petroleum Industry,* New Haven: Yale University Press, 1959.

85. See below pp. 235–36.
86. *U.S. v. Paramount Pictures, Inc.*, 334 U.S. 174 (1948). For a study of the application of antitrust to the motion picture industry see Michael Conant, *Antitrust in the Motion Picture Industry: Economic and Legal Analysis,* Berkeley: University of California Press, 1960.
87. 15 U.S.C.A. §§ 18 and 21 (1950).
    The Bank Holding Company Act of 1956 is designed to prevent lessening of competition in banking by the use of the holding company device. See 12 U.S.C.A., §§ 1841–1848 (1956).
88. For a review of the merger movement and the literature concerning it see RALPH L. NELSON, *Merger Movements in American Industry, 1895–1956,* Princeton: Princeton University Press, 1959; JESSE W. MARKHAM, "Survey of the Evidence and Findings on Mergers," in *Business Concentration and Price Policy,* pp. 141–212 (followed by comments of Walter Adams and George W. Stocking); J. FRED WESTON, *The Role of Mergers in the Growth of Large Firms,* Berkeley: University of California Press, 1953; Federal Trade Commission, *Report on Corporate Mergers and Acquisitions,* Washington, D.C.: Government Printing Office, 1955.
89. From NELSON, *op. cit,*. pp. 154–56.
90. *Ibid.*, p. 6.
91. J. KEITH BUTTERS, JOHN LINTNER, WILLIAM L. CARY, *Effects of Taxation: Corporate Mergers,* Boston: Graduate School of Business Administration, Harvard University, 1951, p. 17.
92. *Northern Securities Co. v. U.S.*, 193 U.S. 197 (1904).
93. HANDLER, *loc. cit.*
94. Select Committee on Small Business, House of Representatives, 81st Cong. 2d Sess., *Hearings: Steel–Acquisitions, Mergers, and Expansion of 12 Major Companies, 1900 to 1950,* Washington, D.C.: Government Printing Office, 1950; GERTRUDE G. SCHROEDER, *The Growth of Major Steel Companies, 1900–1950,* Baltimore: Johns Hopkins Press, 1953; WHITNEY, *op. cit.*, vol. 1, ch. 5.
95. See above pp. 228 and 259, note 67.
96. *U.S. v. Columbia Steel Co.*, 334 U.S. 495 (1948).
97. U.S. Congress, *House Report No. 1191,* 81st Cong., 1st Sess., 1949, p. 2; U.S. Congress, *Senate Report No. 1775,* 81st Cong., 2nd Sess., 1950.
98. *Arrow-Hart and Hegeman Electric Co. v. F.T.C.*, 291 U.S. 587 (1934).
99. *U.S. v. E.I. DuPont de Nemours and Co.*, 353 U.S. 586 (1957); 167 F. Supp. 957 (1958).
100. *U.S. v. Bethlehem Steel Corp.*, 168 F. Supp. 576 (S.D.N.Y 1958).
101. *Ibid.*, p. 617.
102. For a discussion of these problems see JOHN PERRY MILLER, "Measures of Monopoly Power and Concentration: Their Economic Significance," pp. 119–38 (followed by comments of Joe S. Bain) and TIBOR SCITOVSKY, "Economic Theory and the Measurement of Concentration," pp. 101–13 (followed by comments of William Fellner and Carl Kaysen) both in *Business Concentration and Public Policy, op. cit.* Also see JOE S. BAIN, *Industrial Organization,* New York: Wiley & Sons, 1959, ch. 6.
103. EDWARD H. CHAMBERLIN, "Monopolistic Competition Revisited," *Economica,* vol. 18, November, 1951, pp. 343–62.
104. For a discussion of the economics of tying contracts see M. L. BURSTEIN, "The Economics of Tie-in Sales," *Review of Economics and Statistics,* vol. XLII, February, 1960, pp. 68–73; WARD S. BOWMAN, Jr., "Tying Arrangement and the Leverage Problem," *Yale Law Journal,* vol. 67, November, 1957, pp. 19–36; GEORGE W. HILTON, "Tying Sales and Full-line Forcing," *Weltwirtschaftliches Archiv,* vol. 81,

no. 2, 1958, pp. 265–76; for summary of legal position see Attorney General's Committee, *op. cit.*, pp. 137–40.

105. *Henry v. A. B. Dick Co.*, 224 U.S. 1 (1912).
106. 247 U.S. 32 (1918).
107. 258 U.S. 451 (1922). For a detailed study of the United Shoe Machinery Company and subsequent proceedings in which it was found to violate section 2 of the Sherman Act, see Kaysen, *United States v. United Shoe Machinery Company.*
108. *International Salt Co. v. U.S.*, 332 U.S. 395–96 (1947).
109. *F.T.C. v. Sinclair Refining Co.*, 261 U.S. 463 (1923).
110. *International Business Machines Corporation v. U.S.*, 298 *U.S.* 131 (1936).
111. *Times-Picayune Pub. Co. v. U.S.*, 345 U.S. 594 (1953).
112. For discussion of exclusive dealing and requirements contracts see FRIEDRICH KESSLER and RICHARD H. STERN, "Competition, Contract and Vertical Integration," *Yale Law Review*, vol. 69, November, 1959, pp. 1–129; GORDON SHILLINGLAW "The Effects of Requirements Contracts on Competition," *Journal of Industrial Economics*, vol. 2, April, 1954, pp. 147–63; MILLER, *Unfair Competition*, pp. 203–13. For use of requirements contracts and other practices in tin-plate and tin can industries see JAMES W. MCKIE, *Tin Cans and Tin Plate: A Study of Competition in Two Related Industries*, Cambridge: Harvard University Press, 1959.
113. For a summary of the legal position see Attorney General's Committee, *op. cit.*, pp. 140–49.
114. KAYSEN and TURNER, *op. cit.*, pp. 159–60.
115. WILCOX, *op. cit.*, p. 240; MILLER, *Unfair Competition*, pp. 203–10.
116. *Standard Oil of California and Standard Stations, Inc. v. U.S.*, 337 U.S. 293 (1949).
117. KESSLER and STERN, *op. cit.*, pp. 37–51.
118. *Dictograph Products v. F.T.C.*, 217 F. 2d 821 (1954); *Anchor Serum Co. v. F.T.C.*, 217 F. 2d 867 (1954).
119. See "The Enforcement of Resale Price Maintenance," *Yale Law Journal*, vol. 69, November, 1959, pp. 168–92; "Discriminatory Enforcement of Fair Trade Prices: the Problems and Remedies under State and Federal Laws," *ibid.*, vol. 65, December, 1955, pp. 235–47; WALTER ADAMS, "Resale Price Maintenance: Fact and Fancy," *ibid.*, vol. 64, June, 1955, pp. 967–90; WARD S. BOWMAN, Jr., "The Prerequisites and Effects of Resale Price Maintenance," *University of Chicago Law Review*, vol. 22, Summer, 1955, pp. 825–73; WILCOX, *op. cit.*, pp. 378–89.
120. *Dr. Miles Medical Co. v. John D. Park & Sons Co.*, 220 U.S. 373 (1911).
121. *F.T.C. v. Beech-Nut Packing Co.*, 257 U.S. 441 (1922).
122. *Old Dearborn Distributing Co. v. Seagram Distillers Corp.*, 299 U.S. 183 (1936).
123. 50 Stat. 693, 15 U.S.C.A. § 1 (1937).
124. *Schwegmann Bros. v. Calvert Distillers Corp.* and *Schwegmann Bros. v. Seagram Distillers Corp.*, 341 U.S. 384 (1951).
125. 66 Stat. 632, 15 U.S.C.A. §§ 45, 45n (1952).
126. *General Electric Co. v. Masters Mail Order Co.*, 224 F. 2d 681 (1957); *certiorari* denied 355 U.S. 824 (1957). See also *Sunbeam Corp. v. Wentling*, 185 F. 2d 903 (1950).
127. *Eastman Kodak Co. v. F.T.C.*, 158 F. 2d 592 (1946).
128. *U.S. v. McKesson and Robbins, Inc.*, 351 U.S. 305 (1936).
129. WILCOX, *op. cit.*, p. 389.
130. For discussion of the economics of discrimination see ELI CLEMENS, "Price Discrimination and the Multi-product Firm," *The Review of Economic Studies*, vol. 19, No. 48, 1951, pp. 1–11; FRITZ MACHLUP, "Characterisitcs and Types of Price Discrimination," in *Business Concentration and Public Policy*, pp. 397–435. For reinterpretation of Standard Oil case as not involving predatory practices see JOHN S. MCGEE, "Predatory Price Cutting: The Standard Oil (N.J.) Case," *The Journal of Law and Economics*, vol. 1, October, 1958, pp. 137–69.

131. MILLER, *Unfair Competition*, p. 132.
132. *Mennen Co. v. F.T.C.*, 288 Fed. 774 (1923); *National Biscuit Co. v. F.T.C.*, 229 Fed. 733 (1924); *Loose-Wiles Biscuit Co. v. F.T.C.*, *loc. cit.*
133. *George Van Camp & Sons v. American Can Co. et al.*, 278 U.S. 245 (1929).
134. *Goodyear Tire and Rubber Co. v. F.T.C.*, 101 F. 2d 620 (1939).
135. See two recent and interesting studies: EDWARDS, *The Price Discrimination Law*, and JOSEPH C. PALAMOUNTAIN, *The Politics of Distribution*, Cambridge: Harvard University Press, 1955. For a criticism of the act see M. A. ADELMAN, "The Consistency of the Robinson-Patman Act," *op. cit.*
136. EDWARDS, *Price Discrimination*, pp. 128–130.
137. The story of the application of the Sherman and Clayton Acts to the A & P is instructive. See M. A. ADELMAN, *A & P: A Study in Price-Cost Behavior and Public Policy*, Cambridge: Harvard University Press, 1959. See also JOEL B. DIRLAM and ALFRED E. KAHN, "Antitrust Law and the Big Buyer: Another Look at the A & P Case," *Journal of Political Economy*, vol. 60, April, 1952, pp. 118–32; reply by M. A. ADELMAN, *op. cit.*, vol. 61, October, 1953, pp. 436–41 and rejoinder by J. B. DIRLAM and ALFRED KAHN, *op. cit.*, pp. 441–46.
138. For analysis of the basing-point system and history of public policy with respect to it see FRITZ MACHLUP, *The Basing-Point System: An Economic Analysis of a Controversial Pricing Practice*, Philadelphia: Blakiston Co., 1949; Burns, *op. cit.*, pp. 290–371; GEORGE STOCKING, *Basing Point Pricing and Regional Development: A Case Study of the Iron and Steel Industry*, Chapel Hill: University of North Carolina Press, 1954.
139. 8 F.T.C. Decisions 1 (1924).
140. *Corn Products Refining Co. v. F.T.C.*, 324 U.S. 726 (1945); *F.T.C. v. A.E. Staley Mfg. Co.*, 324 U.S. 746 (1945).
141. *U.S. Malsters Assn. v. F.T.C.*, 152 F. 2d 161 (1945); *Milk and Ice Cream Can Institute v. F.T.C.*, 152 F. 2d 478 (1946); *Fort Howard Paper Co. v. F.T.C.*, 156 F. 2d 899 (1946).
142. *F,T.C. v. Cement Institute*, 333 U.S. 683 (1948).
143. WILCOX, *op. cit.*, pp. 297–98. For cement see SAMUEL M. LOESCHER, *Imperfect Collusion in the Cement Industry*, Cambridge: Harvard University Press, 1959, ch. 8.
144. WHITNEY, *op. cit.*, vol. 1, pp. 281–87; vol. 2, pp. 302–14, 320, 395.
145. See Chapter 8 below and Attorney General's Committee, *op. cit.*, ch. 5.
146. *U.S. v. General Electric Co.*, 272 U.S. 476 (1926).
147. *Ethyl Gasoline Corporation v. U.S.*, 309 U.S. 436 (1940). See also *U.S. v. Univis Lens Co.*, 316 U.S. 241 (1942); *U.S. v. Masonite Corporation*, 316 U.S. 265 (1942); *Hartford Empire Co. v. U.S.*, 323 U.S. 386 (1945) and 324 U.S. 570 (1945); *U.S. v. Line Material Co.*, 332 U.S. 287 (1948); *U.S. v. U.S. Gypsum Co.*, 333 U.S. 364 (1948) and 340 U.S. 76 (1950).
148. GEORGE J. STIGLER, *Five Lectures on Economic Problems*, New York: Macmillan, 1950, pp. 46–65.
149. G. WARREN NUTTER, *The Extent of Enterprise Monopoly in the U.S., 1899–1939*, Chicago: University of Chicago Press, 1951, p. 21.
150. M. A. ADELMAN, "Measurement of Industrial Concentration," *Review of Economics and Statistics*, vol. 33, November, 1951, pp. 269–96.
151. MILLER, "Philosophy and Policies of Woodrow Wilson," pp. 140–41.
152. See Attorney General's Committee, *op. cit.*, ch. 8; KAYSEN and TURNER, *op. cit*, ch. 8.
153. WHITNEY, *op. cit.*, vol. 2, p. 390.
154. *Ibid.*, p. 387.
155. *Ibid.*, p. 390.
156. ADAMS, "Dissolution, Divorcement, Divestiture".

CHAPTER 7

THE ROLE OF COMPETITION AND MONOPOLY IN DISTRIBUTION: THE EXPERIENCE IN THE UNITED STATES[1]

RICHARD H. HOLTON
University of California, Berkeley, California, U.S.A.

I. The Distributive Sector: The Point of View

The definitional problem

The distributive sector of an economy is subject to two quite different definitions. The more common of these we will call the functional definition, the other the industrial view. According to the functional view, distribution includes all those activities generally referred to as "marketing": buying and selling and all the activities auxiliary to buying and selling, namely such functions as transportation, storage, financing of goods as they move from producer to ultimate user, and so forth. For example, when Stewart and Dewhurst in 1939 discussed the magnitude of distribution costs in the United States they included the distribution costs incurred by manufacturers and primary producers as well as those represented by wholesaling and retailing activities.[2] And when one hears complaints of the high cost of distribution, the costs referred to nearly always include not only retailing and wholesaling margins but the expense of maintaining manufacturers' sales forces and promotion programs as well. The U.S. Department of Agriculture, responding to the farmer's perennial complaint about the difference between the amount the consumer pays for food and the amount the farmer receives for that food, in its studies refers to this difference as the "marketing margin" even though the difference includes sizable processing costs in many instances.[3] Not only retailing and wholesaling margins but also the marketing costs incurred by others in the channel are thus included as part of the cost of distribution. The multitude of textbooks in the field of marketing also employ the functional approach. They are invariably concerned not only with retailing and wholesaling but also with the distribution policies of manufacturers and of primary producers as well.[4]

In contrast with the functional definition, the industrial definition of the distributive sector restricts consideration to firms engaged primarily in retailing and wholesaling, these being the two industries most concerned with the process of distribution.[5] If firms in an economy are classified by industry, retailers and wholesalers and possibly transportation firms are clearly in the distributive sector. Concerns in manufacturing, agriculture and construction and the like are just as clearly not operating primarily in the distributive sector. Because so much of the available data are classified only by industry and not by function within all industries, this industrial definition of the sector frequently is forced on the researcher even though he may prefer the functional approach.

For purposes of the present discussion, the functional rather than the industrial definition has been chosen as more suitable. Although we are chiefly interested in the nature of competition among retailers and wholesalers, one must remember that the services which these firms sell can also be provided by producers or, in certain instances, by consumers or industrial customers themselves. So if we wish to discuss the role of competition and monopoly among the sellers of distributive services we should include *all* the sellers.

The producer's role in shaping the distributive sector

A producer of any given commodity realizes that certain distributive services must be performed in order for his product to reach the ultimate user. He may perform those services himself or he may choose to have them performed by wholesale or retail middlemen or even by the ultimate buyers. The effect which producers may have on the nature of the competition among wholesalers and retailers is extensive. More important, the degree and type of competition and of monopoly found at the wholesale and retail levels depend in part not only on whether the manufacturers wish to use retailers and wholesalers but also precisely how they wish to use them.

The manufacturer's objective—the production and marketing of a product for profit—is achieved through selection among many alternative methods of manufacturing and many alternative methods of marketing. He may, for instance, select a manufacturing process which results in lower unit costs and relatively low quality in the final product or he may choose a more costly process which provides a higher quality product and yields greater sales and profits. Similar kinds of decisions are made in the selection of distribution methods: the least cost marketing policy may consist of a combination of price, promotion and channel policies which would bring lower sales and profits than would a more costly marketing policy.

There are a myriad of marketing policies which one finds in use among primary producers and among manufacturers of consumer and industrial goods. For example, the producer of certain industrial supplies may choose to employ his own sales force in selling direct to industrial users. Alternatively a manufacturer's representative could be used, or sales could be made through the wholesalers of industrial goods. The firm could even use its own sales force to handle its own products in addition to complementary products of interest to the same customer group.

Countless distribution processes are also found in the case of consumer goods. Here, for example, the producer may decide on a high price to consumers, high distribution margins and much promotion. Or perhaps the market is price conscious but also responsive to advertising, in which case distribution margins could be trimmed to the bone to permit a low retail price, yet the advertising budget put at a high level to persuade retailers to carry the item despite the low margins. The latter policy is often found in the case of low-priced "impulse" items such as chewing gum. Here the manufacturers' interests are best served if the product is available in a maximum number of stores because the customer prefers not to expend any extra effort to buy the item. No single retailer, therefore, has any significant amount of monopoly power with respect to this item. In contrast manufacturers of other goods may consider sales to be especially responsive to careful personal explanation at the point of sale, in which case the producer may market only via selected retailers, as in the case of automobiles, thereby extending to the retailer some of the monopolistic power enjoyed by the manufacturer.

At the wholesale level, too, the manufacturer's selection of a marketing policy may of course have its influence. The producer may choose to perform the wholesaling functions himself, maintaining strategically located warehouses and using his own sales force from these warehouses or from decentralized sales offices to contact the retail trade. On the other hand, he may enfranchise selected wholesalers who may or may not sell competing products, or he may prefer that a maximum number of wholesalers carry his product.

Thus it is apparent that retailing and wholesaling, as the two industries engaged primarily in distribution, are affected greatly by the particular manner in which producers wish to use them. It is, therefore, difficult to discuss the role of competition and monopoly in retailing and wholesaling without considering just what role retailing and wholesaling play in the marketing policies chosen by manufacturers.

This emphasis on the dependence of retailers and wholesalers on the manufacturers' distributive policies, though crucial to any study of retailing and wholesaling as an industry, is not intended to suggest that the dependence is by any means complete or that retailers and wholesalers are totally subservient to the manufacturer. Indeed, in the last three or four decades retailers and wholesalers have devised various means of increasing their bargaining positions vis-à-vis their suppliers. In some instances integrated retail-wholesale organizations have succeeded in making manufacturers subservient to them. The large corporate chain may buy in such quantities that the manufacturers may fight for their custom. In some cases the chain can thus dictate not only the price and other terms of sale but perhaps even design features as well. A strong, integrated distributor with a sufficiently large sales volume may develop his own brands and contract for their manufacture, thus giving the distributor some measure of independence from other manufacturers' marketing policies.

The best-known case of the integrated distributor who makes its impact felt at the level of the manufacturer is Sears, Roebuck. As early as 1925 Sears began to give to manufacturers its own specifications for products to be sold with the Sears label. The development of the company's own line of tires and refrigerators, which incorporated substantial innovations in design, dramatically illustrated the effect an integrated distributor could have on competition among manufacturers.[6] The practice of close cooperation between integrated distributor and manufacturer is now very common.

This discussion has underscored the point that the nature of competition in the distributive trades depends not only on the strategy of the firms in the distributive trades, but also on the marketing strategies of the producers of the goods moving to ultimate users. In the following discussion, therefore, frequent reference will be made to the producer's marketing policies.

II. The Multi-dimensional Nature of Competition in Distribution

The complexity of competitive patterns in distribution

The pattern of competition in distribution is a complex one. First, there is the sort of competition which seems of most concern to economists, namely competition between roughly similar firms. Competition among independent drug stores, among chain supermarkets, among automobile agencies or among hardware wholesalers is of this sort. Palamountain has called this "horizontal" competition.[7] A second variety of competition, which Palamountain refers to as "intertype," is competition between different types of distributive organizations. The independent retailer competes with the mail order house, the department store and the chain store.[8] This particular level of competition has been important, as we will see below, in shaping legislation affecting pricing and other distributive practices. The result has been a distributive sector which has a rather different complexion than might otherwise have been the case.

It was argued above that a third level of competition, namely competition among manufacturers, must be considered with care in any full-scale discussion of competition in the distributive trades. Typically in economics we think of manufacturers competing among themselves for the favor of their customers, the implication usually being that these are ultimate consumers of the product. For purposes of this paper, such an approach of course will not do. Manufacturers compete not only for ultimate consumers but also for retail and wholesale outlets. Furthermore, the manufacturers compete for certain types of treatment by those wholesale and retail outlets. The food processor, for example, is continually struggling with the retailer and with other food processors to have his product placed in preferred positions in the supermarket.

The emphasis on competitive behavior

The nature of competition in distribution can be discussed in terms of the number of firms and the respective market shares at the retail level, the wholesale level and the manufacturing level. But this paper will emphasize the nature of competition not in terms of numbers of firms and market shares, but rather in terms of the competitive behavior of the firms whose actions determine the structure of the distributive sector of the economy. Therefore, we will concentrate mostly on the tactics which are employed by the firms involved. We will not be as concerned with determining how many firms compete with each other in the market, as with determining why firms behave as they do and how this behavior leads to the different varieties of market structure found in distribution.

The competitive behavior varies greatly from one level to another in the channel of distribution. Competing retailers may choose to attract custom by emphasizing any of the possible components of marketing strategy, i.e., price, the product lines, services, promotion, location, and so on. Wholesalers, facing more knowledgeable customers, are likely to compete much less on the basis of advertising and location than do retailers and to emphasize instead the product line, services and possibly prices. The manufacturer's representative may employ yet a different set of tactics. And so at each of these levels of competition quite different patterns of competitive behavior may be found.

The manufacturer's competitive tactics include not only his price and product policies but also his policies with respect to the channels of distribution which he uses, his control over those channels, the type of promotion he employs and the location of the outlets where the public may find his goods. The location of outlets is generally dependent on the choice of channels. In elementary economics we consider the quantity the manufacturer sells to be a simple function of the price he charges. The realities of the problem are much more complicated than this, of course. The point here is that it is these complications which necessitate strategies in addition to a pricing policy. For example, manufacturers often have only limited control over the price charged the ultimate consumer of the product. The non-price policies which manufacturers institute in establishing their distribution system often are generated by the desire to maintain greater control over price to the ultimate consumer than they would otherwise enjoy. Furthermore the manufacturer often feels that the sales of his product depend not only on the design and the price charged the ultimate buyer but also on the context within which the product is sold. This context consists not only of the physical setting but also the bundle of services (in the broad sense) which are sold with the product. Generally speaking, the manufacturer, who already has control over the design of the product, would like also to have control over the salesman's haircut and smile, to say nothing of the price and credit terms offered the ultimate buyer. In those instances in which the sales are particularly sensitive to the degree of control the manufacturer maintains over the transaction with the final buyer of the product, the manufacturer is motivated to integrate forward if he can do so without incurring excessive additional costs.

The manufacturer's distribution policies may even influence the size of firm. It has been suggested that in some industries, particularly tires and tubes, high-priced men's shoes and farm machinery, the distribution economies which are associated with the large and effective dealer organization may have caused firms in those industries to become larger than production economies alone would justify.[9]

Limitations on the manufacturer's power

The manufacturer's common desire to tell the retailer how to handle the product and how to price it is dampened considerably, of course, if he must compete with other manufacturers for that retailer's favor, as is often the case. The large-scale retailing organizations such as chain food stores and department stores developed in part because of the advantages of being big enough to bargain effectively with the manufacturers and even to do some of their own manufacturing. The rise of the integrated chains has undoubtedly put a check on the control the manufacturers can exert over the independent retailers who must compete with the chains.[10]

To summarize to this point, it seems clear that to define distribution as consisting only of retailing and wholesaling firms is to preclude from the discussion of competition in this sector a number of critical elements. The nature of competition and monopoly in distribution is dependent not only on the structure of retailing and of wholesaling viewed as individual industries, but on the behavior of these firms as well. But the behavior of these firms is so conditioned by manufacturers' marketing policies that distribution must be viewed in the functional, rather than the industrial, sense. This requires that the nature of competition among the manufacturers be considered at certain points, as well as the nature of the competition among retailers and wholesalers. Furthermore, it will not suffice to distinguish merely between price competition and non-price competition. Non-price tactics designed to attain increased (or at least satisfactory) profits are so numerous and so varied and have so many consequences for the distributive sector that they must be considered individually.

The many different competitive tactics have different cost and revenue configurations. The same combination of tactics may be associated with a variety of cost and revenue schedules depending on the type of good to which the tactics are applied. For example, marked economies of scale are apparent in the distribution of some goods but not in the case of others. These differences in cost and revenue patterns help explain why the competitive tactics vary so widely among the sub-sectors of the distributive trades.

III. Competition and Monopoly at the Retail Level

Like the manufacturer, the retailer faces the problem of devising a competitive strategy, one which will assure him of at least a satisfactory rate of profit. This strategy is a combination of several policies: policies with respect to price, product (defined to include not only the assortment of physical products but also the type and quantity of services offered), promotion and location. The particular combination of these policies chosen by the firm establishes the character or, to use the currently popular term, the "image" of the store.

These policies are, of course, interdependent to some extent. The store located in a low-rent section of the city is likely to offer primarily goods at modest prices. And the retailer in the midst of the fashionable stores is generally found to offer not only high quality goods but a full line of services such as credit and delivery as well. One finds particular bundles of these policies reappearing often whereas other combinations of policies, e.g., quality merchandise sold for cash only, are rare.

The "Strategy Scattergram"

It may be helpful to conceptualize the retailer's problem of selecting the appropriate combination of marketing policies by using what we will call the "strategy scattergram." Assume for the moment that the retailer has in his strategy only two marketing policies which are variable. One is the location of the firm and the other is the price line of goods handled. Assume that the quality of the location can be measured in some rough way, e.g., by the average income of the shoppers found there, and that the price lines of goods can also be scaled readily from the low-priced goods up to the high-priced goods. A simple scattergram could be constructed with the quality of the location on the ordinate and the index of the price of goods sold on the abscissa, each point on this scattergram representing the particular combination of price and location policy of competing stores in a particular city. The observations would probably show a positive correlation between these two particular policies. A three-dimensional scattergram could be constructed with, say, promotion policy (measured perhaps by advertising expenditures as a percentage of sales) on the third axis. Again the observations might be clustered, with low-priced stores in low quality locations spending less on advertising than high-priced stores in good quality locations. In this case the scattergram would show the points clustered about a line in three-dimensional space. Or there may be enough departures from this type of promotion policy to give a plane. Of course there may be no correlation among any of these three policies, but casual observation seems to indicate that there is probably some clustering.

Let us suppose that there is a considerable degree of clustering of observations around certain combinations of marketing policies. The new retailer must decide whether he will attempt to establish himself by offering the same policies as the existing firms, serving their market somehow in a "better" way, or whether he will offer some new combination of policies on the presumption that there is in fact a demand for such a combination but that no one has attempted to cater to this demand. In this latter case the retailer would be represented on our scattergram by a point well away from the existing cluster of points. Thus the men's clothing store offering the usual number of items each in a common number of brands within the most common price range in a location near similar men's clothing stores yields a point in or very near the existing cluster of points in the scattergram. If, however, the firm should choose to sell only for cash and to compete by offering its goods at slightly lower prices without sacrificing quality, it generates a point on the scattergram well away, in one or two dimensions, from the existing cluster. It thus has chosen to gamble that the particular combination of policies it has employed is desired by a sufficiently large number of consumers to yield a larger net profit than would have been enjoyed if it had merely copied the policies of the existing men's clothing stores in the area.

Conceived in this manner, the competitive strategy of the retailer is either to offer a combination of policies similar to that of the competition or to differentiate itself by some means in order to establish some small degree of monopoly power.[11] It is common to find in discussions of the economics of retailing considerable emphasis on the degree of spatial monopoly achieved by the firm. The point here is that the firm can be differentiated from its competitors in any of several dimensions, only one of which is location. Just as a geographical location far from similar firms gives that retailer an element of monopoly power over those consumers who find that location especially attractive or convenient, so a comparatively unique product assortment will also give the retailer a degree of monopoly power over those consumers who find that product assortment especially desirable. There would seem to be little reason for emphasizing location as a means of isolating oneself from competition more than other means of achieving the same end.

The manufacturer and the retailer's strategy scattergram

Let us return to the role of the manufacturer of the product in the retailer's formulation of this strategy. The manufacturer is presumably interested in shifting his demand curve to the right out to the point where the marginal cost of this manipulation of demand is equated to the marginal revenue. He may have devised a product which is sufficiently unique to give him a strong competitive position or his advertising may have built up strong brand loyalty among a significant number of consumers. Regardless of how the manufacturer's competitive advantage was achieved, the retailer is interested in appropriating some of this to improve his own profit position, thus riding on the coat tails of the manufacturer. The retailer loves nothing more than to stock a much wanted brand which his competitors do not stock. Thus for those items which the manufacturers choose to market through selected outlets only, the retailers do achieve some degree of monopoly simply because their competitors are denied access to the particular brand in question. If the manufacturer requires these selected outlets to agree not to handle competing brands, he can, by careful selection of the outlets, effectively seal off his competitors from many desirable retailers, thus enhancing the manufacturer's monopoly power.[12]

The extension of the manufacturer's monopoly power to the retail level by means of selective distribution is common but by no means universal. The manufacturers of certain types of goods want them to be available in a maximum number of retail locations. These items, the archetypes of which are chewing gum, candy and cigarettes, are commonly referred to as "convenience goods". They are distinguished by the fact that people do not wish to visit many retailers to compare price and quality among the offerings because the probable gains from such comparisons are small relative to the cost of searching.[13] With shopping goods, i.e., goods for which the probable gains from shopping outweigh the cost of shopping, the manufacturer is more likely to use selective distribution. Under this policy he would choose his retailers carefully, thus giving to those he selects a local monopoly of the brand.

This policy of selective distribution recommends itself when certain conditions are met. If the manufacturer wants his retailers to maintain large inventories of his product in order to provide consumers with an adequate selection, the manufacturer may have to offer each of his retailers a local monopoly on the brand in order to persuade them to invest the requisite funds in inventory.[14] When the manufacturer wishes to control the retail price he may make that control a condition of the franchise, thus avoiding many of the problems of fair trading the product. Alternatively, the manufacturer may sell to the retailer on consignment, retaining title (and hence the right to set the retail price) until the consumer makes the purchase. If the item requires a considerable amount of selling effort on the part of the retailer himself, as in the case of a new product requiring demonstration and explanation to consumers, an exclusive franchise for the item encourages the retailer to contribute that extra effort. And if the physical nature of the product or the nature of the market for the product is such that distribution costs would be relatively high if all willing retailers are permitted to stock the good, as may be true in the case of automobiles and furniture, then selective distribution may be called for.[15]

Selective distribution is appropriate, too, when the demand for the product is inelastic with respect to what we might call accessibility. For some kinds of goods, especially convenience goods, the quantity sold at retail at any given price is very sensitive to the proportion of total retail outlets in which the good is available. In the case of shopping goods, however, buyers are likely to survey the offerings of alternative retailers more carefully before buying, and consequently the sales of this type of good are more inelastic with respect to accessibility.

In general, it can be said that if the demand for the good is inelastic with respect to accessibility, and especially if the demand for the product is sensitive to the amount of personal selling the store promotion directed toward it, selective distribution is more likely to be employed.

Location and the retailer's strategy scattergram

If the manufacturer's brand has no monopoly position of any consequence in the market, however, or if the manufacturer chooses to encourage all possible retailers to stock the brand, then very little of the manufacturer's competitive advantage is appropriated by the retailer. The retailer must devise his own means for insulating himself from his competition.

One means by which the retailer might accomplish this, of course, is by locating at a point distant from stores of a similar sort but closer to some segment of the market, thus removing himself in at least one dimension from any cluster of points in the strategy scattergram. But locational strategy differs markedly among retailers. Frequently such firms find it convenient to cluster. Nearly every city of any size in the United States has its "automobile row," an area where new and used car dealers are side by side for a distance of several blocks on a given street. Furniture stores are frequently concentrated in one shopping area, as are department stores.

When do merchants tend to locate close to their competitors and when do they tend to disperse? The major contributions to the economics of spatial competition have employed for the sake of simplicity assumptions about the geographical distribution of demand, the elasticity of demand, and the operating costs of firms which do not permit direct answers to this question. Without delving into the matter in great detail, an answer can at least be suggested.[16]

Let us first recall the distinction between convenience goods and shopping goods. Convenience goods are those for which the consumer is not likely to engage in a significant amount of shopping because the probable gains are likely to be small relative to the cost of the search. Conversely shopping goods are those for which the probable gains are large relative to the cost of searching. The consumer in the case of shopping goods wishes to compare the offerings of competing retailers and this can best be done if these competing retailers are clustered. But for convenience goods the consumer goes to the nearest store only. Furthermore, the demand for that special class of convenience goods referred to as "impulse" goods is by definition positively associated with the proximity of the retail stores stocking such goods to consumers. The greater this proximity the less effort must be expended by the consumer; and the more frequent his exposure to the good, the greater his demand for it.

Assume a given geographical area over which consumers, all with identical demand functions, are evenly diffused. Assume that the demand for all consumer goods is a function of the price at the retail store plus the cost in time, effort and money incurred by consumers in making the search for the good sought. Let us imagine that the stores in the area selling a particular shopping good are scattered evenly over the market. Total demand for the good in question would stand at a certain magnitude given this particular distribution of stores. Now consider the total demand for the same good if these same stores are concentrated at a central point in the area and are adhering to the same pricing policy as under the assumption that the stores were dispersed. Remembering that the consumer wishes to visit several stores offering the shopping good and that demand is a function of retail price plus searching costs, it is clear that the total demand for the item is positively associated with the geographical concentration of the stores.

But the convenience good presents quite a different case. The cost to the consumer is the retail price plus the cost of getting to the nearest store. Searching costs are minimal because no price or quality comparisons are necessary. Suppose that the stores selling a particular convenience good are scattered evenly over the area in question and that the demand for such goods is independent of the location of other goods. Total demand for the good is at a certain magnitude under these conditions. Now assume that these same stores are clustered at the center of the market and that each offers the item at the same price as when the stores were scattered. The average cost to consumers is greater if the stores are concentrated than if they are scattered since the relevant "cost" here is the retail price plus the cost incurred by the consumer in getting to the nearest store. Therefore total market demand for a convenience good at a given retail price is maximized if the stores offering the good are decentralized; but the total market demand for a shopping good is maximized if stores are clustered.

This view of the problem of retail store location may help explain why one frequently finds an "automobile row" in a city but never a "drug store row." Of course convenience goods stores to some extent will cluster around shopping goods stores because of the customer traffic generated by the latter. Thus convenience goods stores are not distributed geographically in exactly the same pattern as the purchasing power of the residents because convenience goods stores are pulled a bit toward the routes people frequent.

Zoning regulations will also enforce a certain amount of clustering of retail stores. In many of the newer suburbs of the major cities of the U. S., these regulations have caused virtually all new stores to be located in shopping centers. The parking problem so often encountered at the smaller, older neighborhood clusters of small convenience goods stores encourages buyers to drive to the larger, modern shopping center with its ample parking facilities. Once parked, the customer wants to accomplish as much of the planned buying as possible. The cost (in terms of effort, largely) of getting to the shopping center and parking is a fixed cost of the expedition; the consumer then attempts to spread this fixed cost over as much purchasing as is feasible. The growing traffic and parking problems have increased this so-called fixed cost of the shopping expedition, and so the convenience goods stores are motivated more than before to locate in the shopping center near the other stores.

Of course, the shopping good retailer may locate at a point quite distant from other similar stores. This is likely to be successful only if he offers a selection of brands, styles and price lines great enough to make the shopper feel that adequate price and quality comparisons among various manufacturers' offering can be made without visiting other retailers[17]. In a few cases the isolated retailer of a shopping good can succeed with a limited selection if he establishes a reputation with consumers for doing such a careful job of selecting stock that in effect he has performed the price and quality comparison job for them. Thus the small department store is probably wise to locate close to its competition. But the greater the size of its selection, the greater the possibility that it can stand alone.

There is some evidence that major department stores in the United States think in these terms. Some have the policy of establishing a branch in a shopping center only if another major department store also establishes a branch there. Others will go into a new shopping center only if they will be the only major department store in the center. This would indicate some doubt among these retailers as to the critical size of selection beyond which consumers are willing to give up comparison among retailers before making their purchases.

This consideration of the problem of retail location makes it clear that a spatial monopoly is attractive to a retailer only under certain conditions. For the small retailer of shopping goods located far from his competition, the supposed spatial monopoly he enjoys may be quite specious.

The chain store device in retailing strategy

The discussion thus far has concerned the strategy of the retailer and certain aspects of the manufacturer's role in shaping that strategy. We have assumed implicitly that the retailer is a single-unit firm and have ignored the chain (or "multiple") store organization. Why is the chain device an appropriate part of the strategy for some types of retailers but not for others? The chains have been seen by some as constituting a most dangerous threat to the small businessman on the assumption that the chains are certain to continue expanding their share of the market to the point where they are unquestionably monopolists. Here we will not examine the growth of the chains, for this has been done quite adequately elsewhere.[18] But it may be worthwhile to examine the extent to which chain stores are likely to lead to decline of competition in retailing.

The discussion of this question will be based primarily on the experience in the United States. We will first examine data for the country as a whole, implying that the entire United States is a single retail market. Ideally, of course, one would look at each local retail market and derive some index of concentration for that market. But the data do not permit this. Furthermore, we are concerned here only with the relative strength of the chain stores in different kinds of retailing.

In Table I, below, the percentage of sales accounted for by single-unit firms is shown for each of the 35 kinds of business for which these data are available for 1954. The circumstances which are conducive to chain store operations can be surmised in part from the position of the various kinds of business in this array. The five kinds of business

TABLE I. PERCENTAGE OF SALES ACCOUNTED FOR BY SINGLE-UNIT FIRMS, BY KIND OF BUSINESS, UNITED STATES, 1954

Kind of business	%	Kind of business	%
Drinking places	97	Plumbing, paint, electrical stores	79
Passenger car dealers, (franchised)	95	Furniture, home furnishings stores	78
Fruit stores, vegetable markets	93	Lumber, building materials dealers	76
Gift, novelty, souvenir stores	92	Jewelry stores	76
Florists	92	Candy, nut, confectionery stores	75
Passenger car dealers (nonfranchised)	91	Bakery products stores	75
Farm equipment dealers	91	Household appliance, radio, TV stores	75
Sporting goods, bicycle stores	89	Music stores	75
Gasoline service stations	87	Drug stores, proprietary stores	73
Meat markets, fish (seafood markets)	85	Feed, farm garden supply stores	71
Camera, photographic supply stores	84	Liquor stores	66
Eating places (including refreshment stands)	83	General merchandise stores, n.e.c.	64
		Tire, battery, accessory dealers	58
Fuel ice dealers	82	Women's clothing specialty stores	57
Book, stationery stores	82	Grocery stores	52
Hardware stores	81	Shoe stores	44
Cigar stores, stands	81	Department stores	24
News dealers, newsstands	80	Variety stores	17

Source: U.S. Department of Commerce, Bureau of the Census, *Census of Business, 1954*, Vol. I, Table 4A.

with the most sales accounted for by single-unit firms are 1) drinking places; 2) franchised passenger car dealers; 3) fruit stores and vegetable markets; 4) gift, novelty and souvenir stores; and 5) florists. For these kinds of business the percentages range from 92 to 97 per cent. At the other extreme are 1) variety stores; 2) department stores; 3) shoe stores; 4) grocery stores; 5) women's clothing specialty stores. For these latter five kinds of business the percentages range from 57 per cent down to 17 per cent.

What are the distinguishing features which may account for the greater role of the chains in the latter group? The following suggestions are offered only in the most tentative way since none of the hypotheses has been carefully investigated. Furthermore, generalizations in this field may have to be qualified so much in application to specific kinds of business that their usefulness is limited, but they may provide some insight nonetheless.

Perhaps it is accurate to say that, in general, chain store organizations are likely to have a large share of the market in any given kind of business if 1) the volume of goods is so large and the assortment demanded at the retail outlet so standardized that much can be gained from reducing to a routine the physical movement of goods through the wholesale and retail levels; 2) the personal service required at the retail level is limited; 3) pricing can be easily centralized; and 4) entry is sufficiently difficult to prevent the constant entry of large numbers of entrepreneurs who lose their investment and then exit to be replaced by similar firms, thus creating a situation in which a substantial percentage of firms in the industry at any one time is operating at a loss.

An examination of the 10 kinds of business singled out above will provide at least some justification for the above statements. If drinking places were to be integrated horizontally and also vertically into wholesaling, the economies of purchasing might be fairly significant as a percentage of purchases; but the cost of goods sold is so small relative to total sales that the savings might not be significant as a percentage of total sales. Another peculiarity of this type of business may be more critical. Entry is easy and the business is attractive because of the obvious non-monetary benefits to the garrulous. It is conceivable that an unusually high proportion of the proprietors of drinking places work for less than the minimum wage paid to hired help. Not only might a chain acquire little competitive advantage from the centralized purchasing and warehousing of its goods but it might also operate at a serious disadvantage in labor costs. In any type of retailing into which entry is particularly easy and personal service plays a major role chains may be at a disadvantage because retailers of a given caliber are happy to work for themselves for less income than the chains would have to pay them. This amounts, then, to a labor cost advantage to independent retailers. Thus the chain must be able to achieve economies in purchasing and in the handling of goods sufficient to overcome the higher labor costs it must pay.

Several possible explanations for the strength of single-unit firms among passenger car agencies can be offered. Given the number of models available in any single brand and the large number of optional items a customer can have on each model, it is difficult to keep retail stocks neatly tailored to demand. A high proportion of automobiles are, therefore, "made to order" in the factory, shipped to the dealer and delivered quickly to the consumer. Selection of stock at the retail level cannot be completely reduced to a routine under these circumstances. Also the possibilities for economies in wholesaling are obviously limited under such circumstances. Perhaps, too, the difficulties with decentralized pricing may operate to discourage the development of more chain automobile agencies. The majority of new cars are sold to buyers who wish to trade in an older car and pay only the difference between the trade-in allowance on the old car and the list price on the new. It is probably a reasonably accurate generalization that typically in any marketing situation the individual who owns the merchandise in question hesitates to let some other party determine the price at which that merchandise is to be sold. Therefore the owner of the merchandise must devise means of keeping in check his employees who are pricing his goods. Certain rules about allowable percentage markups and the like can reduce this to a routine in most types of retailing. However in the automobile business the condition of the automobile being traded in can vary considerably and so it is especially difficult to establish very clear-cut pricing rules. The owner of the merchandise, then, must either be present to do the pricing or else he must be willing to entrust this aspect of the business to a lieutenant. The latter is done in many instances and there are in existence some successful chain automobile agencies. We are only conjecturing that this aspect of automobile retailing may hamper, though not prohibit, the development of chains. The unusually large investment per outlet may also be a serious obstacle.

We might conjecture, too, about the limited role of chains in fruit and vegetable markets. But first it must be emphasized that the low percentage of sales accounted for by the multi-establishment firms in this kind of business does not mean that few chains sell fruits and vegetables. The chains which do sell fruits and vegetables typically are primarily grocery stores and so are classified in that kind of business rather than as fruit stores and vegetable markets. It is probably accurate to argue that a firm organized as a chain to handle fruit and vegetables can so easily become a full-line grocery chain that it is likely to do so. Furthermore, there seems to be some evidence that the savings resulting from handling dry groceries through centralized warehousing facilities are often greater than the savings stemming from centralized procurement of fruit and vegetables.

In the case of gift, novelty and souvenir stores there is clearly a relatively low turnover of stock and so the economies from buying in quantity are probably quite limited. Or, as in the case of the fruit and vegetable markets, the savings from quantity buying of related lines are so great relative to the savings on quantity purchases of gifts, novelties and souvenirs that a chain in the latter field is tempted to take on additional lines, thus removing itself from this particular kind of business classification and becoming a variety store or department store. And as in the case of drinking places, in many establishments in this type of retailing the return to labor may be less than the wage rate a chain would have to pay. A large number of the gift and souvenir shops are located at resorts and in vacation areas where pleasant living attracts, into this kind of business, people who have income from other sources and simply are willing to live for less money than they might demand under other circumstances.

Chain operations are rare among florists apparently for a variety of interesting reasons. As in the case of automobile dealers, the wholesaling step for the main product is by-passed and so there are no gains from reducing wholesaling to a routine. Furthermore, the rate of stockturn in the florist business is so low that the cost of goods to the retailer is a smaller portion of his total outlays than is true of other kinds of retailing. Also the personal service input is especially great in this kind of business and the decision-making cannot readily be centralized.

At the other end of the array in Table I, the five kinds of business in which the chain stores are strongest show quite a range of percentages, from 17 per cent of variety store sales accounted for by single-unit firms up to 57 per cent in the case of women's clothing specialty stores. It is rather surprising that despite the widespread impression that the chain stores are so very strong in retailing in the United States, in only 3 of the 35 kinds of business for which the data are available do the chains account for more than half of the sales. And this definition of "chain" exaggerates their importance since even a two-unit firm is considered a chain.

In the case of the variety, department, shoe and grocery stores, the possible savings from quantity buying are probably of greater consequence than at the other end of the spectrum. Furthermore, the nature of the personal services provided at the retail level in these kinds of business is not such as to preclude a very considerable centralization of decision-making, permitting the personnel at the retail level to operate according to fairly rigid rules.

It is curious that single-unit firms should be no stronger than they are among the women's clothing specialty stores. One might expect that the problem of tailoring the stock very neatly to local tastes in fashion would give the single-unit firm a decided advantage over the chain, which can operate most economically if the stock offered at each retail outlet is highly standardized. And centralized pricing would seem more difficult. It may be that the multi-unit firms concentrate their efforts on the medium- and low-priced types of merchandise, where perhaps style is at least somewhat less volatile than among the higher-priced specialty lines.

Despite the common observation that quantity buying gives the chains a price advantage which they pass on to consumers, there is some evidence that the major economies arise more because of the efficiency with which the goods are handled than because of the lower purchase prices.[19] In other words, the strength of the chains may lie not in their buying power as much as in their ability to reduce the distributive process to a routine which minimizes labor costs and makes fuller utilization of capital equipment and presumably of managerial talent. It may, therefore, be accurate to conclude that chain operations are clearly not a threat to all kinds of business in retailing alike. Rather they pose a threat to those kinds of retailing in which decision-making at the retail level can easily be reduced to a routine and where substantial savings can be generated by combining retail and wholesale operations. It is quite likely, therefore, that many types of retailing will not become dominated by the chains, at least in the foreseeable future.

IV. Competition and Monopoly at the Wholesale Level

In the United States, wholesalers are widely regarded as losing out in their battle with the integrated marketing firms. The public seems to have been especially conscious over the last 20 years of the attempt to "eliminate the middleman" and the presumption has been that the wholesalers' position has been definitely weakened by the assault of the chains.

Insofar as the U.S. Census of Business permits a comparison of wholesale sales by kinds of business with retail sales by kinds of business, merchant wholesalers, generally speaking, seem to be handling a somewhat smaller proportion of the goods moving into retail stores than formerly. Nevertheless the merchant wholesaler is still the most important type of middleman in terms of the proportion of goods handled. For example, in the case of food wholesalers, sales declined over the 1929–1939 period by 40 per cent while the sales of retail food stores declined only 7.4 per cent.[20] Between 1939 and 1954, however, sales of food wholesalers have increased nearly as much as have retail food sales, leaving the ratio of wholesale sales to retail sales in the food line slightly lower than in 1929. But even though food wholesalers have not regained their 1929 position, their sales nonetheless equal more than 50 per cent of retail sales. In part, of course, the apparent decline in the food wholesalers' position relative to retail food store sales can be explained by the increase in the proportion of nonfood sales in retail food stores.

In dry goods and in general merchandise lines the wholesalers have fared about as they have in foods. The merchant wholesalers of drugs and toiletries and of home furnishings and household appliances appear, on the other hand, to have increased their sales more than the corresponding kinds of business at the retail level. One suspects, however, that this cannot be interpreted as an increase in the merchant wholesalers' share of the volume moving through retail outlets. There is no doubt that retail drug and toiletry sales have shifted away from the drug store and toward the food store, and department stores may have been encroaching increasingly on the home furnishings and appliances retailers. So the increase in the ratio of wholesale to retail sales in these two cases may reflect only that the retailers specializing in drugs and toiletries and those specializing in home furnishings and appliances are losing trade to other types of retailers. The wholesalers may or may not be handling an increased proportion of the total retail volume in these items, total retail volume consisting of the sales through the specialized retailers plus those through other retailers. The available data do not provide answers to thesc questions.

The competitive strategy of the wholesaler

As in the case of retailing, it may be enlightening to examine the nature of competition and of monopoly power in wholesaling by looking first at the strategy of the wholesaler and of those other firms, especially manufacturers and retailers, who themselves play a part in the formation of that strategy. This exercise should lead to some insights into the circumstances under which monopoly power is likely to be especially great or small at the wholesale level.

The typical independent merchant wholesaler supposedly wishes always to improve his profit position. He may attempt to do this by means of price competition; by emphasizing the services offered to retail or industrial accounts; by offering a particularly wide or otherwise unique product line; or by accepting an exclusive franchise from a manufacturer who distributes only through a limited number of wholesalers. As in the discussion of retail strategy above, we might conceive of a "strategy scattergram" in *n*-dimensional space. Wholesalers are likely to be clustered around certain combinations of strategies. For example, cash-and-carry merchant wholesalers in food wholesaling in many cases offer the same general "bundle" of services. Each firm must decide whether it will compete by attempting to perform the same services in the same way as (but better than) its competition or whether it will adopt a strategy quite unlike that of the other firms in the trade, hoping that there is a demand for the unique bundle of policies it proposes to employ. To the extent that these components of the total strategy make the firm unique, it is, of course, more independent of its competition and less likely to lose trade to others.

But as in the case of retailing, the competitive strategy of the manufacturer frequently is a major factor in determining the structure of competition at the wholesale level. Manufacturers of convenience goods may consider it advisable to have as many wholesalers as possible handling their product so that retailers will be certain to have easy access to the item. On the other hand the manufacturer may feel that the nature of his product calls for a very considerable amount of work with the retailer himself in order that the retailer might know all he should about the product. To coax the wholesaler to spend this extra effort on the sale of the product, the manufacturer may give the wholesaler an exclusive distributorship for a given area. Thus the manufacturer can extend to the wholesaler a bit of whatever competitive advantage may have accrued to the product over time.

Vertical integration in wholesaling

This interest of the manufacturer in the wholesaling of his product may extend to the point of full integration into wholesaling. Unfortunately there are few reliable data on the extent to which manufacturers have in fact integrated into the wholesaling functions. Nevertheless common observation leads to certain general propositions about this type of integration, propositions which shed some light on the circumstances which cause vertical integration of manufacturing into wholesaling to be more common for some types of goods than for others.

The competitive strategy of the retailer also has its effect on the nature of the competition at the wholesale level. In those kinds of retailing where horizontal integration is common one generally finds at least some vertical integration backward into wholesaling as well. Some of the generalizations which apply to integration of manufacturers into wholesaling can also apply to integration of retailing into wholesaling.

These observations must be stated in *ceteris paribus* terms. One often finds that although one of the conditions generally thought conducive to vertical integration into wholesaling seems to hold in a particular case, vertical integration in fact is not found. This may only indicate that some other set of conditions not conducive to vertical integration is overruling.[21]

The first proposition is one of the most important. The greater the geographical density of a manufacturer's product sales, the greater the probability that he will integrate forward into wholesaling. A certain minimum sales volume is required to support an economical warehousing operation because of the increasing returns to scale in wholesaling at very low levels of output. If a manufacturer's sales of a product (or group of products) in a given region is too small to support a warehousing operation, he will distribute through a firm which handles other lines as well.[22] But if the manufacturer's volume in a region is relatively large, it may be profitable to perform his own wholesaling services.

Second, the greater the average order placed by the retailer for an item (or group of items produced by the same manufacturer), the greater the probability that the wholesaling will be handled by the manufacturer. Given a certain population of retailers who are to be solicited, total distribution costs as a percentage of sales will fall as the average order per call rises. If the average order per call is very low for an item, it is likely to be sold to retailers by salesmen who handle other products as well.

Third, the greater the proportion of the retail firm's sales accounted for by the products of a single manufacturer, the greater the probability that wholesaling will be handled by the manufacturer. This similarity of assortment between manufacturer and retailer encourages integration throughout the channel of distribution and in some cases leads to manufacturer-owned retail outlets.

Fourth, if the services performed by the wholesaler are especially critical in the promotion of sales, then vertical integration is more likely to be found. For example, if it is especially desirable that the inventory commitment at the wholesale level be quite large, or if the sales force calling on retailers or industrial buyers must be especially well trained, or if servicing by wholesalers is particularly important in attracting trade, then integration into wholesaling is more probable than if these conditions do not hold.

Fifth, the greater the perishability of the item, the greater the probability that wholesaling functions will be performed by the producer or by the retailer rather than by an independent wholesaler. It is important here first to distinguish between physical perishability of the sort associated with, say, fresh produce, and perishability of market value arising from style obsolescence or from seasonal changes in demand. It has been estimated, for example, that only about 15 per cent of the shoes sold through retail outlets move through wholesalers.[23] The remainder go directly from manufacturer to retailer. This is explained in part by the style perishability of the product. In order to keep end-of-season stocks to a minimum and to avoid heavy inventory losses on models which prove not to catch the public fancy, it is important that there be especially close contact between manufacturer and retailer. This same feature marks the distribution of the more stylish women's apparel. In the case of men's shoes, the wholesaler plays an especially small role because the similarity of the assortment at the factory and at the retail level encourages integration of manufacturing and retailing. This integration simplifies the problem the manufacturer faces in keeping up to date on the status of retailers' stocks. If the manufacturer owns the retail stores or has exclusive franchises with them, he can insist on periodic inventory reports. These permit efficient production runs, while inventory losses through markdowns are also kept well in hand.

Sixth, the role of the appropriate scale of operation at the various levels in the channel must be recognized. It is difficult to talk of an optimum size of firm in any line of retailing or wholesaling, if one is to judge from the empirical data, because the average unit cost function seems never to turn up. Nevertheless, it does seem clear that if a retail or wholesale establishment is too small, its unit costs are likely to be much too high for long-run survival.[24] We will use the term "optimum" here to mean only some range of output beyond which unit costs fall at a very slow rate. A pair of generalizations about the role of the optimum size, defined in this casual way, seems justified. The greater the optimum size of firm at one level in the distribution channel relative to the optimum size of firm at the next level below, the greater the probability that one will find firms integrating forward. Conversely, if the optimum size of firm at the lower level in the channel is large relative to the optimum size of firm at the level above it, the greater becomes the probability that there will be integration backward. In other words large firms tend to absorb smaller ones vertically related to them in the distribution channel. However, it is entirely possible that although integration may seem warranted because of the relative scale of the enterprises concerned, integration may not be found because of disparity of product assortment or for other reasons.

Finally, as in the case of horizontal integration in retailing, the greater the possibility of reducing decision-making to a routine, the greater the probability that vertical integration will be found either between manufacturing and wholesaling or between retailing and wholesaling.

To summarize, integration of manufacturers or retailers into wholesaling apparently depends, we are suggesting, on the geographical density of the manufacturer's sales, the average order size, the production assortment as compared with the assortment required to support a retail operation, the importance of manufacturer control of the functions performed at other levels in the channel, the perishability of the items, the scale of the optimum size of establishment at the various levels in the channel, and the possibilities for reducing the wholesaling activities to a routine. Perhaps it is for these various reasons that some types of wholesaling are much more susceptible to invasion from either the manufacturer or the retail level than are others.

HORIZONTAL INTEGRATION IN WHOLESALING

We have reviewed the forces at work to tie the wholesaling functions to the manufacturer or to the retailer. We can now turn to the question of horizontal integration in wholesaling to ascertain the extent to which there may be a tendency for wholesale chains with substantial market power to build up at this particular level in the channel of distribution.

The Census data for the United States in 1954 are of some help in answering this question. In Table II the 10 kinds of wholesaling in which multi-unit operations account for the least sales are shown. The number of establishments classified in the given kind of business, the sales per establishment, the operating expense as a percentage of sales and the average inventory are also given. Two things are clear: (1) the kinds of business in which single-unit firms are strong show lower sales per establishment and higher operating expense ratios, generally speaking, than do those kinds of business in which horizontal integration is greatest; and (2) the average inventory is substantially greater for the kinds of business in which horizontal integration is common.

Why should some kinds of wholesaling lend themselves so much more readily to horizontal integration than do others? Although the data of Table II by no means make the case clearcut, we can suggest a few hypotheses which might hold. These are only of the most tentative sort, since more serious answers should be based on careful investigations of the specific kinds of business.

First, there may be a fairly high service input into the kinds of business in which single-unit firms are strongest. Perhaps, competition among wholesalers in such areas is based not so much on the prices of the goods but on the quality of the service. Therefore integration may not be as rewarding as in other kinds of business in which price competition is more important.

Secondly, it is interesting that in at least 6 of the 10 kinds of business in which single-unit firms are strongest, product competition and continual changes in the product line are important in the competitive strategy of the wholesaler. It may be that selection of a profitable product line is an art which is difficult to centralize or to reduce to a routine. This particular managerial skill may be the fixed factor of production which limits the size of firm to one or at least a very few establishments. By contrast, the 10 kinds of business in which chains are strongest include none in which product selection appears to be

TABLE II. TEN KINDS OF WHOLESALING WITH THE LARGEST AND TEN WITH THE SMALLEST PERCENTAGE OF SALES ACCOUNTED FOR BY SINGLE-UNIT FIRMS, UNITED STATES, 1954

Kind of wholesaling	*Number of establishments*	*Total sales $1,000*	*Sales per establishment*	*Inventories per establishment*	*Operating expenses (per cent of sales)*	*Percentage of sales accounted for by single-unit firms*
Largest % of sales by single units						
Undertakers' supply houses	137	14,443	$105,423	$10,913	25.3	100.0
Religious supply houses	134	31,582	235,687	29,813	31.5	100.0
Reconditioned drums, barrels distributors	372	65,360	175,699	7,863	36.6	100.0
Shoe, footwear wholesalers	583	353,979	607,168	75,443	13.6	98.6
Millinery, millinery supplies wholesalers	353	81,953	232,161	27,025	20.8	98.1
Greeting card distributors	248	50,094	201,992	24,427	28.2	98.0
Gift, art goods wholesalers	735	140,213	190,766	20,400	22.8	97.2
Precious stones distributors	498	202,608	406,843	84,863	10.3	97.2
Leather goods wholesalers	454	135,579	298,632	33,302	14.6	97.1
Toy, games, fireworks wholesalers	805	277,626	344,877	32,709	16.6	96.8
Smallest % of sales by single units						
Voluntary group grocery wholesalers	574	2,463,756	4,292,257	315,909	7.4	53.0
General merchandise distributors	594	814,291	1,370,860	107,919	11.2	52.9
Dental supply houses	502	124,125	247,261	46,062	26.0	50.8
General line drug wholesalers	392	1,273,114	3,247,740	448,247	13.6	47.6
Iron, steel scrap dealers (without processing preparation equipment)	1,517	411,788	271,449	11,515	9.6	41.9
Coal wholesalers (with coal yards)	204	226,026	1,107,971	114,863	9.4	40.6
Grain merchants	975	3,989,704	4,092,004	169,974	3.1	26.8
Oil well supply houses	1,208	914,479	757,019	97,988	9.6	18.2
Cash and carry food depots	291	139,950	480,928	27,670	4.2	17.1
General line electrical goods distribution	559	1,567,994	2,804,998	318,116	10.8	13.2

Source: U.S. Department of Commerce, Bureau of the Census, *Census of Business*, 1954, Vol. III, Table 2H.

as critical as in the case of, say, millinery or toys or greeting cards.

Third, the financial economies of scale may be of significance in those types of wholesaling where large inventories must be maintained, since the cost of capital may be smaller the larger the concern.

Perhaps this discussion, even though very limited, is enough to indicate that the merchant wholesaling fields are not equally subject to horizontal integration and the development of large market shares by individual firms. There seems to be considerable evidence that only some of the merchant wholesaling fields lend themselves to large scale operations and that most of the wholesaling sector of the economy is dominated by firms with rather modest market power. But this conclusion calls for some major qualifications, which are covered below.

V. The Threat of Monopoly in Wholesaling and Retailing

The discussion thus far has emphasized that satisfactory comprehension of the role of competition and monopoly in retailing and wholesaling requires some understanding of the competitive strategies of retailers and wholesalers. These strategies and the patterns of price and product competition which result from them in many instances are shaped significantly by the manufacturers with whom the retailers or wholesalers deal. Some of the cost considerations and managerial problems which may limit horizontal and vertical integration in distribution have also been discussed. Even though the various hypotheses suggested have not been well tested, it does seem clear that horizontal or vertical integration is economically attractive to the firm only under certain circumstances and that these circumstances are not found in all types of retailing and wholesaling.

The trend in monopoly power in retailing

With this background, let us consider three related questions: First, has the degree of monopoly in retailing increased over the years? Second, what is the general nature of the *legal* restraints which discourage the development of monopoly in retailing and wholesaling in the United States? And finally, what *economic* restraints on monopoly seem to operate in the distributive sector?

Although the U. S. Census data are not strictly comparable over time, they do permit one to say with certainty that for retailing as a whole, the single-unit firms have not lost any significant proportion of their share of the market since the first Census of Business was taken in 1929.

And there is some evidence, though quite inconclusive, that the single-unit firms may have lost a little ground to the chains between 1929 and 1939, but the chains may have lost ground to the single-unit firms from 1939 to 1954.

The data supporting this conclusion are interesting to examine in some detail. In 1954, single-unit firms accounted for almost exactly 70 per cent of total retail trade in the U.S., the other 30 per cent being accounted for by multi-unit firms of all sorts. It might be pointed out that 6 per cent of the 30 per cent was in the hands of multi-unit firms with two or three establishments. These perhaps should not be called "chain stores" and should probably be considered as small business. For several years, the Census required a firm to have four or more units before it could be considered a chain. For the moment, though, we will work with the single-unit sales figure. Over time, this percentage seems to have changed very little. Although the data for 1929 and 1939 are such that a range of percentages rather than a specific percentage must be given, the share of retail trade for single-unit firms in 1929, 1939 and 1954 seem to be as follows:

1929	between 64 and 72 per cent
1939	between 65 and 69 per cent
1954	70 per cent.

To put the matter in gross terms, single-unit firms have accounted for roughly two-thirds of the total retail trade in the country in the prosperous Census years, the multi-unit stores apparently not increasing their share above the historic one-third at any time. It is even possible that, within the ranges of estimates for 1929 and 1939, the actual percentages would show the single-unit firms gaining ground a bit.

But looking beyond the aggregative data, one finds an interesting contrast between the changes between 1929 and 1939, on the one hand, and the changes between 1939 and 1954 on the other. Without going into the problems of reconciling the data over time, we can say that a review of the individual kinds of business for which the data for firms with four or more units can be made reasonably comparable over time indicates that between 1929 and 1939 the four-or-more-unit firms gained market share in more cases than did the firms with one, two, or three units; between 1939 and 1954, however, the opposite was true, and the chains seem to have lost ground.[25] However, the chains increased their market shares in two of the kinds of business with the largest sales, namely grocery and department stores. But as a counter to this point, it should be mentioned that the sales of single-unit firms is probably understated slightly in the 1954 Census because of the difference in coverage instituted in that year. Only establishments with sales of at least $2,500 were canvassed, whereas in earlier years the cut-off point was $500. It is conceivable that the chains have increased their market share very slightly over the 1939–54 period even though they may have lost ground to single-unit firms in a majority of the kinds of business. The issue must remain in doubt, although it is apparent that the shift of market share has not been large, regardless of the direction.

In one sense the monopoly power of any given retail store has been declining over the years in the United States. Although Detroit has bequeathed the country countless problems, it must be admitted that the automobile, happily, has increased the mobility of the consumer. The shopper's greater range has therefore brought retailers into competition with other retailers who could have been safely ignored in the horse and buggy days. No body of antitrust legislation could conceivably police competition in retailing as effectively as the phenomenon of two cars in every garage.

In wholesaling, the single-unit firms in general lost some ground over the 1939–54 period but largely because of the growth of multi-unit petroleum bulk stations and of manufacturers' sales branches and sales offices. Among the merchant wholesalers the single-unit firms appear to have increased their market share slightly.

Legal restraints on monopoly in the distributive sector

It would be inappropriate to spell out in great detail the application of the antitrust laws to the distributive sector in the United States and to discuss the multitude of problems of legal interpretation and enforcement which can arise in this area. However, in view of the strength of the antimonopoly policy in the U.S., it does seem desirable at least to summarize the legal restraints on monopoly in the distributive sector and to indicate in broadest terms something of the impact of these restraints. We can then proceed to some concluding notes on the manner in which various economic forces operate to minimize the antitrust problem in distribution.

When applied to the distributive sector, antitrust policy in the United States takes on a dual personality. On the one hand there is no question that it is employed to keep the large and powerful firm, regardless of whether that firm be engaged primarily in distribution or in manufacturing, from monopolizing or conspiring to monopolize any portion of the distributive sector. But on the other hand one sees in the legislation and in the enforcement of that legislation definite attempts to encourage what can at best be called noncompetitive behavior. The laws operate in part to prevent rather than to encourage competition.

The reason for this duality is reasonably clear. The political strength of the small businessman (and especially the small retailer) in the United States is so great that he has been blessed with a certain amount of protection from competition, thanks to the antitrust laws themselves. Fair trade pricing, for example, has been exempt from the antitrust laws, thus encouraging what is in effect collusion on prices among retailers. And the restrictions on the discount structure which the manufacturer or distributor may employ discourage the granting of discounts to large buyers even when discounts may be justified on the grounds of cost savings to the seller. Congress has thus taken a strong stand for "hard" competition—for some people but not for others.

The major effects of the federal antitrust laws on competition and monopoly in the distributive sector can be indicated rather briefly by an examination of the major provisions of the relevant statutes insofar as they concern distribution practices. The Sherman Act, passed in 1890, forbids contracts, combinations or conspiracies in restraint of trade and also prohibits any person from monopolizing, attempting to monopolize or conspiring to monopolize any part of the commerce of the country. The most significant recent application of this law to the distributive sector involved the Great Atlantic and Pacific Tea Company, the largest of the corporate grocery chains.[26] The Antitrust Division of the United States Department of Justice filed suit against the A & P in 1944. The Company was found guilty of violation of the Sherman Act and was fined. The government then sought to break the company up into several smaller companies. The affair ended with the signing of a consent decree in 1954, with the government settling for substantially less than it had requested.

Viewing the country as a whole as the relevant market, the A & P was scarcely a monopolist since it accounted for less than seven per cent of the total grocery sales. But in 23 cities the company accounted for more than 40 per cent of the sales and in another 102 cities it had 20 per cent of the market or more. (These contrasting figures on market shares underscore the difficulty of defining the relevant market in antitrust cases, especially cases concerning retail or wholesale trade.) So in many areas the A & P was clearly a power. The government argued that the tactics of the company were in violation of the Sherman Act. It charged that the company deliberately cut prices in some areas but not in others in order to drive out competition. The company agreed that it charged lower prices in some stores than in others, but argued that these prices only reflected the intensity of the competition in the area and not an attempt to monopolize. The company was also accused of using its market power to coerce its suppliers into giving it preferential treatment and prices. This means of lowering its purchasing prices for goods was seen as a device for driving its competition from the market place and establishing a monopoly. The defendant, of course, replied that it was only trying to buy for as little as possible in order to keep its prices at retail low enough to attract more customers.

The A & P moved such a volume of goods through its retail outlets that it had integrated backward not only into wholesaling but into manufacturing as well. The government argued that the company's manufacturing subsidiaries were selling to the A & P's competitors at higher prices than to the A & P itself. The rebuttal is that an internal transfer price standing by itself is nearly meaningless and serves only to help determine the accounting profit of the buying unit or the selling unit. And the Atlantic Commission Company, a subsidiary which purchased produce for A & P outlets, also served as a broker between their suppliers and some of the A & P's competitors. Both uses of the vertically integrated subsidiaries the government considered as part of a pattern of an attempt to monopolize.

Under the terms of the consent decree, that handy device for settling the immediate case out of court while leaving the issues legally in limbo, the A & P agreed to rid itself of the Atlantic Commission Company and not to engage in any further brokerage operations. The decree also stipulated that the A & P would not try to influence its suppliers' pricing practices with respect to its competitors. The company agreed, also, not to operate individual stores at low margins in order to snuff out local competition. But divorcement of the manufacturing subsidiaries and the division of the retail operations of the firm were not granted.

A majority of economists familiar with this case seem to consider it quite clear that the suit was an attempt on the part of the government not to further competition in the market place but rather to protect competitors:

> The growth of the A & P and similar chains has made the grocery business more competitive. It has improved the methods and cut the costs of distribution. It has given the consumer a better product at a lower price. And this is precisely what competition is supposed to do. The chains, moreover, carry no threat of monopoly. Their share of the business is a minor one, and it has not increased for many years. New competitors have entered the market, with new methods, and the door stands open to the entry of many more. The purpose of the government's suit, therefore, was not to enforce competition or to prevent monopoly. It was to protect the independent grocer against the competition of the chains. The attack was on the advantages of size. The legal issue was whether these advantages so seriously restricted the competitive opportunities of small merchants as to constitute restraint of trade. The issue of public policy was whether the small competitor should be protected at the risk of impairing the vigor of competition, or competition preserved at the risk of harming the small competitor.[27]

It may be accurate to say that the net effect of the A & P case on competition in the distributive sector has been to discourage firms from attempting to expand their share of the market too vigorously by means of price competition especially if small competitors, rather than large ones, are bearing the brunt of the attack. And certainly a firm must exercise some care in the design of the buying and selling policies of any processing subsidiaries it may control, at least if that parent firm has what might be called by any stretch of the imagination a significant share of the market.

Of particular relevance to the earlier discussion of the extent of vertical integration by the producer of consumer goods into the channel of distribution is the antitrust policy toward exclusive franchises and tying agreements. The Clayton Act, passed in 1914 and amended significantly by the Robinson-Patman Act of 1936, forbids a firm from requiring that a buyer of its product refuse to handle the products of a competitor if the effect of such a practice "may be to substantially lessen competition or tend to create a monopoly." If a manufacturer were to succeed in signing exclusive agreements with a great majority of the retailers who normally would be expected to handle that particular product, he can, of course, effectively seal off his competitors from that proportion of their possible outlets. If the exclusive franchise device seems to be used with this objective in mind, it is probably illegal. For example in 1922, the Standard Fashion Company was found guilty of violation of the Clayton Act's clause on exclusive dealers.

It had about two-fifths of the dress pattern market in the U.S. and had signed exclusive agreements with a high proportion of the retail outlets in the better market areas.[28] In another case a manufacturer whose retail outlets accounted for only three per cent of the product sales in the relevant market area was found guilty of violating the Clayton Act because of its exclusive dealing arrangements with these retailers. The argument was, in effect, that a substantial *number* of retailers were concerned, so competition might be substantially lessened, even though the *proportion* of retailers concerned was not particularly great.[29] This rather odd interpretation of the substantiality clause appears, however, to have been largely transitory. More recently, substantiality has been interpreted as referring to the proportion rather than the absolute number of the retail outlets concerned.[30]

There is little doubt of the virtue of prohibiting use of the exclusive dealing arrangement for closing the market to competitors. As suggested in the earlier discussion of the circumstances which lead to selective distribution by the manufacturer of consumer goods, certain types of goods require particular attention by the retailer handling them. But whether this necessarily requires that the retailer be prohibited from selling competing lines is another matter. As things now stand, it is probably accurate to say that exclusive dealing in the United States is permitted if competing firms are not thereby denied sufficient access to consumers and if there is clearly no intent to monopolize. This situation is in marked contrast to the situation in the past in Britain, where private agreements among manufacturers served to reinforce exclusive dealing arrangements and to discourage entry into distribution. In the United States the channels of distribution have never been frozen in this manner, and so competition has been more dynamic. The cost of this, of course, has been a high rate of business failures in retailing. We will return to this later.

The structure of prices in the channel of distribution is subject to important regulation in the United States under the Clayton Act as amended by the Robinson-Patman Act. Putting the matter broadly, price discrimination among one's customers is prohibited if the effect may be substantially to lessen competition. Like goods must be sold at like prices, with two major exceptions: 1) price differentials which reflect differences in the cost of manufacturing, sale or delivery to different customers are permitted, and 2) a price difference is permitted if the lower price is set "in good faith" to meet competition.

This price discrimination clause has apparently had a definite effect on the structure of quantity discounts offered in many industries. Quantity discounts must be justified by cost savings, yet the Federal Trade Commission, which shares with the Department of Justice the jurisdiction of certain of the Clayton Act provisions, is empowered to establish limits to quantity discounts, even in cases that can be justified costwise, if it is felt that the quantity discounts promote monopoly. However, the FTC's only attempt to establish such a quantity discount limit was struck down by the courts on the grounds that the rationale for the computation of the limit was improper. So the quantity limit rule remains unused. There is no doubt, however, that even though this particular provision is inactive, the insistence that quantity discounts be justified by cost differences has had a very substantial impact. The FTC has caused any number of firms to revise their discount policies, for it has ruled that the quantity discount is justified only on the basis of the quantity in the single shipment to the single destination. Thus the seller may be vulnerable if the quantity discount is based on the customer's total purchases for the year or on the size of the single order if that single order is to be divided among several destinations. Even quantity discounts based on the size of the single order going to the single destination may have been reduced a bit as a result of the Robinson-Patman amendment because the existence of common costs in a firm's marketing organization make the cost justification of specific quantity discounts so very difficult.

It is general practice among manufacturers of both consumer goods and industrial goods to give "functional" or "trade" discounts, i.e., discounts based solely on the position of the buyer in the distribution channel. The wholesaler may buy a given quantity at a lower price than a retailer even though the retailer is buying in the same quantity. The Clayton and Robinson-Patman Acts do not mention functional discounts as such, so this aspect of pricing in the channel falls under the general prohibition of price discrimination where competition may be lessened.[31] If the wholesaler and the retailer in question are not competing with each other, then clearly competition between the two is not lessened by the practice and it remains legal. But serious and complicated problems arise when a buyer is, say, a wholesaler of some of the goods it buys and a wholesaler-retailer for others. Despite certain recent cases on this point, the area can at best be described as legally cloudy.[32] It seems generally recognized that to the extent that the businessman can from the price discrimination cases distill some pricing rules, these rules would have him relax his pricing tactics and rely more extensively on nonprice devices for increasing his sales and profits.

But these nonprice devices are restricted in yet another provision of the Robinson-Patman Act. The seller cannot provide supplementary services to a buyer nor give any sort of allowance to the buyer for services provided by him unless such services or such allowances are made available on a "proportionally equal" basis to all buyers. A recent case involving a manufacturer of dress patterns illustrates the problem. The firm was providing free to some retailers the catalogues and display cabinets needed for the sale of the patterns, while other retailers were being charged for these items. The Supreme Court ruled that the catalogues and cabinets were services provided on a discriminatory basis, and that, therefore, the practice was in violation of the Robinson-Patman Act.[33] The prohibition of this particular practice applies regardless of whether competition may be substantially lessened as a result.

A remaining provision of the Robinson-Patman Act deserves special mention not only because it affects the structure of the channel of distribution but also because it illustrates the tendency of the law to protect competitors rather than to foster competition. The law prohibits the payment of a broker's commission if an independent broker is not actually involved. Thus the corporate chain which takes over the broker's function of establishing contact with a supplier cannot receive the broker's commission which the supplier would have paid if an independent broker had been used. This provision was clearly instituted to protect the position of the brokers, who were being by-passed by the chains.

Resale price maintenance

Certainly one of the most notable developments in the distribution of consumer goods in the United States in recent years is the erosion of the resale price maintenance laws, which for years were considered exempt from the antitrust laws. In the 1930's and early 1940's, 45 states passed laws which permitted a manufacturer to set the retail price for his product in the given state simply by signing a price maintenance contract with one retailer in that state and notifying other retailers of the existence of the contract. These other retailers, supposedly bound by the price maintenance contract they had not signed, are generally referred to as the "non-signers." The purpose of these laws was to prevent the rapidly growing chain store organizations from selling price-maintained products at lower prices than the independent retailers, who were feeling the intense competition of this new form of retail organization. Such state laws, of course, permitted conspiracies to fix prices at the retail level and so were clearly in conflict with the antitrust laws when the goods had moved across interstate lines and thus had fallen under federal jurisdiction. Accordingly, in 1937 the Miller-Tydings Act was passed, amending the Sherman Act to exempt such contracts from prosecution under the federal antitrust laws.

This means of fixing retail prices should not be confused with price maintenance arrangements abroad, especially in Britain, under which manufacturers may have horizontal agreements designed to reinforce vertical price fixing. Under the U.S. law, collusion among manufacturers is not sanctioned. Thus the manufacturer of Brand A might fix the retail price of Brand A but he would have nothing to do with establishing or enforcing the price the manufacturer of Brand B might wish to employ at the retail level.

"Fair trade" (as resale price maintenance was euphemistically termed) stood undisturbed until 1951. The Supreme Court ruled that a "non-signer" retailer who had been cutting prices on fair-traded merchandise and who was consequently sued by the manufacturer was not bound by the manufacturer's resale price maintenance contract in that state because the defendant had not signed the agreement. The fair trade structure nearly collapsed. For a few weeks wild price wars raged in some cities, especially New York, to the great delight of consumers. But the proponents of fair trade rushed their forces to the breach and arranged the passage of the McGuire-Keogh bill. In this act Congress attempted to enforce the nonsigner clause. At the moment the nonsigner provision of the McGuire-Keogh Act has been upheld in a number of lower courts but the Supreme Court has refused to hear appeals from these decisions. Until it does hear appeals, the lower court decisions stand and the nonsigner clause can be enforced in those states.

Meanwhile, however, in 1957 the Supreme Court refused to review a lower court decision that a mail order house located in Washington, D.C., which has no fair trade law, was not bound by the fair trade laws in New York, where some of its customers were located.[34] This loophole threatened to be so big that the General Electric Company abandoned resale price maintenance on all small appliances. The Westinghouse Electric Corporation, the other major producer of consumer electrical appliances, had abandoned fair trade in 1955.

In 1958 and 1959 Congress was considering a group of bills advocated by the fair trade proponents to solve the problem of enforcement of resale price maintenance. In each, the manufacturer would be able to fix the retail price of an item merely by notifying the retailers. This could be done by printing the price on the label. To resell the item for less than this price would constitute a violation of federal law and not just a violation of a private contractual agreement. None of the bills were reported out of committee, however, in the 1959 session of Congress. Meanwhile in about one-third of the states with fair trade laws these laws have been struck down by lower courts, generally on the grounds that they violate the state constitution. In the absence of passage of the federal fair trade law bills which have been put before Congress, the mail order loophole, combined with the unenforceability of the state fair trade laws in a substantial number of states, puts the institution of resale price maintenance on rather shaky footing.

An evaluation of the impact of resale price maintenance requires an understanding of the circumstances conducive to fair trading.[35] First, in order to be fair traded an item must obviously be branded. Second, it is likely to be one not subject to purchase with a trade-in allowance. The trade-in allowance can hide a *de facto* price cut without departing from the fair trade price. Under these circumstances the fair trade price becomes but a gesture.

Branded convenience goods tend to be fair traded at least if the demand for them is elastic with respect to accessibility rather than price elastic. A manufacturer may have two alternative strategies from which to choose. To a given factory price he may add substantial wholesale and retail margins, enforce these by means of resale price maintenance contracts and thus encourage many retailers to stock the item even though the turnover may be rather low for each retailer. The alternative is to avoid resale price maintenance and let the wholesale and retail margins be competed down to some lower level than would have obtained under the price maintenance contracts. This would result in a lower price to consumers but presumably fewer retailers would stock the item. If the manufacturer considers his sales to be more sensitive to the accessibility of the item than to the price to the consumer, he will enjoy greater unit sales at the given factory price by following the former rather than the latter alternative and hence he will employ resale price maintenance contracts.

Resale price maintenance may also be used because the sales of the item are especially sensitive not only to the proportion of outlets in which the product is sold but also to the amount of promotion (display space, etc.) given the item by the retailer. If promotion by the retailer is important, resale price maintenance may be necessary to permit the retailer a return for his effort.

Fair trading is also common among goods the demand for which is responsive to advertising. In order to obtain the maximum benefits from national advertising, a manufacturer must have his product available to those who see the advertisements. In the case of convenience goods, the item must be available in a very large number of outlets. Shopping goods, however, need not be available in such a large proportion of outlets because people will engage in price and quality comparisons of such goods anyway. Nevertheless if the demand for this type of good is particularly sensitive to the extent of the advertising, the manufacturer may properly prefer to establish resale price maintenance contracts to prevent his retailers from competing with each other on a price basis and to encourage them instead to stress promotion at the retail store level.

Resale price maintenance is not appropriate for some convenience goods. If the buyer can easily see the quality difference between two items, he can judge whether the price difference is warranted. Perhaps this is one reason why so few branded food items are fair traded. But a related factor in the case of food items is the variability of prices of competing brands over time. It is troublesome for the manufacturer to change the agreed price when resale price maintenance is employed, so if any substantial number of the manufacturers in a given consumer goods industry choose to let their prices follow raw material costs, those manufacturers who fair trade their product are clearly at a disadvantage.

Gift items seem to be especially suited to fair trading. Such goods are often widely advertised in part so that the recipient of the gift will have a greater appreciation for it. The demand for gift items in general is undoubtedly less elastic with respect to price than are other consumer goods, and there is a premium on the recipient knowing how much the giver paid for the gift. It may be true that "it's the sentiment that counts," but for many the sentiment counts for more if the gift is costly.

Most independent retailers favor resale price maintenance, of course, because it prevents larger retailers from using fair traded merchandise as loss leaders to attract trade.[36] They argue that loss leaders deceive the public and that fair trade pricing is necessary to prevent consumers from being gouged by retailers who use them to trick people into paying higher than normal margins on other goods. The hapless manufacturer finds that those retailers not using his item as a loss leader are refusing to stock the item or at least to promote it. So the manufacturer faces a problem of dealer morale. He is at a competitive disadvantage vis-à-vis the integrated manufacturer-retailer or the manufacturer who sells on consignment, for the latter can obviously control the retail price on his products because he still owns them. It is this competitive disadvantage which both the non-integrated manufacturers and the independent retailers bemoan. This is reflected in the title of one of the federal fair trade bills, which describes it as a bill "...to equalize rights in the distribution of identified merchandise."

There is little question of the effect of fair trading pricing on the prices paid for merchandise which is fair traded. A price survey by the Department of Justice has been reported to show that in eight cities not covered by fair trade laws the prices of 132 drug, houseware, appliance and similar items averaged 19 per cent below the fair trade prices fixed for other areas.[37] But the fair trade proponents argue that in the absence of fair trade consumers would have to pay more on the average for all products (fair-traded and nonfair-traded) because the loss leaders would be used as bait to sell items with unusually high mark-ups.[38] They refuse to grant that large scale retailers are more efficient than the nonintegrated retailer. What they seem to be saying then is that consumers would not be paying less for all the goods they buy if consumer trade in general were concentrated in fewer, larger outlets, thus denying that there are any economies of scale in retailing. Clearly they are on uncertain ground here.[39]

Resale price maintenance surely perpetuates some excess capacity in retailing by restricting the amount of price competition which is practiced. But much of the protection which the independent retailer expects from resale price maintenance is illusory. If a retailer cannot use price competition as a means of attracting trade, he is likely to turn either to service competition or to price competition on nonfair-traded items. If there is no serious barrier to entry into the type of retailing being considered, any profits above normal will be competed away not through price competition on the fair traded products, but rather through price competition on other products or through competition on the basis of costly services which are offered to attract trade. Furthermore, the existence of the fair-traded item merely encourages the large scale retailer to market a private brand version of the item at a price below the fair traded item, thus making the advantage of shopping at the chain more apparent to consumers. It could be argued that fair trade does not reduce the amount of competition the independent retailer faces but merely changes the nature of that competition; the protection is largely fictitious.[40] It may be accurate to conclude that although the practice of resale price maintenance may be exempted from the Sherman Act, this particular type of conspiracy to maintain prices provides the retailer only with an uncertain shield against competition from the larger firms.

Economic deterrents to monopoly in distribution

Undoubtedly there is some truth in the suggestion that antitrust suits against wholesalers and retailers are comparatively rare because these citizens are sheltered politically.[41] But possibly, too, all but the very largest firms in the distributive sector have such a small share of the market that their monopoly power is very small when compared with the situation of the major manufacturing industries. The Antitrust Division of the Department of Justice may be allocating its time appropriately to the most significant problem areas by concentrating on manufacturing and giving retailers and wholesalers relatively little attention. Cases often involve the marketing practices of manufacturers, but the point here is that it is the manufacturer and not a retailer or wholesaler who is typically the defendant.

Another reason for the relative lack of antitrust action against retailers and wholesalers may stem from the difficulty of generating any significant monopoly returns in retailing or wholesaling in the long run. Unlike the manufacturer, the retailer or wholesaler has almost no opportunity to develop a patent monopoly. The distributor operating under an exclusive franchise may handle an item on which the manufacturer has a patent monopoly. But even though the manufacturer may be enjoying a monopoly return from the sale of the product in question, he is not motivated to hand over much if any of that return to his distributors. The marketing margin will be only great enough to persuade the distributors to give the item the amount of attention the manufacturer thinks it deserves. Neither does the distributor have a monopoly over any natural resource. He may have some degree of monopoly of location, but even power of this sort is being eroded by the increasing mobility of the consumer.

But the major forces at work to keep monopoly in distribution to a minimum stem from the flexibility of the "plant" involved. Freedom of entry into an industry helps insure against long-run monopoly profits. In distribution the merchant eager to charge a particularly high price for an item or a group of items must consider not only the possibility of new stores entering the market. He must also anticipate that other retailers, some of whom may be in quite different lines of business, may "enter" the market in the sense that they will begin to stock the profitable item. This raiding of profitable merchandise lines has led to "mixed" or "scrambled" retailing in the United States. The high retail margins on certain high-volume drug store items induced the food stores to enter this field. Many drug stores have retaliated by adding to their stock such high margin food items as ice cream.

This kind of entry is possible in distribution because the physical plant of any single firm is not as committed to a particular product as is generally the case in manufacturing. In some instances the incremental investment associated with a merchant's adding a new product line is nearly zero. In few if any cases does the risk capital required for such entry compare with that required of the manufacturer. This type of entry may or may not, however, lead to lower prices to the consumer. If retail prices are enforced by the manufacturer in any way or if the new retailers choose not to compete on a price basis, the monopoly profits of the original distributors may be competed away not because the margin is reduced but rather because the volume of sales declines.

A more certain protection against monopoly profits in retailing in the long run is provided by the ease of entry of the new firm. Although data on the number of new firms are not available, we do know that six or seven thousand retailers fail each year and that the majority of these have been in business less than three years.[42] These six or seven thousand represent about one-half of one per cent of all retail firms in the country. The number of retailers who enter is, of course, greater than this, since many do succeed and many who exit are not listed as commercial failures. The point here is that this continual entry is an especially strong deterrent to the growth of monopoly in retailing. Before World War II the development of the chain stores and especially the spread of the supermarket served to put pressure on prices and distribution markets. After the war the phenomenon of the discount house swept the country and shook the established retailers of certain product lines. The advent of this new form of retailing organization has generally re-emphasized price competition in distribution. But probably because the retailer's marginal cost is so low compared with marginal net revenue (and perhaps even when compared with average cost), he fights for greater volume by offering additional services or by incurring substantial selling costs. There would therefore seem to be a tendency for new types of retail organizations to grow by offering more services even though initially these firms may compete on a price basis. Even now the discount houses in the United States appear to be offering more and more services. Some are coming to look much like the old line department stores, from which they were originally differentiated so clearly. Although this service competition may lead the discount houses far from their original strategies, it seems doubtful that they could maintain a strong market position for long without the tacit permission of the public. As Adelman has pointed out, "...the greater the size of the gap between what the consumer wants and what he is getting, the greater the inducement to the bolder spirits to offer the leaner and better product."[43]

The ease of entry of the established retailer into the sale of a particularly attractive article and the ease of entry of the entirely new firm but especially the ease of entry of the firm which offers a minimum of services and minimum prices all help to limit whatever monopoly power a retailer may begin to acquire. The chain stores, who have been seen as threatening to establish themselves in monopoly position, must sell in a market which has either a large number of sellers or a potentially large number of sellers.[44] As the discussion of the strength of multi-unit firms in the various kinds of retailing and wholesaling has shown, the multi-unit firm does not have an equally favorable position in all kinds of business. And even in those kinds of business in which the chains are strongest, they have won more than half of the market only in a small number of the many kinds of business.

NOTES

1. I am indebted to Professors F. E. Balderston, D. J. Duncan, E. T. Grether, and D. A. Revzan, my colleagues at the University of California, Berkeley, for their comments on some of the ideas and interpretations in this paper, and particularly to Professor L. E. Preston of Berkeley, and Professor John Perry Miller for having read the manuscript and made several helpful suggestions.
2. P. W. Stewart and J. F. Dewhurst, *Does Distribution Cost Too Much?* New York: The Twentieth Century Fund, 1939.
3. See the U.S. Department of Agriculture periodical, *The Marketing and Transportation Situation.*
4. See, for example, T. N. Beckman, H. H. Maynard and W. R. Davidson, *Principles of Marketing,* 6th ed., New York: The Ronald Press Company, 1957; E. A. Duddy and D. A. Revzan, *Marketing,* 2nd ed., New York: McGraw-Hill Book Company, 1953; C. F. Phillips and D. J. Duncan, *Marketing,* 4th ed., Homewood, Illinois:

Richard D. Irwin, Inc., 1960; and R. S. VAILE, E. T. GRETHER and R. COX, *Marketing in the American Economy*, New York: Ronald Press Company, 1952.

5. This was the approach generally applied by HAROLD BARGER in his study, *Distribution's Place in the American Economy since 1869*, National Bureau of Economic Research, Princeton: Princeton University Press, 1955.
6. B. EMMET and J. E. JEUCK, *Catalogues and Counters, A History of Sears, Roebuck and Company*, Chicago: University of Chicago Press, 1950, p. 389 ff.
7. J. C. PALAMOUNTAIN, JR., *The Politics of Distribution*, Cambridge: Harvard University Press, 1955, ch. 2.
8. It is this type of competition which Schumpeter has emphasized so much. See J. S. SCHUMPETER, *Capitalism, Socialism, and Democracy*, 3rd ed., New York: Harper and Brothers, 1950, pp. 81–86.
9. See J. S. BAIN, *Barriers to New Competition*, Cambridge: Harvard University Press, 1956, especially pp. 133–42.
10. The rise of the chains as a force to neutralize that of the large manufacturer is referred to by J. K. GALBRAITH in support of the central thesis in his *American Capitalism, The Concept of Countervailing Power*, rev. ed., Boston: Houghton-Mifflin Company, 1956. A more general discussion of the factors influencing the relationships within the marketing channel as well as among competitors appears in W. ALDERSON, *Marketing Behavior and Executive Action*, Homewood, Illinois: Richard D. Irwin, Inc., 1957, Especially chs. 2, 4 and 14.
11. The monopoly power of a retailer we will consider to be increased if the firm increases its isolation from competition either by reducing the elasticity of demand curve faced by the firm as a whole or by reducing the cross-elasticity. See E. H. CHAMBERLIN, *Towards a More General Theory of Value*, New York: Oxford University Press, 1957, p. 81.
12. See J. S. BAIN, *Industrial Organization*, New York: John Wiley and Sons, Inc., 1959, pp. 326–31.
13. I have discussed the nature of convenience goods and shopping goods in more detail in a note, "The Distinctions Between Convenience Goods, Shopping Goods and Specialty Goods," in the *Journal of Marketing*, vol. XXIII, July, 1958, pp. 53–56.
14. The investment in inventory may be large because the price per unit is high as in the case of automobiles, or because the number of sizes and styles is large, as in the case of shoes or men's suits.
15. The advantages and disadvantages of selective distribution are discussed in some detail by D. J. DUNCAN in R. M. CLEWETT, *Marketing Channels*, Homewood, Illinois: Richard D. Irwin, Inc., 1954, pp. 375–78.
16. The more outstanding discussions of the spatial competition problem include H. HOTELLING, "Stability in Competition," *Economic Journal*, vol. XXXIX, March, 1929, pp. 41–57; E. H. CHAMBERLIN, *The Theory of Monopolistic Competition*, 7th ed., Cambridge: Harvard University Press, 1956, Appendix C; A. SMITHIES, "Optimum Location in Spatial Competition," *Journal of Political Economy*, vol. XLIV, June, 1941, pp. 432–39; and G. ACKLEY, "Spatial Competition in a Discontinuous Market," *Quarterly Journal of Economics*, vol. LVI, February, 1942, pp. 212–30.
17. For a discussion of the relationship of product assortment to sales volume, see F. E. BALDERSTON, "Assortment Choice in Wholesale and Retail Marketing," *Journal of Marketing*, vol. XXI, October, 1956, pp. 175–83; and W. J. BAUMOL and E. A. IDE, "Variety in Retailing," *Management Science*, vol. III, October, 1956, pp. 93–101.
18. G. M. LEBHAR, *Chain Stores in America*, 1859–1959, New York: Chain Store Publishing Corp., 1959
19. C. F. PHILLIPS, "The Federal Trade Commission's Chain Store Investigation: A

Note," *Journal of Marketing*, vol. II, January, 1938, p. 191. The results of the investigation were published as Federal Trade Commission reports to the U.S. Senate, carrying various subtitles under the main title, *Chain Stores*. The final report was published in 1934.

20. I am indebted to LEE E. PRESTON for these calculations based on the U.S. Census of Business, 1954, as well as for assistance in clarifying a number of points in other sections of the paper.
21. For a detailed empirical study of channels of distribution in Great Britain, see J. B. JEFFERYS, *The Distribution of Consumer Goods*, Cambridge: Cambridge University Press, 1950, especially chapter 2, on the factors influencing the methods of distribution. Some of the following material is an extension of the Jefferys discussion. For discussion of vertical integration in marketing in the United States, see especially VAILE, GRETHER and COX, *op. cit.*, ch. 9; CLEWETT, *op. cit.;* and ROBERT H. COLE, *et al.*, *Vertical Integration in Marketing*, Urbana, Illinois: University of Illinois, 1952. Some of the ideas below also owe much to MARGARET HALL, *Distributive Trading*, London: Hutchinson's University Library, 1948, especially chs. 5 and 6.
22. An alternative, of course, is for the manufacturer in question to open a warehousing operation which handles not only his own but also the products of other manufacturers.
23. R. M. CLEWETT, *op. cit.*, p. 296.
24. See the cost functions in United States Bureau of the Census, *Census of Business*, 1948, vol. IV, p. 16; J. K. GALBRAITH, R. H. HOLTON and others, *Marketing Efficiency in Puerto Rico*, Cambridge: Harvard University Press, 1955, chs. 7 and 8; and J. DEAN and R. W. JAMES, *The Long-Run Behavior of Costs in a Chain of Shoe Stores*, University of Chicago Studies in Business Administration, vol. XII, No. 3, 1942. Although reported expense and sales figures published in M. P. MCNAIR, *Operating Results of Department and Specialty Stores*, Bulletin No. 152, Division of Research, Harvard Business School, Boston: 1958, show no indication of decreasing costs, it can be argued that the data could not be expected to reflect decreasing costs, strictly defined, even though they might be present. A study by F. M. BASS, "Expense and Margin Functions in Drug Stores," *Journal of Marketing*, vol. XX, January, 1956, pp. 236–41, reflects at least short-run decreasing costs.
25. This appears to be true of shoe stores, furniture stores and cigar stores and stands and possibly in bakery products; fruit and vegetable markets; dealers in tires, batteries and accessories; plumbing, paint and electrical stores; and news stands.
26. The basic reference for the A & P case is M. A. ADELMAN, *A & P, A Study in Price-Cost Behavior and Public Policy*, Cambridge: Harvard University Press, 1959.
27. CLAIR WILCOX, *Public Policies Toward Business*, rev. ed., Homewood, Illinois: Richard D. Irwin, Inc., 1950, p. 377.
28. *Standard Fashion Co. v. Magrane-Houston Co.*, 258 U.S. 346.
29. *U.S. v. Richfield Oil Corp.*, 99 F. Supp. 280, 1951.
30. For a more detailed discussion of the exclusive dealing problem see *Report of the Attorney General's National Committee to Study the Antitrust Laws*, Washington: U.S. Government Printing Office, 1955, pp. 137–49; C. D. EDWARDS, *Maintaining Competition*, New York: McGraw-Hill Book Company, Inc., 1949, pp. 175–78; and WILCOX, *op. cit.*, pp. 238–44.
31. Recent bills introduced to cover functional discounts are discussed in *Functional Discounts*, Hearings before the Antitrust Subcommittee of the Committee on the Judiciary, 86th Congress, Washington, 1959.
32. See particularly the discussion of the functional discount problem and the price discrimination case against Standard Oil Co., Indiana, in J. B. DIRLAM and A. E. KAHN, *Fair Competition, the Law and Economis of Antitrust Policy*, Ithaca, New

York: Cornell University Press, 1954, pp. 245–56. For an earlier discussion of price discrimination as well as the use of tying agreements and exclusive dealing, see J. P. MILLER, *Unfair Competition*, Cambridge: Harvard University Press, 1941, chs. 9 and 10. A detailed study by C. D. EDWARDS, *The Price Discrimination Law*, Washington: The Brookings Institution, 1959, has been received too late to be reflected in this paper.

33. *Federal Trade Commission v. Simplicity Pattern Co.*, 79 S. Ct. 1005 (1959).
34. *General Electric Company v. Masters Mail Order Company of Washington, D.C.*, 78 S. Ct. 32 (1957).
35. See E. R. COREY, "Fair Trade Pricing: A Reappraisal," *Harvard Business Review*, vol. XXX, September-October, 1952, pp. 47–62.
36. The loss leader can be defined in several ways. It may be an item 1) sold at less than wholesale cost plus the "normal" margin, whatever that may be; 2) sold at less than wholesale cost plus distribution costs; or 3) sold at less than wholesale cost.
37. *New York Times*, March 24, 1959.
38. See, for example, Bureau of Education on Fair Trade, *Facts and Myths about Fair Trade*, New York: n.d.
39. That the available studies do *not* indicate the effect of resale price maintenance on the average of prices paid by consumers is emphasized by M. FRANKEL, "The Effects of Fair Trade: Fact and Fiction in the Statistical Findings," *Journal of Business*, vol. XXVIII, (July, 1955), pp. 182–94.
40. For a strong defense of resale price maintenance laws, see WALTER ADAMS, "Resale Price Maintenance: Fact and Fancy," *Yale Law Journal*, vol. LXIV, June, 1955, pp. 967–90. This is in reply to the strong anti-fair trade stand in the *Report of the Attorney General's Committee to Study the Antitrust Laws*. See also C. I. KANTOR and S. G. ROSENBLUM, "The Operation of Fair Trade Programs," *Harvard Law Review*, vol LXIX, December, 1955, pp. 316–52 and E. R. COREY, "Fair Trade, A Reappraisal," *Harvard Business Review*, vol. XXX, September-October, 1952, pp. 47–62. The basic work in the economics of resale price maintenance is E. T. GRETHER, *Price Control under Fair Trade Legislation*, New York: Oxford University Press, 1939.
41. M. A. ADELMAN, "The 'Product' and 'Price' in Distribution," *American Economic Review*, vol. XLVII, May, 1957, p. 271.
42. U.S. Department of Commerce, Bureau of the Census, *Statistical Abstract, 1959*, Washington: U.S. Government Printing Office, 1959, p. 502.
43. ADELMAN, *op. cit.*, p. 272.
44. R. B. HEFLEBOWER has concluded that the mass distributor faces a demand function which is quite elastic. See his "Mass Distribution: A Phase of Bilateral Oligopoly or of Competition?" *American Economic Review*, vol. XLVII, May, 1957, p. 281. With retailing in Great Britain primarily in mind, P. W. S. ANDREWS and R. K. ROTHSCHILD come to nearly the same conclusion. See ANDREWS, "Some Aspects of Competition in Retail Trade," *Oxford Economic Papers*, vol. II, June, 1950, pp. 137–75 and ROTHSCHILD, "Price Theory and Oligopoly," *Economic Journal*, vol. LVII, September, 1947, pp. 299–320. I have discussed the possible significance of the fact that the multi-product retailer sells products which have quite different elasticities of demand in "Price Discrimination at Retail: The Supermarket Case," *Journal of Industrial Economics*, vol. VI, October, 1957, pp. 13–32.

CHAPTER 8

THE ROLE OF PATENTS[1]

ALFRED E. KAHN

Cornell University, Ithaca, N.Y., U.S.A.

The patent law is rooted in capitalism. To grant to "any person who has invented any new and useful process, machine, manufacture, or composition of matter, or any new and useful improvement thereof,"[2] the privilege "of the sole working or making"[3] of whatever he has discovered is a peculiarly capitalistic device. Its philosophic justification is that of property itself: that the artisan is entitled to the exclusive enjoyment of the product of his labor—in this instance "a new trade" or idea—and that to protect him in the enjoyment of what he has contrived will encourage assiduity and ingenuity in economic pursuits beneficial to the community at large. It was, therefore, no accident that the historic common law cases and Statute of Monopolies, of the early seventeenth century, which formally stated the right of individuals to pursue callings of their own choosing, against the British Crown's indiscriminate issue of letters patent, likewise set forth as an exception the permissibility of such grants of monopoly privilege "where any man by his own charge and industry, or by his own wit or invention doth bring in new trade into the realm, or any engine tending to the furtherance of a trade that was never used before..."[4]

I. The Theory of Patents

The history of the patent law has been marked by continuous controversy over its ethical, social and economic premises. The disputes are reminiscent of those over the basic institutions of capitalism itself: for example, is property theft, as Proudhon asserted, or an inducement and reward for productive effort: so with the patent, the question has been raised, over and over: is it legalized monopoly, a license to exploit consumers, capriciously distributed, or does it merely provide the necessary institutional framework for competition by assuring that rewards will be equated with the value of one's contribution to society?[5]

In contrast with the property right in a particular reproducible commodity or service, the right to exclude others from the use of a particular *idea* is obviously inherently monopolistic. The restriction which it imposes on entry permits a price in excess of marginal cost, both short and long run. Yet, as the historic decisions and statutes recognized, the patent is or may be different from other monopolies; the critical distinction is the element of invention. Blackstone defined monopoly as "a license or privilege allowed by the King, for the sole buying and selling, making, working or using of anything... whereby the subject in general is restrained from that liberty of manufacturing or trading *which he had before*."[6] The inventor, the legal authorities averred, discovers something which the people never had before; to give him a patent, therefore, does not make him a monopolist. If the exclusive right conferred is over the idea of a process or product that society had not previously known, and would not have known but for the practice of granting inventors such privileges, the patent is no more objectionable than the artisan's property right in the particular commodities he has produced.

So long as the critical condition is met, the only kind of competition with which the patent is necessarily incompatible is pure or perfect competition. Assume that the practice of offering patents, considering all its consequences direct and indirect, elicits a greater flow of innovation than would otherwise be forthcoming: then clearly that inducement, exclusive in character though it is, contributes positively to the quest for and achievement of new cost-reducing processes—which is compatible with competition of any and all definitions*—and new alternatives with which to entice customers. The latter kind of rivalry is impure, to be sure; but the limited effectiveness of pure competition and the possible incompatibility between purity and innovation are sufficiently familiar to require no further consideration in this essay.[7] No matter how high the monopoly profits or quasi-rents earned by patentees, society would under these assumptions almost certainly be better off by virtue of having a patent system.**

* Neither perfect nor pure competition is necessarily incompatible with the exclusive control over a superior process for producing a standardized good: the patentee in this event really earns not monopoly profit but economic rent.

** It is of course theoretically possible, even if the assumption in the text is valid,

These considerations are aptly illustrated by the controversial antitrust suit charging E. I. Du Pont de Nemours and Co. with illegal monopolization of cellophane.[8] The outcome of the appeal to the United States Supreme Court turned on the single economic question of whether the defendants enjoyed a monopoly by virtue of their predominant patent-based market position in cellophane. The majority answered in the negative, because of what it believed to be a very high cross-elasticity of demand between cellophane and other flexible packaging materials. By the criteria of pure competition, its conclusion was clearly erroneous. Even if the cross-elasticity of demand were infinite at their respective current prices, the products were not identical; cellophane sold at twice the price of its main competitor materials. Du Pont was able to hold the price far above the marginal costs of producing it, and therefore to earn supernormal, authentically monopolistic profits.[9]* Yet assume that this monopoly did indeed stem simply from possession of a valid patent; and that without the prospect of this reward, neither Du Pont nor anyone else would have undertaken the effort of developing and bringing forth cellophane. In that event, clearly, the patent system would have made for effective competition, by any sensible definition. Patents may thus be one of the kinds of monopoly elements that Schumpeter so eloquently defended as required for the dynamically competitive process of "creative destruction."[10]

Schumpeter's defense of "monopoly" effectively demonstrated that pure competition is not a sufficient guide to public policy;[11] but it fell far short of erecting a defense of all monopoly, of all kinds, origins, and degrees.[12] Even innovation requires the stick of competition as well as the carrot of monopoly. The task of economic planning is to differentiate the useful from the harmful forms, manifestations, and degrees of monopoly; to see to it that society pays the price of monopoly power only for value received or promised, and only in such degree and for such time as are minimally required. Whether these conditions were

that the net effect of weakening the patent privilege would be a higher level of economic welfare. This would be so if the undesirable effect, the reduced rate of innovation, were outweighed by the desirable one, the lesser degree of monopoly control over the exploitation of such innovations as continue to be forthcoming. We consider below whether the economist can assume that patent-induced innovation is without limit conducive to economic welfare.

* If the cross elasticity of demand were infinite *and* cellophane sold at the same price as its major competitors, Du Pont's supernormal profits would instead be appropriately considered economic rents, attributable to its control over a superior process for producing an economically undifferentiated product.

met in the case of cellophane was a question the Supreme Court never reached.

So there can be no absolute and complete defense of patents. The issue is not one of principle but of practical social engineering: *how much* protection against competitive appropriation or imitation and of what kind is required and worth paying for the optimum rate of innovation in a capitalistic economy? Are there other stimuli that would produce the same results at less costs? To these questions there can be no single answer appropriate to all circumstances, even if the social engineer were omniscient and could define his goal; for what must be offered by way of patents (setting aside for the moment the devising of alternative stimuli) will depend upon the character of the innovation, and the strength of other motivations and protections for the successful innovator. For some inventions, the patent protection granted will be greater than necessary, for others less.[13] And while the law may be so fashioned as to provide some flexibility in the price society pays—patents of varying durations, patents in some circumstances subject to compulsory licensing, in others not, discretionary payment of variable cash awards—it can never permit the perfect monopsonistic price discrimination by which society could in each instance pay only the marginal costs of each innovation.*

The real price society pays by granting patents has several dimensions. The first is the monopoly power of the patentee to determine the rate at which he will exploit the invention, or, to put it in terms of effects, the delay in competitive imitation.[15] So long as the innovation would not have been forthcoming without the patent, this social cost must always be less than the benefit; but of course the converse is equally true.

The second social cost is the effect of the patent in blocking access of other potential innovators to use of the invention, with a consequent obstruction of the continuing innovative process itself. The patent

* The marginal costs that would have to be covered would be the long run costs of maintaining innovative effort rather than the short run incremental costs of individual inventions already perfected. The latter must be close to zero; but the economic function of a system of rewards is to guarantee a *continuing* undertaking of the innovative function in the first place. Still it must be true that some innovators and kind of innovation require less inducement than others.

This observation is usually made incident to proposals to permit variation of the time span of the patent. (As WALTON HAMILTON points out, a news agency requires protection for a few hours, a dress designer for a season. For most of their "inventions" automobile or appliance manufacturers surely need no more than a year.[14]) It would equally justify varying other aspects of the privilege as well.

that may not represent a socially excessive price by virtue alone of the monopolistic restriction it permits in exploiting the particular invention it covers may become excessive by virtue of its obstructing the proliferation of other innovations.* Defenders of the system often count it as a virtue that patents stimulate efforts by competitors to invent around them, in which process often superior expedients are devised.[16] But surely this tendency is appropriately regarded as mitigating the various social costs of the patent, rather than ordinarily constituting a positive net benefit. Surely scientists and engineers would agree that it is usually better to have free access to all possible products and processes, and to be in a position to make rational choices among them on their technical merits, rather than to be precluded from using certain ones, even though that preclusion may in certain instances force the exploration of alternative channels that (a) would not otherwise be explored and (b) prove in the end to be more fruitful.[17] There are, of course, great social advantages in competitive research. The ideal, however, would probably be competition accompanied by the fullest possible disclosure and availability of results to all. So the obstructive effect of patents is on balance a cost—possibly an inescapable one, if private parties will compete in research only when permitted to keep the results to themselves, but nonetheless a cost.

The third cost is the patent's tendency to extend or protect monopoly beyond the individual innovation, a tendency thoroughly discussed and documented elsewhere.[18] The profusion of patents and the high costs of testing their validity in the courts, the cumulative character of technological growth and the possibility hence of piling patents on patents, undoubtedly tend to confer on those who own patents a market power broader and more enduring than the legally permissible control over their own true inventive contributions, even apart from

* Of course, if the particular invention would *never* have been forthcoming except for the patent, society could never suffer a net loss even taking into account the second-order costs as well; no one could be blocked in the utilization of knowledge of which he would otherwise be totally ignorant. Suppose however the patent system has the tendency merely of causing an invention to appear sooner than otherwise. So far as social costs of the first order are concerned, the question would then be whether the discounted cost savings of a given patented process innovation (for example), with earlier discovery but impeded imitation, exceed the cost savings in the absence of patents, with later discovery but earlier imitation. Conceivably this comparison would more often vindicate than condemn the patent system, so far as primary effects—the direct application of particular inventions—are concerned, yet show a net social loss once one takes into account additionally the patent's obstruction of the cumulative innovation process, by retarding the availability of individual inventions to others who might possibly build on them.

the widespread resort to such practices as tie-ins, full-line forcing, cartel agreements with other patent owners, mergers and patent acquisitions.

The foregoing list of social costs considers only the restrictive effects of patents once issued. But the production of innovations is itself not costless; the question has therefore been raised whether the patent system may not produce an excessive allocation of resources (a) to innovation in contrast with other economic activities, or (b) to those activities contributing to "progress in science and the useful arts" that produce patentable results at the sacrifice of those that do not.[19]

Innovation is a species of investment. As such, it ought to be subject to the economic test that the prospective future flow of net revenue, appropriately discounted for uncertainty and the opportunity cost of capital, be at least equal to the original expenditure. It is, of course, particularly difficult to make such close profit-maximizing calculations in determining the level and direction of research expenditures, because of the unusual uncertainty about the results of any given outlay. But while, in consequence, businesses rely heavily on intuition and rules-of-thumb in making these decisions, still there is little reason to believe the ends they seek to serve by these expenditures differ significantly from the ends they seek to achieve from other investment outlays.[20] The criteria they *try* to apply are similar. The question we must ask, then, is whether the possibility of earning patents distorts these judgments so as to cause the private calculation of costs and benefits to diverge from the social.

The answer to this question depends on the validity of the ancient distinction between the patent and other monopolies. To the extent the patent confers control over a trade *that would otherwise be free,* to the extent in short that it is like any other monopoly, it appears that the system would recommend to private managements research expenditures that would not be justified by a consideration of prospective social benefits alone. In this event, patent-oriented research is similar to competitive advertising—most obviously so in the case of the research designed to circumvent patent-protected positions of competitors—privately necessary but to a very large extent mutually offsetting and socially worthless. To the extent, however, that the patent elicits innovations that would not otherwise be forthcoming, the private and social calculations coincide. The patent in this event is best viewed as an institutional arrangement necessary for the private appropriation of the benefits of innovation, without which private investors could not make or act upon a rational comparison of social costs and benefits.[21]

There are two reasons for believing that the analogy to competitive advertising overstates the possibly wasteful impact of patents. First, research tends to be productive in a way that salesmanship cannot duplicate; expenditures of this kind are much more likely than are television commercials to add to social capital by creating new technical knowledge. Second, against the tendency above-mentioned for the private benefits of such expenditures to exceed the social, should be posed the fact that the private innovator can seldom, even with the help of the patent, fully appropriate all the true social benefits of his contributions. His patent will inevitably give rise to some incremental stimulus and assistance to the inventive contributions of others. This information and stimulus tend to limit the value of the patent to the individual and to assure that the average period of effective economic protection will be less than the legal term (although of course the possibility of extending monopoly beyond the nominal term of the individual patent operates in the opposite direction), while the direct and indirect benefits continue to flow to society at large.

What of the possibility that patents may divert research energies and resources undesirably to pursuits promising patentable results and away from other activities, like education or pure research, that may be at least as productive of scientific and technological progress? There can be little doubt that the patent does encourage only certain kinds of innovative effort and that these are not necessarily the most productive. But it seems unreasonable to criticize the system on this account for two reasons. First, insofar as it does tend to draw scientists and engineers away from those other pursuits, its impact is significant in the short run only. Over time the effect of a patent-inflated demand can only be to elicit an expanded supply: we seem far from having exhausted the native capacities that can be trained for tasks such as these. Second, we do not and can not in any event rely primarily on profit-seeking enterprises for undertaking these other activities, because of the wide discrepancy between social and privately appropriable benefits. If they are slighted, the basic explanation is not the pull of the patent system and the remedy is not to weaken that pull.

The benefits of patent-oriented research, in contrast, are in large measure privately appropriable. But should they be appropriated? Samuelson has suggested that the essential economic characteristic of public goods is not the private inappropriability of their benefits but the fact that, like Hotelling's famous bridge, they can be made available to additional users at zero marginal cost, and that charging a price for them therefore offends against the welfare principle that price should not exceed marginal cost.[22] Knowledge, Francis Bator states, is the purest kind of public good, by this definition; and where its fruits are privately appropriated and priced it will be badly underutilized.[23] This observation raises intriguing questions about the validity of the patent system even for technological contributions the benefits from which can be privately appropriated. Should their costs, too, be borne by the taxpayer rather than by consumers?

The idea that direct government support or awards might be a preferable method of stimulating technological progress, precisely because of the monopoly consequences of patents, is a familiar one. The difference between price and the marginal production cost under a patented process or a patented product is in fact a charge for the use of patented knowledge, the marginal cost of which is zero. Does the imposition of such a charge really offend against the welfare optimum?

It would seem that it does. It uses no more of society's resources to make an item of patented knowledge, once discovered by A, available to B, C, and D as well. For A to impose a royalty on licensees or a monopoly charge on customers is to deny to marginal buyers a satisfaction that it would have cost society nothing to provide. The evil is compounded because technological progress is cumulative in character; by virtue of the second social cost of the patent, above-described, the deprivation extends to the customers of other goods and services as well.

These considerations do not, however, definitively answer the question of whether then the patent system ought to be scrapped in favor of taxpayer support of all research. Government subvention for most of the "public goods" described by Samuelson and Bator usually has other justifications besides zero marginal costs—notably a strong "public interest" in providing them, distributive justice, and externality of benefits.[24]

The bridge has an effect on real estate values; the taxpayer in New York has a strong stake in the literacy of his fellow voter in Kentucky—the marginal costs of providing which, incidentally, are far from zero; all consumers benefit directly and indirectly from the improved shipping made possible by the lighthouse that can as easily assist one hundred ships a night as one. While the familiar welfare criterion would be met in the case of taxpayer-subsidized research, i.e. that it would be theoretically possible for the beneficiaries to reimburse the taxpayers and still be better off than before, in fact such reimbursement is infeasible; government support thus has inevitable distributional effects.

In these circumstances it is clearly arguable that, zero short term marginal costs or not, it is preferable to have the owners of high-compression-ratio cars pay the costs of continuing oil company research on higher-octane gasolines and to have the patron of the laundry that wraps shirts in polyethylene pay the costs of continuing chemical company research on other plastics, than to impose these costs on the taxpayer. The administrative problems and possible threat to competition inherent in replacing the patent incentive and the market test with a system of discretionary government grants likewise argue against such a general reform, despite the strong theoretical case that can be made for it.* We will, therefore, henceforth assume a continuation and possible expansion of governmental support of and awards for innovation in pure science and in areas of applied research, like medicine or defense, that are generally conceded to be of broad public interest, still leaving to consumers of patented products the burden of paying the costs of all other patent-promising innovation.

The criticism that the patent leads to a slighting of non-patentable research and education is illustrative of a general tendency to criticize this law when the true culprit is the market system generally. For example, Machlup points out that the profits earned by various inventors under protection of patents are little correlated with either relative costs and sacrifices on the one hand, or the social value of their respective inventive contributions on the other.[26] These observations do to some extent reflect on the patent law itself. They sup-

* Following the logic of the Samuelson-Bator analysis, the government agency would likewise have to apply a (hypothetical) market test to decide which research deserved taxpayer support and which did not. The appropriate test would be the willingness of all potential beneficiaries to pay the opportunity costs of the resources devoted to the research if they faced a perfectly discriminating monopolist.

These remarks are not to be understood as dismissing the case for this reform, or, even more, for a system of *ex post* government awards in exchange for patents.[25] Part II, below, will show that most research and development today is already financed by the government, and much private innovation does not depend importantly on the patent. Nor is it clear that the imperfections of government decisions would be any greater than those of a patent-ridden market system. But if only on grounds of the political probabilities, the subsequent discussion will ignore the possibility of its adoption as a general practice.

port our earlier observation that an ideal system would discriminate among inventions, adjusting the price society pays to their respective costs or contribution. The failure of some deserving inventors to reap the reward they have earned is in large measure attributable to the uncertainties of the legal protection the patent affords, uncertainties that a better-designed system might diminish. But the injustices Machlup describes are basically the injustices of the market system. For the deserving but unrewarded we must have some other system, outside the market, to finance and reward their generation of unpatentable great ideas. As for the undeserving but heavily rewarded, every economy in the world abounds with them. True, the patent may further enhance their rewards; but to the extent the patent is responsible for their inventions, the high profits represent no net cost to society.

The same observation applies to Melman's arresting contention that the patent system encourages secrecy and incomplete disclosure of technological information—the very opposite of its intended effect. His argument, convincingly documented, is that companies discourage publication or discussion of research in process until patents have issued; that applications are designed to disclose as little as possible—the proof of this is that licenses must typically arrange for provision of "know-how" as well; and that, in consequence, publication of such complementary information is often discouraged even after patents have issued.[27] It has often been observed that the social contribution of a patent system in persuading inventors to disclose what they have found can easily be exaggerated: companies presumably keep secret whatever they can and patent what they cannot; the recourse to greater secrecy, which it is almost universally conceded they would attempt in the absence of a patent system,[28] would therefore be largely futile.

Here again, certain valid criticisms are suggested: patents ought obviously not to be granted except upon full disclosure, as the law actually but ineffectually provides; and the 17-year term is too high a price to pay for disclosure of what inventors could not keep secret anyhow. But the tendency of companies to try to keep their results secret is the fault not of the patent system but of capitalism.* To the extent we rely on private investors for innovation, it is necessary to permit them somehow to reap the rewards of their efforts. And if they

* Of course, economic Commissars might try to do the same, so as to show better results than their competitors; but it would presumably be government policy in a collectivist economy to insist on the fullest and most rapid possible disclosure of technological information.

can protect what they find *neither* by patents *nor* by secrecy and society is unwilling to reward them with cash grants *ex post,* as Polanyi has urged, the incentive to innovation may be impaired. The effect of the patent system is unquestionably to encourage firms to seek one form of protection rather than another. If the free, unrestricted pursuit and exchange of pure scientific knowledge is essential to technological progress, and private business firms do not find it profitable, the remedy is not to abolish the patent system but to supplement it with other, non-capitalistic methods of promoting research, at least in fields of strong public interest.[29]

Manifestly, the critical economic question about the patent law is to what extent it induces private parties to engage in innovative activity they would not otherwise undertake, to what extent instead it genuinely enhances monopoly. Part II considers the first tendency, Part III the second. If the foregoing argument is correct, these are merely two sides of the same coin: the stronger the first tendency the weaker is the second. The present state of knowledge permits only the vaguest general answers to these questions. A more modest but more manageable question might be whether the patent law might be altered to strengthen the first tendency and correspondingly to weaken the second.[30] The remainder of this essay summarizes the evidence bearing on these questions and surveys some of the main ways in which various countries have attempted so to fashion their patent laws as to maximize the net social advantage derived from them.

II. The Patent and Innovation

The presence or absence of a patent law is not, of course, the principal determinant of a country's technological progressiveness. Even within this country, a full three-fifths of the research and development effort is financed by agencies—preponderantly the Federal Government, and to a much smaller extent the universities—for whom patents cannot possibly be an important consideration.[31] As for commercially-financed innovational activity, its sharp increase in recent decades, both absolutely and relative to gross national product,[32] has occurred within the framework of a patent law that has if anything become less generous in its rewards: there has been a markedly increased tendency since the 1920's for the United States Courts to strike down patents presented to them for adjudication,[33] and to draw more tightly the legally permissible boundaries of the privilege.

Indeed, it has been widely remarked that the enormous expansion of these efforts, as well as the spread of industrialism generally in the last century, has been accompanied by secular stagnation in the resort to patenting in all major industrialized countries: patent applications per capita levelled off in the latter portion of the 19th century and have declined sharply since the 1920's.[34] The significance of this phenomenon is not certain. It may indicate, as Gilfillan, Dirlam and Melman strongly assert, that the ratio of patented to non-patented invention has declined, attesting to a diminishing importance of the patent for innovation.[35] It may reflect instead a declining ratio of results to efforts, and therefore permit of no such inference.[36] The first inference seems more likely than the second. The soaring research expenditures of private industry hardly suggest that the results have been progressively disappointing. The long run stability, especially since World War I, in the annual percentage increase in productivity per weighted unit of labor and tangible capital input combined[37] suggests a sustained level of innovative results despite the sharp decrease in per capita patent applications. True, the productivity figures do not show strong evidence of the expanded research and development efforts since the 1930's; but it is doubtful that gross national product figures reflect the welfare contribution of product innovation, to which so much of these efforts have been applied. It seems probable thus that even apart from the great increase in non-profit research, the patent has in recent decades been a decreasingly important stimulus to innovative effort. It does not follow, of course, that it has become unimportant.

Case studies of individual industries and inventions present a mixed picture of the role of patents. Their influence clearly varies from one phase of the innovation process to another, from one kind of innovation to another, from one industry to another, and from one inventor to another. Patent protection has probably been more important to financial backers than to individual inventors; to the corporate employer than to the salaried professional. It apparently counts for little where innovation takes the form of frequent changes in models and styles, where a head start of a month or a year makes the difference between competitive success and failure; or where inventions can be kept secret. It has been more important where results are readily patentable—like antibiotic drugs—than where they are not; for firms whether small or large entering a new field than for companies already established in a field; for radical inventions requiring lengthy and expensive development.

The United Shoe Machinery Corporation has made vigorous use of patents to protect its inventions and market position. Manufacturers of machine tools and textile machinery apparently place less reliance on them in the steady perfection of their products.[38] In aircraft engines, the need for such protection has been asserted much more emphatically by manufacturers of specialized accessories than by the engine builders, just as in automobiles, suppliers of parts seem to be far more patent-conscious than the car manufacturers themselves;[39] but Whittle could not have raised capital for developing his turbojet without it.[40] The prospect of patents could not have been significant to Herz and Lodge in their original scientific work on the principles of wireless. But, in Maclaurin's opinion, it was an important stimulus after 1900 to the individual inventors and their financial backers, as patent protection was also to the backers of Philo Farnsworth in television, to R.C.A. in authorizing the large, long-drawn out and critically successful expenditures in the same field, and to General Electric and Westinghouse in entering the radio field. It was of less importance to the American Telephone and Telegraph Corporation, which would in any event have been impelled to work in the wireless field because of the threat to the company's position in wire telephony.[41] Patents were similarly important in the development of the electric lamps. But Bright makes it very clear that their social contribution was far greater in the protection they gave to the individual inventors who made the radical contributions in the early years than thereafter in buttressing and extending the monopoly of General Electric, whose contributions were mainly product and process improvements, and whose patent position seriously interfered with competitive research.[42] The electronics, chemical and drug companies make heavy use of patents; rubber, paper, and heavy and light machinery manufacturers do not.[43]

When specifically asked about the "importance of patents" to them, some 11 per cent of the patent-owning corporations responding to a questionnaire circulated by students at the Harvard Business School said they were extremely important—a representative of the Polaroid Corporation said "patents are our life blood." Another 22 per cent said they were "not very important"; but two-fifths of the latter said patents had played a major role in their earlier history. The rest of the respondents fell somewhere in between, all agreeing, however, that patents were not "of primary importance."[44] Approximately half of the respondents to a survey of their clients conducted by the members of the Patent Bar Association of Los Angeles said they would engage in less research and development if patent protection were unavailable; significantly, this was the response of 27 out of 34 individual inventors, 74 out of 141 firms with less than 100 employees, but only 35 of the 105 larger companies.[45]

The critical economic question is the elasticity of supply of commercial inventive efforts to greater or lesser patent protection. A plausible argument can be made that it is relatively low. Most companies—and something like 60 per cent of all patents are taken out by corporations or assigned to them[46]—seem to respond that patents are not the critical goal or determinant of their innovative efforts, that innovation recommends itself to them for familiar competitive or other commercial considerations.[47] The large established companies that do most of it would seem to have sufficient resources (consider that they can charge research expenditures against current income in computing their 52 per cent income tax liability), sufficient insulation of market position, sufficient incentives to engage in product-differentiating, as well as production-cost-reducing, innovation, and a sufficient recognition of the contribution of such efforts to long-term growth, to continue them at not much less than the present level, even if the patent law were flatly repealed.[48]

What is impossible to tell, however, is to what extent competitive pressures would continue to impel firms into heavy research and development expenditures if neither they nor their competitors had the inducements and protections of the patent. Just as one must be suspicious of answers to questionnaires that the respondent firms depend heavily on patents—as indeed one would expect them to do so long as patents are available—as guides to how they would act if patents were not available, so one must be equally skeptical of responses that emphasize the superior pressures of competition, in a general context in which patent protection is available to all, as a guide to how companies would act in a different context. Even for entrenched oligopolists, competing strenuously in product innovation, the loss of patent protection would surely militate against certain long-range, risky ventures whose results if successful could easily be copied.[49]

As for individual inventors who have continued for at least two decades, without apparent trend, to take out 40 per cent of total United States patents issued annually,[50] there is strong positive evidence of the important contribution patents make in motivating them and their financial backers. It is not necessary to agree completely with the exaggerated evaluation Jewkes, Sawers and Stillerman place on the contribution of the individual inventor today[51] to regard this fact as establishing a strong continuing contribution of patents to innovations in the modern economy. This is not to deny that the system often does a very poor and unfair job of protecting and rewarding the individual inventor and that it may even be said to tend to give the most effective protection to the powerful companies who need it least. But if it rewards some and motivates many—as it undoubtedly does[52]—the patent may still perform an important social function. As Machlup suggests, one of the strongest possible defenses of the system is that it permits society to take advantage of the overoptimism of inventors; we get a bargain precisely because the patent does a better job of motivating than fairly rewarding the individual inventor.[53]

To emphasize the importance of the patent reward in motivating the efforts of the individual inventor or firm might seem to conflict with the conception of technological progress as an organic, collaborative social process—a conception which the present writer has set forth, drawing on Ogburn, Gilfillan, Usher, and Veblen:

> "But the basic assumption behind the patent law is not economic, but technological. In order to look upon a single inventive contribution as patentable and exploitable, one must look upon each invention as an entity, self-contained and distinct from all others.... The progress of science and the arts is, therefore, conceived to be a series of fortuitous self-contained innovations (steamship, steam engine, locomotive) which are the singlehanded contributions of geniuses (Fulton, Watt, Stephenson). If the patentee had not made this particular synthesis, no one else would have made it, and society loses nothing when it grants the patentee his monopoly. Invention is, in short, not an organic cooperative process... but... an unpredictable patchwork of random formulations.
>
> "And yet the interpretation of all social institutions as the end-results of an impersonal evolutionary process marked by gradual accretion... has become part of the common sense of modern science. Social change... is conceived of as a group process, the unfolding of an "organism" which contains within itself the dynamic factors that make for constant cumulative movement. Each novel element arises inevitably from the past and itself sets up a complex interplay of causes and effects which in turn induce still further change. These novel elements are what we call inventions. They are, of course, created by individuals; but these individuals merely make explicit what was already implicit in the technological organism... Strictly speaking, no individual makes an invention, in the usual connotation of the term. For the object

> which, for linguistic convenience, we call an automobile, a telephone, as if it were an entity, is, as a matter of fact, the aggregate of an almost infinite number of individual units of invention, each of them the contribution of a separate person....
>
> "Invention, or any particular invention, is then a social growth and adheres to certain fairly definite patterns of impersonal causation. To say that no single inventor is indispensable—is it not to say that inventions are inevitable?"[54]

It does not follow that the patent is unimportant, if not for the inventive *conception*, then for the inventive effort and the innovation *investment* (and it is often difficult, especially in the modern research laboratory, to tell where one leaves off and the other begins).

> "This especially must be understood about the "law" of inevitable invention. It does not operate *in vacuo*.... We cannot reason that since inventions are inevitable we need no system for rewarding inventors. Any given invention may be regarded as inevitable only given a certain set of social conditions: among them the prior art, the amount of social encouragement, the social need... Other things being equal, when the state of the industrial arts is adequate, and when the need is perceived by a number of people, the required invention will be forthcoming. The patent system is one of these 'other things'."[55]

It is only when "viewed from a high perspective," Maclaurin contends, that technological change appears as a completely smooth process the inevitability of whose course can be taken for granted. Particular innovations often await the right combination of creative vision and action; radical innovation usually calls for new men, new firms, new money, for whom the patent may provide an indispensible protection.[56]

In sum: government-financed and university research do not depend primarily on patents. Nor does a great deal of private, commercial innovation, the results of which are often non-patentable, or more profitably kept secret.[57] But the fact that the patent incentive is unnecessary in the public sector of the economy does not demonstrate that it is likewise unnecessary in the private. And within the private sector, the fact that certain kinds of invention do not require the patent in no way proves that other kinds do not require it either. The area in which the patent is effective is clearly far narrower than most defenders of the system seem to say; but there is no basis for concluding it is unimportant.

III. The Patent and Monopoly

The first, direct monopolistic consequence of the patent is the retarded exploitation of the invention it covers. As we have already observed, this effect does not give rise to a net social loss, provided patents are granted only for inventions that would not appear in the absence of this or some other, equally costly alternative system for encouraging innovation. Since we have now concluded that the patent does make an important net contribution to the incentive of private investors and business men to innovate, it follows that if a properly administered patent system—that is, one which confers this legal right to exclude only for types or classes of invention that would not otherwise appear—has a net monopolistic effect, it must be because it entails large second- and third-order costs—interference with additional innovation by others, and the extension of monopoly beyond the patented contribution. The significant question then is not whether patents delay exploitation of successful individual inventions—that is inevitable—but whether they produce blockaded entry and monopoly to an unworkable degree in some market more broadly defined.

These observations suggest that to the extent the suppression of inventions, which it is widely believed the patent system makes possible, amounts to nothing more than an inventor's slower-than-optimal exploitation of an individual invention that is truly "his," in the sense above-defined, it is not ordinarily a matter of concern.[58] What greatly accentuates the possibility of net social loss is suppression or insufficient exploitation out of deference to a preexisting monopoly position outside the scope of the patent. Suppose for example that the patent covers a novel production process, lower in average total cost than the old but not below its average variable cost (at which point it would pay even a monopolist to introduce it).[59] Under preexisting conditions of pure competition in the product market, the new process would not be suppressed. The monopolist-patentee might retard its introduction in order to protect his investment in the old. The patent on the new invention, of course, makes the suppression possible, but what increases the cost to society is not the patent itself but its ownership by a monopolist. Where the preexisting monopoly is itself based on patents, the evil consists in the concentrated control over competing patents in the hands of a single owner.

Patent "suppression" of the first order is undoubtedly widespread;

the ability to practice it is the essence of the patent privilege. The very high rates of return, before the basic patents expired, on rayon,[60] cellophane,[61] electric lamps[62] and the newer antibiotics[63] manifestly reflect this phenomenon.

The real issue over alleged suppression concerns the frequency of retardation of the second order, to protect some other monopoly position. In view of the ubiquitousness of monopoly elements in the economy, it would be amazing if secondary retardation as well were not widely practiced. Is has taken several forms. (1) Monopolists have delayed or declined to introduce the new because of their own equities in the old, probably more typically out of simple conservatism or myopia than with deliberate intent to suppress competitive inventions of proved commercial feasibility.[64] (2) Dominant firms individually or collusively have acquired competing patents, less often again to suppress completely something new and better than to control or share in its exploitation.[65] (3) Dominant firms have bought off the competition of a patented process by supplying its owners on unusually favorable terms with requirements they threatened to produce for themselves.[66]

The most serious monopolistic consequences of patents, thus, arise not so much from the possession of individual patents by individual innovating companies, as from the concentration of control over numerous overlapping patents, or the combination of patents with preexisting monopoly.

Moreover, when individual companies have piled patents on patents to an extent sufficient to confer on them monopoly power objectionable in its scope and duration, they have rarely done so by virtue of their own innovating efforts exclusively. The fifty year monopoly of the Aluminum Corporation of America was based originally on the Hall patent; but at the very outset Alcoa's predecessor company was involved in strenuous competition and infringement litigation with the Cowles brothers, and when finally it was held to have infringed the competitive Bradley patent, it purchased the patent for $1,429,000 plus royalties. In so doing, according to Donald Wallace, it obtained a few additional years of legal protection for its monopoly at a time when opportunities for competitive entry were but for that obstacle "perhaps more favorable than they have ever been since."[67] United Shoe Machinery was formed by the merger of several companies, each with controlling patents; and it continued thereafter vigorously to buy up competing patents. The Radio Corporation of America was the patent beneficiary in the American radio field of all the giants in electronics. General Electric's long-continued use of patents to dominate the production of electric lamps owed much to the company's own research; but it owed much also to patent diplomacy and, after the expiration of the important improvement patents in the early 1930's, to a system of domestic and international cross-licensing agreements.[68] According to the Government complaint, the International Business Machines Corp. has "systematically acquired developments, inventions, and patents made or owned by others relating in any way to tabulating machines..."[69] Similar observations can be made about the patterns of market concentration in plate glass, photographic equipment, mimeographing equipment and supplies, and concrete-block machinery.[70] And, of course, it was patent diplomacy rather than the innovations of any single company that produced industry-wide monopoly in glass containers, explosives, petroleum refining, bathtubs, titanium, gypsum, dyestuffs, plastics, fertilizers and the others whose records of industry-wide cartelization-by-patent have been graphically detailed in antitrust proceedings.

If patents contribute to monopoly, patent-induced innovation helps break it down. The question is whether, under these conflicting influences, competition is workable in "the market", appropriately defined. A definition of the market confined to the individual patent is meaninglessly narrow for this purpose; "the business of inventing and patenting" is obviously too broad: the inventor of a triangular doorknob poses no significant limit to the social cost of a patent on the transistor. The question can be answered only with reference to "industries," and the answer will inevitably vary from one to another.

Can we draw no conclusions about the net effect of the patent system on competition in the economy at large? There are various possible approaches to an answer. One might, for example, compare various aspects of the performance of two samples of industries making heavy and light use of patents respectively—perhaps drugs, chemicals, and electronics on the one hand, tires, paper, machinery and automobiles on the other. The rate of profits of the former group has since World War II run consistently above that of the first three of the latter group, as well as above the average for all manufacturing,[71] and there can be little doubt that the protection of patents has contributed importantly to this result. That competitive entry into the business of inventing and patenting in the first group was insufficiently effective to eradicate supernormal profits is not necessarily contradicted by the equally high or higher profits in automobiles,[72] for which other explanations are readily available. But the critical question is whether supernormal profits are the necessary price of competitive innovation. The answer depends on how the innovative record of these industries would look in the absence of patents, a question there is no way of answering in such general terms.

Ineffective competition attributable to patents may be reflected also in wasteful expenditures on duplicative research, just as in drugs it is apparently reflected in excessive selling costs. We have already considered this possibility and concluded that some such tendency almost certainly prevails. But we lack any quantitative basis for indicating its importance; and we have no way of determining whether such waste is too high a price to pay for patent-induced innovation, in the absence of some other system under capitalism that could achieve the benefit without entailing the cost.

Another possible approach would be to make a cross-sectional study of all industry, to appraise the importance of patents among other sources of monopoly at a given point of time. Bain has made a limited though significant effort along these lines, attempting to measure barriers to entry in a sample of twenty American manufacturing industries. Patents played a significant role in almost none of the twenty at the time of his study.[73] Such a static approach would, however, miss the possible effect of patents in helping importantly to fasten upon some of these industries at a critical historical juncture a pattern of concentration that persisted thereafter for other reasons. This has undoubtedly been the case in aluminum, shoe machinery, plate glass, photographic equipment and supplies, Ethyl fluid, braking systems, and, among Bain's industries, at least gypsum products, cigarettes, rayon, and cans. On the other hand, as our discussion in Part II above has already suggested, the positive contribution of patents is likely also to have been relatively great in the early stages of an industry's growth; and patents at times also afford vital protection to new entrants into an established field.

A more modest effort would be to assess the role of patents in antitrust law violations. Cases importantly involving patents have accounted for a large proportion of the total, something like thirty to forty per cent in the five-year period 1952–56, for example.[74] However, this numerical comparison apparently exaggerates the relative importance of patents as a source of the monopoly problem, for several reasons. First, patent transgressions, usually involving restrictive licensing agreements or patent acquisitions, have proved far more vulnerable to antitrust prosecution than most other forms or sources of monopoly power. Second, even in the patent cases, the Government seems all too often to have seized upon the overt patent offenses and settled for patent remedies when there were other, more important sources of monopoly, calling for other remedies more difficult to achieve.[75] The notorious consent settlement of the divestiture suit against AT & T and Western Electric is an excellent example.[76] In any event, a survey of cases in which patents have been instrumental in anti-competitive restraints does not, of course, provide a balanced picture of their net effect on competition in the economy generally. The search for any simple answer to the latter question ends inevitably in frustration.

The foregoing considerations, though necessarily indecisive, seem nevertheless to justify the following conclusions. (1) The net effect of patents on competition will vary from one situation to another; no assessment is possible except in individual markets. (2) One cannot conclude that the patent system is so inherently monopolistic that its major effect is to suppress competition, or (3) that it is a major source of monopoly in the economy today. (4) Yet patents have had as one of their effects at one time or another in a exceedingly large number of markets the suppression or discouragement of competition beyond the scope of the individual inventive contributions they severally represented. (5) This effect has typically been felt where patents were controlled by firms with preexisting monopoly power, or where several patents were subjected to unitary control—and especially where several owners put their patents together.

IV. Striking the Balance

The granting of patents is a matter not of private right but of public convenience. The Statute on Monopolies sanctioned their issuance only on condition that they be not contrary to the law, nor mischievous to the state, by raising of the price of commodities at home, or hurt of trade, or generally inconvenient...

The methods of asserting and protecting the superior public interest may with some oversimplification be classified under two headings: those embodied in procedures for issuing and enforcing patents; and substantive limitations on the legal scope of the patent privilege, including provisions for modifying or rescinding it if need be.

The procedures of staking out and enforcing property rights in the field of ideas are inevitably highly complex. There are significant variations from one country to another in the level of fees; the intensity of examinations of the prior art before patents are issued; the treatment of so-called interferences in the Patent Office between one patent application and either another application or an issued patent; provisions for opposition proceedings, in which interested parties may contest a patent application; opportunities for dilatory tactics in prosecuting applications, by mean of which applicants have extended their period of effective protection; and methods of trying infringement suits, whether in the regular or in special courts, and for protecting business firms against harassing threats of infringement litigation.[78]

The substantial economic importance of provisions like these has already been indirectly emphasized. The social costs of the patent are not worth paying except for a genuinely novel contribution: so the laws (or the administrative or judicial interpretations thereof) typically set forth a standard of patentable invention which requires a demonstration or claim of novelty.[79] They are worth paying only for the inventive contribution, nothing more; applications may, therefore, be denied or patents subsequently voided for claiming too much, or their enforceable scope restricted to the novel elements. And American courts will not enforce contracts by means of which patentees attempt to expand the effective scope of their monopoly by tying sales, leases or licenses of patented products or processes to the purchase of unpatented goods or services.[80] The patent is a reward for prompt disclosure. The failure to disclose related technical information sufficient to enable one "skilled in the art" to duplicate the invention, or the undue delay of an application, will therefore in theory result in a denial of the application or a subsequent declaration of invalidity.[81] Actual practice, as we have already noted, falls far short of this ideal.

The original term of the patent in England was fourteen years, time to train two sets of apprentices; the present American seventeen years resulted from a simple compromise when a provision permitting extension for an additional seven years proved unworkable. Most of the major industrialized countries fall within the 14 to 20 year range. Most observers agree that a term settled on for such reasons, so long ago, would only by the remotest coincidence be appropriate under modern conditions; but few speak very convincingly about what period *would* be appropriate today. Hamilton suggests that the increased pace of technological change—a condition itself probably very difficult to document—means that seventeen years is unnecessarily long.[82] Machlup leans in the same direction, mainly on the ground that the value of protection many years hence—say in the twelfth to seventeen year of the patent—cannot be too influential a consideration motivating innovative effort today, because (1) of the slight (discounted) present value of benefits so far in the future,* (2) the fact that "circum-invention" in any event deprives patents of most of their economic value before their legal term has expired, and (3) the longer the patent period, the harder competitors will strive to "circum-invent" and the sooner on the average they will therefore succeed.[83] The third reason is most unconvincing, and in fact seems to conflict with the first: the possibility of having a patented invention available to them in seventeen rather than twelve years ought to have no greater current effect on competitors' efforts to "circum-invent" than the longer prospective term has in motivating inventors themselves. Moreover, to the extent Machlup's second observation is valid the real social cost of the last five years of the patent is slight anyhow, while its benefit may still be high; so long as the average inventor errs on the optimistic side in appraising the possible gains of the last years, society gets a bargain in seeming to offer them.[84]

The reason why arguments for changing the patent term are usually unconvincing is suggested by our earlier conclusions: the impossibility of making a general determination, valid for all circumstances, concerning the effect of patents on invention on the one hand and competition on the other has as its necessary counterpart the impossibility of concluding with assurance that a single term shorter or longer by so many years would produce a superior result. Agreement seems to be much more general about the desirability of devising periods of varying length for different major categories of invention. The economic virtue of such flexibility is that at least in principle it permits a closer approximation to the kind of monopsonistic social price discrimination alluded to in Part I, above. We may not be able to ascertain whether a uniform period of ten or twenty-four years would be superior in its net effect, but we can be reasonably certain that seventeen is an unnecessarily high price for society to pay in some cases, an inadequate one in others. Certain kinds of invention typically involve less risk,

* It might appear that a similar discounting process would correspondingly reduce the present value of the costs to society of the last five years' protection, but it does not. Society is paying those costs *today* on patents in their thirteenth to seventeenth years in order to persuade inventors to continue their efforts, on the strength of an anticipation of similar *future* returns on anything they may discover and patent.

uncertainty and effort than others, and can safely be given shorter patents in recognition of this fact.[85] Correspondingly, it would be appropriate to provide patent terms longer than the present uniform period for certain inventions—unless society preferred to provide some other inducement or reward in such instances.

Much of what such a reform would seek to achieve is in fact accomplished by the market itself: ordinarily the kind of invention that would qualify for shorter-period protection is in any event quickly outdated or circumvented. Its major contribution would be to reduce the possibly obstructive and monopolistic influence of sheer masses of patents regardless of their individual merits. England, Germany and several other countries apparently achieve a similar result by imposing annual, progressive taxes on patents. Germany's reach a cumulative total of no less than DM 10,230 over the full eighteen year term; they are reduced, however, if the owner endorses the patent, indicating that it is available for licensing. The result is said to be a very high percentage of lapses.[86] The American law, in contrast, requires no more than the $20 filing fee. The graduated tax does not achieve all the purposes served by varying terms; it presumably permits the continuation of obstructive patents that remain on that account valuable to their owners. The two reforms are not mutually exclusive; the case would seem to be strong for adopting both.*

The legal standard of invention is the other side of the coin. If certain inventive contributions require or merit a less generous bundle of privileges than others, then for any given patent term certain inventions require and deserve protection, others do not. The difficulties of determining from a bare patent application whether or not it reflects "genuine invention" or the use of mere technical skill, the definitions of utility and novelty (both of which are prerequisites to patentability), the comparative merits of subjective, "flash of genius" as contrasted with objective tests have all been too thoroughly canvassed elsewhere to call for summary here.[87] As long as there is to be a patent system, or any other system of rewards for that matter, the line must somehow be drawn. It is difficult to set forth any economic principles for drawing it other than the truisms that (a) only those inventions should be permitted to pass the test that require patents to elicit them and that are worth the costs such patents impose on society,[88] and (b) society could

* The graduated tax might be excessively onerous for the individual inventor who requires time to get into commercial production. It might therefore be imposed only on corporations holding patents in excess of a given number.

do a better job if it were not limited, as under the United States patent law, to granting seventeen-year protection or none.[89]

The laws of almost all countries except the United States explicitly preclude the issuance of patents for certain kinds of inventions. The apparently universal preclusion of inventions whose exploitation would be contrary to law, morality, public health or national security requires no additional comment. The denial of patents in most countries on medicines, articles of food, or chemical compounds are more intriguing, since they appear to involve a serious contradiction. The rationale must be that the dangers of monopolistic retardation are intolerable in areas so closely affecting the public interest. But by the same scheme of values, technological progress in these areas ought to be exceptionally desirable. If the patent system is conducive to such progress, it makes little sense for society to refuse to pay the price when the public benefits are greatest; if it is not, there would seem to be little point in having a patent system anywhere. The only possible reconciliation, which does in fact find some support in practice, is that in areas of such general social interest society prefers to pay the price in other ways—for example, by taxpayer-financed research, public awards, or very indirectly by protective tariffs. We have already outlined the sound economic logic supporting the first two courses.

The most common substantive limitation on the patent—every major capitalist country imposes it except the United States—is the obligation that it be worked within a reasonable period of time, typically three years, after issuance. Non-working is ordinarily defined as failing to meet demand "to an adequate extent" or "on reasonable terms" by production within the host country. The typical remedy used to be revocation of the patent; today it is compulsory licensing of all qualified applicants at reasonable royalty.

Where, as is often the case, patents are not worked because the inventions they cover are as yet commercially impracticable, it would be both unfair and in conflict with the purposes of the patent grant to rescind them. Moreover, while patents have often been used to prevent the installation of production facilities within the host country, working provisions directed against such practices might well conflict with the principle of comparative advantage. Where the sanction is merely compulsory licensing, however, these objections lose much of their force.[90] If a patent is not worked, it is because the owner either (1) sees no commercial point or possibility of doing so, considering the invention entirely apart from the effect its exploitation would have on profits elsewhere, or (2) is protecting some other monopoly position. If the reason is the first one, compulsory licensing will have no effect or will confer on the patentee an income that he was unable to earn by his own efforts alone. Particularly if the owner is permitted several years in which to find a use for his own exclusive exploitation, he can hardly object to either of these outcomes. If the reason is the second one, non-working involves one of the second- and third-order monopoly costs to society analyzed in Part III above—the protection or preservation of some preexisting monopoly position. In this event, compulsory licensing restores to patent-induced innovation its proper, competitive function of breaking down rather than preserving monopoly.

The one possible danger of such provisions is that they might in principle be used to attack inventors merely for a slower-than-purely-competitive exploitation of what they have invented. The experience is if anything excessively reassuring on this score. The Canadian law calls for the widest possible use of the invention, but "consistent with the patentee deriving a reasonable advantage" from it; the British law has a similar provision.[91] The courts have been reluctant to decree compulsory licensing merely because prices charged by the patentee were high,[92] and in fact the number of such decrees has been very small. While the number of judgments probably does not fully reflect the salutary effect on business practice of the mere existence of such legal sanctions, it does seem to indicate they have not produced a serious infringement of the patent privilege or impairment of its social usefulness.[93]

The various national laws provide for compulsory licensing of qualified applicants under other circumstances as well. One common occasion is when it is found one patent cannot be practiced without conflicting with another, and particularly when the one covers a notable improvement of the other. Several countries provide also for compulsory licensing of all patents involving food, drugs and chemicals, a provision superior to a flat prohibition of patents in these fields, it would seem, for the reason already indicated. Finally, several of the laws provide for compulsory licensing whenever the "public interest" requires it. Notable examples are those of Switzerland, Holland, Austria and Germany. Such provisions have been successfully invoked when the inventions in question promised to improve the balance of trade, enhance employment, "promote the safety and rationalization of industrial production," or contribute to public health.[94] The criteria seem broad enough to cover all patents of significance, but the provision has been applied sparingly, and compulsory licensing has been decreed only upon a showing that the public interest was importantly involved.[95]

The point is often made by both critics and defenders of the American patent system that the law of this country is unique in its failure to impose limitations of these kinds on the patent privilege. These observations have some substantial validity; but no conclusion is possible until one takes into account the unusually active application of the American antitrust laws to patents, and the unusually well-developed doctrine of patent misuse developed in its courts. As for the first, the Department of Justice obtained patent relief—almost invariably compulsory licensing, and in about half the cases royalty-free for at least some of the patents involved—in no less than 107 suits terminated between August 1941 and January 1959.[96] As for the second, the courts have come generally to refuse to enforce against alleged infringers patents that have been employed by their owners to effect a restraint on competition extending beyond the scope of the patent itself.[97] Finally, where the government itself finances research and development, as in atomic energy, medicine, public health or defense, there are various, and incidentally varying and not at all consistent, limitations imposed on the opportunity of private contractors to take out unrestricted, exclusive patent rights over the technology thus developed.[98]

But these limitations fall considerably short of what is at least theoretically possible in most other countries. The reasons are instructive. The American antitrust laws strike at excessive monopoly power, patent-based or otherwise, only when acquired or maintained by combination or oppression of rivals. Neither they nor the doctrine of patent misuse permit an appraisal of the economic results from the standpoint of the consumer, but only of whether monopoly power has been employed in such a way as to exclude others from a fair opportunity to compete. In short, the test of legality is not market structure or economic performance but market behavior or conduct.[99]

Thus the individual company may take out patents without limit, and without the penalty of the progressive taxes to which such ownership is subject in England and Germany. It may acquire the patents of others, provided this course of action is not construed as part of a deliberate policy of seeking or preserving monopoly. It may work its patents or not, license them or not, as it chooses. If it issues licenses it may limit the quantities and delimit the markets in which the licensee may sell, specify his prices, and require him in exchange to grant back a license under any patents he develops. In all cases, according to the legal rationalization, the patent owner is merely sharing with others, in proportions and for a quid pro quo which he is free to determine, a legal monopoly that he is perfectly free not to share at all if he chooses. The patentee may *exchange* licenses with such other patent owners as he chooses. In this event, the various above-mentioned restrictions may not be imposed on competition between the parties, because they take on the character of collusive restraints of trade;[100] but merely by making available to each of the participants all the patents of all the members, the patent pool still strengthens the competitive position of the members against non-members, and contributes to a community of interest among them. Moreover, by agreeing to take out a license rather than contest a patent whose validity it considers doubtful, a potential competitor may legally accept output, price and market limitations, and thus in effect enter into a cartel agreement with the patent owner—unless the government can prove that they entered into a conspiracy to do so.[101]

If our conclusions of Part I–III, above, are correct, a strong case can be made for the American antitrust approach to the problem of patent-based monopoly. Monopoly control over the individual inventive contribution may be essential for certain kinds of competitive innovation under capitalism. The antitrust laws have no quarrel with market power achieved in this manner. Society's major protection against paying too high a price in the primary exploitation of the patent must be in the standards it sets for patentable invention; or, where it is unwilling to pay even this price, in using taxpayers' resources to finance the innovation directly, rather than rely on the profit motive. The major monopoly problem, we concluded, arises out of the piling of patents on patents, far more as a result of diplomacy, combination and acquisition than the unassisted inventive efforts of the individual company. It is precisely against such combinations that the antitrust laws are directed.

This is not to say that they might not well be strengthened along these very lines. It is not clear that the benefits of permitting an individual patent owner to license others selectively, attaching restrictions on price or output, outweigh the disadvantages of permitting potential or actual competitors to be brought in this way into a common, patent-protected community of interest. Owners of conflicting or interdependent patents must, of course, be permitted to pool them; but here again the consequences for competition among themselves and with outsiders, already suggested, indicate it might be desirable in this event to require compulsory licensing of all applicants, at least where the participants enjoy a dominant position in the market.[102] If patent owners find it preferable to foreswear solitary, competitive exploitation of their inventions and resort instead to patent diplomacy, such diplomacy ought perhaps to be required to be "open." By the same token, dominant firms might be more strictly denied the right to purchase the patents of others; or, alternatively, required in that event to offer licenses to all applicants under patents so acquired.

Reforms of this sort would not be costless. They might discourage the salutary exchange of licenses, abandonment of costly infringement litigation, and acquisition of patents by those who can make the best use of them. The net effect would be somewhat less technological collaboration—how much it is impossible to say—but also more competitive innovation and exploitation.[103] In this writer's judgment the benefits would outweigh the costs: if cartelization were truly necessary for technological progress, it would be necessary to reexamine the entire philosophic basis of not just the patent law but capitalism itself.

No single reform of the patent system is likely to produce superior results in all situations; neither does the system as it now stands. While thus it is possible to devise modest general changes in the law, like those mentioned at various points in this paper, that offer a probability of doing more good than harm in most instances, in the end the optimum social policy must provide for flexibility and selectivity. One instance of such a policy is direct governmental conduct and support or reward of research and innovation in areas of basic public concern. Another is the provision in most countries for compulsory licensing in extreme instances where patents are unworked or interdependent, or where for whatever reason the monopoly costs prove unacceptably high. Even where the patent laws contain no explicit proviso, there is always the right of eminent domain to assert the superiority of the public interest if need be. A freer resort to public purchase with compensation could provide a more felicitous balance than we now have between reliance on patents for most commercial research, and placing technological knowledge in the public domain where it is most clearly in the public interest to do so. Given such safeguards and alternatives, to be applied when the occasion demands, it is difficult to envisage any alternative within the framework of a capitalist economy superior to the patent system for commercial innovation generally.

NOTES

1. I should like to acknowledge with gratitude the assistance of my graduate student, Mr. Laurence Rosenberg.
2. *United States Code*, Title 15, Sec. 31.
3. *The Statute of Monopolies*, 21 Jac. 1, ch. 3, 1623, as reproduced in ANTHONY W. DELLER, *Walker on Patents*, Deller's Edition, New York: Baker, Voorhis and Co., 1937, p. 20. The laws of other capitalist countries are basically the same, although there are important differences in detail; see Part IV below.
4. *Darcy v. Allein*, 11 Coke 84b, K.B. 1602, as reported in Noy's Reports 1656, p. 182. The historic case of the *Clothworkers of Ipswich* adds that patents are permissible also "if a man hath made a new discovery." DELLER, *op. cit.*, p. 17.
5. For an annotated summary of these arguments, see FRITZ MACHLUP and EDITH PENROSE, "The Patent Controversy in the Nineteenth Century", *Journal of Economic History*, vol. 10, May, 1950, pp. 1–29, and MACHLUP, *An Economic Review of the Patent System*, U.S. Senate, Committee on the Judiciary, Subcommittee on Patents, Trademarks and Copyrights, 85th Congress, 2nd Session, Study No. 15. (The above-mentioned Committee has issued a large number of these studies or monographs between 1956 and 1960; references to the individual studies henceforth will therefore be truncated.)
6. DELLER, *op. cit.*, p. 9 (stress supplied).
7. Cf. MACHLUP, *An Economic Review, op. cit.*, pp. 26 n. 141, 53–54, and ARNOLD PLANT, "The Economic Theory Concerning Patents for Inventions," *Economica*, vol. 1, February, 1934, pp. 42–43.
8. *U.S. v. E.I. du Pont de Nemours and Co.*, 76 S. Ct. 994 (1956).
9. See the dissenting opinion, *ibid.*, 1017–23; also GEORGE W. STOCKING and WILLARD F. MUELLER, "The Cellophane Case and the New Competition," *American Economic Review*, vol. 45, March, 1955, pp. 29–63.
10. JOSEPH A. SCHUMPETER, *Capitalism, Socialism and Democracy*, London: Allen & Unwin, 3rd ed., 1950, chs. 7, 8. For some interesting corroboratory illustrations, see GEORGE E. FROST, "The Patent System and the Modern Economy," Senate Patents Subcommittee, *op. cit.*, Study No. 2, pp. 4–28.
11. To some extent he was demolishing a straw man. See SHOREY PETERSON, "Antitrust and the Classic Model," *American Economic Review*, vol. 47, March, 1957, pp. 60–78.
12. See P. HENNIPMAN, "Monopoly: Impediment or Stimulus to Economic Progress?" in Edward H. Chamberlin, ed., *Monopoly and Competition and Their Regulation*, London: Macmillan, 1954, pp. 421–56.
13. See MACHLUP, *An Economic Review, op. cit.*, pp. 39–40, and especially the quotation from Joan Robinson.
14. WALTON HALE HAMILTON, *Patents and Free Enterprise*, U.S. Temporary National Economic Committee, Monograph No. 31, Washington: 1941, p. 157.
15. See MACHLUP, "The Optimum Lag of Imitation Behind Innovation," Reprint from *Festkrift til Frederick Zeuthen*, Copenhagen: 1958, pp. 239–56.
16. On the frequency of these practices, see both SEYMOUR MELMAN, "The Impact of the Patent System on Research," Senate Patents Subcommittee, *op. cit.*, Study No. 11, pp. 23, 33, and the answer to Melman, RICHARD F. CARR, "Our Patent System Works," *Patent, Trademark, and Copyright Journal*, vol. 4, Spring 1960, pp. 68–70, based on a questionnaire survey among the clients of the Los Angeles Bar. Of the respondents 43 per cent said that they had been "hindered by patent considerations" in their research activities; 67 per cent said they had at times tried to invent around the patents of others, and of the latter, 61 per cent *said*

they had achieved results superior to the patent they were trying to circumvent; 13 per cent said they had come out less well.

17. See MACHLUP, *An Economic Review*, *op. cit.*, pp. 50–52.
18. See, e.g., FLOYD L. VAUGHAN, *The United States Patent System*, Norman, Oklahoma: University of Oklahoma Press, 1956, *passim* for a thorough compendium of the literature on this subject, drawing mainly on American antitrust proceedings; CORWIN D. EDWARDS, *Maintaining Competition*, New York: McGraw-Hill, 1949, pp. 216–35; GEORGE W. STOCKING and MYRON W. WATKINS, *Monopoly and Free Enterprise*, New York: Twentieth Century Fund, 1951, ch. 14.
19. MACHLUP has drawn attention dramatically to this question, "An Economic Review," *op. cit.*, pp. 44–52.
20. See RICHARD R. NELSON, "The Economics of Invention: A Survey of the Literature," *Journal of Business*, vol. 32, April 1959, pp. 101–26, *passim;* ALBERT H. RUBENSTEIN, "Looking Around: Guide to R & D," *Harvard Business Review*, vol. 35, May-June, 1957, pp. 133–46.
21. See A. C. PIGOU, *The Economics of Welfare*, 4th ed., London, Macmillan, 1952, p. 185; MICHAEL POLANYI, "Patent Reform," *Review of Economic Studies*, vol. 11, Summer, No. 2, 1944, pp. 61–62. Plant's criticism of the effect of patents on resource allocation is based on an explicit adoption of the first assumption, and a rejection of the second: he says there is no reason why investment in innovation requires special protection as compared with any other kind of investment. *Op. cit.*, pp. 40–44.
22. PAUL SAMUELSON, "The Pure Theory of Public Expenditure," *Review of Economics and Statistics*, vol. 36, November, 1954, p. 387; see also vol. 37, November, 1955, p. 350 and vol. 40, November, 1958, p. 332–38.
23. FRANCIS BATOR, *The Question of Government Spending*, New York: Harper, 1960, pp. 99 n., 107–08. See also his "The Anatomy of Market Failure," *Quarterly Journal of Economics*, vol. 72, August, 1958, p. 351. The identical point was made by POLANYI, *op. cit.*, pp. 62, 65.
24. See JULIUS MARGOLIS, "A Comment on the Pure Theory of Public Expenditure," *Review of Economics and Statistics*, vol. 37, November, 1955, p. 347.
25. See the persuasive argument by POLANYI, *op. cit.*, pp. 65–76.
26. MACHLUP, *An Economic Review*, *op. cit.*, pp. 29–30, 54.
27. MELMAN, *op. cit.*, pp. 34–35, 46–48. See also POLANYI, *op. cit.*, pp. 71, 75–76.
28. MELMAN, *op. cit.*, pp. 50–51; CARR, *op. cit.*, pp. 62–63; JESSE W. MARKHAM, JAMES S. WORLEY and DWIGHT S. BROTHERS, "The Value of the American Patent System: An Inquiry into Possible Approaches to its Measurement," *Patent, Trademark and Copyright Journal*, vol. 1, 1957, pp. 35–36.
29. It is an interesting and important question whether patents should be employed in these areas of non-profit research. MELMAN demonstrates the genuine dangers of universities encouraging their scientists to pursue lines of inquiry that promise to produce patentable results (*op. cit.*, pp. 37–43). His exposition suggests that when universities take out patents they may not be performing their appropriate function, which ought to be the "impractical" pursuit and widest possible dissemination and utilization of knowledge.

    The question has for similar reasons come to be actively debated whether the Government should permit the issuance of patents to private contractors conducting government-financed research. The issue is one not of principle but of strategy: will private parties be willing to invest their own attention and staffs on projects from which they cannot obtain patents? The American experience with research in synthetic rubber after World War II was not encouraging on this score; seeROBERT A. SOLO, *Synthetic Rubber: A Case Study in Technological Development Under Government Direction*, Senate Patents Subcommittee, *op. cit.*, Study No. 18, ch. 9.

30. See the convincing discussion by MARKHAM *et al.*, *op. cit.*, p. 20, and especially 53–55. Also the conclusion of MACHLUP, *An Economic Review*, *op. cit.*, pp. 79–80.
31. According to the McGRAW-HILL estimates, the Federal Government financial contribution has run at 60 per cent of the total or slightly better from 1956 through 1960, with the universities and other non-profit institutions accounting for another 2 to 3 per cent. "The Enormous Growth of Research and Who Pay for It," *Business Week*, December 26, 1959, p. 51. Most of the research and development is actually conducted by private industry, however. On the basis of an estimate that private industry paid only 32 per cent of total research expenditures in 1947, and a consideration of the many kinds of private innovating activity not eventuating in patents, GILFILLAN has estimated that patents motivate only 15 to 20 per cent of research conducted today. S. C. GILFILLAN, "The Prediction of Technical Change," *Review of Economics and Statistics*, vol. 34, November, 1952, pp. 374–77. See the detailed appraisal of this figure by MARKHAM *et al.*, *op. cit.*, pp. 43–44.
32. Private expenditures on research and development, estimated at $166 million in 1930 and $234 million in 1940 (*Science and Public Policy*, A Report to the President by JOHN R. STEELMAN, Chairman, The President's Scientific Research Board, vol. I, August 27, 1947, p. 10) soared to $4.4 billion in 1959–60 (the McGRAW-HILL estimate, note 31 above), or from 0.1 and 0.2 to 0.9 per cent of GNP.
33. H. R. MAYERS, "The United States Patent System in Historical Perspective," *Patent, Trademark and Copyright Journal*, vol. 3, Spring, No. 1, 1959, pp. 33–52; also the compilation by P. J. FEDERICO, United States Senate, Committee on the Judiciary, Subcommittee on Patents, *American Patent System*, Hearings, 84th Congress, 1st Session, October 1955, p. 182. In the 1948–54 period, the Supreme Court declared invalid five of seven patents and the Courts of Appeal 269 out of the 429 that came before them; the latter courts held an additional 83 not infringed. *Ibid.*, pp. 177–78.
34. See ALFRED B. STAFFORD, "Is the Rate of Invention Declining?" *American Journal of Sociology*, vol. 57, May, 1952, p. 540; GILFILLAN, *op. cit.*, p. 376; JACOB SCHMOOKLER, "The Level of Inventive Activity," *Review of Economics and Statistics*, vol. 36, May, 1954, p. 183 and the sources cited there. OTTO J. BACHMANN *et al.* show that even in absolute figures, annual patent applications in the United States reached a peak in the 1920's and fell sharply thereafter, *Patents and the Corporation*, Boston (processed), 1958, p. 120. The recovery of the 1950's failed to reach the earlier peak.
35. GILFILLAN, *op. cit.*; JOEL B. DIRLAM, "Patents and Progress: Is Our Patent Law Obsolete?" *Dun's Review*, April, 1957, especially pp. 54, 92–94; MELMAN, *op. cit.*, pp. 24–32. This hypothesis is lent some support by the convincing and most interesting demonstration by Bachmann *et al.* that corporations in general, and those subject to compulsory licensing by virtue of antitrust decrees in particular, have had decreasing resort to patents, while showing no slackening of their research and development efforts. *Op. cit.*, pp. 121–34.
36. See STAFFORD, *op. cit.*, p. 45; JACOB SCHMOOKLER, "Patent Application Statistics as an Index of Inventive Activity," *Journal of Patent Office Society*, vol. 35, August 1953, pp. 539–50, and SCHMOOKLER, "The Level of Inventive Activity," *op. cit.*
37. SOLOMON FABRICANT, *Basic Facts on Productivity Change*, Occasional Paper, National Bureau of Economic Research, 1959, pp. 10–13 and *passim*.
38. See WILLIAM H. BROWN, "Innovation in the Machine Tool Industry," *Quarterly Journal of Economics*, vol. 71, August, 1957, pp. 406–25; "In Textile Machinery the Improvements Come Slowly," *Business Week*, June 4, 1960, pp. 88–95.
39. C. A. WELSH, "Patents and Competition in the Automobile Industry," *Law and Contemporary Problems*, vol. 13, Spring, 1948, p. 273.

40. Robert Schlaifer, *Development of Aircraft Enginess,* Boston: Harvard, 1950, pp. 103–04, 336–37.
41. W. Rupert Maclaurin, *Invention and Innovation in the Radio Industry,* New York: Macmillan, 1949, pp. 258–60; and W. Rupert Maclaurin "Patents and Technical Progress—a Study of Television," *Journal of Political Economy,* vol. 58, April, 1950, pp. 142–57.
42. Arthur Aaron Bright, *The Electric-Lamp Industry,* New York: Macmillan, 1949, pp. 468–76. For other examples, see Frost, *op. cit.,* pp. 6–19.
43. Bachmann *et al., op. cit.,* p. 107, reporting on the responses to a questionnaire.
44. *Ibid.,* p. 106.
45. Carr, *op. cit.,* p. 74.
46. P. J. Federico, *Distribution of Patents Issued to Corporations,* Senate Patent Subcommittee, *op. cit.,* Study No. 3, pp. 2–3.
47. See Bachmann *et al., op. cit.,* pp. 107–08, 122–34, 136–37; Melman, *op. cit.,* pp. 25–26, 50–56. That the majority of the respondents to the Los Angeles Bar Association survey used patents assiduously and regarded them as important for their business does not prove that they would drastically alter their operations if patents were unavailable—entirely apart from the fact that the sample was not exactly unbiassed, consisting exclusively of clients of patent attorneys. Carr, *op. cit., passim.* A similar observation applies to the finding of another survey: "all persons interviewed felt that there was a significant relationship between the patent system and research activities." Markham *et al., op. cit.,* p. 35.
48. See the observations of Robert F. Lanzillotti, *Patent, Trademark, and Copyright Journal,* vol. 3, Conference No., 1959, pp. 119–20.
49. See Bachmann, *et al., op. cit.,* pp. 137–38; also Frost, *op. cit.,* pp. 6–19, for examples, not all of them convincing. One would have thought, for instance, that the thermal cracking of petroleum (see pp. 9–10) promised large refiners such enormous cost savings and improvements in yields as to justify the research expenditures that developed it even without the protection of patents. According to the president of duPont, only one research dollar's expenditure in five pays out; if the competitor can simply appropriate the product of the one successful dollar, at a possible cost of even less, even the largest corporation would surely be dissuaded from risking the original five. Murray N. Friedman, *The Research and Development Factor in Mergers and Acquisitions,*" Senate Patent Subcommittee, *op. cit.,* Study No. 16, p.14.

   Some of the evidence Melman offers to support his conclusion to the contrary is not convincing. The fact that the large companies he interviewed were not importantly motivated in making research expenditures by the prospective income from patent licenses (*op. cit.,* pp. 25–31) does not at all demonstrate that they were not counting on the patents to protect their own exclusive exploitation of whatever they discovered; nor does the fact that these companies emphasized repeatedly that the main function of patents to them was "to protect and expand the competitive position of the firm" (*ibid.,* p. 33). Nor does the fact that the American Telephone and Telegraph and International Business Machines Corporations have expanded their research activities despite the antitrust consent decrees requiring compulsory licensing of future patents at reasonable royalties (pp. 52–53). The former is a collection of regulated monopolists the cost of whose research expenditures can be incorporated directly or indirectly in their regulated rates; it need hardly worry about rivals appropriating its ideas for exploitation in telephony (and one can for the same reason hardly explain its continued research, as Melman does, primarily in terms of "pressures for competitive product design"). IBM continues subject to competitive pressures of other firms who continue to have the patent incentive; and both it and AT & T continue to enjoy the assurance at least of royalties on what they develop in the future.

50. See FEDERICO, *op. cit.*, p. 12. On the sharp upward trend in the issuance of patents to corporations before 1940, see U.S. Temporary National Economic Committee, *Investigation of Concentration of Economic Power*, Hearings, vol. 3, Washington: 1939, p. 1127.
51. JOHN JEWKES, DAVID SAWERS, and RICHARD STILLERMAN, *The Sources of Invention*, London: Macmillan, 1958. See the review by S. C. GILFILLAN, *Current Economic Comment*, vol. 21, February, 1959, pp. 58–60. One of GILFILLAN's major criticisms is that the authors really define invention in terms of the incipient great idea, and in so doing over-estimate the importance of the individual in innovation. Interpreting the JEWKES case studies of 50 important modern inventions, and assigning fractional valuations where responsibility was divided, DANIEL J. ARNOW, an honors student of mine, found that individuals were responsible for 51 per cent, companies within the industry for 25 per cent, outside companies for 15 per cent, and universities for 9 per cent of the inventions (as the authors would define the concept), and 21 per cent, 60 per cent, 11 per cent, and 8 per cent respectively of the developmental efforts. Obviously the importance of the outside individual in the generation of ideas remains great; but in the process of innovation, the insider corporation at some point clearly takes over major responsibility.

   For a graphic account and explanation of the diminished importance of the "classical inventor" in modern technology, see MELMAN, *op. cit.*, pp. 8–18. On the other hand, none of these demonstrations obliterates the importance of the individual inventor and the necessity for giving heed to his motivations. See JACOB SCHMOOKLER, "Inventors Past and Present," *Review of Economics and Statistics*, vol. 39, August, 1957, pp. 321–33; NELSON, *op. cit.*, pp. 107, 111–19; and the present author's similar contention in "Fundamental Deficiencies of the American Patent Law," *American Economic Review*, vol. 30, 1940, pp. 481–82.
52. See, in contradiction of the specious argument that the "instinct of contrivance" renders the patent incentive unnecessary, PLANT, *op. cit.*, pp. 33–41; JOSEPH ROSSMAN, *The Psychology of the Inventor*, Washington: Inventors Publishing Company, 1931, ch. 10, and the present author's observation some time ago:

   > "it is hard to see how inventions would have been so poorly distributed through history, were not the degree to which society offered [inventors] fame or fortune, or both, of importance. The degree of inner motivation or inner capacity to invent has certainly not so varied from age to age."

   The Efficacy of the American Patent System, unpublished MA thesis, New York University, September, 1937, pp. 57–58.
53. MACHLUP, "The Optimum Lag," *op. cit.*, pp. 251–52.
54. KAHN, "Fundamental Deficiencies of American Patent Law," *op. cit.*, pp. 478–480.
55. KAHN, *The Efficacy of the American Patent System*, pp. 42–43.
56. W. RUPERT MACLAURIN, "Innovation and Capital Formation in Some American Industries," in *Capital Formation and Economic Growth*, A Conference of the Universities-National Bureau Committee for Economic Research, Princeton: Princeton University Press, 1955, pp. 551–68.
57. See PLANT, *op. cit.*, p. 45; and on the wide spread importance of unpatented "know-how", IRVING H. SIEGEL, "Patents and Other Factors in the Creation and Growth of Small Firms: Preliminary Synthesis," *Patent, Trademark, and Copyright Journal*, Vol. 3, Conference No., 1959, pp. 49–50.
58. Of course, though it might be no worse off for having to wait seventeen years for the full exploitation of an invention that would not otherwise have been invented, society might in individual instances be so much better off from a fuller and more rapid exploitation as to justify appropriating the patent and providing some alternative reward for the inventor—even a reward approaching the full monopoly

value of his patent—as our discussion in Part I suggests. See also POLANYI, *op. cit.*, pp. 67–68 and *passim*.

59. This ignores what FELLNER terms "anticipatory retardation," because it would be practiced by rational investors under both pure competition and monopoly, and would not therefore affect the contrast between them. WILLIAM FELLNER, "The Influence of Market Structure on Technological Progress," *Quarterly Journal of Economics*, vol. 65, November, 1951, pp. 567–72.
60. JESSE W. MARKHAM, *Competition in the Rayon Industry*, Cambridge: Harvard University Press, 1952, p. 227. The subsequent history of profits in rayon affords an excellent illustration of the possible compatibility of patent-protected innovation with effective competition. See the present writer's chapter on "The Chemical Industry," in WALTER ADAMS, ed., *The Structure of American Industry*, 3rd ed., New York: MacMillan, 1961.
61. STOCKING and MUELLER, *op. cit.*, pp. 57–63.
62. BRIGHT, *op. cit.*, pp. 149, 250–51, 270–71.
63. Federal Trade Commission, *Economic Report on Antibiotics Manufacture*, Washington: 1958, pp. 214–24.
64. See, e.g. MACLAURIN and BRIGHT, "Economic Factors Influencing the Development and Introduction of the Fluorescent Lamp," *Journal of Political Economy*, vol. 51, October, 1943, pp. 436–41 and especially pp. 446–47, 449. Analogous cases were the Western Union (telegraph) Company's rejection of the Bell telephone patents, United Shoe Machinery's failure to see the possibility of the Bresnahan patents when they were offered to it (see CARL KAYSEN, *United States v. United Shoe Machinery Corporation*, Cambridge: Harvard University Press, 1956, pp. 184–85), and the Standard of New Jersey holding company's veto over the commercial exploitation of the Burton cracking processes, developed in laboratories of its then subsidiary, Standard of Indiana.
65. See Standard of New Jersey's acquisition of patents covering the synthesis of liquid fuels by hydrogenation, and pourpoint depressants, in GEORGE W. STOCKING and MYRON W. WATKINS, *Cartels in Action*, New York: Twentieth Century Fund, 1946, pp. 492–93, 497–98. See also the thorough survey of the evidence on "suppression of patents" in VAUGHAN, *op. cit.*, ch. 8. This survey documents conclusively very few cases of outright suppression of manifestly superior products or processes. But it equally clearly documents the threat of monopolistically retarded exploitation, and the probability that, by being in a position to exploit one patented invention in preference to another while preventing competitors essaying the rejected one, patentees have in some instances precluded the development of other, possibly superior, alternatives.

    Studies of patent utilization by JOSEPH ROSSMAN and BARKEV S. SANDERS indicate that most patents are in fact practiced. However, there is also some fairly clear indication that large corporations use a smaller percentage of their patents (something like 50% in the sample study) than do small corporation (about 75%). "Variations in Patent Utilization by Different Types of Companies," *Patent, Trademark, and Copyright Journal*, vol. 3, Conference No., 1959, pp. 58, 110–12.
66. See the cases of magnesium and methanol in STOCKING and WATKINS, *Cartels in Action*, pp. 280–96 and the same authors, *Cartels or Competition?*, New York: Twentieth Century Fund, 1948, pp. 139–41.
67. DONALD WALLACE, *Market Control in the Aluminum Industry*, Cambridge: Harvard University Press, 1937, pp. 5–6, 10.
68. See *U.S. v. General Electric Company et al.*, 82 F. Supp. 753 (1949); STOCKING and WATKINS, *Cartels in Action*, ch. 8; and BRIGHT, *op. cit.*, *passim*.
69. *U.S. v. I.B.M.*, Civil Action C-72-344, S. D. N.Y., filed January 21, 1952, Par. 47.
70. VAUGHAN, *op. cit.*, pp. 56–57, 72–73, 90–91, 94–95.

71. The median rates of return on net assets, 1946–52, were 20.7, 17.3, and 16.9 in drugs, electrical equipment, and chemicals, and 16.1, 15.9 and 14.2 in paper, tires and rubber products, and machinery, according to the National City Bank's annual compilations. In 1953–59, the respective medians in the patenting group were 21.9, 13.9, and 14.4 per cent, and in the non-patenting, 12.2, 12.8 and 11.7 per cent. For all reporting industries, the 1946–52 median was 14.4, for 1953–59 12.7 per cent.
72. For automobiles and trucks, the median rates of return from the same source were 20.7 per cent in the 1946–52 period and 17.4 per cent in 1953–59.
73. They appeared to pose a slight barrier in metal containers, and a slight to negligible one in gypsum and petroleum refining. JOE S. BAIN, *Barriers to New Competition* Cambridge: Harvard University Press, 1956, pp. 147–53. Moreover, their role in the economy at large is almost certainly much less than in manufacturing.
74. In that period 40 *judgments* were filed in civil antitrust cases in which the Department of Justice obtained patent relief. MARCUS A. HOLLABAUGH, *et al.*, *Compulsory Patent Licensing under Antitrust Judgments*, Senate Patent Subcommittee, *op. cit.*, Staff Report, 1960 pp. 55–78. This figure may be compared, very roughly, with the 105 civil proceedings or the 131 civil and criminal proceedings (companion suits or groups of suits being combined) *instituted* by the Department in the same five years. Counted from the *Federal Antitrust Laws, 1952–56 Supplement*, Chicago, Commerce Clearing House, 1957.
75. See HOLLABAUGH, *op. cit.*, *passim.*
76. See JOHN SHEAHAN, "Integration and Exclusion in the Telephone Equipment Industry," *Quarterly Journal of Economics*, vol. 70, May, 1956, p. 249, and U.S. House of Representatives, Committee on the Judiciary, Report of the Antitrust Subcommittee, *Consent Decree Program of the Department of Justice*, 86th Congress, 1st Session, January 30, 1959.
77. 21 Jac. I, ch. 3, in DELLER, *op. cit.*, vol. I, p. 20.
78. See, e.g., DAVID L. LADD, "Business Aggression under the Patent System," *University of Chicago Law Review*, vol. 26, Spring, No. 3, 1959, pp. 353–75.
79. In most cases these claims are investigated by a public agency before patents are issued. The French, Italian and until 1958 the Swiss laws, however, like the American between 1793 and 1836, provide merely for registration of patents, leaving it to subsequent litigation to settle conflicting claims about their merits and proper scope. STEFAN A. RIESENFELD, "The New United States Patent Act in the Light of Comparative Laws", *Journal of Patent Office Society*, vol. 36, June, 1954, pp. 411–12; HAMILTON, *op. cit.*, pp. 25–26; WILLIAM WALLACE WHITE and BYFLEET G. RAVENSCROFT, *Patents Throughout the World*, New York, Trade Activities Inc., 1959.
80. Cf. *Henry v. A. B. Dick & Co.*, 224 U.S. 1 (1912); *Motion Picture Patents Co. v. Universal Film Manufacturing Co.*, 243 U.S. 502 (1917); and *Mercoid Corp. v. Mid-Continent Investment Co.*, 320 U.S. 661 (1944). See also HAMILTON, *op. cit.*, pp. 62–70; RIESENFELD, *op. cit.*, pp. 435–43.
81. On the disclosure requirement, see DELLER, *op. cit.*, vol. II, pp. 743–53; on the need for promptness, *Pennock v. Dialogue*, 2 Peters (27 U.S.) 1, 1829.
82. HAMILTON, *op. cit.*, p. 157.
83. MACHLUP, "Optimum Lag," *op. cit.*, pp. 243–45, 254–56.
84. The last years of the patent grant will indeed play a disproportionately large role in affecting inventors' anticipations to the extent inventions take some time to move into the stage of full commercial exploitation. The observation of GILFILLAN that the period of protection is much too short for most important inventions supports such a view, although GILFILLAN does not himself propose that the period be lengthened. "The Prediction of Technical Change," *op. cit.*, pp. 371–72.

85. Germany, for example, offers without examination petty patents for minor inventions or improvements, with a three year term extendible to six. See ALFRED F. CROTTI, "The German Gebrauchsmuster," *Journal of Patent Office Society*, vol. 39, August, 1957, p. 566.

In principle the kind of discrimination called for would equate individual rewards not with the value of each inventive contribution, desirable though that might be on grounds of equity, but with its "marginal cost." Cf. C. MICHAEL WHITE, "Why a Seventeen Year Patent?" *Journal of Patent Office Society*, vol. 38, December, 1956, pp. 844, 856. It is not surprising, however, that the usual proposal is to adjust the term with reference to the value or character of the invention. It is difficult to see how the law could provide for ascertaining the relevant cost, except as it would ordinarily be reflected in the character of the invention. Moreover, the underlying philosophy of the system is that the inventor is entitled to whatever value the market places on his contribution: society cannot under capitalism eliminate all the quasi-rents of highly risky and uncertain ventures like these even if it could measure them. But since it must in any event decide for each invention whether it is sufficiently novel to justify a patent, society can readily decide that some inventions are more novel or important than others, hence deserve different rewards.

86. Only about five per cent of all German patents issued are said to remain in force for the full term. BACHMANN *et al.*, *op. cit.*, pp. 10, 83. VAUGHAN reports that of the patents issued in the United Kingdom in 1933, 45.6% were dropped by 1939 and 85.5% by 1948. *Op. cit.*, p. 301.

87. See, among others, the controversial decision in *Potts v. Coe*, 145 F. 2nd 27 (1944); *Great Atlantic and Pacific Tea Co. v. Supermarket Equipment Co.*, 340 U.S. 147 (1950); FROST, *op. cit.*, pp. 47–60; RIESENFELD, *op. cit.*, pp. 420–29; LADD, *op. cit.*, pp. 358–62.

88. See EDWARDS' arresting suggestion for the introduction of such economic considerations into Patent Office decisions: that patents be issued only on a demonstration that the inventions required systematic and expensive research, and that they be denied where their issuance would so accentuate concentration of control over a field of technology as to interfere with rather than promote technological progress. *Op. cit.*, pp. 237–38.

89. See the lucid discussion by JOHN C. STEDMAN, "Invention and Public Policy," *Law and Contemporary Problems*, vol. 12, Autumn, No. 4, 1947, pp. 664–68. Also the persuasive suggestion by Maclaurin that patents be refused on minor improvements of an old art, "Patents and Technical Progress," *op. cit.* pp. 153–54. Crotti feels the German *Gebrauchsmuster* permits the Patent Office to hold to a much higher standard of invention for its regular (18-year) patents than is possible in the United States, and to give such patentees more effective protection. *Op. cit.*, pp. 566–68.

90. See the excellent discussion in EDITH T. PENROSE, *The Economics of the International Patent System*, Baltimore: Johns Hopkins, 1951, pp. 143–62.

91. FREDERIK NEUMEYER, *Compulsory Licensing of Patents under some Non-American Systems*, Senate Patent Subcommittee, *op. cit.*, Study No. 19, pp. 16, 31.

92. *Ibid.*, pp. 35–36.

93. See *ibid.*, p. 50. According to FEDERICO, seventy-three applications for compulsory licensing were filed under the English law between 1919 and 1939; only sixteen went to hearing and decision, and in the end compulsory licenses were ordered in only five cases. Under the German law, which as we point out in the text is less restricted in the opportunities it offers for compulsory licensing, the number of successes ran higher—slightly more than one a year between 1911 and 1934, and seventeen in the eleven years 1924–34. "Compulsory Licensing in Other Countries,"

Law and Contemporary Problems, vol. 13, Spring, 1948, pp. 300–03. See also PENROSE, *op. cit.*, pp. 178–80. On the allegedly wide gap between promise and performance in the Canadian law, see HAROLD G. FOX, "Patents in Relation to Monopoly," *Canadian Journal of Economics and Political Science,* vol. 12, August, 1946, pp. 332–33, the comment thereon by I. M. MACKEIGAN, *ibid.*, November, 1946, pp. 470–82, and Fox's rejoinder *ibid.*, vol. 13, February, 1947, pp. 68–80. In any event, between 1935 and 1959, only nine applications in Canada eventuated in compulsory licensing orders; two others were settled by agreement. Royal Commission on Patents, Copyright and Industrial Designs, *Report on Patents of Invention,* Ottawa: 1960, pp. 77, 95. All the foregoing statistics cover the recourse to compulsory licensing for all causes, of which non-working is the most frequent.

94. NEUMEYER, *op. cit.*, p. 45.
95. See especially RICHARD REIK, "Compulsory Licensing of Patents," *American Economic Review,* vol. 36, December, 1946, pp. 819–22; see also pp. 824–26, and note 93 above. The generality of the German provision for compulsory licensing "in the public interest" is in a sense balanced by the broader interpretation accorded to the enforceable scope of patent claims by the German than by most other patent laws. A. F. CROTTI, "The Allgemeine Erfindungsgedanke in the German Patent," *Journal of Patent Office Society,* vol. 39, July, 1957, pp. 477–501.
96. HOLLABAUGH *et al.*, *op. cit.*, pp. 1, 55–78. Of course other countries as well impose antitrust limitations of various kinds on patent practices. Canada's Combines Investigation Act, for example, empowers the Attorney General to grant compulsory licenses under patents if production is unduly restricted, price unreasonably enhanced, or trade unduly restrained. NEUMEYER, *op. cit.*, p. 16.
97. See FROST, op cit., pp. 36–38; also pp. 31–33 for a summary of the occasions on which American courts have refused to enforce patents; also FEDERICO, "Compulsory Licensing in Other Countries," *op. cit.*, p. 309.
98. See U.S. Senate, Select Committee on Small Business, *Patent Policies of Departments and Agencies of the Federal Government,* 1959, Hearings, 86th Congress, 1st Session, 1959, especially pp. 170–72. Also the Senate Patent Subcommittee series, *op. cit.*, contains a number of studies of the patent practices of individual departments of government.
99. See this writer's "Standards for Antitrust Policy," reprinted in American Economic Association, *Readings in Industrial Organization and Public Policy,* Homewood-Irwin, 1958: pp. 352–57, and "Economic and Legal Approaches to Antitrust: An Attempt to Clarify the Issues," *Antitrust Bulletin,* vol. 2, 1957, pp. 267–79.
100. For a survey of the state of the antitrust law respecting patents, see the Attorney General's National Committee to Study the Antitrust Laws, *Report,* Washington: 1955, ch. 5.
101. See e.g., the minority views in the *Report* of the Attorney General's National Committee *op. cit.*, pp. 235–37, 247. The anti-competitive motivations and consequences of such an agreement are clearly illustrated by the memorandum a du Pont patent attorney wrote summarizing the views of the general counsel of the Sylvania Industrial Corp. expressed in negotiations between the two, as a result of which the two companies settled the contest between them over the validity of the du Pont cellophane patent and Sylvania accepted a license setting a quota limitation on its output:

> "During the conference Mr. Menken stated that in his opinion the case should be settled. He said that they were very fearful of what the result would be to their company in the event they succeeded in having the claims of the patents... held invalid. He seemed to realize the old adage that the defendant can never win.... If the Du Pont Cellophane Corporation succeeds

> and the patents are held to be infringed, Sylvania... will be obliged to stop manufacturing.... On the other hand, if they succeed in having the broad claims of the patents held invalid, they will throw the art open... to anyone and therefore will have additional competition."

Quoted by Stocking and Mueller, *op. cit.*, pp. 42–43. Similar considerations apparently motivated the settlement of the patent conflict over the broad spectrum antibiotic tetracycline. See Federal Trade Commission, *Economic Report on Antibiotics Manufacture*, pp. 245–57, and the Commission's complaint, *In the Matter of American Cyanamid Co. et al.*, Docket No. 7211, July 28, 1958; and for other examples, Edwards, *op. cit.*, pp. 220–22. On the effect of its General Electric license in dampening the incentive of the Westinghouse Company to engage in significant competitive research in incandescent lighting, see Bright, *op. cit.*, pp. 344–45, 456–61.

102. This is the recommendation not only of Corwin D. Edwards, *op. cit.*, pp. 243–44, but also ("where... monopoly results") of the entire Attorney General's Committee, *op. cit.*, p. 245.
103. See the discussion in Penrose, *op. cit.*, pp. 194–200, and Joel B. Dirlam and A. E. Kahn, *Fair Competition, the Law and Economics of Antitrust Policy*, Ithaca: Cornell University Press, 1954, pp. 274–75.

CHAPTER 9

COAL AND STEEL COMMUNITY: RULES FOR A COMPETITIVE MARKET AND THEIR APPLICATIONS

RICHARD A. HAMBURGER

Councillor of the High Authority of the European Coal and Steel Authority, Luxembourg

I. The Experiment with the Common Market for Coal and Steel

The establishment of the common market for coal and steel was an experiment in various respects. When Robert Schuman, at that time Minister of Foreign Affairs of France, invited the European countries in 1950 to establish this market, even the extent of it was unknown. Some months later, the governments of the six countries (France, Germany, Italy, Belgium, the Netherlands and Luxemburg) had decided to participate, while all other countries refused. The regional limits of the future common market were fixed and limited to continental Europe with exclusion of the parts, dominions and colonies of the participating countries in other continents.

To start European integration with two sectors of the economy leaving all others under national control was a new and daring idea. The definition of the products, given in Annexe I of the Treaty, resulted in a rather arbitrary distinction between products which are subject to integration under the Treaty and the vast field of non-integrated products. Everybody realized at that time that this partial integration could not survive indefinitely but must be followed by further steps. The initiators of the Treaty thought and hoped that success in these two sectors would lead to similar efforts in other sectors of the European economy. Therefore, this first Treaty for the integration of coal and steel was proposed and propagated as a model Treaty for partial integration.

As a consequence of this expectation of further integration along these lines, which afterwards was not fulfilled, the Treaty of the European Coal and Steel Community defines in one of the fundamental articles the general criteria of a common market, though they are put down as criteria for the common market for coal and steel. This article 4 reads as follows:

> "The following are recognized to be incompatible with the common market for coal and steel, and are, therefore, abolished and prohibited within the Community in the manner set forth in the present Treaty:
> a) import and export duties, or charges with an equivalent effect, and quantitative restrictions on the movement of coal and steel;
> b) measures or practices discriminating among producers, among buyers or among consumers, specifically as concerns prices, delivery terms and transportation rates, as well as measures or practices which hamper the buyer in the free choice of his supplier;
> c) subsidies or state assistance, or special charges imposed by the state, in any form whatsoever;
> d) restrictive practices tending towards the division of markets or the exploitation of the consumer."

The statements of this article condemn discrimination and restrictive business practices without introducing expressly a free enterprise system as the postulate for state and interstate commerce in the Community of the six states. However, such a statement does not have the value of an antitrust law, because it does not explain what would happen if the "abolished and prohibited" discriminations or restrictive practices should be established in spite of the prohibition. By the limitation of the application of the Treaty with regard to products and enterprises, the statement itself becomes less efficient than similar prohibitions in a common market, which comprises all products and all enterprises of a country. Such a forbidden practice, employed with respect to one of the raw materials for steel production, may influence competition between steel producers, but it would not be incompatible with the common market for steel. Likewise, a concerted action in the field of steel selling could restrain the competition of a final product, e.g. tubes. Such restriction would not be prohibited by article 4, because only the tube market, which remains outside the common market, is affected.

When article 4 was formulated, there was a total lack of experience as to the effects of abolishing and prohibiting restrictive business practices in a partially integrated market. It was recognized from the beginning, however, that the desired effect could not be realized without extending the abolition of these practices to dealers and sales organizations which, with one exception, are not submitted to the jurisdiction of the Community. According to article 80 of the Treaty, article 65 concerning the prohibition of agreements between enterprises, and article 66 asking for prior authorization of any transaction bringing about a concentration, are, contrary to the rest of the Treaty, valid for any enterprise or organization regularly engaged in distribution and sale. In a somewhat weaker form the prohibition of discrimination by article 60 is extended by article 63 2a) to first hand dealers.

The European Community for Coal and Steel was regarded as the predecessor of a future European federation. Accordingly, it has four quasi-federal institutions: the High Authority as an executive, the Council of Ministers as representation of the Member states, the Supreme Court and an Assembly for parliamentary control of the Executive. But this Assembly has no legislative power; this was reserved by the Member states to their own governments and parliaments.

The history of the last century has proved that antitrust laws need amendments, because they generally are not as effective as they should be for the protection of the consumers and because they have to be adapted to changes in the economic structure and the competitive situation. In a democratic country the initiative is taken by the government or by the parliament itself, and a change of the original law may be brought about by the agreement between the government and the constitutional majority of the parliament. These democratic procedures made progress in legislation sometimes hard to achieve even within one state, but any development of antitrust legislation inside the Community is much more difficult, because each amendment has to be accepted by the governments unanimously and by the majority of all parliaments in conformity with their respective constitutional rules.

When the Community was agreed upon, a decision had to be taken as to how the abolition and prohibition of discrimination and restrictive business practices were to be enforced. All agreed that the Supreme Court of the Community was to pronounce the final judgment from which there would be no appeal. Should the enforcement be laid into the hands of lower national courts and the prosecution assigned to a public attorney or to an agency like the Federal Trade Commission in the United States? Or should a special independent institution for prosecution be established like the Kartellamt in Germany? Or should the enforcement become one of the tasks of the High Authority itself?

As a matter of fact, the High Authority has been entrusted with the execution of the Treaty in all details and expressly with the application of its articles 65 and 66. "In the coal and steel market the High Authority has exclusive competence to rule on the conformity of agreements" between enterprises with the provisions of article 65, though its decisions are of course subject to appeals to the Court. This procedure was unprecedented in the history of antitrust enforcement. It was one of the decisions which made the common market an interesting and daring experiment in this field of the application of the Treaty.

II. The Significance of the Common Market

The protection of a market against restrictive business practices and abuse of power on the part of cartels and monopolists is all the more urgent if the market is of a size and importance to make these particularly profitable. We append to this brief account of the subject various statistics which will enable the reader to appreciate the significance of the common market of the Six.

A comparison of the coal and steel production of the common market with that of the United States, the United Kingdom, the Soviet Union and the rest of the world shows that the volume of Community production is comparable with that of the largest national markets of the world.

It was eminently necessary to provide the new market with some measure of protection against practices which could have resulted in its redivision into the old markets of the Member states following private agreements among producers.

Apart from this general conclusion, however, the above figures (representing overall production) should be treated with some caution. Consumption per head of population is rather small in the common market as compared with that in the United States. Some rather sanguine thinkers expect common market consumption per head to catch up with American in a relatively short space of time, but even were Europe to equal the American standard of living its consumption of coal and steel would be lower, since the high American consumption figure is due in part to the very large area inhabited, the distances being bridged thanks to coal and steel. In addition, it is necessary to be cautious in the extrapolation of coal requirements, in view of the increasing extent to which coal is being replaced by fuel oil, natural gas and nuclear energy, which may well work out quite differently in each of the major markets.

TABLE I. 1957 COMMUNITY PRODUCTION OF COAL, COKE, PIG IRON AND CRUDE STEEL, AND ITS POPULATION AND AREA, COMPARED WITH THOSE OF OTHER AREAS

	Coal	*Metallurgical Coke**	*Crude Ore*	*Pig Iron*	*Crude Steel*	*Popu-lation*	*Area in '000*
	(millions, metric tons)					*(millions)*	*sq. km.*
Community	247.4	74.4	86.6	45.1	59.9	164.4	1,165.9
U.S.A.	467.6	52.3	107.9	72.0	102.3	171.2	7,828.0**
U.K.	227.6	19.9	17.2	14.5	22.0	51.6	244.0
U.S.S.R.	327.0	50.9	84.2	37.0	51.0	200.2	22,273.0
Rest of world	461.8	—	106.1	39.9	57.9	2,112.6	—
Total	1,731.4	—	402.0	208.5	293.1	2,700.0	—

* 1958 figures.
** = 3,022,300 square miles.
Sources: E.C.S.C. Statistical Pocketbook 1958, 1959.

The common market is not protected by quantititative restrictions against imports from third countries; there are no import duties on coal, and those on steel are low. Only in certain well-defined emergencies can the Community's free market policy be replaced by import restrictions in accordance with the rules of GATT. In normal circumstances, however, third-country competition will limit abuses of power and render restrictive practices ineffective. The position will be thus regulated by outside forces, however, for just so long as imports continue a major item in the flow of supplies to the common market, and even then only provided third-country producers are not handicapped by freight costs in the case of shipments from overseas. Table II shows the position as it developed during the boom year 1957.

Competition does not affect the Community iron-ore market. All the iron-ore mines in the common market area are "captive" mines, and it was always possible to meet excess demand from other consumers at world market prices, so that imports did not interfere with common market production.

The situation in the coal market was, of course, entirely different: 2% of the Community's production was exported, but more than 18% of the total had to be imported, mainly from the United States. These imports were not competitive, as freight-rates had risen to abnormal levels. However, though the price of imported coal rose well above that of Community-mined coal, common market producers increased their prices only to the extent required to offset the rise in their production costs, and consequently two different sets of prices were charged for the same product in the same market. The reason for this

TABLE II. SUPPLY POSITION OF THE COMMUNITY IN 1957 IN RESPECT OF COAL, COKE, CRUDE ORE AND STEEL
(Millions metric tons)

	Coal	*Coke*	*Crude Ore*	*Steel Products* **
I. Production	247.9	77.2	87.4	59.8
II. Imports	44.0	0.6	24.8	—
III. Exports	5.1	3.8	0.9	10.5
IV. Stock changes *	+1.1	+1.5	+10.9	+1.1
V. Supply position (= I + II — III — IV)	285.7	72.5	100.4	48.2

* Additions to stocks.
** In gat tons.
Sources: E.C.S.C. Statistical Pocketbook 1958, 1959.

abnormal behavior of the market can only be conjectured: presumably the individual Governments managed to exert some kind of moral pressure on the producers to keep their price-level either unchanged or within the limits of the increases in production costs, while the producers themselves were not anxious to induce or encourage inflation leading to higher wages, which would not have been easy to reduce again in the event of a subsequent recession.

The soundness of this policy was demonstrated in the following year, when common market producers' sales fell off as a result of competition from imported coal and the increasing supply of fuel oil. A structural crisis developed, more particularly in some of the coalfields, in connection with which the competent authorities are proposing to take appropriate action.

As regards supplies to steel consumers, imports from third countries were of minor importance, representing less than 2% of the demand. On the other hand, one-sixth of the Community's production, amounting to some 10 million tons, was exported to third countries, so that the Community ranks as the biggest seller in world trade. The recession in the steel market in 1958 did not last long enough to affect the competitive capacity of the rising supply. No major pressure seems to have been forthcoming in respect either of supplies or of prices, and common market producers made only moderate use of their right to meet third-country competition by quoting prices lower than those in their published schedules. My own view is that the geographical protection (considering freight charges, etc.) enjoyed by the European iron and steel industry against imports from overseas (and especially from the United States), together with its high technical standards and pro-

TABLE III. PRODUCTION OF COAL, COKE, CRUDE ORE, PIG IRON AND CRUDE STEEL IN THE COMMUNITY COUNTRIES IN 1957 (BOOM YEAR) WITH NUMBERS OF ENTERPRISES, PITS AND WORKS

(Production: millions metric tons)

Country	*Coal*			*Metallurgical coke Production*	*Crude Ore*		*Pig Iron Production*	*Crude Steel*		
	No. of enterprises	*No. of Pits*	*Production*		*No. of mines*	*Production*		*No. of enterprises*	*No. of works*	*Production*
Germany (excl. Saar)	70	155	133.1	45.2	64	18.3	18.4	82	105	24.5
France	8*	110	56.4	12.6	81	57.8	11.9	94	130	14.1
Belgium	55	120	29.1	7.2	1	0.1	5.6	31	38	6.3
Italy	1	3	0.9	3.7	13	2.6	2.1	132	156	6.8
Saar	1	17	16.5	4.3	—	—	3.1	6	6	3.5
Luxemburg	—	—	—	—	24	7.8	3.3	3	7	3.5
Netherlands	5	12	11.4	4.2	—	—	0.7	4	5	1.2
Community	140	417	247.4	77.2	183	86.6	45.1	352	447	59.9

* Nationalized under Charbonnages de France.

Sources: Statistical Pocketbook 1958, 1959, published by the E.C.S.C.

ductivity and comparatively low wage costs, acted as an effective buffer against an increase in imports of American steel. At all events, the table shows the Community to be self-supporting in steel, while we have as yet no reason to think that cartellization and abuse of power could necessarily be checked by liberalized imports.

A point of importance in connection with the development of competition within the common market is the distribution of production and producers, as shown in table III.

The breakdown of coal production is determined by the distribution of the natural coal deposits: Luxemburg and Italy are dependent on imports for the whole of their coal supplies, and the Netherlands for over one-third. In France and in the Saar the coalmining industry is nationalized, apart from a few small collieries producing negligible tonnages, while in the Netherlands very much the largest of the five concerns is State-owned; in Germany, on the other hand, the industry is mainly run by private enterprise, and in Belgium entirely so. There are traditional flows of trade between one country and another, and in some areas, such as Southern Germany, good openings exist for competition between one Community coalfield and another, and also for competition with coal imported from third countries.

Trade in steel products between one country and another is partly determined by each country's traditional pattern of imports and exports in relation to its production and consumption. Belgium and Luxemburg export more than one-half of their steel production, principally to third countries; in the case of the big producer countries, Germany and France, on the other hand, although they do trade both with other Community countries and with third countries, exports and imports represent only a fraction of total production, so that the export surplus of both countries together is considerably lower than that of Belgium and Luxemburg. Consequently, Belgian and Luxemburg steel production is very sensitive to movements in demand both in the common market and in the world market. It is therefore not surprising that competitive pressure on Belgium and Luxemburg is felt in other parts of the Community also.

As a consequence of the common market, the Netherlands is dependent on imports, since its own steel production is specialized and covers only one-half of its requirements. In 1957 it exported approximately one-quarter of its production to common market countries and one-fifth to third countries, and imported only one-tenth from third countries but thirteen times as much from Community countries. These figures are a demonstration that the steel production of the common market is competitive.

To sum up, it will be apparent from the foregoing facts and figures that the market is in no way closed to outside competitors; at the same time, its size and the geographical protection enjoyed by certain areas and products may tend to encourage practices limiting or restraining competition.

III. The Normal Competition within the Common Market

There can be no doubt that the Member states intended to create a free competitive coal and steel market. They knew quite well that their national markets of coal and steel at that time were neither free nor competitive. During the post-war years some governmental interference was inevitable in Europe, and especially the principal basic materials like coal and steel had to be kept under price control and had to be distributed among the consumers in a fair but non-competitive way. Control and distribution were in the hands of the governments and of the occupying powers in Germany respectively. Import and export were restricted by duties and quantitative restrictions which limited the interstate commerce by bilateral agreements.

It seemed quite impossible to substitute a free competitive common market for the national controlled markets over night. Therefore, the Treaty provided a transitional period of five years during which the restrictions of commerce between the states had to be abolished step by step and during which period restrictive business practices had to be suppressed.

But even for a period of five years, it is rather ambitious to ask for the establishment of a competitive market and we should learn from the example of the United States how many difficulties have to be overcome.

Coal and steel are not the products which offer themselves as models for free competition. The difficulties which had resulted from the shortage of the post-war years were fresh in everybody's memory, nor were the social hardships of the labor force in the 1930's forgotten. The consuming industries asked for fair distribution in times of shortage, while labor pressed for fair chances of employment in times of recession. These demands resulted in provisions of the Treaty which gave to the High Authority the task of ensuring fair distribution if a boom should cause shortage and of enforcing a production quota system during a business decline. These rights can only be exercised in a rather complicated procedure, in which the concurrence of the Council plays a major role (see articles 58 and 59). In these periods of excessive demand or excessive production capacity, the High Authority is entitled to fix maximum or minimum prices.

These provisions of the Treaty evidently tend to limit free competition in the extreme phases of the economic cycle by preventing abuse of power during the boom and cut-throat competition during the depression. Some of the major objectives of prohibited agreements between enterprises were thus realized by authoritative intervention. The discussion about these stipulations of the Treaty began during the year when it was negotiated in Paris and it has not yet ended, nearly ten years later. The critics of the Treaty on the one hand pretended that the Community was a super-cartel because the executive could exercise so-called cartel activities restricting competition. These critics overlook the fact that the High Authority has to act in the common interest of producers, consumers and labor, while cartels have the purpose to serve the interests of their members and to neglect or even frustrate those of the consumers. The intervention of the High Authority is limited by the rights of the Council and can only be exercised after a hearing of representatives of the producers, consumers and labor, united in a Consultative Committee.

On the other hand, these stipulations of the Treaty were criticized as leading to a guided market without competition, because the coal and steel markets would always stay in one of the extreme situations of the economic cycle, either in the state of excessive production capacity or in shortage. These critics forget that the common market is an open market, which can be protected neither by the governments nor by the High Authority nor by cartels against competition from third countries. The possibilities of import restrictions are limited to the special cases enumerated in article 74 of the Treaty, which provide only a reasonable protection against dumping and against increased imports which could inflict or threaten to inflict serious damage on production within the common market.

Both criticisms—that the High Authority would act as a super cartel and that it would tend to dirigism without competition—forget that all decisions of the High Authority are subject to appeal and that the Supreme Court would object to any abuse of power by a High Authority which neglected the rules of the Treaty, forbidding anything like cartel activities.

During the first six years since the establishment of the common market, the Community had periods of rather great demand for coal and steel followed by a considerable recession during the last two years. However, the situation never deteriorated to such an extent that the High Authority and the Council of Ministers agreed to apply the exceptional rules for serious shortage or manifest crisis. During the period of rising demand it was always possible to supply the consumers inside the common market from third countries, though sometimes at higher prices. The recession came to the point where an application of a quota system for production was considered, but until now the Council of Ministers has refused to accept a quota system proposed by the High Authority.

All experts agree that discrimination endangers the normal operation of competition and, therefore, antitrust laws generally prohibit discrimination as far as it restrains competition. It is obvious that competition cannot operate in a normal way, if the competitive customers are supplied by the same producer at different arbitrary prices or conditions. In the Treaty of the Community the abolition of discrimination is not limited to the cases in which it is likely to restrain competition. There were special reasons for going farther than usual. The contracting countries were afraid of discrimination on a national scale, e.g. that producers of one country would make other prices or other conditions for consumers of their own nationality than for those of another Member state. By these rules, there are uniform prices for the same quantities of the same product for all consumers, even if they are not competing with one another. In order to make control of the prohibition of discrimination easier, the Treaty prescribes the publication of the prices.

This rigid system of non-discrimination is likely to restrain competition and to be an incentive to keep prices on a high level as long as possible. The producer cannot reduce his price for a certain category of consumers where he is meeting an extraordinary form of competition, e.g. by a substitute product. He would be compelled in such a case to lower the price for all categories of consumers, which in many cases is too expensive.

The publication of prices involves another danger for competition. The High Authority and its administration have to see that sales take place in conformity with the published prices. If these prices result from agreements or concerted actions, the High Authority, unintentionally and often unknowingly, requires the participants of an illegal practice to keep their illicit promises.

This is not the place to discuss the very interesting problem of enforcing a non-discriminatory system, but it is necessary to enumerate certain restrictions of competition as stipulated by the initiators of the Treaty, in order to appreciate the role which competition may play inside these limits.

IV. Prohibition—Authorization—Control

The philosophy of the Treaty in the field of restrictive practices is laid down in article 4 of the Treaty quoted above. The prohibition is general and not limited to abuse. All agreements among enterprises, all decisions of associations of enterprises and all concerted practices which would tend directly or indirectly to prevent, restrict or impede the normal operation of competition within the common market, are forbidden. This general prohibition is mitigated to a considerable extent by the obligation of the High Authority to authorize certain forms of agreements, if they fulfill certain conditions. This authorization is limited to agreements for joint selling, joint buying or specialization, and to those which are strictly analogous to those in nature and effects.

The conditions which must be fulfilled are as follows: the agreements should contribute to a substantial improvement in production or marketing, they should not be more restrictive than necessary for the achievement of these improvements, and finally they should not give to the interested enterprises the power to determine the prices, to control or limit production or sales of an appreciable part of the products in question within the common market, or to protect themselves from effective competition.

The High Authority has the right to subject the authorizations to certain conditions and to revoke or modify authorizations, if it finds that as a result of changes in circumstances the agreement no longer fulfills the general conditions or that the actual effects of the agreement are contrary to the special conditions under which the approval was given. This task of the High Authority can only be fulfilled by periodic control of the organizations established for joint buying or selling.

Compared with this rigid prohibition of agreements and concerted actions restraining competition, it may be surprising that monopoly and monopolizing is not forbidden by the Treaty. It is recognized in article 66 § 7 that a dominant position, protecting an enterprise from effective competition in a substantial part of the common market may be legally acquired. The High Authority thus has no right to dissolve an enterprise which has acquired a dominant or even a monopolistic position in the common market. However, these enterprises are forbidden to use their power for purposes contrary to those of the Treaty. Compared with this vague formulation, the prohibition of article 86 of the Treaty on the European Economic Community gives more detailed criteria on the same subject, which could be useful for interpretation. This article begins with the prohibition of abuse of a dominant position by one or several enterprises, which could restrain interstate commerce. Some forms of abuse are subsequently mentioned:

a) indirect or direct enforcement of inadequate prices or conditions,
b) restriction of production, sales or technical developments contrary to consumer interests,
c) discrimination between consumers resulting in a restriction of competition,
d) enforcement of conditions asking for additional accomplishments by the consumer outside the objective of a contract.

There is no doubt that all the activities enumerated above would not be admissible under the Treaty of the Community for Coal and Steel either. They are forbidden and cannot be authorized by the High Authority under any conditions. As it has to suppress these forms of abuse, it is entitled and even obliged to exercise control of the activities and behavior of enterprises in the relevant market.

While the powers of the Executive are thus rather limited in all cases where a dominant position is acquired by legal means, the High Authority is entrusted with the prior authorization of all forms of concentration or mergers by § 1 of article 66. The notion of concentration is rather limited. In the sense of the Treaty, a concentration takes place if two enterprises which until now were independent from one another, come under the same control. Control may be exercised by the following rights or contracts: property, rights or contracts granting influence over the decisions of the management, rights or contracts which provide for nomination of a general manager or trustee, contracts limiting the making or spending of profits, and finally contracts with regard to supply or sales if they exceed the normal relations between supplier and consumer.

These criteria of control are laid down in the decision no. 24 of the year 1954 by the High Authority after consultation with the Council of Ministers. These rights are regarded to establish control, if they grant the possibility—one alone or jointly—to determine the activities of an enterprise with regard to production, prices, investments, supply, use of the production or the profits.

The High Authority has to grant authorization of any concentration, if it will not give the interested persons or enterprises the power

> to determine the prices, to control or restrain production or marketing or to impair effective competition in a substantial part of the market; or
>
> to evade the rules of competition of the Treaty, particularly by acquiring an artificially privileged position involving substantial advantage in the access of sources of supply or markets.

Obviously these criteria prevent the forming of monopolies by means of concentration. Under the jurisdiction of the Treaty, the High Authority could never authorize a concentration which would provide a monopoly of one of the products in a substantial part of the common market, because a monopolist always has the power to influence the market in accordance with the above-mentioned criteria. The criteria under which the High Authority has to refuse a demand for concentration are, however, not limited to the cases in which a monopoly would be established. They include—especially by the second criterion—the so-called vertical concentrations between producers and suppliers and producers and the transforming industry.

Transactions leading to concentrations are submitted to prior authorization, even if only one of the participating enterprises is a steel or coal producer or dealer in the terms of the Treaty. Consequently, persons and enterprises outside the coal and steel market may be involved in such transactions and are, with regard to them, submitted to the jurisdiction of the Treaty and the decision of the High Authority. Accordingly, they have the right to appeal to the Court.

The procedure of prior authorization of transactions having the effect of bringing about a concentration has not been prescribed for the European Economic Community. It seems as if the fear of abuse of power by giant enterprises was limited to steel works and coal mines, as no prior authorization is asked for concentrations of producers or dealers of other products.

The High Authority has a right to subject an authorization to any condition which it deems appropriate for the purpose of article 66 of the Treaty. If a concentration is authorized, the High Authority has no right to control its development or to prevent if from gaining a dominant position as long as this is not done by further concentration. Therefore, the control of such enterprises is limited to the requirement that they observe the conditions imposed. The double task of the High Authority as guardian against illegal practices restricting competition and as a body to grant authorization, is so interwoven with its market policy that prohibition, authorization and control had to be united in the hands of the Executive.

V. Rights of the High Authority with Regard to Information, Verification, Fines and Penalties, issuing Regulations

The decisions of the High Authority have to state their reasons and are based on the findings gathered during the investigation of the case. The administration of the High Authority has to observe the market and the activities of the enterprises which might be contrary to the dispositions of the Treaty tending to warrant normal competition. The sources for such a survey of the market consist of press publications and the publications which are made by the enterprises themselves whether voluntarily or according to legal prescriptions in such as their financial reports, other reports and statistical surveys. In addition, the High Authority may be informed of illicit behavior of enterprises submitted to the jurisdiction of the Treaty by interested parties, competitors, suppliers or consumers. Last but not least, the governments of the Member states, the members of the Council of Ministers and of the Assembly (Assemblée Parlementaire Européenne) may draw the attention of the High Authority to agreements or transactions they consider incompatible with the Treaty.

Examination and investigation are designed to prove whether the suspicion aroused by such general information is well-founded. The means by which the High Authority may produce proof is limited to gathering information directly from each of the enterprises, or by a regulation defining the nature of the agreements and practices which must be communicated, and the right to carry out a verification of the given information (article 47). The High Authority does not have the right to put information under oath or to administer an oath, but it may impose fines and daily penalties upon enterprises which evade their obligations or which knowingly furnish false information. The right to administer an oath is reserved to the Supreme Court.

The officials of the High Authority who are charged with verifying information in the territories of the Member states, enjoy such rights and powers, to the extent necessary for the accomplishment of their mission, as are granted by the national laws to the officials of their own tax services.

As long as the activities concern agreements, mergers or concentrations, the investigation will produce the necessary documents in the form of letters, contracts or notes on the results of conferences, sufficient for a decision of the High Authority. The gathering of information is less effective and even insufficient, if the existence of a concerted action has to be proved. To what extent a proof based on circumstantial evidence will be accepted and how far the Court itself will use its rights to administer the oath for the factfinding in such cases will depend largely upon the attitude of the Court. The period of application of the Treaty has been too short and the number of cases too small to determine the effectiveness of these limited rights.

The obvious lack of power given to the High Authority to establish clear evidence in the cases of contravention is to some extent compensated by the risks the enterprises meet if they act illicitly. Agreements preventing, restricting or impeding the normal operation of competition—if not authorized by the High Authority—are automatically void and may not be invoked before any court or tribunal of the Member states. That means practically that no member can be forced by a lawsuit to fulfill his obligations from such an agreement. Most cartel agreements contain severe penalties for not strictly observing what was agreed as an irremissible clause. If all participants fulfill their obligations, there will be no risk of this kind. However, even then the risk remains of being fined as the Treaty entitles the High Authority to pronounce rather severe penalties against enterprises which have concluded an agreement that is automatically void, have applied an agreement for which approval has been refused or revoked, have obtained an authorization by means of information known to be false or misleading, or have engaged in forbidden concerted practices.

The risks for enterprises bringing about a concentration without asking prior authorization by the High Authority are of quite another nature. As long as a concentration would have been authorized on prior demand, the damage inflicted on competitors or consumers is nihil. The fault is regarded as a violation of the existing administrative rules; in these cases the High Authority will subject the approval of the concentration to a payment up to 10% of the value of the assets acquired or regrouped. Such penalty may never be less than half of the maximum amount in any case where it is clear that the authorization should have been requested, in order to prevent the parties concerned from being punished too leniently.

If such a payment is refused or if a concentration should occur which the High Authority recognizes cannot satisfy the conditions to which an authorization would be subject, it will establish the illegal character of it and enforce a deconcentration. The procedure is rather complicated and described in the second paragraph in the fifth section of article 66 of the Treaty. If a prior authorization was needed, a fine of 10% of the value of the assets acquired or regrouped may be imposed likewise. Fines which exceed the above mentioned percentage by 5% may be imposed against enterprises under the Treaty's jurisdiction which have participated in or lent themselves to the realization of transactions contrary to article 66. In the cases of deconcentration, the interested persons and enterprises may appeal against the decision and the Court in such a case is entitled to judge whether the operation effected was illegal or not, although generally it may not review the conclusions of the High Authority drawn from economic facts and circumstances which formed the basis of such a decision (articles 33/36).

Under these circumstances it is not very likely that enterprises will knowingly disregard the stipulations of article 66. Concentrations of major importance cannot be made secretly, at least not in the coal and steel market. Smaller concentrations which might escape the vigilance of the High Authority, generally will not fall under the criteria leading to the refusal of a demand.

With regard to article 66, the High Authority had to issue three regulations, the first of which is indispensable for the application of this article. It defines the elements of control which enterprises may employ only after receiving prior authorization. The second regulation enumerates the criteria for cases exempted from the general obligations to demand prior authorization. These exceptions were published in the decision no. 25 of the year 1954 and comprise bagatelle cases which without any doubt would not be refused by the High Authority. The third regulation is of greater importance. By this regulation the High Authority extends the possibility of getting information, not foreseen by article 47, from persons and enterprises outside coal and steel production and marketing, as far as they take part in transactions which might produce a concentration with or between enterprises of which at least one is a coal or steel enterprise in the sense of the Treaty (decision 26/1954).

Still another way had to be chosen to prevent the abuse of power by legally established monopolistic enterprises and by enterprises occupying a dominant position. The action that may be taken by the High Authority in such cases is limited to enforcing a cease and desist from the abusive activities and practices. To this purpose the High Authority addresses any recommendation required to put an end to the abuse. (A recommendation in the sense of the Treaty is binding upon enterprises with respect to the objectives, but the enterprise is free to choose the appropriate means by which it will put an end to the abuse of its position). If the recommendation is not complied with satisfactorily within a reasonable period, the High Authority will, in consultation with the interested government, take the necessary decisions concerning pricing, sales conditions, production programs, and delivery programs to ensure that there will be an end to the abuse.

If a guess is allowed about the reason for this limited power against monopolistic enterprises, it may be due to the fact that there existed only one monopoly in the coal and steel market when the Treaty was concluded, the nationalized French coal production coordinated by les Charbonnages de France. After the deconcentration of German industry, which by application of the law 27 the occupying powers had performed in Germany during the postwar period, there were no other dominating positions in the market left. The establishment of monopolies by concentration had been made impossible by the stipulations of article 66 of the Treaty, so that it seemed unlikely that monopolies could develop in a legal way. If this is true, article 66 section 7 is only a safeguard which was put in a general form, but aimed practically at the nationalized coal production in France to prevent it from abusing its dominant position. At the same time it was insured that nationalized coal and steel industries in Member countries, which might follow the French example, would not be exempted from the general rules of the Treaty.

VI. The Application of the Treaty during the First Six Years of the Existence of the Community

The dispositions of the Treaty are the same for coal and steel and the fundamental rules were thought to be applicable for any other product. In practice, however, and especially with regard to competition, the conditions are very different for different products and even for coal and for steel. Among the steel products submitted to the rules of the Treaty, we find iron ore and scrap, which again differ quite considerably in their market behavior from real steel products. Scrap, for example, is collected and distributed under conditions which cannot be compared with those of a product which is really produced and of which the production will be increased or reduced according to the ups and downs of the demand. Though these markets are not fully independent of one another, it seems necessary to have a look at each of them separately.

A. The competition in the coal market

The common market for coal was established in February 1953. The transitional period of five years had thus started according to point 4 of section I of the Convention. During the transitional period, the Belgian coal mining enjoyed special protection and a subvention and was in some sense partially separated from the common market. A temporary subvention was also granted to the Italian coal mines and some protective tariffs were established to protect the Italian coking plants (section 27 of the Convention). There were some provisions made to protect French coal mining against abrupt reduction of the production, but these were never applied. These transitional measures in the coal market were necessary to avoid social repercussions and to give the enterprises a limited time to increase their productivity to be able to meet the competition of other producers after the transitional period was over.

In none of the three coal producing countries with a considerable production (Germany, France and Belgium) was the market competitive. In France, as mentioned before, the nationalization of coal mining had eliminated the possibility of competition on the national market by establishing a monopoly, and the production of the Saar was coordinated with the Charbonnages de France since the Saar-district stood under French administration and coal mining was under a sequestrator. In Germany, the dominant district was that of the Ruhr producing nearly half of the whole production of the Community. For more than a generation, the selling of the coal of the Ruhr had been centralized in an organization, called the Rheinisch-Westfälische Kohlen Syndikat (RWKS). After the war, this organization was replaced by another one, controlled by the Allied High Commission, which ordered its transformation into six independent sales agencies which were allowed to coordinate some of their activities by a common body. The general lines for this reorganization were laid down in Regulation 20 of the Committee for Decartellization of the Allied High Commission.

A few days before the establishment of the common market, this reorganization took place: six selling agencies were established with a overhead organization called: Gemeinschaftsorganisation Ruhrkohle mbH (GEORG).

In Belgium the coal mines had a common selling agency too, limited to the sales of certain categories of consumers and to the export market. 40% of the production was sold directly by the mines themselves, but at the prices and under the conditions fixed by the common organization, the Comptoir Belge de Charbons (COBECHAR). This agency had the right to fix production quotas if necessary, and was in this respect more powerful and even more restrictive of competition than the German cartel.

The existing circumstances under which the national markets functioned before the establishment of the common market were of course known to the Contracting Parties and amply discussed during the negotiation of the terms of the Treaty. It was recognized that more or less centralized organizations could be useful in times of shortage to ensure a fair distribution among consumers or to avoid hardships for labor (in a serious crisis), if the weaker mines should have to close down while others could continue with nearly full-time work. The trade unions regarded the central sales organizations as a safeguard against unequal employment in times of recession. They were not satisfied with the stipulations of article 58 giving to the High Authority the power to fix production quotas in a manifest crisis. They insisted that in the case of liquidation of existing cartels the High Authority should be obliged by the Convention to avoid an inequitable distribution of reduced employment resulting from reduced demand. Section 12 of the Convention deals with the rules to be applied during the transitional period with regard to agreements or organizations restraining competition in the sense of article 65 (Section I). The Convention asks the High Authority to gather all information necessary to examine these agreements. If the High Authority does not grant the authorization provided in Section 2 of article 65 it shall fix reasonable time limits at the expiration of which the prohibitions provided in article 65 shall take effect.

In the case of the liquidation of an existing organization, the High Authority had not only to avoid the inequitable distribution of employment among labor, but also the closing down of the production capacity in periods of reduced demand which would be needed again in a following period of prosperity. Finally it had to ensure the most economic distribution and use of the product and particularly of the different sorts of coal. The means given to the High Authority to attain these aims were rather limited. If, for example, a central sales organization for the Ruhr were regarded as incompatible with a normal operation of competition and these activities were forbidden, the High Authority could not enforce the establishment of a less centralized organization by the mine enterprises nor could it ensure that the sales organization would be efficient in distribution and that it would prevent inequitable employment of the miners. "The High Authority had to study the problem and to establish any procedures or organisations permissible under the Treaty, which it may deem appropriate to the solution in the exercise of its powers."

The trade unions argued that this clause of Section 12 of the Convention had to be regarded as an exception from the prescriptions of article 65 and the same view was taken by some scientists. The opponents of this opinion stressed that the High Authority had to act within the powers given to it by the Treaty and, therefore, would not be entitled to reestablish a central organization contrary to article 65. In a procedure which was just foreseen for cases in which prohibition had to be ordered in application of this article 65, a central organization contrary to this article could not be established. At the beginning, the task seemed insolvable. Section 12 of the Convention was a compromise formula reached in the last days of the Paris negotiations, and is open to different interpretations.

High Authority's decision no. 37 issued in July 1953, asked the adherents of existing cartels to request authorization or to stop the common activities. During the fall of the year 1953, the demands were submitted, and in the year 1954 the studies of how to solve the problem within the lines of article 65 on the one side and Section 12 on the other could begin.

Not until February 1956 was the High Authority ready to take the decisions 5, 6, 7 and 8 concerning a reorganization of the sales organization of the Ruhr district. As the High Authority had not the right to impose a sales organization, it had to negotiate agreements with the coal mines, which were acceptable to the High Authority. Hearings took place with consumers and their organizations, with interested governments and with the trade unions.

The result was that the existing GEORG with its six sales agencies was dissolved. In their place, three independent sales agencies were established for the supply of dealers and consumers with less than 50,000 tons of yearly consumption. Further authorization was given to establish a central body, called "Bureau Commun", which was allowed to negotiate with consumers a yearly consumption of more than 50,000 tons, if they would be interested to do so. The hope was that this common bureau would dispose of a limited quantity of orders, which could be distributed between the mine enterprises, so that equitable distribution of employment would be possible in a recession and a fair distribution of coal could be attained in a period of rising demand. As nobody could predict the effect of the system, the authorization was limited to three years.

During the years 1956–1957 demand was increasing on such a scale that a sufficient supply for the consumers could only be provided by the large importation of coal from third countries at higher prices. As long as these imports were available there was no serious shortage of coal in the sense of article 59 of the Treaty, but a noticeable shortage of the cheap European coal. The High Authority asked the authorized cartels to distribute the coal production of their adherents fairly among their traditional consumers. By these and some other interventions and pressures from the side of the Federal Government and the High

Authority, a rather fair distribution resulted. But the market was not competitive and particularly the three sales agencies had no reason to compete with one another.

At the end of 1957 a recession of coal consumption could be observed for some varieties and qualities of coal, but there was still a considerable demand for others, which could not be satisfied from the European sources. At the beginning of 1958, at the end of which year the expiration of the authorization was approaching, the market for nearly all qualities turned from a sellers' market to a buyers' market. If the system as such were competitive, competition would now have become manifest. As a matter of fact, the system did not lead to competition between the sales agencies which was recognized by the High Authority during the session of the Assembly in spring 1959.

During the boom the consumers were willing to accept deliveries of any mine producing the quality ordered without insisting on a certain origin and to accept even lower grades, but now all, and especially the big consumers, designated the mines from which they wanted to be supplied and raised their prescriptions with regard to quality. As a consequence, the common bureau had no possibility to manoeuvre. Under these circumstances the sales agencies joined under the leadership of the common bureau for general distribution of the orders to avoid inequitable distribution of them among the enterprises. This practice was evidently incompatible with the authorizations.

The effect of the recession of consumption was aggravated by long-term import-contracts concluded during the boom and by the revolutionary extension of the use of other fuel than coal. This emergency situation came as a surprise to everyone, above all to the experts of the governments and of the High Authority, who had predicted a long-term shortage of coal and of energy supply for the Community which could only be surmounted by great efforts in building up nuclear plants. Meanwhile, oil and natural gas deposits were found inside the Community, and last but not least the efficiency of industrial coal furnaces rose on an unexpected scale. The situation became serious in Germany and Belgium, where a reorganization of coal mining became indispensable, even after the effect of the import-contracts had been diverted by financial efforts.

The coal mines tried to defend themselves by common action against the competition of other forms of energy. The coal market had started to compete with the coal substitutes. Nobody dared, however, to aggravate the serious situation of the coal mines by enforcing competition between the mine enterprises, or by prohibiting their sales organizations, though in their present form these had turned out to be incompatible with article 65 of the Treaty. So the High Authority took the decision no. 17 in February 1959 authorizing prolongation of the existing sales organizations requested for one year. In this decision the High Authority states that the different organizations frequently had not acted in conformity with the conditions under which the common selling had been authorized and that these had not had the expected results, particularly that the agencies had not developed independent sales policies. The High Authority declared in its considerations that the present difficulties of the mining industry do not allow the prohibition of the existing system at this moment. Besides that, the High Authority announced in this decision which principles should govern future sales organizations, if authorization would be asked for:

> The sales agencies must be fully independent in their decisions and the High Authority will take care, by fixing certain rules, that no uniform system would be established again;
> the marketing should become as efficient as possible to improve the competitive situation of coal in the energy market;
> the High Authority will authorize, as far as necessary, institutions to ensure employment and income of the miners.

At the same time the High Authority had pledged herself to control during this transitional period the activities of the sales organizations and to see to it that they will be working along the lines of the authorizations, which were, apart from some modification of minor importance, the same as in those of February 1956.

In France the activities of the High Authority were limited to insuring that the Charbonnages de France did not abuse their power. This control took place and resulted in only minor objections which did not touch the sales policy of the French organization. During the first years of the existence of the common market, the Saar district was reunited with Germany in two steps which put an end to the sequestration and established the state-owned coal enterprise (Saarbergwerke). During the transitional period some interstate obligations laid down in the Saar Treaty had to be fulfilled. A common selling of Saar coal and the coal of the French state mines of Lorraine will take place in southern Germany. The authorization of this common selling by the High Authority was asked for.

At the time when the nationalization of the French coal mining took place, a semi-official organization was established under the control of the French government, which obtained a monopoly for coal import from all countries. This system later became incompatible with the Treaty since it restrained the French buyer in the free choice of his supplier. Though the French government had modified the system after the establishment of the common market, the High Authority could not agree with the restrictions of competition, which according to its view remained although the French government did not admit it. This divergence of opinion could not be settled according to the rules of the articles 65 and 66, but had to be treated as a supposed contravention of a Member state. The states had bound themselves by article 86 to refrain from any measures incompatible with the existence of the common market. The High Authority had to act in conformity with article 88. After long negotiations resulting in an appeal by the French government to the Court, an appeal not yet decided, some important points have been agreed upon. The only rather important limitation of the freedom of the French consumer and dealer, which still exists and which is still being negotiated, is the role of the organization as sole and obligatory agent for the signing and the execution of import contracts. The parties are trying to find a solution by which the agent would be refrained from unduly influencing the buyers.

At about the same time as the sales agencies of the Ruhr district were authorized, the High Authority took a similar decision with regard to COBECHAR. The activities of the institution were limited to common selling as the control of the production of the mines previously permitted, was incompatible with the Treaty. During the transitional period, competition in the Belgian coal market was more limited by the protection which was granted to the Belgian coal mining industry by the Treaty, than by the common selling to certain categories of consumers by COBECHAR. Protection and subvention of Belgian coal mining was necessary, because these mines had cost prices which were too high to compete with neighboring European competitors, but during the boom of the years 1956 and 1957 their prices were still lower than the prices of imported American coal.

As a consequence of this situation, the transitional period passed without the necessary rationalization. It is not surprising that the following recession put Belgian mining in a serious position which was aggravated because it coincided with the end of the protectional system of the transitional period. The Treaty provides for a limited extention of protective measures after the end of this period and the Council of

Ministers together with the High Authority made emergency measures involving an efficient reorganization as a condition for prolongation.

This development weakened the position of the selling agency with the result that three rather important mine enterprises withdrew during the year 1958, while others followed in 1959. Considering the serious situation, the High Authority had no objection to the continuation of joint selling by the rest of the enterprises insofar as these activities would not endanger the reorganization plan.

Southern Germany always was a contested area between the surrounding coal districts. In order to limit this competition, to organize transport on the Rhine and its major tributaries, and to provide stock piling for the periods of low or high water and drifting ice, the four mining districts of the Ruhr, Aachen, the Saar and Lorraine established a joint sales agency with the participation of the first-hand dealers of the district. The activity of this cartel prevented competition between the traditional coal suppliers of this part of the common market and, therefore, could not be authorized by the High Authority. It was replaced by a cartel of the dealers of Southern Germany for joint buying. Their interests in efficient transport and stock piling along the Rhine could be taken over by this institution without harm to competition, as joint selling by these dealers was neither asked for nor authorized.

B. The steel market

The features of the steel market differed considerably from those of the coal market. In none of the countries was joint selling practised on a large scale. There was no nationalized steel industry and the group of leading enterprises in the different countries of the Community was approximately of the same size after the deconcentration of the larger German units had taken place. The prices were under the control of the national governments. The establishment of the common market in May 1953 abolished the right of the governments to fix prices or to limit interstate commerce by tariff restrictions.

By decision of the High Authority with regard to discrimination, steel enterprises were allowed to meet competition by way of price-absorption provided in Section 2 of article 60. All conditions for a competitive steel market seemed to be present. Some existing smaller joint sales agencies were dissolved by the enterprises themselves, because they preferred to regain their freedom in the competition they had now to face with producers from other countries of the common market. All demands for authorization were granted by the High

Authority. The restrictions of competition provided for the transitional period were of minor importance compared with those of the coal market. The provisions of Section 31 were never applied. There was only a protective decreasing tariff for Italy.

The common market started with uniform prices inside the different steel producing districts. Without any doubt, this uniformity of prices, which existed before as a result of the interference of the national authorities, now resulted from contacts between the steel producers of the districts. During the following months, the market showed some signs of recession and this decline provoked the first price competition in the common steel market.

As a matter of fact, the prices gave way, varying from enterprise to enterprise. However, the behavior of the enterprises was incompatible with the rules for price quotations. The enterprises granted individual rebates for certain transactions. They discriminated and did not apply the prices of the price list they had published. If they had been compelled by the High Authority to apply the published prices, they probably would not have reduced the quotation of the lists, but would have abstained from giving any more individual rebates. The High Authority tried to legalize the rebates by the decision no. 2/1954 by which the firms were allowed to a certain extent, as an exception from the rule, to sell for other than published prices. The Court abolished this decision by its judgment of 21/12/1954 upon a complaint by the Italian government, and stated that the High Authority had to insure that the prices of the offers and invoices corresponded with the price lists. This judgment was a severe blow to competitive pricing.

Some months later the market recovered, the rebates disappeared and growing demand made the prices rise above the previous level. New price lists with higher prices were published and deposited. Like the first price-lists after the establishment of the common market, the enterprises of the same district published the same lists, which roused the suspicion that the enterprises had acted concertedly. The suspicion proved to be justified, but the enterprises pleaded that their national governments had asked them to agree on a price-list.

In the national markets, the governments tried to keep the prices on a moderate level in order to fight inflationary tendencies. They were afraid that their own price policy would be endangered by rising coal and steel prices. They consequently tried to influence the price level of these industries by direct or indirect measures and asked the steel industry to limit the rise of their prices only to the extent of cost increases. The High Authority asked the governments to refrain from interventions, which would result in concerted actions incompatible with the Treaty. The negotiations about this matter were not successful, but before the question had been settled, the recession put an end to this form of undue interference.

The last rise of prices, before the recession started, occurred in Germany contrary to the advice of the Federal Minister of Economic Affairs, who asked the state-owned steelworks to keep prices at their existing level. Consequently, there existed at last different prices for the same product on the market. Nine months later, the difference was eliminated by a halfway rise and halfway reduction from both sides. In this case, concerted action was evident and the High Authority decided to impose fines. The recession of the following period lessened the pressure of the governments on the enterprises to keep prices low; detailed investigations about concerted actions in making steel prices have since become routine work of the High Authority.

The steel industry of the common market has established an export cartel treating the exports to third countries. This cartel is not forbidden by the terms of the Treaty as long as it exercises no influence on the competition inside the common market. Until now the activities were limited to the fixing of minimum prices for export. Several attempts to establish export quotas failed. It is the duty of the High Authority to control the level of the export prices in order to prohibit excessive pricing within the limits of article 61 c). There was no reason for intervention.

C. The scrap market

When the common market for scrap was established, the market situation differed considerably from country to country. The reason was that the markets were closed and separated from one another. The scrap supply of a closed market depends upon iron and steel consumption of preceding decades and the demolishing of ships, while the demand for scrap depends upon iron and steel production and the price relation between scrap and pig iron. The possibility of substituting pig iron for scrap is quantitatively limited for SM-steel and cannot happen at all in electro-furnaces. Consequently, the countries with a relatively great production of electro-steel and SM-steel had a greater demand for scrap. Both sides of this balance varied from country to country, so that some of the Member states were scrap exporters, while others had limited or even forbidden the export by regulations. The restrictions of export artificially increasing the domestic supply kept the price level low. Contrary to other products the availability of scrap cannot be increased considerably by rising demand and higher prices.

When the High Authority established the common scrap market, it was difficult to predict what would be the effect. But it was sure that there would be a tendency to raise prices, the more as demand seemed to be higher than supply and as the artificial price level was lower than that of imported scrap. One was afraid that the dealers would hold back their stocks and that there would be a speculative artificial restriction of supply.

The scrap consuming industry would have liked to have gone on fixing prices and controlling them by national cartel organizations, but the High Authority had, from the beginning, to prohibit such price fixing or controlling organizations, though evidently such a control would not have been contrary to steel consumers' interests. By decision no. 44/1953, it fixed maximum prices for scrap, but it could not by these means prevent stocks being withheld by scrap dealers. There was no shortage of scrap, as it could be imported from third countries, above all from the United States. But even these sources were not unlimited and American consumers repeatedly asked for export restriction. In this respect the situation ressembled that of the coal market: the supply was possible, but at higher prices than those in Europe. To avoid a rise of prices to the marginal level of imported scrap, the consuming industry established an organization to negotiate imports jointly and to equalize the difference between import and European market by an equalization fund. The High Authority agreed and later even forced enterprises to contribute to the fund when part of the enterprises refused to join this organization voluntarily.

During the boom which brought European steel production to unprecendented levels, the market situation for scrap showed signs of growing shortage without a need to declare that the Community was faced with a serious shortage. Several times, the supply system was changed to improve its effectiveness, especially to limit, by special charges for the benefit of the fund, the use of scrap where substitution was possible. The enterprises tried again and again to be allowed to allocate the resources of supply, but the High Authority had no right to grant such authorization. It insisted on dissolution in one case, where such an organization had been established without authorization.

During the recession the interference by the equalization fund and joint importing was abandoned and illegal allocation disappeared. This does not mean that the problem has been solved. The High Authority and the consuming industry will be confronted with the same difficulties as in the past as soon as supply depends upon import and import prices are higher than the consuming industry can enforce by concerted action inside the common market.

VII. The Policy of the High Authority with Regard to Concentrations

When the common market was established, the size of the enterprises of the steel and the coal mining industry did not differ very much from country to country. The only exception was coal mining in France which was integrated by nationalization. The big steel enterprises which had existed in Germany had been deconcentrated by the Allied High Commission. The largest coal enterprise of the Community, besides the Charbonnages de France, had an output of 15 million tons a year, and the largest steel works had a crude steel production of 2.5 to 3 million tons. The greatest part of the steel production was produced by enterprises with capacities between 1 and 2 million tons of crude steel, while a great number of smaller steel mills without crude steel production provided for the rest.

It seems that there was no interest in concentrating these existing and rather modest units in large enterprises as they existed for instance in the United States or had existed in Germany. The demands for horizontal concentration between steel works and steel works or coal mine and coal mine were not numerous at all. In the steel sector, they were asked for by enterprises which by concentration would attain a joint production between 2 and 3 million tons moving up from an average size to the size of the largest enterprises without becoming larger than the existing leaders in this group.

Among concentrations authorized by the High Authority were the merger between Ougrée Marihaye and Jean Cockerill, the concentration between August Thyssen-Hütte, Deutsche Edelstahl-Werke and Niederrheinische Hütte, being directly or indirectly controlled by Countess Zichy, the daughter of the late Dr. Fritz Thyssen, and finally the concentration of Rheinhausen AG, the steelwork of Krupp, with the Bochumer Verein, which had been separated from the Vereinigte Stahlwerke during the deconcentration of this largest prewar unit.

Though these concentrations centered about the building up of larger steel units, in most of the cases some vertical concentrations of minor importance were involved as nearly all steelworks are in some way or another integrated with transforming industries or coal mines outside France. This vertical concentration was the object of another group of concentrations for which prior authorization was asked from the High Authority. Most of them were bagatelle cases which had only to be submitted, because the exemptions from prior authorization had been fixed in decision no. 25/1954 on a very low level. In most of these cases, it was evident that they gave the enterprises no power to escape effective competition or to gain an artificially privileged position.

The more interesting cases of vertical concentration were submitted by deconcentrated German enterprises who asked for a reconstitution of their relations with coal mines and steel consuming industries with which they had been connected in the past. The attitude of the High Authority with regard to these requests was determined by the stipulations of the Treaty and not by the deconcentration law no. 27. It was agreed between the Member states, and laid down in the Treaty, that all institutions of the Community and particularly the High Authority had to make decisions without any discrimination. Accordingly, it had to determine whether these vertical concentrations were compatible with the criteria of article 66, and nothing else.

There was not a single case which had to be rejected. The Market Commission of the Assembly examined the granting of authorizations by the High Authority, which gave full particulars about the cases which had been treated. Following the report of its commission, the Assembly agreed that none of the requested authorizations should have been refused. The High Authority declared in the Assembly that it would not grant authorization for concentrations uniting production capacities like those which were united in the Vereinigte Stahlwerke, 9 million tons, and added that this did not mean that every demand inside this limit would be authorized.

The general conclusion drawn from these experiences is that until now competition has not been threatened by any attempt to concentrate on an excessive scale.

VIII. The Balance of the First Six Years

It may be too early to draw a balance in view of the short transitional period since the establishment of the common market. If we compare the experiences of this period with the development which antitrust law application has taken in other countries, especially in the United States, we should not be surprised that a real competitive market has not yet been established. The partial integration and the special features of the coal and steel markets were handicaps for a rapid evolution. Most of the time the economic situation in the market was unfavorable for the development of competition. Last but not least, the common market was formed by uniting national markets which were not competitive but were controlled for decades either by cartel agreements or by governmental interventions aiming at price fixing or at limiting the distribution in the market.

The threat to the successful functioning of the common market was above all the establishment of supra-national cartels or monopolies in which the producers of coal and steel of the six countries would unite their forces to eliminate competition. The practical effect of the Treaty and of the activity of the High Authority has been that such a combined action was not even attempted. There is no doubt that the various districts of the common market are in competition with one another and that by this competition and by the policy of the High Authority, the power of the existing cartels, authorized or not, has decreased and some of them already show signs of increasing centrifugal forces.

If the High Authority is vigilant and enforces the prohibition of article 65, the rest of national cartellization will disappear gradually with the growing competition between the industrial districts and the competition of the substitute products for coal, because it will be easier to protect the market against new illicit agreements after a period of competition imposed by law and induced by the situation of the coal market.

CHAPTER 10

ECONOMICS AND POLITICS OF THE COMMON MARKET

PIERRE URI

Formerly Director General with the European Communities

I. Introduction

The Common Market grew out of the Schuman Plan. Some of the men who were instrumental in formulating and setting up the Schuman Plan were equally prominent in the preparation and the success of the Common Market. The political inspiration was the same: to create a united Europe. The first effort toward integration, accomplished in a limited sector, had suffered from the failure of the European Defense Community, and would have lost all momentum had it not been extended to new fields. One of the most spectacular of these fields appeared to be that of Atomic Energy. But it rapidly became evident that there was no particular reason why six countries should get together to explore the unknown possibilities and promises of atomic energy if they were not united in other areas by ties broader than those of two basic industries. A step toward the formation of a general common market was required by the creation of the Euratom. At the time of the negotiation of the Schuman Treaty, a special clause had been discussed for the case integration should remain limited to the two sectors the Treaty endorsed. Although this clause was economically justified, since the conditions of equilibrium for two integrated sectors are different from what they normally would be in a case of general integration, it was considered politically untimely. It illustrated, however, the degree to which this first effort called forth the idea of a general common market.

Stated another way, the Schuman Plan had no intention of providing the prototype for integration brought about by the successive integration of sectors. If it succeeded in establishing common bases for development, it served also, in what was at first a limited sector, to bring to light the problems and the solutions peculiar to a case of broader integration. Nevertheless, it was still necessary to avoid copying provisions suited to another framework and to bring about, in order to satisfy the same ends, their necessary adaptation to this form of integration. Such is the work of economic imagination presented in the Brussels report and continued in the negotiation of the Rome Treaty. This adaptation does not exclude, but on the contrary implies, the same inspiration: the search for a solution that will be a synthesis which, at the same time, makes room for the full initiative of economic agents and the responsibility of government. It is a question of dealing with our economic world just as it is. The fusion of markets can not be brought about from one day to the next nor maintain itself without conscious attention to the establishment and preservation of those conditions which prevent its breakup.

Integration, therefore, involves two basic interpretations which are mutually complementary: economic fusion and the creation of common institutions.

1. The meaning of integration

Integration is far more than a simple freeing of exchange such as had been understood by the European Organization of Economic Cooperation. To arrive at a rational distribution of economic activity it is not enough to eliminate the bilateral quotas, whose effect is to assure protection against imports as well as assure protection for exports. It is not enough to transform them into multilateral quotas, nor even to eliminate these quantitative restrictions. When duties are high, they, too, block imports effectively or arbitrarily increase the price of foreign goods by permitting a higher cost on the domestic market.

These forms of protection are merely the most obvious ones. State trading, especially if purchases from abroad only cover the excess of needs over domestic resources, constitutes even more restrictive screening. But the manipulation of transport rates may also lead to insuring a kind of protection comparable to that of duties. If rates are allowed to differ depending on the origin of the products and if there is discrimination between domestic and foreign goods, there will be an arbitrary rate differential which tends to vary with the value of the products, just as duties vary, but here also they will vary with distance. It is, therefore, absolutely necessary to deliminate these discriminatory measures. We must go even further. Internal transport rates always taper off in proportion to the total distance covered. If, in cases of transportation across borders, rates taper off only within the boundaries of each country, the sum of the charges is higher than for a similar distance covered in a single country. Such "load breaking" must be eliminated. Finally, in addition to interfering with a rational allocation of economic activities, subsidies given domestic production mean that foreign goods must compete under unequal conditions. The situation resulting from this inequality of prices is the same as if, because of a duty, there were a rise in the price of foreign goods. But these public obstacles to free exchange do not constitute the only means by which markets can be divided. They could be eliminated and everything would remain unchanged if producers agreed to use systematically the prices in the market for which the goods were destined or if the producers themselves agreed upon a division of markets. International cartels and economic integration are incompatible.

Naturally all these principles have been recognized by the Rome Treaty. But since it is interested in a rational distribution of activities, it can not restrict itself to industrial goods: it must cover agricultural products as well. It cannot even be limited only to material goods: a growing part of activities, whether in the course of production, or final consumption, takes the form of a wide range of services. In order that the conditions of production will not be distorted and that each country can benefit from its own comparative advantage, whatever form they may take, the free sale of services must be assured.

The theory of international trade shows the advantage of exchange, even if the factors of production cannot cross boundaries freely. This is not, however, an acceptable situation from the perspective of economic integration for, in the long run, we are dealing with problems of business enterprise as well as human problems. We must know which firms will be able to undergo a broader development. They must be able to obtain either the manpower or the capital necessary for expansion without being limited by the available resources of the country to which they belong. Inversely, firms which are in poor positions to compete and workers whose jobs are threatened must have the right to prove that their situation is not due to their organization or lack of competence but rather that they suffer merely from a bad location for their operations. This is the second justification for free movement of workers or the right of establishment: the right to set up shop either as individuals or as firms in all the countries of the integrated zone.

This policy by which a group of territories is assimilated into one single territory is not based on the excessively naïve idea that modern techniques of production are incompatible with the boundaries of a given country. There are few branches of industry where a market of 40 million consumers does not permit the utilization of the most modern techniques or the attaining of the optimum size of an enterprise. It would be much more correct to note that the dimensions of a national market such as Western Europe's often permits only one enterprise, or perhaps a small number of enterprises, to reach an optimum size in each sector. A larger market, then, is needed to reconcile this optimum size with the need to maintain competition. The example of the United States shows that the strength of a large market is derived from the fact that it finds new openings large enough to support firms which are very narrowly specialized. Much more than absolute size, it is specialization which permits long continuous mass production and the price advantages which are its result. Above all, the wiping away of boundaries by exposing firms to competitors heretofore largely unknown provides completely new incentives to modernize and rationalize. Its result is a quick abandonment of restrictive attitudes and a breaking up of those tacit or explicit agreements by which certain companies sacrifice their possibilities of expansion in order to maintain the status they have attained. This security runs the risk of being upset by the abolition of external protection. A modification in business practices, a stimulus to increased investments, the desire to obtain competitive prices—these are the major effects of a common market and the source of accelerated expansion and growing productivity.

If this movement toward integration is to overcome traditional opposition, it must be able to counter effectively all legitimate objections. We cannot ask a country to eliminate those protective arrangements which benefit its producers if that country does not have some insurance against acts of economic aggression committed by other nations or their business firms. Dumping committed with or without government subsidy leads to prices which have no relationship to competitive position. It must be effectively controlled. There is a kind of indirect dumping which consists of supplying domestic consumers with certain essential materials at lower prices than those which are imposed on foreign consumers. These double prices falsify the conditions under which competition operates. Thus, we arrived at a general formula according to which discrimination in terms of one's nationality or location is forbidden, a formula that alone permits fair competition and the elimination of protection but which must be effectively supervised. Likewise, in modern market structures, producers may indeed fear the impact of large concentrations which do not necessarily have the advantage of efficiency but which assemble financial resources enabling them to pursue for a time competitive methods designed to give them later a monopoly position. Such abuses of economic power must be defined and repressed. It is already obvious that a common market cannot do without rules, a jurisprudence of its own, and some kind of supervision.

The conditions which permit its maintenance again touch upon the question of a general policy. That part of the national income withheld by public finance, whether to cover the direct cost of goods and services or to cover transfer payments, is so large that it cannot fail to have an important effect on manufacturing costs. Therefore, we must make certain that the forms in which revenues are raised do not have the effect of establishing artificial inequalities of competitive position, and that this essential element of the economy, i.e., the level of public expenditures, is handled so as to affect the various sectors equally.

In addition, the more protective arrangements are reduced, the more each country is exposed to the spread of a case of inflation or deflation which may develop in another country. As a result, a common market necessarily tends toward the creation of a true economic union.

2. Regional union

The enumeration of those conditions which make integration economically sound and politically acceptable has presented enough evidence to show that it cannot be extended to all countries. The simple lowering of duties, such as might be desired and negotiated in as broad a framework as possible, allows the continued existence between sectors of discrimination, which alters the distribution of economic activities. It is sufficient to mention, for example, the demand for a free movement of manpower, a revision of transport rates, a correction of fiscal systems, and a coordination of monetary policies. It is easy to see that these demands can be met only by countries which feel they are closely tied together and whose mutual desire for unity allows them to overcome an accumulation of habitual practices and individual interest. Therefore, we must be resigned to the impossibility of integration on a world scale and seek solutions at the regional level. Such regional tendencies have not obstructed free exchange in the world. On the contrary, the experience of recent years suggests that the movement toward liberation throughout the world has received a completely new stimulus by the creation of the European Common Market.

This regionalism raises the political objection of discrimination. The answer to this objection is that the mutual advantages which the member countries grant one another are but the counterpart of special obligations to which they agree, and there would be, on the contrary, discrimination in extending the same advantages to others without demanding the same obligations. Regional union revives the economic argument of the "diversion of trade" since the member countries are prompted to import from their associates what they used to import from a third country. All the same, it is odd that this argument should be brought against a group of nations when it is infinitely more valid against individual nations. Every national system leads to discriminations between members of that nation and outsiders and to the assuring of a preference for national products over foreign products; a regional preference based on an economic union diminishes that very "diversion of trade" which a system of isolated countries brings about. Moreover, this argument is essentially a static one. If economic union permits accelerated expansion, the normal result will be not a contraction but an expansion in buying in third countries. The fact that foreign trade may develop less rapidly than trade within the union does not in itself bring about any adverse effect; what is important is that there be a more extensive flow of trade with the third country. For, one of the obstacles to such a flow of trade is not only protection but that rapid cessation in expansion which most countries, even those whose size seems to assure complete autonomy, are obliged to make in view of the difficulties arising from their balance of payments. One of the most important effects of a regional union—not only on the member countries but also on their non-member associates—is the transformation into internal trade of a sizeable part of their external trade and, as a consequence, the establishment of a surer basis for expansion without disturbance.

3. The economies of the six countries

Here, the formulation of a common policy is made easier because of the fundamental similarities between the economies of the six countries and, above and beyond the obvious differences in their ideologies or administrative practices, their identical objectives and orientation in economic policy.

We are dealing with six countries, five of which have a real income per capita which is approximately equal to half that of the United States. Given the difficult adjustments necessary to arrive at this comparison of real income, by offsetting exchange disparities and differences in prices we can say that the discrepancies between those countries are within the margin of error. The only exception is Italy, whose average income per capita is not more than two-thirds that of the other countries. But the comparison is distorted by the fact that two fundamentally different areas have been included in the same figure, the North and the South of the same country. Especially since last year's boom, the north doubtlessly comes within 80 percent of the level of the other member countries; per capita income in the South is less than one-half that of the North. Although they affect regions that are relatively less important, equivalently appreciable differences could be found in each of the other countries. Between Corsica and the region around Paris, between Schleswig-Holstein and Hamburg or the Ruhr, between West Flanders and Brussels, between the Drenthe region and Amsterdam, and even between South and North Luxembourg, the disparity is infinitely greater than between Italy's average income and the average income of the five other countries. What permits us to distinguish these six countries, one from another, is the role the three great economic sectors, agriculture, industry and services, play in the working population and in the national product. The role of industry is greatest in Germany and Belgium and least in Italy. Service industries play a particularly important role in the Dutch economy. Within the industrial sector, however, there is a striking similarity in structure, and through developments in recent years the role of each large industrial branch has become nearly the same in France and Germany. To state it another way, differences in the volume of production as between major sectors of industry are the same as the differences between the global volume of industrial production which is 50 percent higher in Germany than in France.

In the agricultural sector, however, the differences are major ones. The proportion of the active population which is employed in this area varies from 35 percent in Italy to 12 percent in Belgium. France alone has half the farm land available in the six countries of the Community. The choice of crops, yields, and methods of production that are used, all differ widely from one country to another. Competition, however, is reduced by great distances and by differences in climate, which, as a result, demand different kinds of production. On the other hand, we may note a rapid progress in the use of equipment by agricultural countries which have been relatively backward. Above all, we must note again that the differences between countries are much less pronounced than those existing within each country. Not only Italy but also Germany and especially France provide spectacular illustrations of such disparity by having within the same boundaries certain regions with the highest yields in the world and others where an archaic form of cultivation exists practically as a closed family economy.

After suffering from the crisis which occurred between the two world wars, all these countries underwent, one by one, destruction and occupation. All have shown remarkable vitality in the process of reconstruction: higher investment rates and a new attitude in all economic circles toward the progress of productivity. Starting at the very low levels to which production had fallen at the end of the war, they have, within a short period of time, passed their pre-war levels. Since 1953, industrial production has grown by 80 percent. Progress in industrial productivity of the three largest countries is almost exactly parallel. In all countries economic policies have aimed at reconciling—with varying degrees of success in different countries and at different times—a high level of employment and rapid growth with balance of payments equilibrium and price stability.

France and also Italy and the Netherlands have resorted to establishing general plans, which Germany avoids and Belgium abstains so far from using. In any case these plans have no function other than to indicate the direction of the country's policies and by presenting an over-all view to clarify the actions of interested parties. Direct controls have lost their importance everywhere, and the spectacular progress in production, the rise in the standard of living, the establishment of an external equilibrium have, in point of fact, permitted the return in all these countries of a policy which is essentially liberal.

As a result of this general discussion, it should be clear that of the two types of economic union—either between mutually complementary countries or between relatively homogeneous countries—the European Common Market belongs to the second type. If we stop to reflect, does it not represent that situation in which an economic union produces its most important effects? Between complementary economies, such as the economies of the United Kingdom and the British Empire have been for a long time, there exists a spontaneous absence of protection and an intensity of trade based on the obvious necessity to supply certain needs. It is, rather, between economies which resemble one another closely that we have to overcome opposition in order to eliminate obstacles to trade. There, competition and specialization produce effects which would never have been achieved without this decisive action. Above all, due to the realities of the modern world, the maintenance of a Common Market requires rules and a policy which, in the last analysis, can be instituted only between countries which have a common structure and a common tradition.

II. The Functioning of the Common Market

1. The transition

The mechanisms which establish the Common Market have as a basic aim the avoidance of any lack of equilibrium between various sectors. To put it another way, they are careful not to eliminate too quickly obstacles to trade in certain products while keeping these barriers on other products; their intention is to maintain a front which is approximately balanced. Therefore, they are fundamentally different from the steps followed in the freeing of trade in the OEEC. There the point of reference was imports originating in other countries of the Organization during a given year and the elimination of quotas was expected to cover a growing percentage of these imports. The difficulty here is that a liberalization percentage calculated on the basis of a year which recedes continuously further into the past, may represent a much lower fraction of later imports in an expanding economy.

Above all, what seems to be a gradual procedure for the whole economy is carried out without transition in each of the sectors as they are affected one by one by these measures. As a result there is a tendency to free the last vulnerable sectors first—that is those in which the country concerned is anyway a large importer and those where it possesses a competitive advantage. The most difficult cases are constantly put off and experience has shown that it was more difficult to go from 90 to 100 percent of the imports of a base year than it was earlier to reach 90 percent. In addition, this freeing of trade permitted the re-establishment of custom duties; and it is difficult to say which is more restrictive—quotas which are broad enough or custom duties that are excessively high.

On the contrary, the method selected for the elimination of quotas is progressive for each sector concerned as well as for the whole of the economy. It follows a geometric progression by allowing a growth in percent from year to year over the preceding year. It has the automatic result of providing a length of time that is geared in a practical way to the difficulties of each sector and at the end of which the quotas, which are greater than the actual imports and have become ineffective, can be eliminated without any shock to the economy. In effect we may presuppose that the more poorly placed a sector is competitively, the smaller the quota will be compared to the potential import demand; and although it was necessary to set up some minimum point of departure in order to apply this geometric progression, it is none the less true that a spontaneous harmony exists between these delays and the acuteness of the problems involved.

In particular, the elimination of quotas goes hand in hand with the lowering of custom duties which is carried out in successive stages. After the first reductions in duties, the countries have the means (which they really do not use) to put into effect merely an average reduction at each stage, rather than a linear application of the reduction percentages. Favorable general business conditions, the harmony between the economies concerned, and the French financial reform have in fact permitted an acceleration of the elimination of quotas and of the reduction in custom duties compared to the schedule provided by the Treaty. In place of any effort to provide in advance for the difficulties a particular sector or country might have to face and which are likely to be eliminated by more rapid progress, a certain flexibility within the mechanisms themselves has been preserved to permit the handling of delicate situations as they arise. Thus, there is a safeguard written into the mechanisms themselves that eliminates any recourse to so-called safety clauses *per se*.

2. Rules governing competition

This same flexibility can be seen in a consideration of the rules for competition as they are applied to actions of business firms. No Common Market would be possible if dumping were permitted. But we can observe its tendency toward self-elimination as the Common Market becomes more established. A dealer's local clients would have the possibility of buying their products in another market where these price reductions were in effect. Therefore, only in so far as a firm's own market is protected can the firm engage in dumping elsewhere. Thus, we are dealing with a problem that arises only during the transition period. As of the time the Treaty is being put into effect, a provision has been devised which permits goods sent to another area of the Common Market to be reimported without duties or restrictions into the national market from which they came.

Regarding agreements, we must expect that they will be harder to establish and maintain between the industries of several countries than on protected national markets. Nevertheless, some common action will be necessary to thwart these agreements. The action can be limited to restrictive practices which would affect trade between the member countries thereby leaving to each country the problem of suppressing those practices that have a purely local effect. This limitation reflects the care taken not to entrust common institutions with any tasks other than those they can handle effectively. It recognizes that not all parts of the economy of the countries will be affected by the setting up of the Common Market. In particular, retail distribution, even in its most integrated forms, preserves by definition its local nature. Modernized distribution is a necessary complement to the Common Market in order to permit the disposal of goods to keep pace with increased production and to prevent the loss of cost advantages. But this is not a problem the Common Market can solve by itself. The right of firms to choose where they may set up business will extend the effects of European competition even to the commercial sector by permitting one country's most dynamic distributive firms to settle in another country. In addition, a broad market is likely to attract distributive organizations which have proven themselves in countries outside the Common Market.

3. Transport and agriculture

The rules of the Market, and the different mechanisms by which competition is to spread, are extended to all the sectors: in other words, the provisions of the Treaty apply to all, with the exception of special clauses concerning agriculture and the transport of goods. We have already noted how transport rates may have an important role in restraining trade between countries and providing hidden protection. In a more general sense, the way in which transport rates are set up has a fundamental effect on the determination of industrial sites and on firms' competitive positions. Certain industries or certain sites may find they have an advantage depending upon whether there are very general rules governing rates or, on the contrary, special rates for different regions or industries; whether the rates are modeled on the cost of each shipment or are, on the contrary, uniform throughout the country whatever the nature of the routes may be; or how rates are tapered according to distance. In addition, no country has solved in a completely satisfactory way the problem of coordinating the different means of transport which are so frequently subjected to very different operating regulations and charges. Thus, we are dealing with a sector where some governmental policy is always at work even if it is not clearly formulated, coherent, or effective. There is, then, an area where a common policy must be developed. Taking into consideration the effect of transportation on industrial location and on competition, this policy would seek to eliminate those differences between countries which distort competition; it should facilitate those transport services which are essential to the movement of goods within the Common Market. This is not to say that there should necessarily be a greater transport volume, but that transports will be directed according to that rational allocation of markets which will accompany integration. Finally, it is not impossible to hope that the principles on which governments must agree will lead to a more rational solution—in the terms of the natural advantages of each form of transport—of the problem of mutual coordination, a problem which national policies have largely failed to solve. Although no country has adopted a systematic doctrine, the search for a common policy will have to face the conflict between the doctrine which, because of the effect of the transport agencies on the economy as a whole, imposes upon them duties of common interest and the doctrine which believes that the best interest of the whole economy is served by an effort on the part of each type of transport to seek its own system for optimum revenue and those conditions under which it operates most favorably. It is not certain that by a rational consideration of prices and costs we can succeed in eliminating those authoritarian regulations which seek to correct the effects of a poor policy by occasional intervention.

The meaning of a common agricultural policy must be clearly understood. It does not apply necessarily to all products, rather only those products will come under a free market whose markets are expanding or which are grown exclusively in certain regions and certain climates. Basic difficulties, however, arise with those products which constitute an essential part of agricultural activity and income and have a market which undergoes no substantial growth along with the general development of a country's revenue. We are dealing here with grains and, in a certain sense, with sugar and dairy products. European agriculture, moreover, represent a family structure which cannot be modified without changing the whole social structure. The policy to be formulated will seek to increase productivity and lower cost and to favor specialization whatever the regions or the types of cultivation involved. It is none the less true that there is a limit to the rates at which various types of cultivation can be changed or a surplus agricultural population reabsorbed by other sectors. These reasons alone would justify the use of precautions both within and without the Common Market. In addition, there is yet another essential consideration: how can a country comply with external competition and market prices when it is well known that there is no longer any country which, even under the most favorable operating conditions, does not subsidize its grain production. These subsidies lower prices to artificial levels or, on the contrary, increase the incentive to produce in such a way that the surpluses unloaded on the world market are offered up at lower prices.

The agrarian policy of the Community of Six ought to serve as a point of departure and should be considered a temporary measure until a more concerted and more coherent agrarian policy can be set up for the countries being developed. The feeling that the agricultural world is threatened by surpluses which lower prices is based, in the case of the six countries, on the important progress that has been brought about in productivity. This has led to a volume of production which exceeds domestic demand and which in view of the massive surpluses developed by other countries, is hard to dispose of on foreign markets. In a broader sense, however, this is only a temporary situation. Within a few years the rapid increase in world population will pose a problem of food supplies and the lack of sufficient arable land. Everything depends upon the success with which an indispensable policy of aid to development is carried out: we would no longer speak of surpluses when the greater part of the world is tragically underfed.

Therefore, the elimination of differences in the price levels of the various agricultural systems within the Community must be conceived of in terms of a wider perspective. The necessary reconcilation of these differences should not be based on some simple averaging of prices. The level toward which prices should converge must, rather, be conceived in terms of the world situation and of more concerted policies which will eliminate competitive subsidies as well as wastes in all the countries which have a decisive influence on the world market.

III. Harmonization and Coordination

The idea of a common policy as it has been arranged for agriculture or transport allows us to define, by contrast, the meaning of harmonization and coordination necessary for the functioning of the Common

Market. These are two terms which are both distinct from unification in legislative arrangements and in the conception of the action to be undertaken. Both presuppose that differences exist between countries in terms of the way they act and the framework in which they act. Although they are often confused, they fill two very distinct requirements. The need for coordination has not raised any problems of principle, although the terms and conditions may be hard to define. On the other hand, the idea of harmonization is among those which stirred up the liveliest controversies, and its exact importance had to be clarified before any agreement on the Common Market was reached.

A naïve and biased conception of harmonization was, in effect, that for competition to be acceptable conditions had to be the same everywhere, the same salary scale, same power costs, same taxes: such would have been the prerequisite for the Common Market. A great deal of work was necessary to show that, in actuality, equal salaries, when productivity differs or when other elements of the cost of production such as the cost of supplies, of transport, or power themselves differ, would be incompatible with the functioning of a market because they would prevent absolutely the establishment of comparable prices. A preliminary equality, then, far from being a prerequisite for a Common Market, would be impossible to set up and would even render the Common Market impossible. It was necessary to return to the valid aspects of the harmonization concept, i.e., the elimination of those artificial factors which would distort competition by introducing into monetary costs differences which do not correspond to real cost relationships.

Harmonization, like coordination, takes into consideration the differences within economic conditions: they both allow to persist those basic differences which are the very foundation of trade. Harmonization, far from eliminating such differences, seeks rather to bring them to light by eliminating the elements which hide or reverse them. Its target is the framework of economic action, the legislative or statutory arrangements affecting the behavior of firms, salaries, social security or taxes. Coordination concerns action itself. It presupposes not that the same measures should be taken despite a difference in situations but that different measures, taking into consideration the respective situations, should work toward a common objective.

1. Harmonization and distortions

The greater part of the necessary harmonization must originate either from the actual workings of the Common Market or from the application of the basic clauses of the Treaty. Moderate salaries in one region should attract industries requiring a great deal of manpower, and at the same time by increasing job possibilities, this development will raise salary scales. More generally speaking, if industries are in an unequal situation as far as competition is concerned, the tendencies—toward contraction on the one hand and toward expansion on the other—must lead to an equilibrium situation through the action of increasing costs. Finally, putting the economic systems of different countries into communication with one another brings about a kind of contagion which eliminates the most glaring examples of disparity in group action. It is easy to imagine that there will be a tendency on the part of the workers to insist upon the benefits of the system of remuneration which they consider to be the most favorable. By the same token, the most productive methods, the most profitable forms of organization will spread throughout the whole Common Market.

One of the important sources of differences in production costs arises from costs of supplies which, themselves, are influenced by the customs policies of the countries involved. Certain industries find themselves priced out of the market because of the preference given the production of raw materials coming from the same country or from the same monetary zone, whereas their competitors can obtain their supplies on the World Market. A common trade policy and the creation of a common customs tariff will tend to eliminate these cases of disparity.

Thus, we are discovering the deeper meaning of the transition and the steps in establishing the Common Market. It is not simply a question of assuring firms some delay during which they can adjust their methods of production and reorient eventually their activities in terms of their comparative advantages. As the fusion of markets proceeds, it affects in its turn the conditions of production and costs. Positions of equilibrium are thus constantly modified and the ability to compete will be noticeably different at the end of the transition period from what it was at the beginning of the Common Market. But more particularly, the steps involved in establishing this Common Market, each forming approximately a four-year cycle, require the agreement upon and carrying out of a group of actions which must all be effected at the same time. Thus, the reduction of differences in the conditions of production, deriving not from an arbitrary and economically unmaintainable attempt but rather from the effects of the integration and the conditions it requires, will go hand in hand with the elimination of obstacles to trade.

This spontaneous harmonization is complemented by a concerted harmonization whose demands and limits can be minutely defined. Distortions must be done away with; we must eliminate them by deliberate action in cases where they lead the process of competition to results that are contrary to the fundamental objectives of the economic policy. Examples of working rules, of certain social security arrangements, and of certain tax problems, will make clearer what the notion of distortion entails and, at the same time, why concerted efforts to correct it are necessary.

Consider two countries, one of which observes the international agreement of equal pay to both sexes for equal quantity and quality of work and the other of which either has not signed, has not ratified, or does not enforce effectively such an agreement, but allows the unimpeded functioning of the difference in the markets for male and female labor. The difference in systems does not affect over-all competition between these two countries. But, in the case of industries where female labor plays an important or even preponderant role, it has a considerable effect. If there is an over-all equilibrium of wage scales and productivity between the two countries in question, the industries employing a high percentage of female labor will be in a more favorable situation concerning manufacturing costs in that country which pays its female labor lower wages than its male labor. The spontaneous tendency, then, would be a lowering of female wages in that industry now open to competition; the reverse of what is considered a more favorable social arrangement. Such a disparity in legislation allows a specific distortion in particular industries, the correction of which cannot be expected from the spontaneous action of the market but only from organized intervention.

One striking disparity is that which separates the countries where social security is financed essentially by contributions from the employers in proportion to the wages they pay and those countries where it is paid for out of public funds. In the latter case all activities, even those which employ very little manpower, participate in financing the plan; and industries with a large labor force are to the same degree relieved of a heavier load. The full financial burden, on the other hand, falls upon the industries with a larger labor force in countries where social security financing is coupled with the payment of wages. All the countries of the Common Market belong to the second system; Great Britain, however, follows essentially the first.

Problems arising from taxes must be examined more closely. It is helpful in analyzing their effects on international competition to distinguish among other things between taxes which are a part of manufacturing costs, taxes added to prices—taxes on turn-over—taxes which are paid on profits and other forms of income. Those which are a part of manufacturing costs—such as taxes paid by employers on their total payroll, taxes on productive resources, e.g., property taxes on land and buildings—are part of the total costs of economic activity. In as much as these taxes are levied with no intentional discrimination between industries but rather are applied to the basic productive resources, they are compensated for, along with the rest of these costs, by the exchange rate equilibrium.

Taxes added to the price present a problem which at first seems rather delicate. First of all these taxes may take various forms; moreover, they generally differ according to the nature of the products to which they are applied; finally, in international trade, they receive special treatment since exports are exempted while imports are subjected to a compensatory tax, which is in principle equal to the one borne by corresponding domestic products. The basic difference is that between those taxes which are collected on each transaction throughout the production process and which as a result have a cumulative effect on manufacturing costs and those taxes which represent a definite percent of the final product's value, whether they are collected only once at a single level like the British "purchase tax" or the American "sales tax," or collected at every level but only on the difference between sales and purchases such as the French tax on the value added. The second solution offers the particular advantage of allowing an export exemption and an import compensation which are calculated accurately. On the other hand, the effect of cumulative taxes on the value of a product depends on the number of transactions which have taken place in the course of its manufacture and on the relationship between the value of the intermediate transactions and the value of the final product. If the exemption and the compensation are calculated on the final transaction, i.e. only on the price of the product being exported or imported, they represent an unequal fraction of the total incidence of the taxes, depending on the products. If a complementary tax is added to take care of these previous transactions, it must be brought into line with the differences of incidence. Otherwise, national products will be unequally favored in competition: in the absence of correct calculations, the exemption or the compensation may represent more or less than the actual effect of the tax. But, if the scale of complementary taxes is correctly set up between the different products, an inequality still exists between firms in the same industry if the tax is applied only to transactions and not to the stages of production. In this case vertically integrated companies benefit from a less onerous fiscal burden. But, we can see immediately that inequality in conditions of external competition is but one consequence of a much more serious inequality in the conditions of internal competition.

The question has been raised as to whether in a common market there would not be grounds for eliminating the practice of exemption and compensation. It is self-evident, however, that the correct level of exchange rates is not the same if the products exported are burdened with a domestic tax as it would be if they were exempt. Nor is the correct level the same if imported products are subject to the same rates as domestic goods as it would be if they keep the taxes of the country where they originate. Since the exchange rate is the same for transactions inside and outside the Common Market, it is not possible to have two different systems coexisting. Would it then be necessary to eliminate exemption and compensation in all transactions? A modification in the exchange rate could indeed correct for the increase in export prices and the lowering of import prices which would be, on the average, the result. But, it is a fact that taxes on turnover have different scales. They are low for food products, high for luxury items. Only insofar as these differences are eliminated could a modification of the exchange rates be substituted, without distortion, for exemption and compensation of taxes on turn-over.

If a uniform system of indirect taxes could be established between countries of the Common Market with the same rates and the same types of differences, it would become a matter of indifference to competition, if not to the fiscal revenue of each country, as to whether products pay the tax in the country where they originate or the tax in the country where they are sent. This is not a situation necessary to the functioning of the Common Market as long as indirect taxes, thanks to exemption and compensation, do not prevent products from being subject to the same taxes whatever their origin. Nevertheless this would ease considerably the movement of goods since otherwise customs border stations would have to be kept in place, even though they no longer have any duties to collect, for the simple purpose of verifying that exports have really taken place and to collect compensatory duties.

The conclusion here is that there are no noticeable distortions to be corrected, unless it is a distortion which already exists within countries using cumulative taxes, but rather that a harmonization of indirect tax systems, insofar as a convergence of the financial conditions of all countries will permit, would eliminate a source of friction in the development of trade.

The situation is quite different when one examines taxes on profits and on income from capital. The Common Market should protect the right of all firms to choose their location freely, the opportunity for each firm to obtain the capital which it needs and not necessarily within the boundaries of the country where it is located, and finally, the opportunity for each firm to make investments whether purely financial or in the form of the creation or acquisition of manufacturing facilities in areas where the profits seem most favorable. In addition, these movements of capital, whether or not they are associated with the practice of a free choice of manufacturing sites, must correspond to the basic earning ability of the investments and not to fiscal advantages. This does not exclude the possibility that important differences in assessment rates may reverse the relationship between net income after taxes compared to profits before taxes. To avoid this distortion there is no other solution than to effect a radical convergence not only of tax rates but also of the tax bases with particular attention to authorized deductions, amortization provisions, and capital gains provisions. For this harmonization will not come about of itself, at least not in the desirable sense of the word. If no deliberate action is taken, there will be cumulative pressures to favor the inflow of capital through competitive lowering of tax rates which would in the end destroy direct taxes and the financial resources of the countries.

When we try to sum up these analyses, we realize the meaning and limits of this harmonization which has been long sought as the necessary condition for a common market. In the majority of cases, it must be spontaneous. It will be deliberate only if spontaneous harmonization threatens to produce results contrary to those proposed. In no case is it necessary to abolish those differences which arise from basic economic conditions but rather only those distortions which hide them. Differences between countries in their legal or fiscal arrangements are harmful only if they affect unequally all economic activities. In so far as they have a discriminatory effect on different activities, they favor artificially one or the other. The specific distortion is not defined in terms of the discrepancies in effect from one country to another but by the discrepancy of the discrepancy.

2. The levels of development

In opposition to specific distortions we have general cases of disparity which distort competition between economic activities in one country and those activities in the other countries. Whether they are called wage levels or more generally production costs or prices, they amount to a lack of equilibrium in exchange rates. Such a far-reaching problem as this was threatening to arise at the opening of the Common Market due to that overvaluation in the French franc which had been long since noted. The monetary reform that intervened just before the first lowering of custom duties and the establishment of minimum import quotas, has re-established the alignment so that the particular provisions authorizing France to keep special taxes on imports and export subsidies have become pointless and no particular safeguard clause has had to be invoked.

The other general disparity is that between levels of development, which does not necessarily mean that at a given moment one economy less developed than the others is not in a position to compete. It is simply a matter of price levels. The real problem involves future development. Will there be a tendency to make up for lost time, i.e., a more rapid rate of development in less favored areas, or, on the contrary, is there a risk of the disparity becoming cumulative? This is a problem which appears particularly acute in southern Italy.

Integration experiments carried out in the past between regions of different levels and the progress of economic analysis have, on this point, destroyed all confidence in systems that function automatically. Examples include not only the increased poverty in southern Italy after unification but also what happened in the United States between the North and the South after the Civil War. Here traditional theory would argue that in regions where there was relatively less investment the marginal productivity would be higher and the inflow of capital would correct the discrepancy in development. In reality certain basic conditions must be assured before firms can develop in a profitable way: basic investments are necessary to assure collective means of transport, energy supply, and also schools, homes and hospitals. A firm's ability to make profits is not solely a function of its internal organization. It depends on the nearness of its sources of supply and new markets and, what is more important, on the technical capacity of its manpower. This situation is best assured in regions where important industries already exist. Hence, there is a tendency toward concentration in areas where such development is already most advanced. How does one compensate for the disadvantage of retarded areas and solve within a Common Market a world problem, the disparity between the most highly developed areas and underdeveloped areas?

Special temporary protections are not a satisfactory answer. Politically untimely, they succeed only in postponing the problem if the basic conditions are not established to permit an accelerated development. In a sense, the very development of the Common Market contributes to the solution of this problem. Once a certain level of growth of production has been passed in older regions, costs tend to increase rapidly as a result of the scarcity of land, water, housing possibilities and, finally, manpower. Hence, we see the evolution which has been noted in the United States where a higher level of development has led to a decentralization of industry. An analogous point could be rapidly reached in the Community of Six. But to make the scales lean in this direction, special facilities must be made available to underdeveloped areas. An exception is made to the general prohibition of those aids and subsidies that distort competition on behalf of less developed regions; in such cases subsidies are actually legitimate in that they tend toward self-elimination through the development which they further. Their elimination in other regions renders them, by contrast, all the more effective in zones where they will remain in use. Hence it is possible to compensate at the outset for the disadvantage resulting from the absence of these external economies created by the existing basic facilities and by an industrial milieu which offers trained manpower and reciprocal supplies and outlets. But, in addition, a part of the basic investments cannot bring in profits directly and the countries where they are most necessary are not necessarily those countries which have the greatest amount of capital at their disposal. Hence, there arises the conception of complementary financing supported by the cooperation of the countries of the Common Market. The European Investment Bank is set up in such a way that whatever conditions may be, important resources are assured the Bank by subscriptions paid by the governments to its capital and, if need be, by supplementary advances. But the magnitude of the subscribed but unpaid capital and the possibility of having recourse to such advances is designed, by strengthening the credit of the institution immediately, to facilitate its access to the capital market, thus making recourse to the advances and unpaid capital unnecessary. If this abundance of capital at present reduces appeals to the Bank, this does not mean that the Bank is a superfluous institution: the market for capital may become tighter or the Bank may prove to be a useful instrument in the Community's action vis-à-vis underdeveloped countries.

The same philosophy is at the base of the fund for overseas territories. A lower level of development justifies the elimination of loans in favor of outright assistance either for social work or for work on the infrastructure connected with projects that are directly productive.

3. Economic and monetary policy

The true meaning of coordination of economic policies derives from the realization that such differences exist in the initial situation of these countries. Objectives must be common objectives. But they would not be reached if the measures agreed upon were the same in all the countries. As long as economic integration is not achieved, certain elements of independent business conditions continue to exist, as well as problems of the balance of payments between countries and of differences in real income and in the level of public expenditures. One example will make clear the distinction between a coordination of policies and a common policy. If, at the same time, two central banks fearing a rise in prices raise their discount rates when one of the countries has a deficit in its balance of payments, but the other has a surplus, there is a perfect correspondence between actions, a perfect synchronization. But, such action is the very opposite of true coordination. The action of one bank not only cancels the equilibrating effect of the action of the other but tends also to increase the disequilibrium. It is none the less true, that as the fusion of markets proceeds, changes in the level of activity spread more rapidly, economic conditions become more similar and coordination, in its turn, tends to develop into a common policy.

This economic policy affects at the same time business conditions, expansion, monetary stability and policies concerning wages, and the raising of the workers' standard of living. The more a social policy is integrated with a coherent economic policy, the more effective it becomes. The social fund created by the Rome Treaty provides for participation of the Community in the countries' expenditures to help the unemployed. In each case it is a question of not giving them workman's compensation—this remains the country's responsibility—but of facilitating their productive reemployment. The fund provides for expenses incurred in rehousing the worker should a change of residence be necessary, for professional instruction should a change of job occur, and for the possibility of reemployment in the same company after its production has been reoriented. Here the fund contributes to expansion whether the workers are reemployed in the same countries or are absorbed by another country of the Common Market which is retarded in its development by a lack of local manpower. In a sense the Common Market itself brings about a spontaneous coordination of policies. This coordination is oriented toward expansion through the development of investments stimulated by the perspective of an enlarged competition. Above all, the means by which economy situations are disguised (subsidies, import restrictions) are quickly eliminated so that governments are forced to rectify directly the causes of such disequilibrium.

Similar mechanisms have been formulated to insure that the reestablishment of equilibrium will come about in the direction of expansion. If a country is having difficulties with its balance of payments, it can normally count on the assistance of other countries. During the transition period, they will step up, to the country's benefit, the elimination of import obstacles and, at all times, should consent to offer special financial aid when ordinary international means are insufficient.

Nevertheless, we must realize that whenever necessary such mutual cooperation would each time require separate decisions to enlist the agreement of governments to common action, and that no funds are set aside to implement it. Aids are only granted to governments who accept the recommendations of the Community's institutions. In other words, only debtor countries are submitted to any real pressure. This intervention, moreover, does not occur before the difficulties are already present. Each country's situation, the risks countries run of losing their state of equilibrium vis-à-vis one another are doubtlessly subjected to regular scrutiny in a monetary committee. Meetings of Finance Ministers have become customary procedure. If one considers, however, the decisive influence of the whole economic and monetary policy on the development and functioning of the Common Market, one has to recognize the need to create instruments and procedures which will give increased efficiency to a permanent coordination of economic policy, capable of anticipating losses of equilibrium between countries and of resolving them in the direction of expansion. Budgetary magnitudes, the size of deficits, and the regulation of credit are problems of common interest.

As a matter of fact payments do not meet with any particular difficulties. The system of transferability between European currencies alone, set up by the European Payments Union, was superseded by a return to external convertibility at the very time when the first steps towards a customs disarmament were being taken. One of the Common Market countries, Germany, has even established full integral convertibility which includes the right of its own citizens to use their money where they will as well as the right of non-citizens to use, in any other country, the balances or currency acquired in one country. But it is not enough to reestablish convertibility. The conditions under which it will be effectively maintained must also be insured. This is not a problem of the six member countries alone; it involves the whole western world where these six countries are in a position to exercise a broader influence and to make a more effective contribution.

IV. The Community in the World

1. Its commercial situation and policy

Viewed in its entirety, the community already represents the world's greatest commercial power. Its imports of primary products—raw materials, and food stuffs—represent almost a third of total world import trade; they are double the American imports and almost double the imports of the United Kingdom. Its exports of industrial goods are a third of world exports, as against one fourth for the United States and one sixth for the United Kingdom. Nevertheless, we must take into consideration the fact that the trade of each country with other members of the Common Market represents about one fourth of its total trade. Finally, if we exclude their trade with other countries of the Community, with the United States, and with Great Britain in order to evaluate their share of trade with the rest of the world, we find that industrial exports of the Common Market countries are almost equal those of the United States and higher than those of the United Kingdom by one third. As for the purchase of primary products from these other areas of the world, the Community exceeds the United States by one third who in turn buys hardly more than the United Kingdom.

In the last ten years, a remarkable recovery has occurred in each country's balance of payments, France having been the last country to effect this reversal. The Community has a surplus balance vis-à-vis the rest of Europe and the rest of the world. The German and Italian surpluses are even such that they constitute an important fraction of the counterpart of what has become (after those surpluses which seemed permanent and irreducible) the deficit in the American balance of payments.

This situation calls for the creation of mechanisms to finance these surpluses directly, whereas in the present situation (not counting France's assistance to Africa) it is essentially the United States which makes loans and gifts to the rest of the world while Europe accumulates gold and dollars under conditions which threaten the continuation of American aid and the stability of that very currency in which European countries hold a large part of their reserves. Above and beyond the coordination of economic policies and, if necessary, the release of resources for mutual cooperation, there is a major problem which calls upon Europe to complete its economic integration by some common action in monetary matters.

This situation also explains why Europe is ready for a liberal policy toward world trade. In any case, the acceptance of the competition of other countries within the Community eliminated the need for high protection for its industries. In each sector, there is at least one industry in one of the member countries which is on a par with the most advanced industries in the world. A firm which can sustain such competition in the common market can also match its outside competitors. The concept of a restricted market, sheltered by high common protection, was never part of the Common Market's objectives. On the other hand, the capacity of this powerful group to negotiate for counterparts to its own liberalization was never lost from sight. In the end to promote a lowering of tariffs throughout the world in this manner represents a more aggressive liberal attitude than to proceed to a unilateral disarmament without any reciprocal concessions. Experience shows that the formation of this customs union is the moving force behind broader attempts at the reciprocal elimination of protection, e.g. the free trade zone project in Europe or the opening of negotiations within the framework of GATT for the reduction of tariffs in the widest possible area.

A common trade policy, of which these negotiations are a part, rests, first, upon a common tariff rate. It is based fundamentally on the arithmetic average of the tariffs in effect in the four customs zones within the Community. For this purpose the Three Benelux countries are considered to be one zone. This solution is justified in the first place by practical considerations: any attempt to weight the duties to be applied would have prolonged the calculations indefinitely. Moreover, any weighting based on imports would conflict with all harmony between tariffs rates, since in sectors where one of the pre-existent customs areas is not a producer, it levies low tariffs and imports heavily. The common tariff would have presented wide variances without any economic justification whatsoever. Moreover, imports do not constitute a satisfactory basis for such weighting because they reflect past sales under the divergent policies followed by each country, whereas in a common customs rate it is each region's consumption which will constitute the actual basis of importation; but, consumption is a difficult ground on which to base one's weighting, since the future pattern of consumption cannot be accurately gauged. All the same, ceilings have been put on raw materials and on semi-finished products, in recognition of the fact that it was to the advantage of final stages of production not to have their costs raised artificially. For a relatively limited number of products there were conflicting interests, notably between producers and non-producers within the Community, and decisions concerning the duties to apply to them had to be postponed until further negotiation. Such negotiation was completed more rapidly and more easily than had been expected. At the time of the first lowering of customs duties between the members of the community, the reduction in duties was extended to the entire world. When it was decided to accelerate the reduction of customs duties, the counterpart was to advance the date of the first rapprochement between the duties in each country and the common customs rate, but at a level that, itself, was to be lowered. What the common customs tariff will be at the end of the transition period will depend on the success of the negotiations which its very principle will have brought about.

2. Overseas countries

One area where the reciprocity rule has been deliberately pushed aside is that of the overseas countries and territories that have special ties with certain members of the Community. These countries were formerly colonies, protectorates or mandates. Openings will be made to those states which had achieved their independence before the signing of the Treaty to enter into a privileged association with the Community. The program agreed upon for these countries which are bound by the Treaty is intentionally generous. The countries of the Community will eliminate all restrictions and protections when dealing with them. They admit that in certain cases these countries undergoing development will need protection which, it is hoped, will be only temporary. However, the preferential treatment benefiting the country with which the overseas country had special ties must be eliminated as far as the other members of the community are concerned. Here, the territories receive a double advantage as they obtain at the same time a free market for their products and the possibility of getting supplies under the most advantageous circumstances from any one of the members of the Common Market. These arrangements are accompanied by the creation of a development fund to which all the members of the Community contribute. This system, which constitutes a kind of free trade zone in Europe's relations with its associated territories, has aroused the suspicions of primary producers who fear the effect of this preferential treatment. In the majority of cases those who benefit are in fact the countries which are less developed than their competitors. Custom preferences assure them less of a price advantage than the maintenance on the consumer market of prices which they can hope to hold despite higher production costs. Moreover, it is not expected that their production will develop to the point of satisfying all of a country's needs or even the increase in its needs; new markets for foreign producers should, therefore, be able to continue to develop normally. We are dealing with a kind of relief system where assistance is given new primary producers, while others begin to enter an industrial phase.

This is not to say that the general problem of development within the world can be ignored. On the contrary, the place the Community will hold in world trade, the rapid progress of its production and of its financial capacity will give it increased responsibility in this area. It is not a problem that the Community can deal with alone but rather through constant cooperation with Great Britain and the United States. In the end, the relations between these groups are less important than the formulation and execution of a common policy toward the rest of the world.

3. The common market and the free trade area

Such is the true perspective in which the relationship between members of the Common Market and other European countries should be viewed. The idea of a free trade area was born out of the desire to effect the same elimination of custom duties and quantitative restrictions between the member countries of the European Organization for Economic Cooperation that members of the Common Market had agreed to, even if the other members could not accept all the provisions contained in the Rome Treaty. One major difference has long been the center of attention and monopolized the negotiations: the rejection of a common customs rate against outsiders and of a common trade policy. The experts have for a long time leaned toward a compromise which would maintain free circulation of goods between members without one country obtaining any undue advantages resulting from a difference of customs rates in their relations with other countries. This position overlooks the fact that the formula of a customs union had been retained not merely because of expediency but for a fundamental economic reason: customs duties are a part of a whole and enter into various costs and finally into exchange rates so as to establish a competitive equilibrium. Is not competition distorted, if, between member countries, exchange rates alone come into play, while in the world equilibrium of the balance of payments they are combined with customs duties that are not the same from country to country?

More precise analysis has shown that we have been dealing here with a problem that is essentially a false one, that the differences among customs rates were far less than was imagined and were due, moreover, largely to such accidents as pressures of the moment or negotiations that were being carried on. These accidents were not the results of a national policy with which no compromise could be made. The countries which so feared a rise in their customs duties that they would not create a uniform common tariff forgot no doubt that on the other hand a larger part of their supplies would come from within this very zone without any customs duty. For a long time now the problem has ceased to appear as an essential difficulty, although it was the basis for the technical distinction between the customs union and the free trade area. If the customs tariff is made part of the over-all trade policy, this desire to preserve an autonomous trade policy in the name of those advantages it provides in negotiations or in the name of the character of "pure politics" which it maintains in its relation with certain regions of the world, would be a misinterpretation of the very spirit of the undertaking. Even if there were no intention of extending the integration effort, there are self-evident reasons why the countries of Europe should eliminate obstacles in their relations with these areas of the world and adopt a single concerted policy. At the same time they would establish one more basis for intimate relations between themselves.

Another essential difference is that the Common Market Treaty provides common and collective means for overcoming the difficulties which one of the signers might face. Whether it be a lag in development, to which the Bank addresses itself, unemployment, to be mitigated by the social fund, disequilibrium in the balance of payments, where mutual aid applies, solidarity is recognized as the way to avoid retrogression. When this is lacking, there is only recourse to the safety clauses: irreversibility, which is essential in order for integration to make its effects felt since the economic agents will adjust to a situation that is considered permanent, will be continually jeopardized. There, too, it does not seem impossible that a comparable solidarity might be established within a broader framework.

The treatment of agriculture presents a more fundamental difficulty in two respects. Several European countries insist upon preserving their agricultural set-up even to the extent of retaining products whose costs are way out of line with costs in more favored regions, but compensating for these high costs with low cost imports selected so as to favor their own exports. It should be noted that their problem in this respect is not appreciably different from the problem faced by Germany which, quite to the contrary, has admitted that an economic union carries with it necessary revisions even in the agricultural sector. The problem is most acute in the case of Great Britain where the protection of the nation's agriculture is carried out not by raising prices but by using subsidies which bring excessively high prices down to the level of imported supplies. Moreover, these imports constitute a privileged market for the Commonwealth countries which grant in exchange a customs preference to British exports according to different scales varying from country to country and from one product to another. The problems of agriculture and of the Commonwealth are so broadly connected that one must reopen the deeply political question of Great Britain's situation in the world.

The difficulty of both the agricultural and Commonwealth problems cannot be underestimated. The community's agricultural interests sees production growing more quickly than its new markets. The agricultural groups of certain countries watch for new markets which will be found among the fellow members of the Commonwealth, thanks to the common agricultural policy and to the preference or relative isolation that this policy will inevitably establish in the event of over-production. But these same countries cannot envisage submitting themselves to industrial competition without finding counterparts in increased agricultural markets. Thus, some agreement must be found.

Let us imagine that the Community can find directly the means of guaranteeing the Commonwealth the maintenance of their European markets and a part of the growth in the consumption. In this way, they would doubtlessly have a more important advantage than if they were guaranteed the maintenance of British markets protected against competition from European countries. In return they would be able to offer to extend to other countries and in particular to Europe the level of custom duties reserved today for British products. They would have the same advantage as overseas countries associated with the Community, and equal choice among various possible suppliers. Great Britain might then admit that a favorable solution had been worked out for the Commonwealth; she could thus allow competition within her own borders between goods from Europe and the Commonwealth, just as she would find that the loss of preferences for her exports within the Empire would be compensated for by their entry on an equal footing into European markets. By seeking directly the solution to this agricultural problem and the Commonwealth problem, we can find a valid resolution of what has been presented by opponents of the Common Market as a division of Europe. If the Common Market is a coherent system, if the conditions under which protection is being abolished are in the main justified, how could it coexist with another system which would imply, on the contrary, that all these conditions are superfluous? It is through the participation in the Common Market (thanks to a specific solution to the Commonwealth problem) of Great Britain and any other countries that will follow her example, that the end of the schism between them will in time be effected.

V. Conclusion

The institutions

The organizational set-up of the Common Market, if it is correctly interpreted, should not hinder this union nor provoke ideological quarrels concerning a supra-national power versus cooperation between responsible governments.

The institutions have been conceived of in a way that will allow them to fit into a federal system. There is a College responsible to an assembly but which, for its important decisions, needs the concurrence of either all or a majority of the governments of the member States meeting in a Council of Ministers. A Court settles differences either between the States, between the Institutions or, finally, between the

Commission and one of the States at the request of one or the other. Usual commentaries have chosen to see in the details of this system a retreat from the supranational powers vested with the High Authority of the European Coal and Steel Community. This is an impression that has been created purposely so as not to revive opposition. On one particular point a form of supreme power reserved for the common Executive over the governments of the States has been eliminated: according to the Paris Treaty the High Authority itself determined failures on the part of the States to adhere to the Treaty and its decision was binding, subject to a State's recourse to the Court. This arrangement has been done away with in the Rome Treaty because of the confusion it might cause and because it fitted in poorly with a federal system where conflicts between the Union and the States are not settled by the Union executive but by the Supreme Court. By giving the Common Market's Commission the right to bring infringements before the Court, a normal procedure was reestablished. But the Court as well as the Assembly are independent of the respective governments, as is the Common Market Commission. The members of the Court, like the Commission, are named by all the governments together without any one of them keeping its own representatives, and the Assembly mixes the delegates of national representatives.

Upon close analysis we can see that to put the Treaty into action, the Commission has received powers rather analogous to those of the High Authority. The Commission judges whether subsidies or agreements are to be accepted or rejected. All the same it does not have any direct financial resources, although this idea has been accepted for the future; therefore, it depends on contributions from the States. As soon as it deals with problems that go beyond the mere application of the Treaty's fixed rules, the High Authority, like the Commission, requires the consent of the Council of Ministers. Problems of general policy in the Coal and Steel Community require unanimous approval. What is remarkable in the construction of the Rome Treaty is that a time comes, in all cases, when the necessity of a unanimous decision can be discarded; majority votes can decide changes in the system for eliminating trade obstacles, in farm policy, in trade policy, in transport policy, in policies concerning labor, the various services, or the flow of capital. Here we are dealing with actual complements or amendments to the Treaty. It is by finding a valid solution to eliminate the necessity for unanimity and not by entrusting powers to an independent authority that an effective approach to a federal system has been achieved. The role of the Commission must be interpreted with moderation. Formally, except in cases where direct powers are delegated to it, the Commission does not make decisions but rather the Council. The latter makes them upon recommendations from the Commission although it can change their terms if it is unanimously agreed. According to the Schuman Treaty system it was the High Authority which made the decisions but it might need the concurring opinion of the Council. This difference is first of all one of presentation. But it shows how in every case the governments are a party to the Community. And the fruitless debate between integration and cooperation appears to have lost all substance.

In effect, what is essential is that decisions affecting the Community are prepared by an independent body whose duty is to take a common view of common interests. This is carried out with an authoritative influence that a secretariat directly under a Council of Ministers could not possess. Such authority is held not only through common appointment by the governments but independence from these governments because this authority is responsible to an Assembly. Because proposals are objective, agreement is facilitated. Because of this objectivity of proposals, countries can abandon their demand for unanimous action, i.e. for keeping the right to veto. In reality most decisions are unanimous. This is not a situation which is contrary to what had been envisaged: this was the very objective. The unanimity is reached, however, only because it was prepared and because it is possible to do without it if need be. One of the most original innovations of the Treaty is its provision for an evolutionary procedure; the need for unanimity lapses after a number of years varying according to the problem. There is, then, a better chance for these problems to be solved in the shortest period of time and by unanimous agreement before the governments subject themselves to majority rule.

This majority, moreover, is weighted according to a very simple formula: it is not a question of taking into consideration the importance or the development of each country through subtle designs; it is simply a question of defining which countries or group of countries can be overruled in a vote. In the Community there are three large countries which have been put on the same plane, two countries of average importance and one small country. If a large State may not by itself block decisions, it is only reasonable that the three Benelux countries, whose total population is less than half that of each of the large States, cannot block them either. This result is obtained by giving four votes to each of the large countries, two each to Belgium and the Netherlands, and one to Luxemburg, and declaring that twelve votes out of a total of seventeen constitute a majority. Thus, three large countries constitute a majority, or two large countries if at the same time both Belgium and Netherlands vote with them on a Commission's motion. On the other hand, a minimum of four countries is required in exceptional cases, where a majority decision can be made by the Council without any previous motion. Thus in all cases there is a majority of votes; and, moreover, either a numerical majority of the States, or a majority of the members of the Commission, which is necessary to formulate a proposal on which the Council has deliberated. There is no conflict with the system of cooperation between governments: their mutual cooperation is necessary, but it is organized in such a way as to be effective.

The unity of this structure is not, however—we must admit it—devoid of a certain ambiguity. Two contradictory interpretations could be advanced concerning where the true executive power is to be found. The Commission may be considered a kind of government, responsible to an assembly although it is not named by this assembly, but needing the concurrence of a federal council composed of one representative per country: this representative comes directly from the government of each State, as in the Bundesrat of the German Federal Republic, and is not elected as in the United States Senate. But an equally well-founded interpretation, recognizing the importance of the functions of the Commission and of its Statute, finds that the true executive power resides in the intergovernmental college which is the Council of Ministers.

As for the actual functioning of the Economic Community, this discussion has no practical importance. It dominates, however, the directions that will be taken in the future development of united European action. It can be maintained that the existing communities are limited to an economic and almost technical domain. In reality their major effect has been to transform the atmosphere surrounding relations between European countries making them more stable and more consistently amiable, to change dramatically the relations between France and Germany and to preserve the hope of a European unity which will emerge as a new great power. Considered in this light, the Common Market is the most important event since the beginning of the twentieth century.

The step which would make this economic union a political one presents undeniable difficulty. First of all, it means that these countries would agree to a common foreign policy. This is the great stumbling block and once it is passed the rest will follow, i.e. essentially defense. Education and culture represent an area eminently appropriate for common action, although such action is not a necessary condition for political unity. But diplomacy and defense are so intimately related to each government's basic policy that this step is a delicate one. How does one establish cooperation that is neither weak nor disjointed, but leads to a true unity of the overall policies of governments that are still divided?

If, at the present time, it is difficult to conceive common institutions distinct from the governments within these essential areas, it is all the more necessary that the organization which is to be formulated should allow the continuation of that more effectively united and coherent system which has been accepted in the economic domains. In time the problem of the duality of the executive power or of interpretations of the executive power, will disappear if a federal government can be instituted which will necessarily have under its jurisdiction foreign affairs and defense as well as the economy, and as a result, a large share of common budget and finance. At the present juncture, it is necessary to conceive the coexistence of two forms of organization, one retaining an independent authority responsible to an Assembly, the other not yet endowed with such an authority. There lies the opportunity to go forward without delay as well as to hold forth hope for the future.

NAME INDEX

SUBJECT INDEX